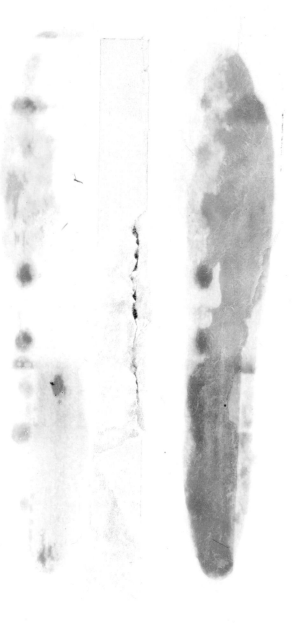

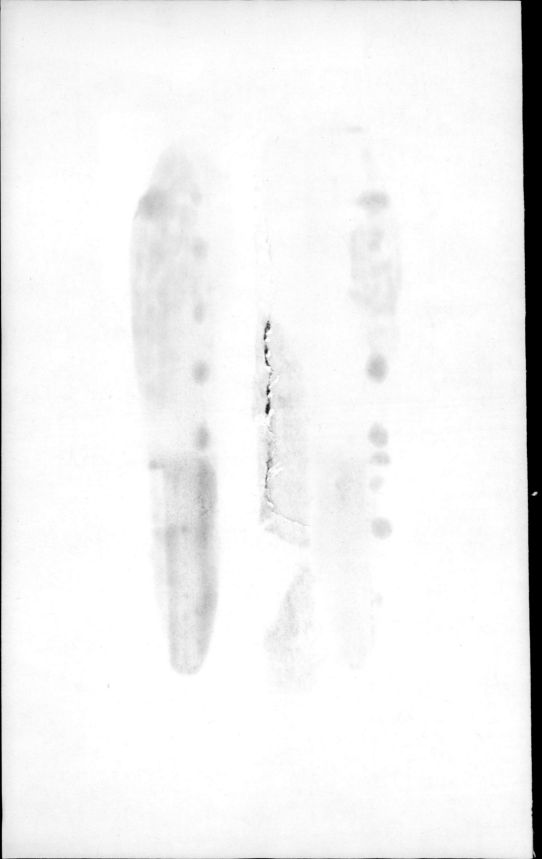

HEIDEGGER
THE MAN AND THE THINKER

Edited by

Thomas Sheehan

Precedent Publishing, Inc.
Chicago

ISBN: 0-913750-16-6
LC: 77-082476

Printed in the United States of America.

Typesetting: North Coast Associates.

Contents

Preface   v
    Thomas Sheehan

Introduction: Heidegger, the Project and the Fulfillment   vii
    Thomas Sheehan

Part I. Glimpses of the Philosopher's Life   1

Heidegger's Early Years: Fragments for a Philosophical Biography   3
    Thomas Sheehan

A Recollection (1957)   21
    Martin Heidegger

Letter to Rudolf Otto (1919)   23
    Edmund Husserl

Why Do I Stay in the Provinces? (1934)   27
    Martin Heidegger

Heidegger and the Nazis   31
    Karl A. Moehling

"Only a God Can Save Us": The *Spiegel* Interview (1966)   45
    Martin Heidegger

Seeking and Finding: The Speech at Heidegger's Burial   73
    Bernhard Welte

Part II. Being, Dasein, and Subjectivity   77

Heidegger's Way Through Phenomenology to the Thinking of Being . . .   79
    William J. Richardson, S.J.

Toward the Topology of Dasein   95
    Theodore Kisiel

Into the Clearing 107
    John Sallis

Heidegger's Model of Subjectivity: A Polanyian Critique 117
    ＼Robert E. Innis

Part III. In Dialogue with Max Scheler 131

Reality and Resistance: On *Being and Time,* Section 43 133
    Max Scheler

Heidegger on Transcendence and Intentionality: His Critique of Scheler 145
    Parvis Emad

In Memory of Max Scheler (1928) 159
    Martin Heidegger

Part IV. Overcoming Metaphysics 161

Heidegger and Metaphysics 163
    Walter Biemel

Metaphysics and the Topology of Being in Heidegger 173
    Otto Pöggeler

Finitude and the Absolute: Remarks on Hegel and Heidegger 187
    Jacques Taminiaux

The Poverty of Thought: A Reflection on Heidegger and Eckhart 209
    John D. Caputo

Part V. Technology, Politics, and Art 217

Beyond "Humanism": Heidegger's Understanding of Technology 219
    Michael E. Zimmerman

Heidegger and Marx: A Framework for Dialogue 229
    David Schweickart

Principles Precarious: On the Origin of the Political in Heidegger 245
    Reiner Schürmann

Heidegger's Philosophy of Art 257
    Sandra Lee Bartky

Part VI. Bibliographies 275

Heidegger: Translations in English, 1949–1977 277
    H. Miles Groth

Heidegger: Secondary Literature in English, 1929–1977 293
    H. Miles Groth

Preface

Thomas Sheehan

The essays and translations that follow provide a glimpse into the life and a clarification of the thought of Martin Heidegger. His thought, for all its breadth and complexity, was quite simple: the meaning of Being as disclosure. His life was almost as simple — that of a German professor — except for a brief but significant period in which he supported the Nazi Regime. While that misguided sally from philosophy continues to haunt his name and work to this day, the question seems to be whether his thought from 1912 to 1976 can be measured by the yardstick of his politics from May, 1933, through February, 1934. The anthology addresses both topics: his complex but simple thought and his simple but complex life.

Part One charts the span of Heidegger's career from his early work and fame, through his political involvement and his attempts to explain it, to his death on May 26, 1976, at the age of 86. Part Two examines the center of his thought: the relation between the disclosure that is Being and the nature of man that is the place of such disclosure. Part Three presents new material on an important polemical discussion between Heidegger and Max Scheler until the latter's death in 1928. Part Four probes Heidegger's claims about the forgottenness of Being, his interpretations of key figures in metaphysics, and his attempt to overcome the tradition. Part Five analyzes Heidegger's statements on technology, politics, and art, and examines the possibility of a Marxist–Heideggerian dialogue. Part Six provides extensive bibliographies of works by and about Heidegger in English up to 1977. The unity of the collection is its concentration on a single thought forged over a lifetime: the meaning of Being—"that ever-puzzling question," as Aristotle says, "that was asked of old, is still being asked today, and will always be asked in the future" (*Metaphysics*, Z, 1, 1028 b 2).

I wish to express my gratitude to the contributors to this collection, to Professor Victor LaMotte for encouraging the volume, and to Professor Kenneth Thompson of Loyola University of Chicago for his support and friendship throughout its compilation.

Introduction:
Heidegger, the Project
and the Fulfillment

Thomas Sheehan

Bergson has written that every great philosopher thinks only one inexhaustible thought and spends his whole life trying to express it: *Et c'est pourquoi il a parlé toute sa vie.*[1] Over the half-century of his professional life, Martin Heidegger liked to insist that his thought was focused on one topic only and that this topic was utterly simple. But defining and articulating that simple topic, *die Sache selbst,* has proven to be no easy matter for either Heidegger or his commentators.

It is a truism to say that the subject matter of Heidegger's thought is the "question of Being" *(die Seinsfrage),* but like most truisms this is both correct and potentially misleading. Indeed, it could be argued that we might enhance the explanation of Heidegger's subject matter by retiring the terms "Being" and the "question of Being" from the discussion.

For one thing, the phrase "the question of Being" is a condensation (its earliest form reads: the question of the meaning of Being), and for another, the full form of the phrase underwent changes throughout Heidegger's career (the question of the *meaning* of Being → the question of the *truth* of Being → the question of the *place* of Being). Furthermore, the word "Being" *(Sein)* has two distinct but easily confused meanings in Heidegger, with the result that Heidegger himself, in order to specify *his* meaning of the term, resorted in his later writings to such stratagems as spelling it archaically *(Seyn)* crossing it out (~~Sein~~), and finally dropping it from his lexicon. There is the added problem that the word (especially when capitalized in English) seems to suggest a metaphysical super-entity, which is anathema to Heidegger's intentions. And when we read about Being "hiding itself" or "sending itself" to man, we find it hard not to think that Heidegger has lapsed into theology or metaphysical anthropomorphism. Moreover, talk of Being "itself" can easily lose sight of the analogical character of Being. Heidegger was not after a univocal something that subsists on its own. Over and above the Being of man, the Being of implements, nature, artworks and ideal objects, there is no second level of "Being itself." Rather, the "itself" refers to the analogically unified meaning of Being (in Aristotelian terms, its *pros hen* unity) which is instantiated in all cases of the Being of this or that.

Moreover, there is the problem of Heidegger's audacious claim that the question of Being has been entirely forgotten by the Western philosophical tradition. Apropos of this, Helmut Franz tells an anecdote about a philosophy conference in 1958 at which Heidegger had discussed this fate of metaphysics. A Protestant participant asked Heidegger whether it were not the case that at least Martin Luther was an exception to this charge. Heidegger quipped: Would you care to guess how many Catholics ask me the same thing about Thomas Aquinas?[2]

Let us pose this as a test case. After the painstaking work of Étienne Gilson and others, is it not the legitimate claim of the neo-Thomist that Aquinas raised metaphysical questioning to a new and creative level by his thematization of the primacy of *esse,* the existential act of Being, over essence? Whereas Aristotle's philosophy was still one of form as highest actuality, Aquinas compared form to *esse* as potency to a higher actuality. "Being [*esse*] is the actuality of every form or nature" (S.T., I, 3, 4, c); "Being itself [*ipsum esse*] is the most perfect of all; indeed, it is compared as act to everything. For nothing has actuality except insofar as it is. Thus Being itself is the actuality of all things" (S.T., I, 4, 1, ad 3). And since in God there is nothing potential, it follows that at the apex of reality essence is existence: "The divine essence is Being itself" (S.T., I, 12, 2, ad 3). "God is Being itself subsisting per se" (S.T., I, 4, 2, c.). Surely there is no forgetfulness of Being here! And indeed, the various attempts to rescue Aquinas from Heidegger's indictment generally consist in demonstrating — irrefutably, as far as I can see — that in Aquinas *existentia* or *ipsum esse* has primacy over *essentia,* indeed that *essentia* is reducible to *esse.*[3]

Far from being ignorant of Aquinas' metaphysical revolution and of its rediscovery in this century, Heidegger freely grants this achievement while still maintaining that in Thomas, as much as in Plato or Nietzsche, "Being" is forgotten. Clearly Heidegger's "Being" means something different from Aquinas' *ipsum esse* or *actus essendi.* As a preliminary and merely formal indication of the difference, we may say that Heidegger is asking for the possibilizing condition of what Aquinas calls *esse,* and that from this viewpoint all the ultimate ontological principles of the tradition — whether Plato's *eidos* or Aquinas' *esse* — are on the same plane.

One way to get at the simple topic that commands Heidegger's thought is to distinguish the two meanings of "Being," the one that is the sole and exclusive topic throughout the history of metaphysics, and the other which is the prerogative only of a pre- or post-metaphysical thinking. In the first sense "Being" refers to the highest ontological or theological principle discoverable by traditional metaphysics. This we shall call generically "beingness" *(Seiendheit)*. In the second sense "Being" refers to a pre-ontological principle undiscovered and undiscoverable by metaphysics: the prior event whereby beingness can "be" at all. And by this Heidegger does not mean creation but, in the most general terms, the happening of the world of sense in which man lives and moves and is. Let us not yet give a name to this, other than to say it is "Being" in Heidegger's sense of the term.

"Being" as Beingness

The problematic of metaphysics is that constellation of questions that ultimately reduces to one: What is the "core" of each and every thing that exists? That is: What is a being insofar as it is at all? This is the question of beings *as being* (Greek: *on hei on*). Aristotle articulates this clearly: "The ever-puzzling question that has always been asked and is still being asked today — namely, 'What is a being?' — comes down to this question: 'What is being-ness?'" (*Metaphysics, Z, 1, 1028, b 2*). Explanation: The uniqueness of a properly philosophical question is that it looks away from and beyond the obvious dimensions of things in order to ask about the "-ness" dimension of things, beyond virtue*s* to virtue-*ness* as in Plato's *Meno,* beyond pious acts to pie*ty,* as in the *Euthyphro,* beyond particular men to man*hood* as in the *De Anima.* The philosophical question is, in the broadest sense, the question of the "essence" or "X-ness" of X. And the highest form of philosophy is not to ask about the "essence" of particular regions of things (the X-ness of all Xs, the Y-ness of all Ys), but to ask about the "is-ness" of all that is. In Aristotle's framework, this is the question which defines "first" philosophy as contrasted with regional disciplines within philosophy: the question of each and every being insofar is it *is* at all, beings with regard to their "is-ness."

Now, to designate this "is-ness" or state-of-being which characterizes beings as beings, Aristotle took over from popular usage of his day the noun *ousia.* It is derived from the present participle of the verb *eimi, einai,* "to be," and specifically from the feminine singular, *ousa,* just as the neuter of that participle supplies the word for "beings" *(on, onta).* The noun *ousia* in its popular meaning referred to that which is properly one's own, one's present possessions or holdings, one's property or substance. When taken up by Aristotle as a philosophical term, it came to mean that which is the "essential property" of beings: their "is-ness" or state-of-being. It was eventually translated into Latin as *essentia* and into English as "substance" or "essence." But lest we be tempted to understand *ousia* as referring exclusively to "essence" as contrasted with "existence" (as Heidegger shows, the Greek word includes both)[4], let us translate it simply as "beingness," that which characterizes a being insofar as it is at all and is what it is. Thus Aristotle can say that the question which defines First Philosophy — What are beings as beings? — comes down to the question: What is beingness?

For Heidegger, the whole history of metaphysics, from Plato through Nietzsche, is structured by this same question, the search for the analogical unity of beingness as the substantial ground and cause of actual beings, regardless of the particular interpretations of beingness that emerge in the tradition. In Professor Werner Marx's phrase, the history of metaphysics as a whole and in each of its parts is an "ousiology" or doctrine of *ousia*/beingness, where beingness has the double sense of what-things-are and that-they-are. Regardless of whether whatness or thatness is given priority, metaphysics still and always moves within the parameters of the doctrine of *ousia*. One may wish to claim that certain forms of beingness are improvements over others (for example, Aquinas' "existential" beingness over Aristotle's form-centered beingness), but specific differences within the genus "beingness" remain instances of that genus.

Moreover, metaphysics works out the beingness of beings in a twofold pattern that makes up a unified science. The question "What is a being as being?" asks about the entity's ontological constitution in general and about the beingness of the highest entity, the divine. In Heidegger's telling, all metaphysics is onto-theo-logical: ontological in that it transcends beings to their beingness, and theological in that it seeks ultimate cause or ground *(theion)*. Heidegger goes so far as to say: "Even Nietzsche's metaphysics *as ontology* is . . . at the same time theology."[5]

So far, our discussion of "Being" as beingness has led to these conclusions: (1) The exclusive prerogative of traditional metaphysics is the question of the beingness of beings, the whatness or thatness of whatever is under discussion. (2) The tradition's name for the "beingness of beings" is the "Being of beings" under a variety of nomenclatures: the *idea* of beings, the *energeia* of beings, the *esse* of beings, and so forth. But thus far Heidegger's discussion of beingness has gotten no further than discovering the unity of the metaphysical tradition in the most general terms. There is a second step in his reading, whereby he uncovers a first level of the hidden meaning of that unity.

Beingness in all its historical forms conceals, in the broadest sense, a certain relation to man. The beingness of beings is not something "out there" in beings but rather is the meaningful relatedness, the intelligible presentness, of things to and for man. Beingness always includes this implicit referredness, even if it is suppressed or forgotten. Beingness means "intelligible disclosure" or "revealedness," in Greek: *aletheia*. When we speak of intelligibility, we mean it in the broad sense of "meaningful accessibility," not just theoretical knowability. And the peculiarity of the Greeks as the spiritual forefathers of the West consists in the fact that in a unique way their culture—their poetry, drama, sculpture, thought—understood implicitly and celebrated at large this openness or revealedness, this up-front-ness, of things. The word *eidos*—the visible shape or meaningful appearance of things—summarizes and typifies this Greek vision. It says that the world of things is open, accessible, present to man. To be is to appear. To be sure, the "to-ness" or relatedness to man is not thematized (and if it were, it would not denote any kind of objectivity before a subject). The implicitness of it all constitutes the beauty and enchanting naïveté of the Greeks. Man is "all eyes" and therefore caught up in seeing the world as just "there." No subjectivity, no anthropocentrism, only captivation by the openness of things.

Thus the word *ousia,* which we initially and very blandly translated as beingness, in fact has overtones of "thereness" or "presentness" *(parousia)* and "openness" *(aletheia),* indeed of "emergence into appearance" *(physis).* All of these really mean the same thing. By pushing the problematic of *ousia* (beingness) back to the problematic of *parousia* (presentness, openness), Heidegger has located the proper issue of Greek philosophy in the disclosive bond *(logos, legein)* between man and beingness: the appearance or openness of things in conjunction with the essence of man as allowing that appearance to happen.

Heidegger is making no claim that this togetherness of beingness/openness and man was explicit and thematic in Greek philosophy (in fact, the first task of his deconstruction and retrieval of the Greeks is to uncover this dimension). But neither can he claim that this conjunction was unknown to the tradition.[6] From its beginnings in Parmenides, philosophy has sought to clarify beingness by reflecting upon the thinking *(noein)* of beingness (cf. Fr. 3). In Plato the disclosure of the Ideas takes its bearings from the soul's monologue *(logos)* with itself (cf. *Sophist,* 245e). In Aristotle the categories of beingness are connected with the assertoric knowledge of *logos.* In Aquinas we find the problematic of the agent intellect as revelatory excess towards beingness. In Descartes First Philosophy is explicitly founded on the *res cogitans.* In Kant, "The conditions of the possibility of experience in general are at the same time conditions of the possibility of the objects of experience." In short, the proper subject matter of philosophy has always implicitly been the bond between beingness and man, between the openness and presence of things and the essence of man.

We may now add two more conclusions to those already made concerning the explanation of "Being" as beingness: (3) The problematic of beingness is implicitly *phenomeno*logical: beingness is the appearing (openness, presentness) of things. (4) The problematic of beingness is implicitly phenomeno*logical*: it implies that man is essential to the event of the appearing of things. And if we pull all four conclusions into a unity, we have a clear, if general, definition of metaphysics: it is the ontological-theological search for the beingness of things (their ultimate what-ness and that-ness), one which unfolds historically in various modes of beingness, all of which are implicitly modes of the presence or appearance of things in necessary conjunction with man's essence as allowing that appearance.

Now, if Heidegger is willing to concede that much to the traditional notion of "Being" as beingness, what is left over as the topic for his own thinking? What could possibly have been forgotten in metaphysics?

Answering this question will require intermediate steps. But for now, a formal indication of the direction in which Heidegger moves. Beingness is the intelligible presence of beings, it is that which allows beings to show up in the specifically human world. Beingness, therefore, is the possibilizing condition *of beings* showing up. But the prior question which Heidegger asks is: what brings it about that *beingness itself* shows up, what puts beingness into action in the specifically human world? Let us ask the question another way: If beingness is the presence of beings, what occasions the presence of presence? Or one last way: If beingness is the "essence" (in the broad sense, including whatness and that-ness) of beings, what is the "essence of essence"?

All such ways of putting Heidegger's initial question indicate a shift of focus from beings towards beingness itself. Of course, metaphysics already is aware of beingness, but only in terms of how it allows beings to be meaningfully present. Heidegger seeks to become aware of beingness in and for itself, while of course never forgetting that beingness is always and only the beingness *of beings*. But the question remains: What brings about beingness? And since, as the tradition implicitly knew, beingness is necessarily tied into man's essence, what about man in his unique relation not to beings but to the happening of beingness? Clearly Heidegger is going to focus on the nature of the *disclosive bond* between man and beingness, a bond which is operative wherever man is man and beingness appears, but which gets covered over both in everyday life and in the thematic science called metaphysics. To look ahead we may say: This bond is *proper* to man, indeed he is *appropriated* unto it willy nilly; and, to truly be what he in fact already is, he must *personally re-appropriate* his state of being already appropriated unto this bond. Moreover, the fact that he is appropriated unto this bond is the possibilizing condition for beingness to happen at all and thus for beings to appear to man. That is, the appropriation of man unto beingness *discloses* beings. Heidegger is trying to thematize this appropriation as the primordial disclosive event; thus he calls his topic *"das Ereignis,"* the event of appropriation whereby disclosure happens.

But these formal indications of Heidegger's topic require more concrete demonstration, and that means an intermediate step. If metaphysics has always asked about the presentness of present beings, or equally, about beings in their beingness, Heidegger's new question, which claims to be *the*

phenomenological question *par excellence,* is: What about presentness or beingness as such? What allows *it* to be present? What is the "Being" of beingness? Now, if phenomenology is about the immediate appearance of
things, and if the above questions are to be answered phenomenologically,
then beingness itself must become a phenomenon, something seen as immediately showing itself to man. Concretely this means focusing on the unique
correlation between man and beingness and, more concretely yet, freeing beingness from its traditional imprisonment in the copula of sentential logic.
These services were performed for Heidegger by Edmund Husserl's ground-
breaking work, *Logical Investigations.*

HUSSERL: PHENOMENOLOGICAL ACCESS TO BEINGNESS

From out of such questions as the above, Heidegger came to the text of
Husserl's which was to remain the most important for him: *Logical Investigations*
VI, chapter 6, "Sensuous and Categorial Intuitions."[7] Although he began
reading this work as early as 1909 when he entered Freiburg University, it was
some years before its import for his own question about the "meaning of beingness" became apparent. The title of this chapter at one and the same time
points towards and away from Kant. Whereas the general theme of the Second
Part of the Sixth Investigation, "Sense and Understanding," certainly recalls
Kant, the specific title of chapter six in that section already heralds a revolutionary break with Kant: "Sensuous and *Categorial* Intuitions." For Kant,
categorial intuitions are impossible, since the categories of the understanding
function merely to bring the hyletic data into categorial form, such that the object known is posited in a synthesis of intuition and concept. But Husserl's
chapter seeks to broaden the range of intuitive givenness beyond Kant's
limitation of intuition to the realm of the senses and sense data. Husserl's aim
in this Investigation is phenomenological clarification of truth or true
knowledge by means of a phenomenological analysis of the identity-synthesis,
specifically by analyzing how categorial as well as sensuous meaning-
intuitions are fulfilled. But for such a *phenomenological* clarification, the
categorial content itself must become a phenomenon, an immediate and intuitable given, analogous to the immediate givenness of sense data. And since
intuition bespeaks an "immediate presence to . . . ," then the dimension of the
categorial must enter presentness.

What is this dimension of the categorial? It is the tradition's name for
beingness, that which makes a thing accessible to understanding as
what and how it is. Both Kant and Husserl stand within the long tradition
wherein the doctrine of beingness *(Seinslehre)* is a doctrine of categories *(Kate-
gorienlehre).* In the tradition, beingness is always — explicitly or not — correlative
to a revelatory enunciation *(logos)* and specifically to a categorical-predicative
one *(logos apophantikos, apophansis).* To that degree, ontology is the

theoretical revealing of beingness-as-categorial. (To be sure, in this sixth chapter Husserl is not explicitly elaborating the categories as metaphysics from Aristotle to Hegel does, but is only establishing the analogy between sensation and categorial intuition. Thus, although the categorial intuition appears in the *Investigations,* it does not become an explicit ontological thematic.)

Husserl discusses the phenomenological presentness of the categorial dimension in terms of a "surplus" *(Ueberschuss)* of meaning over and above the perceptual sensuous presentation. For Kant, only the sense data are given, and the category (e.g., "substance") is simply a form for organizing that data. Husserl, however, demonstrates how the propositional categorial form of a statement can attain to intuitive fulfillment. When one says, "The sea is rough" or just "rough seas," he knows the sea *as* rough. The entrance of the "as-factor" indicates the surplus of meaning beyond the sense intuition. The sea is a sea which *is* rough. But there is nothing in sense perception corresponding to form-words like "is." Rather, the surplus of meaning here requires another act, the categorial, in order to be seen. This categorial act, to be sure, is founded on sense perception, but it also lets the sensuously appearing object be manifest *as* what and how it *is*, i.e., in its *beingness*-dimension beyond the purely formal beingness of the copula. And since for Husserl intuition is the model of knowledge (because true knowledge must have the character of fulfillment and identity), then we will have to broaden intuition beyond that of individual objects to include general and categorial objects in a categorial intuition. The object of categorial intuition is "what is universal, what is merely documented in [sensuous] intuition" *(Logical Investigations,* p. 778).

As far as Heidegger is concerned, this discovery of the surplus of intuitable categorial meaning and the rendering of this surplus as equally present as is sense data, marks the major achievement of the chapter. Beingness is given to a categorial intuition in a way analogous to how the sensuous being is given to sense intuition. Beingness—that whereby I know a thing as what and how it is—is not derived from the Table of Judgements as it is in Kant, but is *given as a phenomenon.* There are two levels of givenness, and man has immediate access to both. Husserl's discovery, his rendering present of the beingness-dimension of beings, may be roughly diagrammed as follows:

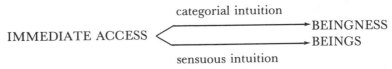

With this discovery of beingness as the presentness of beings, itself immediately present, Heidegger now had a clue for returning to Plato, Aristotle, and the whole tradition, and for reading beingness in terms of temporality. To say something "is" is to say it "is-present-now." All of metaphysics implicitly reads beingness in terms of one moment of time, the present. But Husserl's discovery also opened up for Heidegger the question which his master did not pose. Now that Husserl had broken the stranglehold of the apophantic assertion in ontology, now that he has rescued beingness from the copula and had rendered it present for itself as an immediately intuitable phenomenon, Heidegger could ask how *it* is given. If beingness is the givenness of beings, and if this givenness-of... is itself given, then it too can be treated as a phenomenon and questioned as to the "how" of its becoming present. To use language that Heidegger developed in his earliest courses after World War I, Husserl had uncovered the *Bezugssinn* operative in ontology, the sense of relation between man and beingness; but the *Vollzugssinn* remained to be settled, the sense of the "how" in which the *Bezugssinn* is carried out. For Heidegger that *Vollzugssinn* essentially has to do with man's temporality: his presence-by-absence, his having of himself and his world by being out beyond himself in self-absence. That dimension of *absence* into which man is *appropriated* lets happen the *presence* or beingness of all that is.

With his reading of *Logical Investigations* Heidegger had found the clue to transcending the problematic of the beingness-of-beings so as to ask the question of the meaning of beingness itself. For all his lack of regard for the tradition, Husserl had brilliantly uncovered its major premise, unspoken since the Greeks, that the true field for philosophy was the correlation between *eidos* and *logos,* between the appearance of beings and man's essence as necessary to and bound into that appearance. Husserl read that correlation in terms of immediate phenomenological presentness. He freed the beingness-issue from its captivity in Kantian formalism and opened the way to the promised land of the question about the possibilizing condition of beingness. But he was refused access by his self-restriction to the issues of consciousness and objectivity. It was Heidegger's privilege to enter that land and to chart its topology. And he did so by pushing the *eidos-logos* correlation of immediacy and presentness back to the prior question of the *kinesis* or movement which is the very enactment *(Vollzug)* of the bond between man and beingness. Since *kinesis* is primarily a matter of presence-by-absence (in Aristotle's terms: *energeia* that is still bound up with *dynamis*), Heidegger entered the promised land by reawakening the question of absence (future, past) as the condition of beingness (presence).

THE "KINETIC" MEANING OF BEINGNESS

It is well known that *Sein und Zeit* (hereafter: *SZ*) was projected in two Parts, the first of which was to determine, on the basis of a new understanding of man as temporality, the time-character of beingness in general and of its possible variations, while the second Part would use this time-character of beingness to reduce the traditional ontology to its underlying temporal content. The second Part would confirm by historical "deconstruction" what the first

Part had established by phenomenological "construction": the new doctrine of the analogical unity of all modes of beingness. Unlike the traditional report that claimed that "beingness as stable presentness" exhausted the meaning of beingness, Heidegger would show that the absential moments of temporal movement (no longer, not yet) are what allow beingness as presentness: the meaning of beingness would be read in terms of time. Each of the two Parts had three projected Divisions, but the work got no further than Part I, Division 2.

Part I as a whole is entitled "The Interpretation of Existence in terms of Temporality [= Part I, Divisions I and 2] and the Explication of Time as the Transcendental Horizon for the Question of [the meaning of] Beingness [= Part I, Division 3]." *SZ* I.1 would establish that the structure of man's existence is "care" *(Sorge)*; *SZ* I.2 would interpret the meaning of care as temporality *(Zeitlichkeit)*; and *SZ* I.3, the unpublished Division entitled "Time and Being," would show how *Zeitlichkeit* in its horizon-forming function called *Temporalität,* determines the analogically unified temporal meaning of beingness.

The complexity of the analysis of *SZ* can tend to block a clear view of the overarching movement of the whole work. To state it simply: Man as "excess" (ahead of himself and already in a world) holds open the area of access to (or intelligibility of) beings. As an "excess" which makes possible "access," man is the *"Da,"* the "there," the open area of intelligibility — where "intelligibility" is not to be taken to mean theoretical knowability but rather "accessibility of beings in meaningfulness" in the broadest sense.

SZ I.1 reads human beings as constituted by three moments. (1) Existentiality: man's existence is ahead of itself; (2) Facticity: man is ahead of himself by being already in a world of meaning; (3) Being among *(Sein bei)*: man's already-ahead-ness holds open the realm of intelligibility within which man has access to, and in everydayness is "fallen into," the things of his concern. These three moments are in fact reducible to two: (1) Existence is already projected possibility, (2) which yields possible encounter with things. Excess possibilizes access, and the whole is called "transcendence."

Part I, Division 2, "Existence and Temporality," first shows *what* it is that existence is ultimately already-out-towards, viz., its most proper possibility of dying; and secondly shows *how* man is called to take over and accept that aheadness, viz., in conscience and resolve. Then it spells out the temporal meaning of the whole structure. In the excess-dimension lie the two moments of aheadness and alreadiness. (1) As ahead of itself, existence is *becoming* its most proper possibility. This becoming or "coming towards" *(Zu-kommen)* is man's proper "future" *(Zukunft)*. (2) But what man ultimately comes towards is that which he already and essentially is, his own aheadness, his own finitude, concretized in his dying. Here is the temporal dimension of "what-man-already-essentially-is" or, more briefly, "alreadiness," *Gewesenheit,* which unites the meanings of "already-having-been" and "essence" *(Wesen)*. This "alreadiness" is not a past which lies behind man *(Vergangenheit),* but an essential condition, always already operative, which structures his present and future. The excess-dimension, therefore, is structured as a dynamic of possibility: *becoming* what one *already* is. As excess, man holds open the horizon within which he can "make present," or render accessible in meaning, the beings he meets. The structure of care (being ahead of oneself, already in a world, and among beings) finds its ground or meaning in the structure of temporality as self-transcendence. Human existence is nothing other than this self-transcendence: letting things have access by becoming what one already is. Very roughly:

ACCESS   (letting beings be meaningfully present)

EXCESS   (becoming what one already essentially is)

After *SZ* I.2 had shown that primordial time is the unified structure of man's self-transcendence (and here it is called "temporality," *Zeitlichkeit*), the next but unpublished Division, I.3, was going to specify and work out what was implicit in the foregoing, namely, that transcendence as excess-access forms the analogical unity of the intelligibility of whatever is intelligible. In this horizonal function, primordial time is called the *Temporalität* or time-character of beingness. But what is this "time"? It is not the linear *chronos* (i.e., the number of motion according to before and after) which the West has known explicitly at least since Aristotle. For Heidegger, "time" is the much more original *movement* constitutive of human existence, the movement whereby the domain of intelligibility is opened up. This unique *kinesis* (which is already found implicitly in the Pre-Socratic notions of *aletheia* and *physis* and which is echoed in Aristotle) is the dynamic structure of intelligibility as such, the event or "coming-out" of the meaningful presentness (disclosure) of anything at all, an event which happens only on the basis of man's appropriation unto excess. The e-vent of intelligibility *(a-letheia)* in its specifically kinetic structure *(Ereignis)* is the topic of Heidegger's thought.

Therefore Division 3 of Part I was to look away, as it were, from the excess-access structure of human being in order to focus on the movement of intelligibility itself in its analogical unity. Regardless of which kind of thing is revealed in its meaningful presence, the same process is at work. Just as in motion privativeness allows presentness (a moving being is present *as moving* only because it has *not yet* arrived at its essential completeness: Aristotle's *energeia ateles*), so likewise a meaningful being is present as what it is only on the basis of the privative self-absence (excess) of man. We might speak of a "background" that remains in the background (in recess) in order that beings may emerge into the foreground of meaningfulness. Indeed, man's excess holds open that recessive background-dimension; it is, in fact, his *proper* dimension, he is *appropriated unto* it. In order properly to be what he already is, man must re-appropriate his excessive appropriation unto recess, not in the sense of overcoming and controlling it but in the sense of accepting it *as* recessive. Only because man is already appropriated unto this excess-recess dimension (*Ereignis:* the event of being appropriated unto absence) can he acquiesce in his condition and re-appropriate what he properly is, i.e., achieve "authenticity" (*Eigentlichkeit:* properness). To describe man's condition as appropriated unto the recess-dimension, Heidegger sometimes speaks of man as "called forth" or "tuned in" or "drawn out." But of course there can be no hypostasizing of the recess-dimension as if it were someone or something that calls or tunes or draws. The receding is known only as it is registered in man's ineluctable exceeding of himself. The sameness of excess and recess is equally described as *Ereignis* and *Enteignis:* man's ownness consists in not being his own; he is appropriated into his disappropriation. We may further specify the earlier diagram:

$$\text{ACCESS} \xleftarrow{\hspace{2cm}} \left.\begin{array}{c} \\ \\ \end{array}\right\rangle \text{RECESS}$$
$$\text{EXCESS} \xrightarrow{\hspace{2cm}}$$

The unity of excess-recess on the one hand and access on the other is captured by the fundamental Greek noun *aletheia* or verb *aletheuein*. At the heart of the word is "recess" or "hiddenness" *(lethe)* — not a complete and absolute hiddenness but a withdrawal. This recess is itself present in a unique way, viz., as registered in and held open by man's excess, and experienced, for example, in his being-towards-death. We may equally say: it is present by calling man forth into his excess. In either way, it is present *privately*. And on the basis of this recess, the arena is cleared for beings-in-their-beingness, the accessibility of things as what and how they are. Recess possibilizes access, and *aletheia* bespeaks: the revealment, manifestness, beingness, of some particular being on the basis of a prior withdrawal; the meaningful presence of a being on the basis of a privative absence; or equally, a privative absence that is "present" in man's excess or self-absence. "In *aletheia*, what essentially becomes present is *lethe;* yet this *lethe* recedes in favor of a being which becomes manifest [in its beingness]." The topic for thought is this "pre-ab-sence."

The uniqueness of Heidegger's "question of Being" vis-à-vis the tradition comes into full view. The phrase is to be expanded into (1) the question of the *temporal meaning* or *kinesis* of beingness: Pre-ab-sence is the appropriation of man as excess by the dimension of intrinsic recess such that access can happen; or (2) the question of the *truth* or *aletheia* of beingness: Pre-ab-sence, i.e., presence by withdrawal, allows the revealedness of things; or (3) the question of the *place* or *topos* of beingness: Pres-ab-sence is the "clearing" of the domain in which beings can be meaningfully present.

CONCLUSION

The simplicity of Heidegger's topic is the legacy of his thought, a legacy which he himself inherited from the tradition which preceded him. In a poem from his youth he wrote that:

> ... the yield to me of shining summer day
> Rests like heavy fruit —
> From long eternities
> A burden beyond sense —
> For me in the gray desert
> Of a great Simplicity.[8]

In a very real sense there is no "content" to that topic and legacy, only a "method." But "method" must not be taken here to mean a technique or procedure for philosophical thinking. In that sense there is no "method" in Heidegger as there is, for example, in Husserl. Rather, the topic of Heidegger's thought and the pursuit of that topic, the "what" and the "how," are one and the same simple thing. Heidegger writes, *"Alles ist Weg,"*[9] "Everything is way," and man's Being is to be on-the-way (Greek, *meta tei hodoi, methodos*), i.e., in essential movement. Hence there is no method which could show us for the first time the topic of philosophy or lead us to the place of thought. Rather, we are already there, in our essence we are the topic and *topos,* and the point is not to be led there so much as to come to know what we already know and to become what we already are. In the words of the poet,

> We shall not cease from exploration
> And the end of all our exploring
> Will be to arrive where we started
> And know the place for the first time.[10]

Notes

1. Henri Bergson, *Oeuvres,* Edition du centenaire, ed., André Robinet, Paris: Presses Universitaires de France, 1970, p. 1347. I am grateful to Professor James Felt, S.J., for pointing out this reference to me.
2. Helmut Franz, "Das Denken Heideggers und die Theologie," in *Heidegger und die Theologie,* ed. Gerhard Noller, Munich: Kaiser, 1967, p. 262f.
3. On Heidegger and Aquinas, cf. J. B. Lotz, "Das Sein selbst und das subsistierende Sein nach Thomas von Aquin," in G. Neske, ed., *Martin Heidegger zum siebzigsten*

Geburtstag, Pfullingen: Neske, 1959, pp.180-194; also John N. Deely, *The Tradition via Heidegger,* The Hague: Nijoff, 1971; John P. Doyle, "Heidegger and Scholastic Metaphysics," *The Modern Schoolman,* 49 (1972), 201-220. On the reduction of essence to *esse:* K. Rahner, *Geist in Welt,* Munich: Kösel, 1957, pp. 166-172; English translation, *Spirit in the World,* New York: Herder and Herder, 1968, pp. 156-162.

4. Martin Heidegger, *The End of Philosophy,* trans. Joan Stambaugh, New York: Harper and Row, 1973, pp. 1-10.

5. Martin Heidegger, *Nietzsche,* Pfullingen: Neske, 1961, II, 348.

6. Cf. Martin Heidegger, "The Idea of Phenomenology, with a Letter to Edmund Husserl (1927)," trans. Thomas Sheehan, *Listening* 12, 3 (Fall, 1977), 111.

7. For this section, cf. Edmund Husserl, *Logical Investigations,* trans. J. N. Findlay, London: Routledge, Kegan, Paul, 1970, pp. 773-802; Martin Heidegger, *Vier Seminare,* trans. Curd Ochwadt, Frankfurt: Klostermann, 1977, pp. 110-128; Jacques Taminiaux, "Heidegger and Husserl's Logical Investigations," in *Radical Phenomenology: Essays in Honor of Martin Heidegger,* ed. John Sallis, New York: Humanities Press, 1978.

8. Martin Heidegger, "Eventide on Reichenau" (1917), trans. William J. Richardson, S.J., in Richardson, *Heidegger: Through Phenomenology to Thought,* The Hague, Nijhoff, 1963, p. 1.

9. *Unterwegs zur Sprache,* Pfullingen: Neske, 1954, p. 198.

10. T. S. Eliot, "Little Gidding," V, *(Four Quartets)* in Eliot, *The Complete Poems and Plays of T. S. Eliot,* London, Faber and Faber, 1969, p. 197.

I. GLIMPSES OF THE PHILOSOPHER'S LIFE

Heidegger's Early Years: Fragments for a Philosophical Biography

Thomas Sheehan

Martin Heidegger, perhaps the most influential philosopher of this century, is in many ways "a man without a biography."[1] He once opened a lecture on Aristotle with the information: "He was born, he worked, he died." Much the same could be said of Heidegger. Born in southwest Germany in 1889, he worked there all his life except for five years at Marburg, and died there on May 26, 1976. Yet within the span of those 86 years his thought shook the world of philosophy.

In Heidegger the biography and the course of thinking are virtually coterminous. From beginning to end he lived in his thought. The only biography worth writing, therefore, is a philosophical one which charts the sources and development of his thinking. What follows is not that, but only a collection of fragments to fill in some gaps in the period leading up to the 1927 publication of his major work, *Sein und Zeit* (hereafter: SZ).

FROM MESSKIRCH TO FREIBURG: 1889–1909

Martin Heidegger was born on Thursday, September 26, 1889, in Messkirch, Baden-Württemburg, of Friedrich Heidegger (1851-1924) and Johanna Kempf Heidegger (1858-1927). Both parents were Roman Catholics, his father the sexton of St. Martin's Church in Messkirch. His mother's family traces its origins in the region back in an unbroken line to 1510, and his father's family name kept the resonances of the region: *die Heide*, heath, moorland. He had a sister, Mariele, and a brother, Fritz, who survives him in Messkirch. Everything about his family and youth bespeaks the simplicity of a farming town on the eastern edge of the Black Forest, which Heidegger himself celebrated in his essay "The Pathway." His earliest formal education (until 1903, age thirteen) took place at the local public schools in Messkirch. Just after his fourteenth birthday a promising future as a priest sent young Martin to the Jesuit secondary school at Konstanz, some thirty miles south of his native town, where he spent three years (1903-1906) followed by three more at the Jesuit Bertholds–Gymnasium in Freiburg (1906-1909).

Those six years of secondary school were momentous in the formation of the young thinker. They were the time, he tells us, when "I acquired everything that was to be of lasting value."[2] This was the period of his training in Greek and Latin (he continued to read Greek authors every day of his life except for the war years[3]), his discovery of Adalbert Stifter (1905) and Friedrich Hölderlin (1908), and perhaps most important of all, the first encounter with his abiding question about the meaning of Being. In the summer of 1907, when the seventeen-year-old scholar was home on vacation from the Bertholds-Gymnasium, his "fatherly friend and fellow Swabian," Father Conrad Gröber, then pastor of Trinity Church in Konstanz, later bishop of Meissen (Saxony) and archbishop of Freiburg,[4] gave him Franz Brentano's *On the Several Senses of Being in Aristotle.*[5] This straightforward 220-page treatise examined the meaning of the Greek participle *on* (which has the verbal sense of "to-be-in-Being" as well as the substantive sense of "that-which-is-in-Being") and found it to be a homonym whose analogous meanings Aristotle ordered according to a fourfold distinction: Being as "accidental," being as true, being as potential and actual, and being according to the schema of the categories. Heidegger repeatedly characterized the work as "my first guide through Greek philosophy in my secondary school days," as "the 'rod and staff' of my first awkward attempts to penetrate into philosophy," and as "the first philosophical text through which I worked my way, again and again from 1907 on."[6] More important than the book was the question it awoke in him but could not answer: if that-which-is-in-Being (*das Seiende*) has several meanings, what does "Being itself" (*das Sein*) mean in its unity? From this question, rooted in Aristotle (and not in Husserl!), the line leads, with some wavering, to the publication of SZ.

FREIBURG: FROM STUDENT TO LECTURER: 1909–1916

In 1909, the end of his secondary education, the twenty-year-old Heidegger entered the novitiate of the German Province of the Jesuits at Feldkirch, Austria, near the border with Lichtenstein, but he was dismissed after only a few weeks for reasons of health. Thereupon he entered the archdiocesan seminary at Freiburg, where the spiritual directors were also Jesuits, and simultaneously matriculated at the Albert Ludwig University in Freiburg.[7] From the fall of 1909 through the summer of 1911, he studied theology and some philosophy until he abandoned entirely the idea of becoming a priest and left the seminary. But he continued his studies at the university with a concentration on philosophy until the summer of 1913 when at the age of 23 he completed his doctoral dissertation, *The Doctrine of Judgment in Psychologism*, under the directorship of Arthur Schneider.[8]

From his first semester at the university Heidegger began reading, with little enough success, Edmund Husserl's *Logical Investigations*. The reason, he recalls, is that "I expected a decisive aid in the questions stimulated by Brentano's dissertation,"[9] and Husserl, he knew, had been a student of Brentano's in Vienna. But the "realist" Husserl of the *Logical Investigations* (1900-1901) had already begun to give way to the "transcendental" Husserl who would write the *Ideas* (1913),[10] and from early on, the young Heidegger seems to have understood that whereas phenomenological *method* might help him to "articulate the whole region of 'Being' in its various modes of reality,"[11] Husserl's turn toward *transcendental subjectivity* could only bar the way. For in 1910 we find Heidegger reading Husserl's programmatic essay "Philosophy as Strict Science" and at the end, next to the sentence "Not from philosophies but from issues [*Sachen*] and problems must the impulse to research proceed," writing the following marginal note: "*Wir nehmen Husserl beim Wort*"—"We take Husserl at his word." He had already begun to see that not consciousness, as in Husserl, but rather *alētheia*, as in the Greeks, was the central issue for philosophy. In that regard, he has said, the appearance of Werner Jaeger's *The History of the Genesis of Aristotle's Metaphysics* (1912) awakened his keen interest in the problematic of truth or disclosure (*alētheia*) in *Metaphysics* IX, 10.

Catholic thinkers also exerted great influence on Heidegger during his first two years at the university. Maurice Blondel's *L'Action*, which Heidegger told Henry Duméry he read "secretly" while with the Jesuits, continued to earn his praise until late in his life. And in the spring of 1950 Heidegger told Duméry that he thought a personalist theodicy was conceivable on the basis of Heidegger's own work so long as one rigorously and critically avoided anthropomorphisms.[12] The French spiritualist Ravaisson also worked an abiding influence on him.[13] But during those first two years at the university the influence of Carl Braig, Catholic theologian of the Tübingen school, seems to have been most pronounced, especially through his treatise *On Being: An Outline of Ontology*.[14] Besides offering Heidegger an extensive access to the philosophical texts of the tradition and an introduction to the concept of the onto-theological structure of metaphysics, the work seems to have started him on the path of searching out the etymology of fundamental concepts. For example, Braig traces the word *Zeit* (time) back to the Greek *tanumi*, "I stretch myself" (*ich strecke mich*), and here we may well see the roots of the discussion of temporality and historicity at SZ, p. 373, as a "stretching" (*Erstreckung*).[15] It was Braig who, on walks with the young seminarian, spoke of the internal restrictions of scholasticism and the possibilities inherent in German Idealism. Here was Heidegger's introduction to Schelling and Hegel. And another topic that would be fruitful in his teaching and writing after World War One dawned on him during this period.

> The term "hermeneutic" was familiar to me from my theological studies. At that time, I was particularly agitated over the question of the relation between the Word of Sacred Scripture and theological-speculative thinking. It was, if you will, the same relation, viz., between language and Being, only veiled and inaccessible to me, so that along many detours and wrong paths I sought in vain for a guiding thread.[16]

It was also during these university years that he discovered Kierkegaard, Nietzsche, and Dilthey, Dostoevsky, Rilke, and Trakl, and no doubt countless others. He speaks fondly of the lectures of the art historian, Wilhelm Vöge.

When Heidegger left the seminary in 1911 to devote himself to philosophy, his first wish was to go to Göttingen to study under Husserl, but financial problems kept him at Freiburg. (Within five years the situation would work out to his advantage with Husserl's transfer to Freiburg.) There he enrolled in lectures and seminars given by Heinrich Rickert, the neo-Kantian philosopher of values. Rickert's distinction between history and nature on the basis of individualizing vs. generalizing thought was, for all its primitiveness, basic to the young thinker at that time, and some forty years later he remarked that in those pre-war years when experimental psychology was attempting to become the one and only philosophy, "the value-philosophy school was an essential and decisive support for what was known as philosophy in the great tradition."[17] Through Rickert Heidegger was introduced to the writings of Emil Lask, who mediated between Husserl's *Logical Investigations* and Rickert's neo-Kantian theory of value.

In August, 1914, with the outbreak of the war, Heidegger enlisted in the military but was dismissed on October 9, 1914, for ill health. From 1915 through 1917 he worked in Freiburg with the Control Board of the Post Office, a position that apparently entailed field service. Fairly quickly during this period he finished his work, *Duns Scotus' Doctrine of Categories and Meaning,* which he presented in the summer of 1915 as his *Habilitationsschrift,* the book which, coupled with his lecture on "The Concept of Time in the Science of History" (July 27, 1915), gave him the right to lecture within the German university system. Significantly enough, his first course that fall was on Parmenides, and in the next two semesters he gave lectures on Kant, Fichte, and nineteenth century philosophy, and a seminar on Aristotle. On February 9, 1916, Edmund Husserl, then at Göttingen, received an appointment at Freiburg effective April 1. Apparently the contact between Husserl and Heidegger was immediate, for in September of that year, when Heidegger finished the preface to his Duns Scotus book, we find him thanking Prof. Husserl for his help in getting the work published. The Husserl Archives in Louvain today have the original copy that Heidegger gave Husserl with the inscription "Presented to Professor E. Husserl with most grateful respect."[18] Thus begins a relationship that was to launch Heidegger into the public eye as Husserl's "favorite student"[19] and colleague. In the 'twenties Husserl would often say to Heidegger, "You and I are phenomenology."[20]

THE PATH TO MARBURG: 1917–1923

One year after Husserl's arrival Heidegger was drafted for service on the Western Front with the *Ersatz-Bataillon Infanterie-Regiment* 113, and in 1918 he was at Verdun with the meteorological service (*Frontwetterwarte* 414). During this period, on October 7, 1917, Edmund Husserl received in Freiburg a letter from his friend and colleague Prof. Paul Natorp of the Philipps University at Marburg, inquiring whether the 28-year old Heidegger would be a fitting candidate for the position of professor *Extraordinarius* left vacant by the removal of Georg Misch to a full professorship in Göttingen. Natorp was interested in making this a position in medieval philosophy, and he notes that Heidegger had recently published a work on Duns Scotus. But Natorp wondered whether Heidegger's commitment to Catholicism would affect the matter.[21] On October 8 Husserl replied:

> I hasten to respond to your inquiry. Because Dr. Heidegger is very busy in the war service, I have not had sufficient opportunity up to this point to become closely acquainted with him and to form for myself a reliable judgment about his personality and character. In any case I have nothing bad to say of him.
>
> It is certain that he has confessional ties [*konfessionell gebunden ist*], because he stands, so to speak, under the protection of our "Catholic historian," Colleague Finke. Accordingly last year he was proposed in committee meetings as a nominee for the chair of Catholic philosophy in our Philosophy Department—a chair which we too would have liked to form into a scientific teaching position for the history of medieval philosophy. He was taken into consideration along with others, at which point Finke suggested him as an appropriate candidate in terms of his religious affiliation [*in konfessioneller Hinsicht*].[22]

Husserl goes on to note that a few months ago Heidegger had married a Protestant woman (Elfride Petri), who, he says, "as far as I know, has up until this point not converted [to Catholicism]." He finds him too young and not ripe enough for the position of *Extraordinarius*, and his Duns Scotus book is only a beginner's work (*Erstlingsbuch*). Moreover, "Dr. Heidegger has not yet had the opportunity to prove himself extensively as a teacher because, as I mentioned, some years back he was drafted into the Field Service of the Post Office [*Postfelddienst*]." Concerning Heidegger's teaching, "I have heard some very favorable judgments and also some critical ones—which in any case is connected with the fact that, in order to make headway in the systematic area, he does not give historical lecture courses but systematic ones," and he does manage to attain "a secure position on fundamental questions and methods." Moreover, Heidegger is no longer satisfied with Rickert, and "he now seeks to come to grips with phenomenological philosophy from within. It seems that he is doing this seriously and with thoroughness. This is all I can say at this time."

A week later (October 15, 1917) Natorp responded that, because of his youth and limited area of work, Heidegger was only third on the list after Kuntze and M. Wundt, but that in any case he seemed to show promise.[23] The job went to Wundt, who held it until 1920, when Heidegger was to have another chance at the position.

When he returned from the war and took up teaching again, Heidegger's interests ranged over a wide area that included St. Paul, St. Augustine, and above all Aristotle—all of these studied from within phenomenological method. But Heidegger's method was an adaptation of Husserl's. For one thing, its focus was set on the area of "everyday life" and not on the strictly theoretical areas that Husserl had probed in *Logical Investigations,* vol. II and in *Ideas.* For another, little enough was said about the reductions that Husserl saw as the necessary entry into philosophical work, although a reduction is certainly at work in Heidegger insofar as he approaches all beings from the question of their presence (Being) in the open domain of sense that is man's essence.[24] And there was nothing at all about the transcendental ego, that final goal of phenomenological archeology. Husserl would later attribute Heidegger's divergence from his own work to Heidegger's theological prejudices and to the disorienting experience of the war and its "ensuing difficulties [which] drive men into mysticism,"[25] and he would lament, "Unfortunately I did not determine his philosophical formation; he was obviously already into his own thing when he studied my writings."[26]

Indeed. And that meant Aristotle and the question about the unified meaning of Being which determines all modes of the Being of beings. Phenomenology was a means to, a method for, ontology. To be sure, it put the science of Being on a whole new footing insofar as it no longer asked about Being apart from man but rather focused on the *presence* of beings in and to man's essence and designated this *relatedness* as the problem-area that the tradition inadequately searched for under the title "Being." But if phenomenological givenness and correlativity were now the domain for ontology, the question that began to put distance between the master and his young disciple was: What *is* this area of presence and relatedness? "It is consciousness and its objectivity, or is it the Being of beings in its unconcealedness and concealing?"[27] Yes, the one and only issue (*die Sache selbst*) for phenomenology was the self-showing of whatever immediately appears. But Heidegger had a hunch:

"What occurs for [Husserl's] phenomenology of the acts of consciousness as the self-manifestation of phenomena is thought even more originally by Aristotle and in all Greek thinking and existence as *alētheia,* the unconcealedness of what-is-present, its un-hiding, its showing of itself."[28]

This happy marriage of the Aristotelian problematic of Being and an adapted phenomenological method led Heidegger further away from his master. Husserl's insistence on seeing for oneself "demanded that one give up introducing the authority of the great thinkers into the conversation. However, the clearer it became to me that the increasing familiarity with phenomenological seeing was fruitful for the interpretation of Aristotle's writings, the less I could separate myself from Aristotle and the other Greek thinkers."[29]

There were other components to the revolutionary doctrine being formed by Husserl's apprentice. There was the discovery of what he called "kairological time" in the writings of St. Paul, especially in the fifth chapter of I Thessalonians.[30] The eschatological thrust of early Christianity, the expectation of the Parousia, opens up an absolutely unique understanding of time wherein all questions of "when" are transposed from chronology (*chronos*) into "the moment of insight" (*kairos, Augenblick*). The question of when the Parousia will occur is not answered by reference to objective time but is referred back to factical lived experience and becomes a matter of the way a man leads his life. The "time" of the Parousia and the task of self-understanding are bound together in such a way that to relate authentically to the coming of the Lord means to be awake and vigilant (*wachsam sein*) rather than to look forward to a future event. The question of the "when" of the Parousia reduces back to the question of the "how" of authentic living. Rather than crying out "Peace! Security!" (I Thess., 5:3), the person who is truly awake in his factical experience lives a life of constant, essential, and necessary uncertainty in a *Vollzugszusammenhang mit Gott,* an enactment of that uncertainty before the divine. Out of such an experience, Heidegger asserts, authentic temporality is generated. Clearly at this point he was at some distance from Husserl. Heidegger was captured by the insight that the finitude and temporality of human existence are what open up the primordial realm within which can happen the self-manifestation of phenomena: dis-closure or *a-lētheia.* This was the original and unifying meaning of what the tradition called "Being," and Heidegger was out to "destroy" (i.e., de-construct) that tradition in order to find what it had left unsaid, viz., that man opens up the world of meaningfulness by living into his future and thereby reappropriating his ownmost and already operative state of dying. Here, he thought, was born sense as such and the world of presence.

Sometime between 1919 and June of 1921 Heidegger drew these themes together in a document that only recently has been published: "Remarks on

Karl Jaspers' *Psychology of Worldviews*."[31] The whole essay has received an excellent commentary by David Krell, so here I need only highlight some topics that point towards SZ. Heidegger focuses on existence (*Existenz*), which is not grasped theoretically but only in the experience of living out one's own Being in a concernful having-of-oneself in historical contexts.[32] This basic experience of self-having is constituted by an "authentic historical stretch into my past—not a past which is some baggage I drag along behind me, but a past which I experience historically in such a way that I thereby possess myself as a self within the horizon of expectations which I have already projected ahead of myself."[33] This concernful, historically enacted self-having is the "how" (*Wie*) of man's Being, and: "The phenomenological explication of the 'how' of this enactment of experience according to its fundamental *historical* sense is the decisive task in this whole complex of problems involving the phenomenon of existence."[34] Within that phenomenology, facticity—the lived experience of one's own "here and now"—is crucial. Facticity is a phenomenon enacted only historically, where "the historical" means not "the chronological" but the very content and "how" of the self-concern wherein I experience my specific past, present, and future. In this regard Heidegger speaks of "conscience" as the "renewal of concern" (*Bekümmerungserneuerung*) by the enactment of self-appropriation (*Selbstaneignung*), and he emphasizes that the meaning of the factical "I am" includes in an original way historical living within the problematic of the "how" of concernful appropriation of oneself.[35] Clearly, the kernel of SZ is already present in this essay.

On February 11, 1920, when Heidegger was in the middle of a course that investigated the "hermeneutics of facticity" and the structure of the *Umwelt*, Husserl was at last impressed enough with the thirty-year-old lecturer to write to Natorp recommending that Heidegger fill the position that Wundt was vacating to go to Jena.[36] Natorp responded on March 21 that Hedegger was again third on the list, this time after Nicolai Hartmann and Leser, but now "proposed with more emphasis."[37] No matter. Hartmann got the job.

The third and finally successful chance came in 1922. Paul Natorp, 68 years old and about to retire, would be succeeded in the fall of 1923 by Hartmann with the result that the *Extraordinarius* position would again be open. On February 1, 1922, when Heidegger was between lectures on Aristotle which in fact were a *tour de force* on "falling" and *Reluzenz* (material that would enter SZ at page 21), Husserl wrote Natorp about the "original personality" (*originelle Persönlichkeit*) of this *Privatdozent,* about his command of a range of material from Aristotle through the neo-Platonists to Augustine, and about how "he illustrates fundamental problems through *concrete* exegesis [and] develops, for example, thoughts about the hermeneutical categories, about the sense and the genuine method for history" and so on. He also notes that Heidegger has studied Luther (in fact he had opened his Aristotle course on November 2,

1921, by citing Luther's condemnation of the *Metaphysics, De Anima,* and *Ethics* of the "pagan master Aristotle"!) and that his knowledge of Catholicity would be important at Marburg for linking up philosophy with Protestant theology, which Heidegger also knows well.[38]

In several letters Natorp made positive moves to invite Heidegger to Marburg. On September 22, 1922 he wrote Husserl: Whereas Richard Kroner, also of Freiburg, would certainly qualify because of his book *From Kant to Hegel,* it would be more desirable to widen the range of the philosophical offerings at Marburg by bringing in some new blood. Thus we come again to Heidegger, not only because of Husserl's high recommendations of his assistant, but also because of what the Marburg faculty has heard of his new developments in applying phenomenological method to the history of philosophy, especially to Aristotle and the Middle Ages. In fact, Marburg needs both a professor to teach phenomenology and a professor familiar with the history of medieval philosophy — and Martin Heidegger would be two in one. But there is one hitch (it will occur again in 1925-26): Heidegger has published so little — in fact nothing since his book on Duns Scotus. Therefore the Marburg faculty is thrown back on Husserl's judgment of the man. But doesn't Heidegger have something in the works, a manuscript far enough along to be printed or that could be read? Could he send it to Natorp? And in any case Natorp would be thankful to Husserl for any reports available about Heidegger's lecture courses and seminars.[39]

That letter is the beginning of the famous and much discussed "Natorp essay."[40] Sometime between September 22 and October 30, 1922, Heidegger had his brother Fritz type up two copies of a forty page manuscript which pulled together the major themes and directions of his teaching over the past three years. The manuscript was represented as part of a major work on Aristotle that would be published in Husserl's *Jahrbuch für Philosophie und phänomenologische Forschung.* (On December 14 of that same year Husserl told Ingarden: "In the seventh [volume of the *Jahrbuch*] there will appear a fundamental and long work on Aristotle by Heidegger."[41]) The full manuscript was to deal with texts Heidegger had been discussing in his Aristotle courses: *Nicomachean Ethics* VI, *Metaphysics* I and VII-IX, *De Anima* III, and *Physics* II; and the "Natorp essay" was an introduction to this work. The scope of the essay was enormous: besides Aristotle he spoke of Augustine, the young Luther, Gabriel Biel, St. Paul, Peter Lombard, and the Old Testament. "At that time," Hans-Georg Gadamer writes, "Heidegger would surely have called it a working out of the hermeneutical situation: it tried to make the reader aware of the questions and the intellectual resistance [*Gegenwollen*] with which we might confront Aristotle, the master of the tradition."[42] Heidegger kept one copy for himself (the only one to survive) and covered the margins of the other with handwritten additions, clarifications, and amendments before sending it off to Natorp. (This copy, which Natorp later gave to Gadamer, was destroyed in the bombings of Leipzig.) "The remarkable phenomenological power of intuition Heidegger brought to his interpretation liberated the original Aristotelian text so profoundly and strikingly from the sedimentations of the scholastic tradition and from the lamentably distorted image of Aristotle contained in the criticism of the time (Cohen loved to say, 'Aristotle was an apothecary') that it began to speak in an unexpected way."[43]

The response of Natorp was immediate and enthusiastic. On October 30, 1922, he wrote that he and Nicholai Hartmann had read the document (*"Heideggers Auszug"*) with the greatest interest and had found therein what Husserl's reports had prepared them for: an extraordinary originality, depth and rigor that happily wipes off the map so much of the at best second-quality material that even some full professors of medieval thought at Marburg have written and use to defend their professorships. But apparently Heidegger was negotiating at this time for another position, at Göttingen, and Natorp assures Husserl that Heidegger will have a warm reception at Marburg and that, while they could get by with Kroner or Heimsoeth, neither of them could provide, as well as Heidegger can, such a strong expansion of Marburg's philosophical offerings.[44]

A week later Natorp again wrote to say what strong interest the essay had awakened among his colleagues for its originality of procedure and execution. He himself has read it once more and has an even more intense impression of its worth. He is amazed at Heidegger's view of Greek thought and its decisive influence on the whole of Western "culture," at his position both on and against German thought, and at how, in the case of Luther and Kant, he places himself against the past and seems to agree with and to corroborate Natorp's own views from many new perspectives. He asks whether there is any more that they might see of Heidegger's essay.[45]

The die was cast. Heidegger accepted the call.[46] When he had finished his last course as *Privatdozent* at Freiburg, he gathered some friends, colleagues, and students for a going-away celebration at Todtnauberg in the Black Forest. Gadamer remembers sitting at night around an immense bonfire and listening to a moving talk by Heidegger about the Greeks and about vigilance (*wach sein*).[47] Here, says Gadamer, the romanticism of the Youth Movement of the times and the power of Greek philosophy, the present and the past, met in the decisiveness of a thinker who saw both as one. That unifying vision also explains why the Aristotle essay never appeared. In a very real sense it became SZ.

THE GENESIS OF "BEING AND TIME": 1923–1926

The question: When was SZ conceived and written? can only have a complex answer, only part of which can be given here. As early as 1913 Heidegger stated his goal of "articulating the whole region of 'Being' in its various modes of reality."[48] Soon after the war his lecture course "Basic Questions in Phenomenology" (winter semester, 1919-1920) presented in incipient form the analysis of environment within a hermeneutics of facticity. The following winter his "Introduction to the Phenomenology of Religion" opened up, by a reading of St. Paul, what was to become his doctrine of resolve and existential temporality. His Jaspers essay probed the meaning of *Existenz*, and his two Aristotle courses at Freiburg (winter, 1921-1922, and summer, 1922), which shaped much of the Natorp essay, elaborated the environment analysis through a reading of Aristotelian texts.

During the summer of 1923 his last course at Freiburg began to pull together the analytic of existence (*Dasein*) which was to become SZ. Announced in the catalogue as "Ontology," the course was better known by the subtitle which Heidegger gave it on May 2, the first day of class: "Hermeneutics of Facticity."[49] Facticity: this meant not human Being as the object of some intuition but the Being of man insofar as he lives in his time being and his current "there" (*Da*). Hermeneutics: this meant neither exegesis and commentary as in Hellenism and Christianity nor the theory and art of interpretation as in Schleiermacher and Dilthey, but rather the very event of disclosing one's heretofore undisclosed facticity, a moment already operative within facticity insofar as man is *zōion logon echon*, the living being who has himself and his world in speech. The true self that is facticity is not derived from the ego — rather the ego is derived from it. (Heidegger would seem to be the first philosopher to have ontologically deduced the ego.) And so too this hermeneutics is no mere description (*Abschilderung*) at the service of a theory of rational man, but rather a matter of awakening existence to and for itself. After discussing (May 30 through July 4) "historical consciousness" and "philosophy" as two modes of the current self-interpretation of existence, Heidegger proceeded to spell out what he had earlier called *der Bewegtheitszusammenhang des Lebens*, the world of movement (*kinēsis*) that is existence. To that end he called for a return to the Greeks, especially to Aristotle, and at the same time for a destruction of the tradition (July 11). In the two remaining lectures many of the technical terms of SZ began to make their appearance: *gewesen sein, Neugier, Vorhabe, In-der-Welt-sein, Alltäglichkeit, Bedeutsamkeit*, the *Als, Erschlossenheit, Vorhandenheit*, and even the threefold articulation of SZ Part One, Division One (= SZ I.1): *Welt, In*, and *Wer*. However, the course broke off on July 25 before these themes could be fully developed. Although it would be premature to call this course a "proto-SZ," there could be no question of Heidegger's direction.

The actual writing of SZ belongs to the Marburg period. In December of 1923 Heidegger discussed with Ernst Cassirer "the demand for an existential analytic," and during that winter in Todtnauberg he began the first drafts of

SZ.[50] A few months later, on Friday, July 25, 1924, the "original form" of SZ emerged as a 6000-word speech delivered before the Theologians' Society of Marburg under the title, "The Concept of Time."[51] After introducing his topic by a brief discussion of time in Christian theology, Einstein, Aristotle, and Augustine, Heidegger poses the question of time within the arena of human existence: Could it be that I myself am the "now" and that my existence itself is time? The rest of the lecture (1) provides a very brief eight-point summary of some of what is in SZ Part One, Division One (= SZ I.1): *In-der-Welt-sein als Besorgen, Mitsein, Sprache, Jemeinigkeit, das Man, Worumwillen, Reluzenz,* and *Alltäglichkeit,* and then (2) lays out the essentials of SZ I.2 on death, resolve, authentic temporality, and within-time-ness. It ends with a stirring list of questions which reduce from: What is time? to: Who is time? to: Am I *my* time? With the last question, he says, existence becomes questionable.

A year later, in the summer of 1925, we can at last begin to speak of a "proto-SZ" and it takes the form of the lecture course, "The History of the Concept of Time."[52] Like so many of Heidegger's courses, its title scarcely betrays its contents. After a lengthy discussion (May 4—June 15) of intentionality, categorial intuition, and the *a priori* in Husserl, Heidegger launches into the following ambitious outline:

Part One: Analysis of the Phenomenon of Time
  a. The preparatory description of the field in which the phenomenon of time becomes visible: The elaboration of the Being-question in the sense of a first explication of existence;
  b. The laying free [*Freilegung*] of time itself;
  c. The conceptual interpretation [of time].
Part Two: History of the Concept of Time from the Present Backwards
  a. Henri Bergson's theory of time;
  b. The Concept of Time in Kant and Newton;
  c. The Genesis of the Concept of Time in Aristotle.
Part Three: The Exposition of the Question about Being in General and about the Being of History and Nature in Particular

Let two remarks suffice for our purposes. First: the proposed outline. The three Parts here projected scramble the outline of SZ; they correspond roughly to: (1) SZ Part I, Divs. 1-2; (2) SZ Part II, Divs. 1-3, without Descartes but with Bergson and Newton; and (3) SZ Part I, Div. 3. The "Destruction of the History of Ontology," here called "Part Two: History of the Concept of Time . . .," is to come *between* what we now have as the *published* parts of SZ and the famous *unpublished* division entitled "Time and Being." (With Heidegger's 1927 course, "The Basic Problems of Phenomenology" we will get yet a third outline: first, the "historical-destructive" part, but focused on the question of

Being, not time; secondly, roughly SZ II.3 on Aristotle, followed by SZ I.1-2; and thirdly, a glimpse into SZ I.3[53]) Second remark: what the course actually covered. The lectures got no further than the first division entitled "The Preparatory Description..." or "A first explication of existence." Within those twenty-four lectures we have an occasionally close, occasionally divergent, elaboration of the Table of Contents of SZ up to the chapter on death.

It is well known that a few months after this lecture course broke off, Heidegger was nominated to the Marburg chair vacated by Nicolai Hartmann's removal to Cologne, but on condition that he publish something immediately. The order of events thereafter seems to be the following. During the spring vacation, January 29 through April 30, 1926, Heidegger retired to Todtnauberg and in the house of Johann Brender, a hundred meters below his own cabin,[54] pulled together the lecture notes of "The History of the Concept of Time" into the first 240 pages of SZ, had them printed with Husserl's help, and sent two copies of the page proofs to the appropriate ministry in Berlin. Husserl joined him for vacation in Todtnauberg, and there they discussed the notion of Being-in-the-world as this would be elaborated in SZ sections 12 through 69. On Thursday, April 8, 1926, Husserl's sixty-seventh birthday, Heidegger presented him the dedicatory first page of SZ, covered with flowers and hand-inscribed: "To Edmund Husserl in grateful admiration and friendship."[55] The old man could hardly have surmised that three years later, when reading the book during his vacation at Lago Como, he would scrawl in pencil on the title page: "*amicus Plato, magis amica veritas*." But at this point his jubilation carried over into helping Heidegger correct the page proofs, and by mid-April they were into sections 12 and 13 on "Being-in-the-world in general."

The jubilation was squelched some months later when the minister in Berlin denied Heidegger the appointment and adjudged the 240 pages "inadequate." But the publication of the full text—as much of it as would ever appear—in February of 1927 brought Heidegger immediate fame. Two months later, on April 30, 1927, he began lecturing on "The Basic Problems of Phenomenology," an illuminating restructuring of SZ and a sneak preview of how he intended to complete that work. In October of the same year, while he was helping an already dubious Husserl to write the *Encyclopaedia Britannica* article on phenomenology, the ministry in Berlin reversed its decision and gave Heidegger the position. He stayed on only a year longer, until the retirement of his master brought a call back to the university where he had begun and would end his philosophical career. On November 5, 1928, as he entered Hörsaal 6 of the University of Freiburg to begin his first lecture as Husserl's successor, he was greeted by the applause of an overflow crowd of 280 students. He was thirty-nine years old, at the height of his powers, and the brightest star of German phenomenology.

Notes

Thomas Sheehan is an Associate Professor of Philosophy at Loyola University of Chicago. This essay is part of a work in progress tentatively entitled *The Genesis of "Sein und Zeit."*

1. Cf. Paul Hühnerfeld, *In Sachen Heidegger,* Hamburg: Hoffman and Campe, 1950, p. 9. Besides the usual sources, I am indebted for information in this essay to conversations with Martin Heidegger, spring, 1971; H.-G. Gadamer, E. Tugendhat, and W. Biemel, January and May, 1975; M. Müller, K. Rahner, and F.-W. von Herrmann, fall, 1976; to the Husserl Archives and Prof. Karl Schuhmann's *Husserl-Chronik: Denk- und Lebensweg Edmund Husserls,* The Hague: Nijhoff, 1977, and to information supplied by Heidegger himself to *Das Deutsche Führerlexikon,* Berlin: Otto Stollberg, 1934/35, p. 180, reprinted in G. Schneeberger, ed., *Nachlese zu Heidegger,* Bern, 1962, p. 237.
2. M. Heidegger, "A Recollection...," trans. H. Seigfried, *infra.*
3. Jean-Michel Palmier and Frédérich de Towarnicki, "Entretien avec Heidegger," *L'Express* 954 (Oct. 20-26, 1969), p. 80.
4. On Gröber's relations to the Nazis as archbishop of Freiburg, cf. Gordon Zahn, *German Catholics and Hitler's Wars,* New York: Sheed and Ward, 1962, pp. 119-142.
5. Franz Brentano, *Von der mannigfachen Bedeutung des Seienden nach Aristoteles,* Freiburg: Herder, 1862; reprinted, Darmstadt: Wissenschaftliche Buchgesellschaft, 1960. In English: *On the Several Senses of Being in Aristotle,* trans., Rolf George, Berkeley: University of California Press, 1975.
6. Respectively: *Unterwegs zur Sprache,* Pfullingen: Neske, 1959, p. 92f. = *On the Way to Language,* trans. P. Hertz, New York: Harper and Row, 1971, p. 7 (hereafter: US). *Zur Sache des Denkens,* Tübingen: Niemeyer, 1969, p. 81 = *On 'Time and Being'* trans. J. Stambaugh, New York: Harper & Row, 1972, p. 74 (hereafter: SD). "Preface" to William J. Richardson, *Heidegger: Through Phenomenology to Thought,* The Hague: Nijhoff, 1963, p. x.
7. J. A. MacDowell, *A Gênese da Ontologia Fundamental de Martin Heidegger: Ensaio de caracterização do modo de pensar de "Sein und Zeit,"* São Paulo: Herder, 1970, p. 155, n. 116. MacDowell opines: "Nestas circunstâncias, Heidegger deverá ter practicado mais de uma vez os 'Exercícios Espirituais" (*loc. cit.*).
8. *Die Lehre vom Urteil im Psychologismus. Ein kritisch-positiver Beitrag zur Logik,* Leipzig: Johann Ambrosius Barth, 1914. Also in M. Heidegger, *Frühe Schriften* (hereafter:FS), Frankfurt: V. Klostermann, 1972, pp. 1-129 with omission of the "Lebenslauf" (p. 111 of the original). H. Rickert was co-director.
9. SD 82 = (Eng. trans.) 75
10. On Husserl as a realist, cf. Roman Ingarden, *On the Motives which led Husserl to Transcendental Idealism,* trans. Arnór Hannibalsson, The Hague: Nijhoff, 1975.
11. *Die Lehre vom Urteil...,* original, p. 108; FS, 128.
12. On Heidegger and Blondel: Henry Duméry, "Blondel et la philosophie contemporaine (Etude critique)," *Etudes blondéliennes* (Paris), 1952, fascicule 2, p. 92, n. 1. Also Jean Beaufret's contribution to *Dem Andenken Martin Heideggers. Zum 26. Mai 1976,* Frankfurt: V. Klostermann, 1977, p. 19. Also Jean Guitton, "Visite à Heidegger," *La Table Ronde* 123 (March, 1958), p. 155: Heidegger also read Blondel's *Pensée.*
13. On Heidegger and Ravaisson: Jean Guitton, *loc. cit.* and "Cette paix qui émane d'un long repos de l'être," *Le Monde* (Paris), May 28, 1976, p. 8

divided into an introduction (Being in general and the science thereof) and three unequal divisions: Vom Wesen des Seienden (Wirklichkeit, Wesenheit), Vom Wirken des Seienden, and Vom Zwecke des Seienden. The work opened with a long citation from Bonaventure's *Itinerarium mentis in Deum*, V, 3, 4, which said in part: "Mira est caecitas intellectus, qui non considerat illud [esse], quod prius videt et sine quo nihil potest cognoscere."

15. Braig, p. 88f. Cf. etymologies and explanations of other Greek terms: *energeia* and *entelecheia* on p. 27; *to ti ēn einai, hypokeimenon* and *hypostasis*, p. 49; *topos* (traced back to the Sanskrit!), p. 65; *ratio, logos, archē,* and *aitia,* p. 105; *telos,* p. 140.
16. US 96 = (Eng. trans.) 9f., here slightly revised.
17. Heidegger made these remarks during a discussion in the pro-seminar of Prof. Spoerri in Zürich, Nov. 6, 1951.
18. "Herrn Professor E. Husserl in dankbarster Verehrung überreicht vom Verfasser," Husserl Archives, Louvain, B P 75.
19. R I Albrecht 12. III. 26. My special thanks to Professor Samuel IJsseling, Director of the Husserl Archives, for permission to quote from selected letters of Husserl.
20. Husserl's conversation of 13. VIII. 31 cited in Dorion Cairns, *Conversations with Husserl and Fink,* ed. by the Husserl Archives, The Hague: Nijhoff, 1976, p. 9.
21. R II Natorp 7.X.17.
22. For this and the following: R I Natorp 8.X.17
23. R II Natorp 15.X.17
24. For Heidegger's use of the term "phenomenological reduction," cf. his *Die Grundprobleme der Phänomenologie,* Frankfurt: V. Klostermann, 1975, p. 29. For Husserl's claim that "Heidegger has not grasped the whole meaning of the phenomenological reduction," cf. E. Husserl *Briefe an Roman Ingarden,* ed. R. Ingarden, The Hague: Nijhoff, 1968, p. 42f.
25. Cairns, *loc. cit.* (same date and conversation).
26. Husserl, *Briefe,* p. 41 (Nov. 19, 1927).
27. SD 87 = (Eng. trans.) 79.
28. *Ibid.*
29. *Ibid.,* 86 = (Eng. trans.) 78.
30. See my article "Heidegger's 'Introduction to the Phenomenology of Religion,' 1920–1921," *The Personalist,* LX, 3 (July 1979), 312–324.
31. M. Heidegger, "Anmerkungen zu Karl Jaspers' *Psychologie der Weltanschauungen,*" in *Karl Jaspers in der Diskussion,* ed., Hans Saner, Munich: Piper, 1973, pp. 70-100. Also in M. Heidegger, *Wegmarken,* 2d. ed., Frankfurt: V. Klostermann, 1976, pp. 1-44. Cf. David Farrell Krell, "Toward *Sein und Zeit,*" *Journal of the British Society for Phenomenology,* 6 (1975), 147-156.
32. "Anmerkungen," p. 89f. (= *Wegmarken,* p. 29f.): gehabt im Vollzug des 'bin'; Mich-selbst-haben; *historischen* Zusammenhängen; Grunderfahrung des *bekümmerten* Habens seiner selbst.
33. *Ibid.,* p. 91 (= p. 31). This is more a close paraphrase than a translation.
34. *Ibid.,* p. 91 (= p. 31f.)
35. *Ibid.,* p. 92f. (= pp. 33-35).
36. R I Natorp 11.II.20
37. R II Natorp 21.III.20
38. R I Natorp 1.II.22
39. R II Natorp 22.IX.22
40. To the best of my knowledge Heidegger refers to this essay only once and then to say he will not publish it: Juan Llambías de Azevedo, "Un diálogo con Heidegger," *Marcha* (Argentina) 17 (Dec. 30, 1955). Other mentions of it are: H.-G. Gadamer,

Philosophische Lehrjahre. Eine Rückschau, Frankfurt: V. Klostermann, 1977, pp. 24, 212f.; *isdem, Philosophical Hermeneutics,* trans., David E. Linge, Berkeley: University of California Press, 1976, p. 200f.; Wilhelm Szilasi, "Interpretation und Geschichte der Philosophie," in *Martin Heideggers Einfluss auf die Wissenschaften,* ed. C. Astrada *et al.,* Bern: Francke, 1949, p. 77; (Szilasi erroneously dates the essay from 1923); Hinrich Knittermeyer, *Die Philosophie der Existenz,* Vienna: Humboldt, 1952, p. 212. (Knittermeyer calls it "eine nur handschriftlich vorliegende Interpretation der aristotelischen Metaphysik."). I am grateful to Professor Gadamer for further information on this essay in a conversation held on January 27, 1975.

41. Husserl, *Briefe,* p. 40.

42. Gadamer, *Philosophical Hermeneutics,* p. 200; translation slightly revised.

43. *Ibid.,* p. 201.

44. R II Natorp 30.X.22.

45. R II Natorp 9.XI.22.

46. Did Heidegger go to Marburg as an *Ordinarius* (roughly, full professor) or as an *Extraordinarius* (roughly, associate professor)? Walter Biemel (*Martin Heidegger: An Illustrated Study,* trans. J. L. Mehta, New York: Harcourt Brace Jovanovich, 1976, p. 181) and David Farrell Krell ("General Introduction" to Martin Heidegger, *Basic Writings,* trans., D. Krell *et al,* New York: Harper and Row, 1977, p. 14) have him an *Extraordinarius* at Marburg, and indeed Heidegger's own "Zur Geschichte des philosophischen Lehrstuhls seit 1866," in *Die Philipps-Universität zu Marburg 1527-1927,* Marburg: N.G. Elwert, 1927, p. 687, indicates that Misch, Wundt, and Hartmann (up to 1922) occupied an *Extraordinariat.* But Heidegger himself (*Das Deutsche Führerlexikon,* p. 180 [cf. n. 1, *supra*]) and Husserl (*Briefe,* p. 26, 31. VIII.23) say that he went as an *Ordinarius.* Knittermeyer, *op. cit.,* p. 212, says: "1923 wird Heidegger Ordinarius in Marburg, in der Nachfolge Paul Natorps, neben Nicolai Hartmann."

47. Gadamer, *Philosophische Lehrjahre,* p. 213f. and 33. Heidegger delivered a lecture on "Dasein und Wahrsein" in 1923 at the Kant Society in Cologne, on invitation of Max Scheler.

48. Cf. note 11 *supra.*

49. Oskar Becker, who heard the course, defines its subtitle: "Damit ist gemeint die *Auslegung* (interpretierende Explikation) des tatsächlichen geschichtlichen Lebens als eines faktischen, historisch da seienden, auf die Weise seines *Da-seins* hin." "Mathematische Existenz. Untersuchungen zur Logik und Ontologie mathematischer Phänomene," *Jahrbuch für Philosophie und phänomenologische Forschung,* 8 (1927), 621.

50. On the discussion with Cassirer, cf. SZ, 51, n. 1. On the drafts of SZ, US 95 = 9 says that Heidegger began the first drafts in the summer of 1923, but information from F.-W. von Herrmann confirms that he began in the winter of 1923-24.

51. See my article "The 'Original Form' of *Sein und Zeit:* Heidegger's *Der Begriff der Zeit* (1924)," *Journal of the British Society for Phenomenology,* X, 2 (May 1979), 78-83. Also Oskar Becker, *op cit.,* p. 444.

52. Martin Heidegger, *Prolegomena zur Geschichte des Zeitbegriffs,* Frankfurt: V. Klostermann, 1979.

53. See my article, "Time and Being, 1925-27" forthcoming in *Heidegger Studies* (tentative title), ed. Robert W. Shahan and J. N. Mohanty, Norman, Okla.: Oklahoma University Press.

54. Cf. W. Biemel, "Erinnerungen an Heidegger," *Allgemeine Zeitschrift für Philosophie* 2 (1977), p. 13.

55. The Husserl Archives at Louvain preserve Husserl's own copy of SZ (B P 78) and, glued inside it, the handwritten dedication of April 8, 1926: "Edmund Husserl/in

dankbarer Vererhrung und Freundschaft/ Todtnauberg i. Schwarzwald, zum 8. April 1926." In the final printed draft the dedication reads: "Edmund Husserl in Verehrung und Freundschaft zugeeignet" and adds "Bad." before "Schwarzwald." The citation from the *Sophist* also appears in Greek and German above the dedication, with a slightly different translation ("... denn offenbar versteht ihr doch schon lange..." for SZ's "Denn offenbar seid ihr doch schon lange mit dem vertraut..."). Was the manuscript completed at the time? Frau Husserl writes (*Briefe*, p. 37, 16.IV.26): "Heidegger... brachte eine mit Blumen geschmückte Rolle, die die Widmung 'Edmund Husserl in dankbarer Verehrung und Freundschaft' seines eben vollendeten Werkes enthielt." Husserl (R I Albert 28.IV.26) speaks of "die Widmung seines eben in Druck befindlichen Buches." Heidegger himself, many years later, wrote of showing Husserl on this occasion "Das nahezu fertige [well-nigh finished] Manuskript" of SZ. Cf. Edmund Husserl, *Zur Phänomenologie des inneren Zeitbewusstseins (1893-1917)* ed. Rudolf Boehm, The Hague: Nijhoff, 1966, p. xxiv.

A Recollection (1957)

Martin Heidegger

The chosen path, in retrospect and in prospect, appears at every juncture in a different light, with a different tone, and stimulates different interpretations. Several features, however, although hardly recognizable to oneself, run continuously throughout the regions of thought. Their image appears in the little pamphlet, *The Pathway*, written in 1947/48.

At the grammar schools in Konstanz and Freiburg im Breisgau, between 1903 and 1909, I enjoyed fruitful learning under excellent teachers of the Greek, Latin, and German languages; likewise, besides my formal education — or rather, during it — I acquired everything that was to be of lasting value.

In 1905 I read, for the first time, Stifter's *Bunte Steine*. In 1907 a fatherly friend from my hometown, the later archbishop of Freiburg im Breisgau, Dr. Conrad Gröber, presented me with Franz Brentano's dissertation: *On the Several Senses of Being in Aristotle* (1862). Its many lengthy quotations from the Greek original took, for me, the place of Aristotle's collected works which, however, were on my student desk one year later, after I had borrowed them from my boarding school library. The quest for the unity in the multiplicity of Being, then only obscurely, unsteadily, and helplessly stirring within me, *remained*, through many upsets, wanderings, and perplexities, *the* ceaseless impetus for the treatise *Being and Time* which appeared two decades later.

In 1908 I found my way to Hölderlin through a small, still preserved Reclam paperback of his poems.

In 1909 I began my studies by taking theology at the University of Freiburg im Breisgau for four semesters; in the following years philosophy, the humanities and the natural sciences replaced this course of study. Beginning in 1909 I attempted, although without adequate guidance, to grasp the meaning of Husserl's *Logical Investigations*. Rickert's seminars introduced me to the writings of Emil Lask who, mediating between the two, attempted to listen also to the Greek thinkers.

What the exciting years between 1910 and 1914 meant for me cannot be adequately expressed; I can only indicate it by a selective enumeration: the second, significantly enlarged edition of Nietzsche's *The Will to Power*, the works of Kierkegaard and Dostoevsky in translation, the awakening interest in Hegel and Schelling, Rilke's works and Trakl's poems, Dilthey's *Collected Writings*.

The decisive, and therefore ineffable, influence on my own later academic career came from two men who should be expressly mentioned here in memory and gratitude; the one was Carl Braig, professor of systematic theology, who was the last in the tradition of the speculative school of Tübingen which gave significance and scope to Catholic theology through its dialogue with Hegel and Schelling; the other one was the art historian Wilhelm Vöge. The impact of each lecture by these two teachers lasted through the long semester breaks which I always spent at my parents' house in my hometown Messkirch, working uninterruptedly.

What later succeeded and failed, on the chosen path, defies self-interpretation which could only name that which is not one's own. And that includes everything essential.

Translated by Hans Seigfried

Note

Hans Seigfried is Associate Professor of Philosophy at Loyola University of Chicago and author of *Wahrheit und Metaphysik bei Suarez* (1967) and various articles in professional journals on Kant, Nietzsche, Heidegger, phenomenology, philosophy of science, and literary criticism.

The present text is a translation of the "Antrittsrede" (Inaugural Address) which Heidegger delivered in 1957. It has appeared in *Jahreshefte der Heidelberger Akademie der Wissenschaften* 1957/58, Heidelberg, 1959, p. 20-21 and in Martin Heidegger, *Frühe Schriften* (Frankfurt: Klostermann, 1972), pp. ix-xi. The translation is made from the latter. It first appeared in *Man and World*, 3, 1 (1970), 3-4, and is reprinted here with Professor Seigfried's gracious permission.

Letter to
Rudolf Otto
(1919)

Edmund Husserl

To Rudolf Otto, Marburg

Freiburg
March 5, 1919

Dear Colleague,

I have just heard from Vicar Katz that you would like to take me up on my offer to tell you my impressions of Herr Oxner. I hasten to fulfill your wish.

Herr Oxner, like his older friend, Dr. Heidegger, was originally a philosophy student of Rickert. Not without strong inner struggles did the two of them gradually open themselves to my suggestions and also draw closer to me personally. In that same period they both underwent radical changes in their fundamental religious convictions. Truly both of them are religiously oriented personalities. In Heidegger it is the theoretical-philosophical interest which predominates, whereas in Oxner it is the religious — and so much so in Oxner that I would be inclined to characterize him straightaway as a *homo religiosus*. Yet at the same time he is of a specifically theological nature: he cannot and will not do without a philosophy, but it must be an honest, serious, scientific philosophy which, in concepts of a faithfully ancillary reason, gives to the depths of religious life and to the religious objectivity revealed therein an adequate expression and more: a purification, clarification, rational illumination, and a sure defense against scepticism. In that regard he hopes for quite a bit from pure phenomenology and has already penetrated deeply into the spirit of its work and into its method — if all indications do not deceive. I say "indications": It is indeed hard to break through the extraordinary shyness of this man, to lead him to free and easy conversation, even to engage him personally. For years now, whenever I have run across him (for example, after seminars), I have invited him to come and talk with me at length about the ideas concerning philosophy of religion which came up in the seminar (and which always have a lively interest for me). But only twice did he actually come, and in only one instance did we get down to a conversation of several hours. Hence I do not know him well in the usual sense. Insofar as I have often experienced sharp disappointments with students, I would prefer to be very reserved in my judgment. And yet in those cases my *daimonion* has always warned me often enough. But with Oxner it positively admonishes me to trust him entirely. Only with real difficulty can I imagine how I might be deceived in the case of this completely unassuming man who holds himself timidly in the background, who blushes when one merely looks at him — this man with the inwardly directed gaze, from whom only purity and goodness speak and in whom all trace of fanaticism, maliciousness and camouflage is lacking. Even to think of this possibility seems to be almost like an injustice. Above all I have an impression as if he needed love, as if it were his life-element, but not in the sense of an embittered person whose icy armor one would have to melt. He is not that at all, although I have heard (certainly *he* would never have told me such a thing) that he does have a very hard life. At most, dear colleague, take my words merely as an occasion to approach this person so as to get to know him. I suspect that he (who, by the way, was also strongly affected by your book on the holy) will give himself more freely and open himself more quickly to you the theologian than to me. Yet I must say that he has enjoyed quite great respect here in my small circle of close-knit students.

I am sure that Vicar Katz has told you that I would sincerely like to participate in any "relief action" to help Oxner. But my name must not be mentioned in that connection. I must not endanger my peaceful effectiveness in Freiburg. Nonetheless, my philosophical effect does have something revolutionary about it: Protestants become Catholic, Catholics become Protestant. But I do not think about Catholicizing and Protestantizing; I want nothing more than to educate the youth to a radical honesty of thought, to a thinking which guards against obscuring and violating by verbal constructions and conceptual illusions the primordial intuitions which necessarily determine the sense of all rational thinking. In arch-Catholic Freiburg I do not want to stand out as a corrupter of the youth, as a proselytizer, as an enemy of the Catholic Church. That I am not. I have not exercised the least influence on Heidegger's and Oxner's migration over to the ground of Protestantism, even though it can only be very pleasing to me as a "non-dogmatic Protestant" and a free Christian (if one may call himself a "free Christian" when by that he envisages an ideal goal of religious longing and understands it, for his part, as an infinite task). For the rest, I am happy to have an effect on all sincere men, whether Catholic, Protestant or Jewish.

Through Heidegger and Oxner (I no longer know who took precedence in the matter) I became aware last summer of your book, *Das Heilige [The Idea of the Holy]*, and it has had a strong effect on me as hardly no other book in years. Allow me to express my impressions in this way: It is a first beginning for a phenomenology of religion, at least with regard to everything that does not go beyond a pure description and analysis of the phenomena themselves. To put it succinctly: I cannot share in the additional philosophical theorizing; and it is quite non-essential for the specific task and particular subject matter of this book, and it would be better left out. It seems to me that a great deal more progress would have to be made in the study of the phenomena and their eidetic analysis before a theory of religious consciousness, as a philosophical theory, could arise. Above all, one would need to carry out a radical distinction: between accidental *factum* and the *eidos*. One would need to study the eidetic necessities and eidetic possibilities of religious consciousness and of its correlate. One would need a systematic eidetic typification of the levels of religious data, indeed in their eidetically necessary development. It seems to me that the metaphysician (theologian) in Herr Otto has carried away on his wings Otto the phenomenologist; and in that regard I think of the image of the angels who *cover their eyes* with their wings. But be that as it may, this book will hold an *abiding* place in the history of genuine philosophy of religion or phenomenology of religion. It is a beginning and its significance is that it goes back to the "beginnings," the "origins," and thus, in the most beautiful sense of the word, is "original." And our age yearns for nothing so much as that the true origins might finally come to word and then, in the higher sense, come to their Word, to the Logos.

I am sure that you will not take amiss this free expression of mine. From our Göttingen years you know how highly I esteem you and with what pleasure I seek out intellectual contact with you. Now that you have brought us phenomenologists worthwhile gifts, we would be very happy if new ones were to follow these.

With cordial greetings and constant esteem,

E. Husserl

Translated by Thomas Sheehan

Note

The original copy of this letter is found in the Rudolf-Otto-Nachlass at the Universitätsbibliotek in Marburg, West Germany, catalogued as Hs 797:794. It has been published in Hans-Walter Schütte, *Religion und Christentum in der Theologie Rudolf Ottos*, Berlin: de Gruyter, 1969, pp. 139-142. I have followed the more accurate transcription that is found in the Husserl Archives in Leuven, catalogued as R I Otto 5.III.19. I am grateful to Professor Samuel IJsseling, Director of the Leuven Archives, for permission to translate this text.

Although the letter is chiefly concerned with Oxner and with Otto's book *Das Heilige*, it is one of the earliest documents in which Husserl mentions Heidegger, and specifically Heidegger's religious orientation to Protestantism. Moreover, while this would be the first time that Otto heard the name of Heidegger, it would not be the last. During 1925 Otto worked vigorously to oppose Heidegger's promotion at Marburg to the chair vacated by Nicolai Hartmann. (Tr. note.)

Why Do I Stay in The Provinces? (1934)

Martin Heidegger

On the steep slope of a wide mountain valley in the southern Black Forest, at an elevation of 1150 meters, there stands a small ski hut. The floor plan measures six meters by seven. The low-hanging roof covers three rooms: the kitchen which is also the living room, a bedroom and a study. Scattered at wide intervals throughout the narrow base of the valley and on the equally steep slope opposite, lie the farmhouses with their large over-hanging roofs. Higher up the slope the meadows and pasture lands lead to the woods with its dark fir-trees, old and towering. Over everything there stands a clear summer sky, and in its radiant expanse two hawks glide around in wide circles.

This is my work-world — seen with the eye of an observer: the guest or summer vacationer. Strictly speaking I myself never observe the landscape. I experience its hourly changes, day and night, in the great comings and goings of the seasons. The gravity of the mountains and the hardness of their primeval rock, the slow and deliberate growth of the fir-trees, the brilliant, simple splendor of the meadows in bloom, the rush of the mountain brook in the long autumn night, the stern simplicity of the flatlands covered with snow — all of this moves and flows through and penetrates daily existence up there, and not in forced moments of "aesthetic" immersion or artificial empathy, but only when one's own existence stands in its work. It is the work alone that opens up space for the reality that is these mountains. The course of the work remains embedded in what happens in the region.

On a deep winter's night when a wild, pounding snowstorm rages around the cabin and veils and covers everything, that is the perfect time for philosophy. Then its questions must become simple and essential. Working through each thought can only be tough and rigorous. The struggle to mold something into language is like the resistance of the towering firs against the storm.

And this philosophical work does not take its course like the aloof studies of some eccentric. It belongs right in the midst of the peasants' work. When the young farmboy drags his heavy sled up the slope and guides it, piled high with beech logs, down the dangerous descent to his house, when the [217] herdsman, lost in thought and slow of step, drives his cattle up the slope, when the farmer in his shed gets the countless shingles ready for his roof, my work is of the same sort. It is intimately rooted in and related to the life of the peasants.

A city-dweller thinks he has gone "out among the people" as soon as he condescends to have a long conversation with a peasant. But in the evening during a work-break, when I sit with the peasants by the fire or at the table in the "Lord's Corner," we mostly say nothing at all. We smoke our pipes in silence. Now and again someone might say that the woodcutting in the forest is finishing up, that a marten broke into the hen-house last night, that one of the cows will probably calf in the morning, that someone's uncle suffered a stroke, that the weather will soon "turn." The inner relationship of my own work to the Black Forest and its people comes from a centuries-long and irreplaceable rootedness in the Alemannian-Swabian soil.

At most, a city-dweller gets "stimulated" by a so-called "stay in the country." But my whole work is sustained and guided by the world of these mountains and their people. Lately from time to time my work up there is interrupted for long stretches by conferences, lecture trips, committee meetings and my teaching work down here in Freiburg. But as soon as I go back up there, even in the first few hours of being at the cabin, the whole world of previous questions forces itself upon me in the very form in which I left it. I simply am transported into the work's own rhythm, and in a fundamental sense I am not at all in command of its hidden law. People in the city often wonder whether one gets lonely up in the mountains among the peasants for such long and monotonous periods of time. But it isn't loneliness, it is solitude. In large cities one can easily be as lonely as almost nowhere else. But one can never be in solitude there. Solitude has the peculiar and original power not of isolating us but of projecting our whole existence out into the vast nearness of the presence [*Wesen*] of all things.

In the public world one can be made a "celebrity" overnight by the newspapers and journals. That always remains the surest way to have one's ownmost intentions get misinterpreted and quickly and thoroughly forgotten.

In contrast, the memory of the peasant has its simple and sure fidelity which never forgets. Recently an old peasant woman up there was approaching death. She liked to chat with me frequently, and she told me many old stories of the village. In her robust language, full of images, she still preserved many old words and various sayings which have become unintelligible to the village youth today [218] and hence are lost to the spoken language. Very often in the past year when I lived alone in the cabin for weeks on end, this peasant woman with her 83 years would still come climbing up the slope to visit me. She wanted to look in from time to time, as she put it, to see whether I was still there or whether "someone" had stolen me off unawares. She spent the night of her death in conversation with her family. Just an hour and a half before the end she sent her greetings to the "Professor." Such a memory is worth incomparably more than the most astute report by any international newspaper about my alleged philosophy.

The world of the city runs the risk of falling into a destructive error. A very loud and very active and very fashionable obtrusiveness often passes itself off as concern for the world and existence of the peasant. But this goes exactly contrary to the one and only thing that now needs to be done, namely, to keep one's distance from the life of the peasant, to leave their existence more than ever to its own law, to keep hands off lest it be dragged into the literati's dishonest chatter about "folk-character" and "rootedness in the soil." The peasant doesn't need and doesn't want this citified officiousness. What he needs and wants is quiet reserve with regard to his own way of being and its independence. But nowadays many people from the city, the kind who "know their way around" and not least of all the skiers, often behave in the village or at a farmer's house in the same way they "have fun" at their recreation centers in the city. Such goings-on destroy more in one evening than centuries of scholarly teaching about folk-character and folklore could ever hope to promote.

Let us stop all this condescending familiarity and sham concern for "folk-character" and let us learn to take seriously that simple, rough existence up there. Only then will it speak to us once more.

Recently I got a second invitation to teach at the University of Berlin. On that occasion I left Freiburg and withdrew to the cabin. I listened to what the mountains and the forest and the farmlands were saying, and I went to see an old friend of mine, a 75-year old farmer. He had read about the call to Berlin in the newspapers. What would he say? Slowly he fixed the sure gaze of his clear eyes on mine, and keeping his mouth tightly shut, he thoughtfully put his faithful hand on my shoulder. Ever so slightly he shook his head. That meant: absolutely no!

Translated by Thomas Sheehan

Translator's Note

Heidegger's "Warum bleiben wir in der Provinz?" was published in *Der Alemanne* on March 7, 1934, a month after he had resigned the rectorate of Freiburg University. Within the context of events from the winter of 1932-33 through September-October, 1933, it describes Heidegger's "work-world" at his Black Forest retreat above

Todtnauberg, 25 kilometers south of Freiburg. The text invites comparison with his *Aus der Erfahrung des Denkens* (Pfullingen: Neske, 1954; written, 1947), English translation by Albert Hofstadter, "The Thinker as Poet" in *Poetry, Language, Thought* (New York: Harper and Row, 1971), pp.1-14, and with "Bauen Wohnen Denken," *Vorträge und Aufsätze* (Pfullingen: Neske, 1954), p. 161 = "Building Dwelling Thinking," *Poetry, Language, Thought,* p. 160.

Heidegger received and refused a first call to the chair of philosophy at Berlin in 1931; Nicolai Hartmann then accepted it. A second call, which came in the fall of 1933, while Heidegger was rector of Freiburg, was refused by early October of that year. Heidegger's meeting Todtnauberg with his neighbor, Johann Brender (at whose farmhouse Heidegger had composed *Sein und Zeit*) is discussed by Walter Biemel in "Erinnerungen an Heidegger," *Allgemeine Zeitschrift für Philosophie,* 2/1 (1977), 14. In southern German homes, the "Lord's Corner" (*Herrgottswinkel*) is the corner near the common table, where a crucifix hangs (cf. "Building Dwelling Thinking," p. 160).

My thanks to Guido Schneeberger for permission to translate the German text as it appears in his *Nachlese zu Heidegger* (Bern, 1962), pp. 216-218.

Heidegger and the Nazis

Karl A. Moehling

For more than half a century Heidegger's thought has attracted widespread public and scholarly interest. His career marked by growing numbers of followers and disciples, a veneration of the man and his thought which sometimes bordered on hagiolatry. It was also a career marked by much controversy and acrimony. The literature on existentialism and Heidegger is replete with countless allegations and vituperations which not only challenge the validity of his thought but also call into question his very humanity. The most serious episode in Heidegger's public life was his membership and active involvement in the Nazi Party from April, 1933, to February, 1934. This political interlude is well known, but it is poorly understood in terms of its motivations and the details of events. The reasons why this political digression remains shrouded and blurred are not difficult to discern. One the one hand, there has been a written and oral tradition sustained by rumor and canard which has passed among Heidegger's friends and enemies alike, a spurious tradition which has confused more than enlightened. On the other hand, there has been Heidegger's virtually complete silence on the whole matter, which implied at least that the content of his life was not important, that one must get on with the task of thinking. He had always shunned the approaches of biographers and in this way only helped to perpetuate the aura of mystery which surrounded the events of his life especially those of 1933 and 1934.

But Heidegger's silence on his political involvement was not complete. In November and December of 1945 Freiburg University conducted an investigation of his political activity. This investigation was largely urged upon the university by the French occupation authorities who, like the other occupation powers, were concerned that no ex-Nazis hold positions of responsibility in post-war Germany.[1] In response to the de-Nazification committee's investigation, Heidegger wrote a statement of explanation to the rector of Freiburg University and a statement to the de-Nazification committee.[2] Since 1945 these two documents have floated surreptitiously among a small group of Heidegger scholars. More significant is the interview Heidegger granted the German news magazine *Der Spiegel* in September of 1966. This interview dealt almost solely with his Nazi past and with his life during the Third Reich. It was his request that the interview not be published during his lifetime, for he felt the sensationalism of the topic would interfere with his philosophical work.[3] What is fundamental is that the veracity of the two 1945 letters and the 1966 interview is sustained by the conclusions of the independent investigation Freiburg University conducted in 1945.

I.

Since Heidegger's most active involvement in the Nazi Party is coterminous with his holdings of the office of rector at Freiburg University, it is basic that one understand the events which led to his election to the rectorate. From the nineteenth century on, the rector was the administrative head of the German university. The rector was elected to his office by the university senate, a body comprised of full professors. He was elected for one year but could be re-elected indefinitely. Legally the administration of the university was subject to the individual state governments, but the state governments rarely interfered in the internal affairs of the universities. Academic freedom was a rich and deep tradition in Germany. The universities jealously guarded it, and the governments sought to honor it. In December of 1932, Wilhelm von Moellendorf, professor of anatomy, was elected rector of Freiburg University. Moellendorf was officially to take office on April 15, 1933. Heidegger related that during the winter semester of 1932-33 he and Moellendorf spoke often not only of the political situation in Germany but also of the situation of the universities (*Interview*). All through the Weimar years the universities were hotbeds of rightist political activities with the Nazi student organizations growing larger and more vocal. After the naming of Hitler to the chancellorship on January 30, 1933, Heidegger spoke often with his colleagues about the growing political crisis and its meaning for German learning. In April the nation witnessed the first serious attempts by the Nazis to institute anti-Semitic policies, a boycott against Jewish businesses and legislation against Jewish professionals and intellectuals. It was in this growing anti-Semitic hysteria that Moellendorf became rector on April 16th. Less than two weeks later he was relieved of his office by the Baden Cultural Minister. The probable cause for this was Moellendorf's refusal to allow the hanging of anti-Jewish posters within Freiburg University. On the day of his dismissal from office, Moellendorf approached Heidegger and urged him to stand for election for the rectorate. Moellendorf was joined by the other faculties at Freiburg in this plea to Heidegger. As the de-Nazification Committee discovered in 1945, his colleagues believed that his international reputation would best put him in a "position to preserve a certain independence for the university and to protect it against the most unbearable imputations from a part of the Nazi party" (*Freiburg Report*, 262). Heidegger was elected unanimously by the university senate and took over the rectorate in late April.

On the second day after his assumption of the rectorate, three members of the Nazi student organization appeared at his office and again demanded that he allow the hanging of the anti-Jewish posters which Moellendorf had prohibited. Like Moellendorf, Heidegger refused. The three students left after saying the prohibition of the displaying of the posters would be relayed to the national student leadership. After some days, a Dr. Baumann of the SA communicated to Heidegger a demand that Freiburg follow the lead of the other German universities and exhibit the anti-Jewish posters. It was also made clear that failure to meet this demand could mean Heidegger's termination as rector and the closing of the university. Even confronted with these dire threats, Heidegger still adamantly refused to rescind his prohibition against the posters.

This early confrontation with state power convinced Heidegger that he needed sources of influence other than his international reputation as a scholar to deal with the party functionaries. He decided that he would be in a better position to protect the university if he were a member of the Nazi Party. If he were to remain outside of the political vortex, he would be just as vulnerable as Moellendorf was in administering the university. "It was never my intention to deliver the university to the party doctrine but, conversely, to attempt from *within* National Socialism and while having a point of reference to it to bring about a spiritual change in its development" (*Letter-Committee*, 269).

Heidegger looked upon his inaugural address as rector, *The Self-Assertion of the German University*,[4] in a dual sense. On the one hand, he wanted to attempt to protect the university by defining the meaning of learning; and on the other hand, he wanted to attempt to influence the new government's view of German learning and its part in the national awakening. He asserted that his inaugural address was not a political tract. It sought primarily to define the meaning and value of learning (*Interview*). The address, which was given on May 27, 1933, was nothing less than a demand that the status and function of the university in Germany be completely rethought. It was a revolutionary appeal in that he argued the time had come in German history when an examination of the relationship between the university and the nation was not only desirable but an absolute necessity. He urged the reassertion of the university and learning in the life of the nation so that pressing and urgent spiritual issues could be confronted.

> For us the German university is the institution of higher learning which, from and through scientific knowledge, undertakes the education and training of the leaders and guardians of the destiny of the German people. The will to the essence of the German university is the will to scientific knowledge as a will to the historical intellectual mandate of the German people as one which knows itself in its nation (*SU*, 6f.).

This passage from the inaugural address is central to the question of how Heidegger interpreted the purpose of the German university in the new Germany the National Socialists were creating. It was an argument for the priority of learning, which for Heidegger primarily meant meditative and spiritual thinking. In 1933 he maintained that the purpose of the university was to educate the nation and through learning provide the leaders and guardians of the nation. He reiterated this claim in his speech on "The University in the New Reich," delivered at Heidelberg University in late June, 1933: "The university must again become an educational force which through knowledge educates the leaders of the state to knowledge."[5]

Clearly, Heidegger's thinking in 1933 on learning and the German university demonstrates a serious departure from the Nazis' understanding of the university as a place for training a racial elite subservient to the state. It also reflects the unpolitical nature of his perception of the Nazi revolution. In an indirect though positive way, he saw the university—the place of national learning—as the arbiter of state power. Without the clarification of learning and meditative thinking, nations like individuals become spiritually rudderless and sink into nihilism.

How far Heidegger thought the university had become divorced from the spiritual needs of the German nation is made clear by his statement: "The much vaunted 'academic freedom' will be driven from the German university, for this freedom was spurious because purely negative. It meant predominantly a lack of concern, arbitrariness in one's aims and intentions, licence in acting and not acting" (*SU*, 15). This most inflammatory and controversial passage from the inaugural address must be understood in the light of how Heidegger saw the meaning of the university's autonomy—that is, its isolation from the nation's spiritual life. In Heidegger's understanding, academic freedom in the modern age had come to mean academic specialization and the fragmentation of learning into distinct and isolated areas. It was the modern trend towards specialization, relativism, and irrelevancy which molded the university into a corporate entity which took pride in its autonomy but failed to recognize its isolation from the spiritual needs of the nation. University scholars had come to nurture and sustain such ideals as art for art's sake and science for science's sake, while true spiritual questions went unasked and unthought. For Heidegger the university faculty could be a genuine faculty only if it "developes itself into a force for spiritual legislation, a force rooted in the essence of its scientific knowledge" (SU,18). The university professor as a spiritual legislator was a concept straight out of the Idealist heritage. In many ways Heidegger's activity and thought in 1933 and 1934 can be seen as an attempt to infuse such Idealist values into a profoundly altered political climate. He admitted in 1966 that he had made compromises with the regime in an attempt to get his views to as wide an audience as possible. He came to regret the compromises, but at the time they appeared to be the only real alternatives open to him.

It is important to understand that in the early months of his political activity Heidegger did not consider himself to be totally outside the mainstream of National Socialist thought, precisely because he interpreted the thought to be essentially undefined.

> Already in 1933-34 I was likewise opposed to the National Socialist worldview, but at that time I was of the belief that the movement could be intellectually guided into other paths, and I believed this endeavor to be compatible with the social and general political tendencies of the movement. I believed that Hitler, after he became responsible for the *whole* nation in 1933, would rise above the party and its doctrines and that everything would come together on the basis of a renewal of and a gathering unto a responsibility for the West [*zu einer abendländischen Verantwortung*].... In 1933 I had brought myself to a middle position, in that I affirmed the social and national—but not nationalistic—[principles] of party doctrine while denying the intellectual and metaphysical laying of its foundations by biologism, because the social and national principles, as I saw it, were not essentially joined to the biological-racial world-view doctrine...(*Letter-Committee*, 270f.).

What is significant in Heidegger's written testimony in the 1945 de-Nazification proceedings is his claim that in 1933 and 1934 he considered Hitler and National Socialism as not only important for the future of Germany but also for the future of the West.

> But at that time I was certainly also convinced that through the independent assistance of the intellectuals many essential tendencies of the "National Socialist movement" could be deepened and changed in order to make the movement capable of assisting in its [own] way to overcome the confused situation of Europe and the crisis of the Western spirit.... In addition, because the will of the overwhelming majority of the German people, expressed in free election [the national plebiscites], assented at that time to a work of construction in the sense of the National Socialist movement, I

thought it necessary and possible to assist as well in the realm of the university to encounter in a consistent and effective manner the general confusion and the threat to the West. And precisely because in the realm of the sciences and the intellect, many so-called "impossible" people were pushing for influence and power, it seemed to me necessary to make visible, in opposition to them, essential intellectual goals and horizons and to attempt, from out of a responsibility for the West, to lend my concern for their diffusion and realization (*Letter-Rector*, 264f.).

Thus Heidegger was both attracted to and repelled by Nazism. He was put in what he called "a middle position" of believing in the social and national ideas of the movement while rejecting its essential racism. He attempted to contribute to its fund of ideas from his own conceptions of spirit and value, while attempting to hold at bay party functionaries who wanted to alter the university's autonomy and its administrative structure.

This kind of juggling act between what was politically possible and what was intellectually non-negotiable brought Heidegger into increasing confrontations with the Nazi idealogues. In a direct rejection of Nazi policy, he was able to protect Freiburg University's library from the notorious book burnings in the spring of 1933. He made special efforts to protect his Jewish students and assistants, Werner Brock and Helene Weiss, both of whom eventually emigrated to Britain with Heidegger's strong recommendation for academic placement. It is true that during the time he was a member of the party Heidegger's relations with his Jewish mentor, Edmund Husserl, were strained. But the source of this strained relationship was philosophical disagreement rather than political hostility. In fact, it antedated the political upheavals of 1933 by some years. The most notorious tale about Heidegger at this time — that he prohibited Husserl from using the university library — is simply untrue.[6]

That the Nazis were becoming more and more uncomfortable with Heidegger both as a party member and as rector of Freiburg University becomes clear as one examines the captured files from the Nazis Office of Learning. The early documents reflect a guarded yet cordial relationship between Heidegger and the party functionaries, but it quickly becomes confused, and Heidegger is finally talked about as being "dangerous."[7] The official discomfort with his growing intransigence on both party and ideological concerns finally broke into the public arena with a series of hostile articles by the race theorist and rector of Frankfurt University, Ernst Krieck. In response to a laudatory article on Heidegger's use of the German language in the journal *Muttersprache*, Krieck wrote about Heidegger's philosophy in the journal *Volk im Werden:*

The meaning of this philosophy is outspoken atheism and metaphysical nihilism, as it formerly had been primarily represented by Jewish authors;

therefore, a ferment of decay and dissolution for the German nation. In *Being and Time* Heidegger philosophizes consciously and deliberately about "everydayness"—there is nothing in it about nation, state, race, and all the values of our National Socialist view of the world.[8]

With Krieck's linking of Heidegger with Jewish authors, there could no longer be any doubt that the theoreticians of Nazism were purging him from the intellectual ranks of National Socialism.

During the fall of 1933 Heidegger struggled to get the university back on its scholarly and educational course, but he was unable to do this because of the general involvement of the government in university affairs. He also became aware that he was having no impact upon the thought of National Socialism:

> During several quiet days during Christmas vacation, it became clear to me that it was an error to think that my intellectual position, which had developed in me through long years of philosophical work, could exert an *immediate* influence to change the intellectual—non-intellectual—bases of the National Socialist movement. In early 1934, I decided to resign from the rectorate at the end of the semester (*Letter-Rector,* 265f.).

The Nazis themselves provided Heidegger with the opportunity to resign. In February of 1934 Otto Wacker, the Baden Minister of Culture, called Heidegger to Karlsruhe where he demanded that Heidegger immediately dismiss Wilhelm von Moellendorf, dean of the School of Medicine, and Erik Wolf, dean of the School of Law. It was well known that both men were hostile to the regime. Moellendorf had been Heidegger's predecessor as rector and was active in the Social Democratic Party. Wolf made no secret of his hostility towards the Nazi philosopher of law, Carl Schmitt. Heidegger refused Wacker's demand and resigned the rectorate. It was customary in German universities for the outgoing rector to install his successor. Heidegger refused to do this. Moreover, the Nazi press hailed his successor as "the first National Socialist rector of [Freiburg] University."[9]

Heidegger's act of defiance which led to his resignation of the rectorate, coupled with Krieck's continued attacks upon him in *Volk im Werden,* set the future character of his relationship with National Socialism. In the words of the de-Nazification proceedings:

> From the time he had resigned as rector in the spring of 1934, all of his lectures and seminars got suspiciously controlled by the Nazi authorities. Heidegger's literary work was outlawed in the whole Nazi press at the instigation of the Nazi pseudo-philosopher Krieck, whom Heidegger deeply despised. A great part of Heidegger's books were no longer permitted to be printed. The mentioning of Heidegger's name and of his works was suppressed as far as possible (*Freiburg Report,* 263).

In 1934, Alfred Rosenberg prevented Heidegger from being a member of the German delegation to the International Philosophers' Congress. In 1937, he was prevented from attending the Descartes Congress in Paris, even though the French twice expressed their desire for Heidegger to attend (*Letter-Rector*, 267).

After his clash with Wacker and his purge from the intellectual ranks of the party by Krieck, Heidegger withdrew into his own philosophical work and teaching. But it would be an error to see him as just another German intellectual who chose "inner emigration" as his response to the German situation under National Socialism. For Heidegger, even to teach his philosophy would have meant resistance to the Nazi program. As he wrote in 1945:

> After I resigned from the rectorate, it was clear to me that my continuation as a teacher would have to lead to increasing resistance against the principles of the National Socialist world-view. It was not required that I first make particular attacks; it was enough that I discuss my basic philosophical position in opposition to the dogmatic obduracy and primitiveness of the biologism proclaimed by Rosenberg. . . . In the first semester after I resigned the rectorate, I lectured on logic, and under the title "The Doctrine of *Logos*" I dealt with the essence of language. It had to be shown that language was not a structure of expression of the essence of man thought of in biological and racist terms, but rather that conversely the essence of man is grounded in language as the fundamental reality of spirit (*Letter-Rector*, 266f.).

In like manner, Heidegger's lectures on Nietzsche from 1936 to 1940 were outspoken assaults upon the Nazi's attempts to assimilate Nietzsche into the pantheon of National Socialist forerunners. He vehemently rejected Alfred Baeumler's view of Nietzsche as a political and racial theorist.

Of course, all this was not going unnoticed by the authorities. Members of the Security Service enrolled in Heidegger's seminars and attended his lectures for the purpose of monitoring his remarks. Two of Heidegger's students during the Nazi era came forward in 1945 with testimony about his behavior during the Third Reich. Walter Biemel, a Husserl scholar, testified:

> Heidegger was one of the very rare professors who never began his courses with the "German salute" (*Heil Hitler*), even though it was administratively obligatory. His courses . . . were among the very rare ones where remarks against National Socialism were risked. Some conversations in those times could cost you your head; I had many such conversations with Heidegger. There is absolutely no doubt that he was a declared adversary of the regime.[10]

And Siegfried Broese, Heidegger's teaching assistant during the thirties, wrote to the de-Nazification hearing on Heidegger:

One could see—and this was often confirmed to me by the students—that Heidegger's lectures were attended *en masse* because the students wanted to form a rule to guide their own conduct by hearing National Socialism characterized in all its non-truth. . . . Heidegger's lectures were attended not only by students but also by people with long-standing professions and even by retired people, and everytime that I had the occasion to talk with these people what came back again and again in these conversations was the admiration these people had for the courage with which Heidegger, from the height of his position as a thinker and in the rigor of his philosophical approach, attacked National Socialism. I know as well that precisely for this reason Heidegger's lectures were being watched politically, for his open rupture did not remain ignored by the Nazis.[11]

In the summer of 1944, the Nazi authorities designated Heidegger as "the least indispensible of the professors at the university,"[12] and he was drafted into the *Volkssturm*, the Third Reich's last remaining army reserves, composed of old men and young boys. The *Volkssturm* was Hitler's last ditch effort to save the Reich from invasion. Heidegger could not have escaped the irony of his and the nation's situation: what he thought in 1933 could be transformed into a spiritual example for the salvation of the West was now being besieged with a vengeance and resolve unprecedented in western history.

With Germany's defeat in 1945 and the coming of the occupation governments, Heidegger's life became entangled in the human and bureaucratic chaos of the immediate post-war period. In September of 1945 the French military government ruled that Heidegger's status at the university was one of "dispensible."[13] Recognizing the course of future events, Heidegger, before any formal action was taken against him, asked the university to place him on emeritus status, and he voluntarily gave up the right to hold the *venia legendi* (the right to teach in a German university). However, with his application for ermeritus status, he explained that he would retain the right of the *venia legendi* if the university expressly desired it. In November and December of 1945 the university investigated his political activity and the de-Nazification committee recommended that no action be taken against him.

Not having had anything to do with the Nazis before the spring of 1933, Heidegger can no longer be regarded as a Nazi after April, 1934. We, therefore, would regard it as a most serious loss if Heidegger would have to leave the university because of his short political error in 1933 (*Freiburg Report*, 263).

Thereupon Heidegger's application for emeritus status was placed before the university for consideration, and he was to retain the right of the *venia legendi*.

However, in the summer and fall of 1946, the French military government, "meeting behind closed doors, therefore, without information or even a statement from the accused" (*Explanations*), conducted general de-Nazification proceedings against all former party members in Baden. For Heidegger this meant he was prohibited from teaching for an indefinite length of time. Contrary to the general misunderstanding, the French directive was not a dismissal from the university, and Heidegger remained in the employ of the university as a research professor. His first concern was that he maintain his affiliation with the university; thus, "I did not ask for a revision of the directive which prohibited me from teaching, because in no way was this seen as a dismissal; this was also repeated by the dean and the French liaison officer at the university" (*Explanations*).

The military government issued its final statement on Heidegger's Nazism in July of 1949, classifying him as a "fellow traveler without reconciliation" (*Explanations*). And in September of that year, the prohibition against his teaching was terminated. Later, in September of 1951, the Baden government granted him emeritus status.

II.

The emphasis of this essay has been upon a factual consideration of Heidegger's political and academic activity during the Nazi years, but there are larger interpretative issues which compel examination. An interpretative framework becomes compelling if one is to make biographical, philosophical, and historical sense out of Heidegger's support of National Socialism. In his *Introduction to Metaphysics*, originally a series of lectures from 1935, Heidegger himself offers an insight into this interpretative framework, when he speaks of

> [t]he works that are being peddled about nowadays as the philosophy of National Socialism but have nothing whatever to do with the inner truth and greatness of this movement (namely the encounter between global technology and modern man). . . .[14]

His original and sustaining view of Nazism was its political power to confront the spiritual crisis engendered by modern, post-industrial man's encounter with the meaning of his own technological devices. Consistent in Heidegger's philosophy is a vision of modern man as striving and seeking, yet as greatly threatened by his technology and by the thinking which has given technology its character. For Heidegger as for Oswald Spengler, the twentieth century is not only the apotheosis but the apocalypse of Faustian man. In Germany, early National Socialism appeared to be the only political party seeking state power which was willing and strong enough to confront the twin evils of modernity: corporative capitalism and international Marxism. For all their differences, these two opposing ideologies both remained firmly anchored in technological-positivist modes of thought. Of course the history of Nazism was an outrageous betrayal of this early promise, if indeed it ever was a promise and not just a veil for more sinister intentions.

Heidegger in many of his works often linked modern technological development with what he perceived to be the spread of nihilism. The threat of nihilism is one of the abiding philosophical concerns which spans Heidegger's career. Nihilism for him means the abandonment of meaning, the rejection of value and spirit. The primary representations of incipient nihilism in the late nineteenth and early twentieth centuries were doctrines of relativism, pluralism, determinism, and positivism. For Heidegger and other German neo-conservatives during the 1920's the generic manifestation of nihilism-positivism was not only science but its abuses: unrestrained industrialization and technology, the sprawling, malignant growth of the city, crude economic materialism, and social manipulation. Conservative German intellectuals during the Weimar years saw the ideals of positivism pervading every aspect of German life. The early support for National Socialism in 1933 may be seen as not simply support for Hitler, but perhaps more decisively as a profound rejection of the Weimar Republic and its culture.

It may very well be that Heidegger's fundamental error in 1933 was not his failure to perceive clearly the nature of Nazism; rather it may have been his belief that an authoritarian government would be able to re-establish the unity of spirit and state which had been split apart by the arrival of modernity. In light of the modern state with its pluralistic-industrial society, there may be something anachronistic about the ideal of the cultural state — it was an ideal which had been formulated in a pre-industrial and less complicated time. One may still want to maintain that the ideal of states guided and restrained by transcendent values is not only desirable, but necessary. During the early twentieth century many German intellectuals, looking back to the nineteenth-century concept of the cultural state reasserted the ideal in such a way that there could be no compromise with modernity. The ideal of the cultural state was formulated in terms of at least a spiritual rejection of the industrial-technological world.

There is in Heidegger's life and thought a strong element of this spiritual rejection of the technological world; it is expressed in his life by his close personal identification with the simple, rural life of the Swabian peasant. As a thinker and as a Swabian peasant himself, he was disturbed by the fact that the modern world had become insensitive to the dignity and truth expressed by the life of the peasant. The personal view found its corollary in a marked strain of anti-intellectualism in Heidegger's thought, a rebellion against the ideals of art for art's sake, science for science's sake. This rebellion against intellectual activity for the sake of intellectual activity — in conjunction with his reverence for the values of rural life — are not in themselves reprehensible. But in 1933 they helped to lead him into making a political error which almost destroyed his reputation as a serious scholar and thinker. What saved this reputation was the sheer might of his philosophical vision and the awareness of many serious-minded people that no matter what Heidegger's political association may have been, his contribution to thought in this age of crisis has been too important to ignore.

Notes

Karl A. Moehling received his doctorate in European intellectual history from Northern Illinois University in 1972. He is currently with the Educational Services of the Illinois State Department of Mental Health.

1. The summation of this "Bereinigungsausschüsse" is in Appendix A of my doctoral dissertation: Karl A. Moehling, *Martin Heidegger and the Nazi Party: An Examination* (unpublished Ph.D. dissertation, Northern Illinois University, 1972, Ann Arbor Microfilms, No. 72-29,319) pp. 262-263. I am indebted to Dr. Medard Boss of the University of Zurich for this document. Dr. Boss did the translation. Hereafter notes to the "Bereinigungsausschüsse" will be cited as "Freiburg Report" with page references to Appendix A of my dissertation. Hereafter notes to my dissertation will be cited as *MHNP*.

2. The German text of Heidegger's letter to the rector of Freiburg University ("An das Akademische Rektorat der Albert-Ludwigs-Universität") is in Apprendix B of *MHNP*, pp.264-268. Hereafter notes to this document will be cited as "*Letter-Rector*" with page references to Appendix B of *MHNP*. The German text of Heidegger's letter to the de-Nazification Committee at Freiburg University ("Einige Auszüge aus einem Brief an den Vorsitzenden des politischen Reinigungsausschusses") is in Appendix C of *MHNP*, pp. 269-272. Hereafter notes to this document will be cited as "*Letter-Committee*" with page references to Appendix C of *MHNP*. I am indebted to Dr. Stanley Rosen of Pennsylvania State University for these two documents.

3. "Nur noch ein Gott kann uns retten," *Der Spiegel*, Nr. 23 (1976), pp. 193-219; English translation by William J. Richardson, "Only a God Can Save Us," immediately following in the present volume. In the text I refer to this document as: *Interview*.

4. Martin Heidegger, *Die Selbstbehauptung der deutschen Universität* (Breslau: Korn, 1933), hereafter cited as *SU*.

5. Martin Heidegger, "Die Universität im neuen Reich," *Heidelberger Neueste Nachrichten*, July 1, 1933, p. 4. Reprinted in Guido Schneeberger, *Nachlese zu Heidegger. Dokumente zu seinem Leben und Denken* (Bern: Suhr, 1962) p. 74.

6. The error and distortions of fact which pervade both the written and oral tradition on Heidegger's political involvement are treated in Chapter I of *MHNP*. See also the bibliography of *MHNP* for an extensive listing of the literature on this problem. Two important additions are Otto Pöggeler, *Philosophie und Politik bei Heidegger* (Freiburg & Munich: Karl Alber, 1972) and Karsten Harries, "Heidegger as a Political Thinker," *Review of Metaphysics*, (1976), 642-669.

7. Records of the National Socialist German Labor Party (NSDAP), National Archives Microcopy No. T-81, Roll 239, Serial 457, Folder 253-d/38, frames 5025060-62; Roll 243, Serial 461, Folder 253-d/57, frame 5030188; Roll 244, Serial 462, Folder 253-d/61, frame 5031076. See also the document from the Centre de Documentation Juive Contemporaine reprinted in Leon Poliakov and Josef Wulf, *Das Dritte Reich und seine Denker. Dokumente* (Berlin: Arani, 1959), p.548. See also *MHNP* pp. 35-40.

8. Ernst Krieck, "Germanischer Mythos und Heideggersche Philosophie," *Volk im Werden*, II (1934), 247.

9. See also François Fédier, "Trois attaques contre Heidegger," *Critique* XXII, No. 234 (1966), 901.

10. See also François Fédier, "A propos de Heidegger,: une lecture dénoncée," *Critique* XXIII (1967), 681; cf. also Jean-Michel Palmier, *Les Ecrits politiques de Heidegger,* (Paris: L'Herne, 1968), pp. 283-284. Prof. James Luther Adams has informed the author that he personally witnessed Heidegger standing with his students and giving the Nazi salute during Heidegger's 1936 lectures on Schelling. Adams' testimony would not be in conflict with Biemel's testimony, since Biemel joined Heidegger in April of 1942, a time when the totalitarian features of the regime had become clearly defined.

11. I am indebted to Dr. Medard Boss for procuring this letter of Jan. 14, 1946, from Heidegger's files. A French translation of this letter appears in Fédier, "Trois attaques contre Heidegger," *Critique,* 903-904.

12. *Ibid.,* 901.

13. The account of Heidegger's status at Freiburg University in the immediate post war period is based upon "Erklärungen zu den Vorgängen in den Jahren 1945-1951 meine Stellung als ordentl. Professor a.d. Universität betreffend," which Heidegger wrote in 1954 for his files. Hereafter cited as "*Explanations.*" I am indebted to Dr. Boss for this document.

14. Martin Heidegger, *An Introduction to Metaphysics,* trans. by Ralph Manheim (Garden City, New York: Doubleday, 1961.) p. 166.

"Only a God Can Save Us": The *Spiegel* Interview (1966)

Martin Heidegger

[*Although Heidegger was one of the seminal thinkers of the twentieth century, few such men of his time were criticized more severely or resented more bitterly than he. Much of this criticism arose because of an association with the Nazis while Rector of the University of Freiburg, 1933-34, one that publicly he neither repudiated, justified, nor explained. In 1966 the editors of the German news weekly,* Der Spiegel, *requested of Heidegger an interview to discuss these issues. In granting the interview, which took place on September 23, 1966, Heidegger insisted that it remain unpublished during his lifetime. (It appeared in* Der Spiegel on May 31, 1976, *five days after his death.) Its substance goes far beyond the personal issues involved and rephrases his entire philosophical experience. He saw this as an opportunity to meditate upon the meaning of Being, particularly under the guise that most profoundly characterizes contemporary culture — labeled by him "technicity" (die* Technik). *In these terms the interview takes on the quality of a last will and testament.*

In the translation which follows I have inserted the pagination of the German publication, Der Spiegel, Nr. 23 (1976), 193-219, *directly into the text in brackets. I was assisted in historical matters by the researches of Dr. Kurt Maier of the Leo Baeck Institute, New York City.*

— *William J. Richardson, S.J.]*

SPIEGEL: Professor Heidegger, we have noted repeatedly that your philosophical work has been overshadowed somewhat by [certain] events of short duration in your life that you never have clarified.

Heidegger: You mean 1933?

SPIEGEL: Yes, [both] before and after. We would like to set this in a larger context and thus arrive at certain questions that seem to us important, namely: what possibilities does philosophy offer for having an influence upon actuality *(Wirklichkeit)*—even upon politicial actuality?

Heidegger: These are indeed important questions, whether or not I can answer them. But first I must say that before my rectorate I was in no way politically active.[1] During the winter semester of 1932-33 I was on leave and spent most of the time in my mountain hut.[2]

SPIEGEL: How did it happen, then, that you became Rector of the University of Freiburg?

Heidegger: In December, 1932, my neighbor, Professor (of Anatomy) von Möllendorf, was chosen Rector. The installation of the new Rector here takes place on April 15. During the winter semester of 1932-33, we discussed the [current] situation often, not only the political one, but especially that of the universities and the partially hopeless situation of the students. My judgment went like this: to the extent that I can judge things, the only possibility still available [to us] is to try to seize upon the approaching developments with those constructive forces that still remain alive.

SPIEGEL: You saw, then, a relationship between the position of the German University and the political situation of Germany as a whole?

Heidegger: To be sure, I did follow the political events of January-March, 1933, and also spoke about them from time to time with younger colleagues. My own work, however, was concerned with a more comprehensive interpretation of [196] pre-Socratic thought. With the beginning of the summer semester I returned to Freiburg.[3] Meanwhile, Professor von Möllendorf had assumed the office as Rector on April 16. Hardly two weeks later he was removed from office by the then Minister of Culture of Baden. What presumably gave the desired occasion for this decision of the Minister was the fact that the Rector had forbidden the so-called "Jewish poster" to be displayed in the University.[4]

SPIEGEL: Mr. von Möllendorf was a Social Democrat. What did he do after his dismissal?[5]

Heidegger: On the very day of his dismissal, von Möllendorf came to me and said: "Heidegger, now you must take over the rectorate." I protested that I had absolutely no administrative experience. However, the Pro-Rector at the time, Professor (of Theology) Sauer, also urged me to become a candidate in the new election, for there was a real danger that otherwise a [mere] functionary would be named Rector. Younger colleagues with whom for several years I had discussed questions of university management besieged me [with requests] to take over the rectorate. I hesitated a long time. Finally, I declared myself ready to take over the office only in the interests in the University, provided I could be certain of the unanimous support of the entire Academic Senate. Meantime, the doubts about my qualifications for the rectorate remained, so that on the very morning of the election I went to the Rector's office and told the dismissed colleague, von Möllendorf, and the Pro-Rector, Sauer, that I could not take over the office. Both replied that the election already had proceeded so far that at that point I could no longer withdraw from the candidacy.

SPIEGEL: And so you declared yourself definitively ready. What form, then did your relationship to the National Socialists take?

Heidegger: On the second day after I took office the "Student Leader" and two companions appeared at my door and demanded once more that the "Jewish poster" be displayed. I refused. The three students left with the remark that my prohibition would be made known to the Student Leadership Division of the government. Several days later a telephone call came from Dr. Baumann, S.A. Group Leader in the office of Higher Education of the Supreme S.A. Command.[6] He demanded the hanging of the poster in question, as this already had been done in other universities. Should I refuse, I could expect my own dismissal, if not, indeed, the closure of the University. I tried to gain the support of the Minister of Culture of Baden for my prohibition. He explained that he could do nothing against the S.A. Nonetheless, I did not retract my prohibition.

SPIEGEL: Up to now, this was not known in that way.

Heidegger: The motive that above all determined me to take over the rectorate was mentioned already in my inaugural lecture at Freiburg in 1929, "What is Metaphysics?"[7] "The fields of sciences lie far apart. The manner of handling their objects is essentially different. This disintegrated multiplicity of disciplines is held together today only through the technical organization of universities and faculties, and through the practical direction of the disciplines according to a single orientation. At the same time, the rooting of the sciences in their essential ground has become dead." What I attempted to do during my administration, in view of this condition of the universities — in our own day degenerated to the extreme — is laid out in my rectoral address.[8]

SPIEGEL: We are trying to find out whether, and how, this statement of 1929 coincides with what you said in your inaugural address as Rector in 1933. We take here one sentence out of context: "The much celebrated 'academic freedom' is repudiated by the German university; for this freedom was not genuine, insofar as it was only [a] negative [one]." There seems good reason to infer that this statement at the very least gives expression to certain conceptions that even today are not foreign to you.

Heidegger: Yes, I agree, for this academic "freedom" was only too often a negative one: freedom *from* the effort to surrender oneself to what a scientific study demands in terms of reflection and meditation. Moreover, the sentence that you have excerpted ought not to be taken alone but read in its context, for then it becomes clear what I wanted to have understood by "negative freedom."

SPIEGEL: Fine, that is understandable. But we seem to perceive a new tone in your rectoral discourse, when, four months after Hitler's designation as Chancellor, you there talk about the "greatness and glory of this new era *(Aufbruch)*."

Heidegger: Yes, I was also convinced of it.

SPIEGEL: Could you explain that a little further?

Heidegger: Gladly. At that time I saw no other alternative. Amid the general confusion of opinion and political tendencies of 22 parties, it was necessary to find a national and, above all, social attitude, somewhat in the sense of Friederich Naumann's endeavor. I could cite here, simply by way of example, a passage from Eduard Spranger that goes far beyond my rectoral address.[9]

SPIEGEL: When did you begin to become involved in political affairs? The 22 parties were long since there. Already in 1930 there were millions of unemployed.

Heidegger: At that time I was still completely preoccupied with the questions that were developed in *Being and Time* (1927)[10] and the writings and lectures of the following years—fundamental questions of thought that touched also national and social questions [though not im]mediately. Immediately what faced me as a university professor was the question about the meaning of the sciences, and with it the determination of the mission of the university. This concern is expressed in the title of my rectoral discourse,"The Self-Assertion of the German University." No other rectoral discourse of the time bore a title as audacious as this. But who among those who attack this discourse has read it carefully, thought it through, and interpreted it in terms of the situation at that time?

SPIEGEL: Self-assertion of the university in such a turbulent world—isn't that a bit much?

Heidegger: Why? "The Self-Assertion of the University" went against the so-called "political science" that at that time was already demanded by the Party and by the National Socialist Student Organization. "Political science" at that time had a completely different sense; it did not signify "the science of politics" as we know it today, but meant: science as such—its meaning and value—is appraised according to its practical utility for the people. Opposition to *this* politicizing of science is directly expressed in the rectoral discourse.

SPIEGEL: Let us make sure we understand you correctly: insofar as you led the University into what you experienced at that time as a new era, you wanted to affirm the University against otherwise overwhelming tendencies that no longer would have left to the University its proper function?

Heidegger: Exactly. But at the same time the self-assertion had to assume the task of winning back a new meaning for the University, in opposition to its merely technical organization, through a reflection upon the tradition of Western European thought.

SPIEGEL: Should we understand this to mean, Professor, that at the time you thought that you could bring about the restitution of the University in conjunction with the National Socialists?

Heidegger: That is the wrong way to put it. Not "in conjunction with the National Socialists," but the University ought to renew itself through a reflection all its own and thereby gain a firm position against the danger of the politicizing of science — in the sense that I just mentioned.

SPIEGEL: And for that reason you proclaimed in your rectoral discourse these three supporting columns: "service by labor," "service under arms," "service through knowledge." Accordingly, "service through knowledge," or so you thought anyway, was to be raised to a position equal [to the others] that the National Socialists had not conceded to it?

Heidegger: It is not a matter of "supporting columns." If you read [the text] carefully, service through knowledge stands in third place numerically, to be sure, but in terms of its meaning it is placed first. The task remains to consider how labor and the bearing of arms, like every human activity, are grounded in knowledge and illumined by it.

SPIEGEL: But we must mention here another statement — we are soon finished with these distressing citations — that we cannot imagine you would subscribe to today. You said in the fall of 1933: "Let not doctrines and ideas be the rules of your Being. The Führer, himself and he alone, is today and for the future German actuality and its law."

Heidegger: These sentences do not appear in the rectoral discourse but only in a local Freiburg student newspaper at the beginning of the winter semester of 1933-34. When I took over the rectorate, it was clear to me that I would not survive without compromises. The sentences you quote I would no longer write today. Such things as that I stopped saying by 1934.

SPIEGEL: May we throw in again another question? So far in this interview it has become clear that your position in 1933 oscillated between two poles. In the first place: You had to say many things *ad usum Delphini*. [11] This was one pole. The other pole, however, was much more positive, and this you express as follows: I had the feeling that here was something novel, here was a new era.

Heidegger: That's it exactly. Not that I spoke for the sake of mere appearances — I saw this as the one possibility.

SPIEGEL: You know that in this context several accusations have been made against you that concern your cooperation with the Nazi Party and its organizations, and these still persist in the public mind as undenied. Thus, you are accused of having taken part in the book burnings of the student body, or of the Hitler Youth.

Heidegger: I forbade the planned book-burning that was scheduled to take place in front of the University building.

SPIEGEL: Then you are accused of having books of Jewish authors removed from the library of the [199] University or from the Philosophical Seminar.[12]

Heidegger: As Director of the Seminar, I had jurisdiction only over the Seminar Library. I did not comply with repeated demands that the books of Jewish authors be removed. Former participants in my seminars can testify today to the fact that not only were no books of Jewish authors withdrawn but that these authors, above all, Husserl, were cited and discussed just as [they were] before 1933.

SPIEGEL: How do you explain the origin of such rumors? Is it malice?

Heidegger: According to my knowledge of the sources, I would like to assume that, but the reasons for the calumny lie deeper. My taking over the rectorate was probably only the occasion for it, not the determining cause. For that reason the polemic probably will flare up again and again whenever the occasion is offered.

SPIEGEL: Even after 1933 you had Jewish students. Your relationship to some of these Jewish students is supposed to have been cordial.

Heidegger: My attitude after 1933 remained unchanged. One of my oldest and most gifted students, Helene Weiss, who later emigrated to Scotland, took her degree in Basel (after continued study at Freiburg became impossible) with a work on *Causality and Chance in the Philosophy of Aristotle* (Basel, 1942). At the end of the foreword, the author writes: "The attempt at a phenomenological interpretation that we present here in Part I owes its possibility to M. Heidegger's unpublished interpretation of Greek philosophy." You see here a copy with a dedication of the author. I visited Dr. Weiss several times in Brussels before her death.

SPIEGEL: You were friendly for a long time with Karl Jaspers. After 1933, this relationship began to deteriorate. Rumor has it that the deterioration must be seen in conjunction with the fact that Jaspers had a Jewish wife. Would you like to say something about that?

Heidegger: My friendship with Jaspers began in 1919. I visited him and his wife during the summer semester of 1933 in Heidelberg. He sent me all his publications between 1934 and 1938 "with heartfelt greetings."

SPIEGEL: You were a student of Edmund Husserl, your Jewish predecessor in the chair of philosophy at the University of Freiburg. He had recommended you to the Faculty as his successor in that chair. Your relationship to him cannot have been without gratitude.

Heidegger: You know, of course, the dedication of *Being and Time*.

SPIEGEL: But later the relationship deteriorated. Can you, and do you want to, tell us what led to this?

Heidegger: The differences in matters of substance became sharper. In the beginning of the 1930's Husserl had a public reckoning with Max Scheler and me, the explicitness of which left little to the imagination. What moved Husserl to oppose my thought in such public fashion I was unable to learn.

SPIEGEL: What was the occasion for this?

Heidegger: Husserl spoke to the students in the Berlin Sportspalast. Erich Mühsam reported it in one of the large Berlin newspapers.[13]

SPIEGEL: The controversy as such is of no interest to us at the moment. Of interest only is that there was no controversy [between you] that had anything to do with the year 1933.

Heidegger: Not the slightest.

SPIEGEL: You have been criticized for the fact that in the publication of the fifth edition of *Being and Time* (1941) the original dedication to Husserl was omitted.

Heidegger: That's right. I explained this affair in my book *On the Way to Language.*[14] There I wrote: "To counter widely circulated allegations, let it be stated here explicitly that the dedication of *Being and Time. . .* remained in *Being and Time* until its fourth edition of 1935. In 1941, when my publishers felt that the fifth edition might be endangered and that, indeed, the book might be suppressed, it was finally agreed, on the suggestion and at the desire of Niemeyer[15], that the dedication be omitted from the edition, however, on the condition imposed by me, that the note to page 38 be retained — a note which in fact states the reason for that dedication, and which runs: "If the following investigation has taken any steps forward in disclosing the 'things themselves,' the author must first of all thank E. Husserl, who, by providing his own incisive personal guidance and by freely turning over his unpublished investigations, familiarized the author with the most diverse areas of phenomenological research during his student years in Freiburg." (*Being and Time,* [New York: Harper and Row, 1962] p. 489.)

SPIEGEL: Then we hardly need to raise the question whether it is correct that as Rector of the University of Freiburg you forbade the retired Husserl access to, or use of, the University library or the library of the Philosophical Seminar.

Heidegger: That is a calumny.

SPIEGEL: And there is no letter in which this prohibition against Husserl is contained? How, then, did such a rumor start?

Heidegger: I don't know either. I have no explanation for it. The impossibility of the whole thing can be shown by another little-known fact. During my rectorate I went before the Minister of Culture and defended the Director of the Medical Clinic, Professor Thannhauser, and the later Nobel Laureate, Professor (of Physical Chemistry) von Hevesy — both Jews — whom the Ministry gave orders to be dismissed. That I supported these men and at the same time took shabby action against Husserl, a retired professor and my own teacher, is absurd. I also prevented the students and teachers from organizing a demonstration [201] against Professor Thannhauser. At that time there were [some young] instructors waiting [for a formal appointment] who thought: now is the time for advancement. When these people presented their case to me, I turned them all away.

SPIEGEL: You did not attend Husserl's funeral in 1938.

Heidegger: Let me say this. The criticism that I had broken off my ties to Husserl is unfounded. In May, 1933, my wife wrote a letter to Mrs. Husserl in the name of both of us in which we assured them of our unaltered gratitude, and sent this letter with a small bouquet to Husserl. Mrs. Husserl answered briefly with a formal 'thank you' and wrote that the ties betweeen our families were broken. That I failed to express again to Husserl my gratitude and respect for him upon the occasion of his final illness and death is a human failure that I apologized for in a letter to Mrs. Husserl.

SPIEGEL: Husserl died in 1938. Already in February, 1934, you had resigned the rectorate. How did that happen?

Heidegger: Here I have a point to make. In the interest of reorganizing the technical structure of the university, i.e., of renewing the faculties from the inside out in terms of the very substance of their task, I proposed to nominate for the winter semester of 1933-34, younger and, above all, professionally outstanding colleagues to become deans of the individual faculties, and this, indeed, without considering their relationship to the Nazi Party. Thus, Professor Erik Wolf was appointed Dean of the Faculty of Law, Professor Schadewalt of the Philosophy Faculty, Professor Soergel of the Science Faculty, and Professor von Möllendorf, who had been dismissed as Rector the previous spring, of the Medical Faculty. But already by Christmas of 1933 it became clear to me that I would be unable to carry through the pending renewal of the University against either the resistance of the academic community or [the opposition of] the Party. For example, the Faculty reproached me for introducing students into responsible administration of the University—exactly as is done today. One day I was called to Karlsruhe where the Minister, through one of his Councillors, demanded, in the presence of the Student District Leader, that I replace the deans of the legal and medical faculties with other colleagues who were acceptable to the Party. I refused this request and offered my resignation from the rectorate if the Minister insisted on his demand. That's just what happened. This was in February, 1934. I resigned after ten months in office while [other] rectors of that time remained in office for two or more years. While the national and international press commented on my assumption of the rectorate in the most diversified fashion, not a word was said about my resignation.

SPIEGEL: Did you have at that time the opportunity to present your thoughts about university reform to the appropriate government minister?

Heidegger: What time are you referring to?

SPIEGEL: We are referring to the trip that Rust made to Freiburg in 1933.[16]

Heidegger: There were two different occasions involved. On the occasion of the Schlageter celebration in Schönau (Westphalia), I took the initiative of making a short formal call upon the Minister.[17] On a second occasion in November, 1933, I spoke with him in Berlin. I presented to him my conception of science and of the possible restructuring of the faculties. He took careful account of everything that I said, so I nurtured the hope that what I presented to him would have some effect. But nothing happened. I do not see why exception is taken to this exchange with the Party's then Minister of Education, while at the same time all foreign governments were hastening to recognize Hitler and to extend to him the ordinary international signs of respect.

SPIEGEL: Did your relations with the Nazi Party change after you resigned as Rector?

Heidegger: After my resignation, I limited myself to my teaching responsibilities. In the summer semester [204] of 1934, I lectured on "Logic." In the following semester 1934-35, I gave my first course on Hölderlin. In 1936, the Nietzsche courses began.[18] All who could hear at all heard this as a confrontation with National Socialism.

SPIEGEL: How did the transfer of office take place? You took no part in the celebration?

Heidegger: That's right. I refused to take part in the ceremonial transfer of the rectorate.

SPIEGEL: Was your successor a committed member of the Party?

Heidegger: He was a member of the Law Faculty. The party newspaper, Der Alemanne, announced his designation as Rector with banner headlines: "The First National Socialist Rector of the University."

SPIEGEL: What position did the Party take toward you?

Heidegger: I was constantly watched.

SPIEGEL: Did you notice this?

Heidegger: Yes—for example, the case of Dr. Hanke.

SPIEGEL: How did you know about it?

Heidegger: He came to me himself. He had just taken his doctorate in the winter semester of 1936-37, and in the summer semester of 1937 he was a member of my advanced seminar. He was sent here from S.S. Security Service to keep watch on me.

SPIEGEL: How did it happen that he suddenly came to you?

Heidegger: On the basis of my Nietzsche seminar in the summer semester of 1937, and the manner in which the work proceeded, he acknowledged to me that he could no longer sustain the role of watchman and wanted to bring the situation to my attention in the interest of my subsequent teaching.

SPIEGEL: So the Party kept a watchful eye on you?

Heidegger: I knew only that my publications were not allowed to be reviewed, e.g., the essay, "Plato's Doctrine of Truth."[19] The Hölderlin lecture[20] that I gave at the German Institute in Rome in the spring of 1936 was maliciously attacked in the review of the Hitler Youth Movement, *Wille und Macht*. Anyone interested today might read the polemic against me in E. Kriecks' journal, *Volk im Werden*, that began in the summer of 1934. At the International Philosophical Congress in Prague, 1934, I was not one of the German delegates. In like manner, I was excluded from the International Descartes Congress in Paris, 1937. In Paris, this seemed so surprising that the Director of the Congress, Professor Emil Bréhier of the Sorbonne, asked me, of his own accord, why I was not a member of the German delegation. I replied that the administration of the Congress might inquire about the matter at the National Ministry of Education. Shortly afterward, an invitation came to me from Berlin to join the delegation belatedly. I declined. The lectures "What is Metaphysics?" and "On the Essence of Truth"[21] were sold under the counter with jackets that bore no title. After 1934, the rectoral discourse was withdrawn immediately from the bookstores at the instigation of the Party.

SPIEGEL: Did it get even worse later on?

Heidegger: In the last year of the war, 500 of the most important scientists and artists were released from any kind of war service. I was not among them. On the contrary, in the summer of 1944, I was ordered up the Rhine to build fortifications.

SPIEGEL: On the other side of the border, Karl Barth did the same thing for the Swiss.

Heidegger: What is interesting is how this took place. The Rector had invited the entire teaching faculty [to a reception]. He gave a short talk to this effect: he was speaking by special arrangement with both the circle and the district leaders of the Party. [Accordingly,] he would now divide the entire teaching faculty into three groups: first, those who were completely expendable; second, those who were half-expendable; and third, those who were not expendable at all. In the first group of completely expendable was Heidegger, and along with him Gerhard Ritter.[22] In the winter semester of 1944-45, after the termination of the manual labor on the Rhine, I began a course that bore the title, "Poetizing and Thinking." In a certain sense it was a continuation of my Nietzsche courses, i.e., of my confrontation with National Socialism. After the second hour, I was conscripted into the Civil Defense Forces, the oldest member of the teaching body to be called up in this way.

SPIEGEL: To summarize then: In 1933, as an unpolitical person in the strict sense, if not in the broad sense, you became involved. . .

Heidegger: . . .by way of the University. . .

SPIEGEL: Yes, by way of and through the Unversity you became involved with the politics of this supposedly new era. After about a year you relinquished the function you had taken over. But in 1935, in a course that in 1953 was published as *Introduction to Metaphysics*, you said: "What today" — this was, therefore, 1935 — "is bandied about as the philosophy of National Socialism but has absolutely nothing to do with the inner truth and greatness of this movement (namely, with the encounter between technicity on the planetary level and modern man) casts its net in these troubled waters of 'values' and 'totalities'."[23] Did you add those parenthesized words for the first time in 1953, i.e., at the time of the publication, in order to explain to the reader of 1953, so to speak, in what way you saw the "inner truth and greatness of this movement" (i.e., of National Socialism) in 1935 — or did you have this explanatory parenthesis already there in 1935?

Heidegger: The parenthesis stood in my [original] manuscript and corresponded precisely to my conception of technicity at that time, and not yet to the later explication of the essence of technicity as "pos-ure" (*Ge-Stell*).[24] The reason I did not read the phrase publicly [206] was that I was convinced of the proper understanding of my listeners, although stupid people, informers and spies understood it differently — and also wanted to.

SPIEGEL: Surely you would include here the communist movement?

Heidegger: Yes, unquestionably — insofar as that, too is a form of planetary technicity.

SPIEGEL: Americanism also?

Heidegger: Yes, I would say so. Meantime, the last 30 years have made it clearer that the planet-wide movement of modern technicity is a power whose magnitude in determining [our] history can hardly be overestimated. For me today it is a decisive question as to how any political system — and which one — can be adapted to an epoch of technicity. I know of no answer to this question. I am not convinced that it is democracy.

SPIEGEL: But "democracy" is only a collective term that can be conceptualized in many different ways. The question is whether or not a transformation of this political form is still possible. Since 1945, you have commented on the political efforts of the Western World, hence also on democracy, on a politically expressed Christian view of the world (*Weltanschauung*), even on the system of constitutionally guaranteed citizens' rights. All of these efforts you have called "half-way measures."

Heidegger: First of all, please tell me where I have spoken about democracy and the other things you mention. I would indeed characterize them as half-way measures, [though] because I do not see in them any actual confrontation with the world of technicity, inasmuch as behind them all, according to my view, stands the conception that technicity in its essence is something that man holds within his own hands. In my opinion, this is not possible. Technicity in its essence is something that man does not master by his own power.[25]

SPIEGEL: Which of the trends just sketched out, according to your view, would be most suitable to our time?

Heidegger: I don't see [any answer to] that. But I do see here a decisive question. First of all, it would be necessary to clarify what you mean by "suitable to our time." What is meant here by "time?" Furthermore, the question should be raised as to whether such suitability is the [appropriate] standard for the "inner truth" of human activity, and whether the standard measure of [human] activity is not thinking and poetizing, however heretical such a shift [of emphasis] may seem to be.[26]

SPIEGEL: It is obvious that man is never [complete] master of his tools—witness the case of the Sorcerer's Apprentice. But is it not a little too pessimistic to say: we are not gaining mastery over this surely much greater tool [that is] modern technicity?

Heidegger: Pessimism, no. In the area of the reflection that I am attempting now, pessimism and optimism are positions that don't go far enough. But above all, modern technicity is no "tool" and has nothing at all to do with tools.

SPIEGEL: Why should we be so powerfully overwhelmed by technicity that. . .?

Heidegger: I don't say [we are] "overwhelmed" [by it]. I say that up to the present we have not yet found a way to respond to the essence of technicity.

SPIEGEL: But someone might object very naively: what must be mastered in this case? Everything is functioning. More and more electric power companies are being built. Production is up. In highly technologized parts of the earth, people are well cared for. We are living in a state of prosperity. What really is lacking to us?

Heidegger: Everything is functioning. That is precisely what is awesome, that everything functions, that the functioning propels everything more and more toward further functioning, and that technicity increasingly dislodges man and uproots him from the earth. I don't know if you were shocked, but [certainly] I was shocked when a short time ago I saw the pictures of the earth taken from the moon. We do not need atomic bombs at all [to uproot us]—the uprooting of man is already here. All our relationships have become merely technical ones. It is no longer upon an earth that man lives today. Recently I had a long [209] dialogue in Provence with Réné Char—a poet and resistance fighter, as you know. In Provence now, launch pads are being built and the countryside laid waste in unimaginable fashion. This poet, who certainly is open to no suspicion of sentimentality or of glorifying the idyllic, said to me that the uprooting of man that is now taking place is the end [of everything human], unless thinking and poetizing once again regain [their] nonviolent power.

SPIEGEL: Well, we have to say that indeed we prefer to be here, and in our age we surely will not have to leave for elsewhere. But who knows if man is determined to be upon this earth? It is thinkable that man has absolutely no determination at all. After all, one might see it to be one of man's possibilities that he reach out from this earth toward other planets. We have by no means come that far, of course—but where is it written that he has his place here?

Heidegger: As far as my own orientation goes, in any case, I know that, according to our human experience and history, everything essential and of great magnitude has arisen only out of the fact that man had a home and was rooted in a tradition. Contemporary literature, for example, is largely destructive.

SPIEGEL: The word "destructive" in this case is bothersome, especially insofar as, thanks to you and your philosophy, the word has been given a comprehensive context of meaning that is nihilistic [in tone]. It is jarring to hear the word "destructive" used with regard to literature, which apparently you are able to see—or are compelled to see—as completely a part of this nihlism.

Heidegger: Let me say that the literature I have in mind is not nihilistic in the sense that I give to that word.

SPIEGEL: Obviously, you see a world movement—this is the way you, too, have expressed it—that either is bringing about an absolutely technical state or has done so already.

Heidegger: That's right.

SPIEGEL: Fine. Now the question naturally arises: Can the individual man in any way still influence this web of fateful circumstance? Or, indeed, can philosophy influence it? Or can both together influence it, insofar as philosophy guides the individual, or several individuals, to a determined action?

Heidegger: If I may answer briefly, and perhaps clumsily, but after long reflection: philosophy will be unable to effect any immediate change in the current state of the world. This is true not only of philosophy but of all purely human reflection and endeavor. Only a god can save us. The only possibility available to us is that by thinking and poetizing we prepare a readiness for the appearance of a god, or for the absence of a god in [our] decline, insofar as in view of the absent god we are in a state of decline.[27]

SPIEGEL: Is there a correlation between your thinking and the emergence of this god? Is there here in your view a causal connection? Do you feel that we can bring a god forth by our thinking?

Heidegger: We can not bring him forth by our thinking. At best we can awaken a readiness to wait [for him].

SPIEGEL: But can we help?

Heidegger: The first help might be the readying of this readiness. It is not through man that the world can be what it is and how it is—but also not without man. In my view, this goes together with the fact that what I call "Being" (that long traditional, highly ambiguous, now worn-out word) has need of man in order that its revelation, its appearance as truth, and its [various] forms may come to pass. The essence of techriicity I see in what I call "pos-ure" (*Ge-Stell*), an often ridiculed and perhaps awkward expression.[28] To say that pos-ure holds sway means that man is posed, enjoined and challenged by a power that becomes manifest in the essence of technicity—a power that man himself does not control. Thought asks no more than this: that it help us achieve this insight. Philosophy is at an end.

SPIEGEL: Yet, nonetheless, in former times (and not only in former times) philosophy was thought to accomplish a great deal indirectly—directly only seldom—but was able indirectly to do much, to help new currents break through. If we think only of the great names of German thought, like Kant and Hegel down through Nietzsche (not to mention Marx), it can be shown that in roundabout ways philosophy has had a tremendous effect. Do you mean now that this effectiveness of philosophy is at an end? And if you say that the old philosophy is dead—that there is no such thing any more, do you also include the thought that this effectiveness of philosophy, if it was ever there in the past, is in our day, at least, no longer there?

Heidegger: A mediated effectiveness is possible through another [kind of] thinking, but no direct one—in the sense that thought will change the world in any causal way, so to speak.

SPIEGEL: Excuse me, we do not wish to philosophize—we are not up to that—but we have here the point of contact between politics and philosophy. That is why you notice that we are drawn into a dialogue of this kind. You have just said that philosophy and the individual would be able to do nothing but. . .

Heidegger: . . . .but make ready for this readiness of holding oneself open for the arrival, or for the absence, of a god. Even the experience of this absence is not nothing, but a liberation of man from what in *Being and Time* I call "fallenness" upon beings.[29] Making [ourselves] ready for the aforementioned readiness involves reflecting on what in our own day. . .is.

SPIEGEL: But for this we still would need, in fact, the well-known stimulus from outside—a god or someone else. Hence, [we are asking:] cannot thought, relying completely on its own resources, have a greater impact today? There was a time when it had an impact—[at least] so thought the contemporaries then, and many of us, I suspect, think so too.

Heidegger: But not immediately.

SPIEGEL: We just mentioned Kant, Hegel and Marx as men who moved [the world]. But even from a Leibniz came stimuli for the development of modern physics and consequently for the emergence of the modern world as such. We believe you said a moment ago that you no longer take account of efficacy of this kind.

Heidegger: Not in the sense of philosophy—not any more.[30] The role of philosophy in the past has been taken over today by the sciences. For a satisfactory clarification of the "efficacy" of [philosophical] thinking we would have to analyze in greater depth what in this case "efficacy" and "having an effect" can mean. Here we would need fundamental distinctions betwen"occasion," "stimulus," "challenge," "assistance," "hinderance" and "cooperation," once we have sufficiently analyzed the "principle of ground ['sufficient reason']." Philosophy [today] dissolves into individual sciences: psychology, logic, political science.

SPIEGEL: And what now takes the place of philosophy?

Heidegger: Cybernetics.

SPIEGEL: Or the pious [one] that holds himself open.[31]

Heidegger: But that is no longer philosophy.[32]

SPIEGEL: What is it then?

Heidegger: I call it another [kind of] thinking.

SPIEGEL: You call it another [kind of] thinking. Would you please formulate that a bit more clearly?

Heidegger: Are you thinking of the sentence with which I closed my lecture, "The Question of Technicity": "Questioning is the piety of thought"?

SPIEGEL: We found a phrase in your Nietzsche courses that was illuminating. You say there: "Because philosophical thinking takes place within the strictest possible bounds, all great thinkers think the same [thing]. But this same [thing] is so essential and rich that no individual ever exhausts it, but rather each [individual] only binds other individuals [to it] the more rigorously." But indeed it is precisely this philosophical edifice that in your opinon apparently has reached a certain termination,

Heidegger: It has reached its term. But it has not become for us [simply] nothing—rather, precisely through dialogue it has become newly present again. My entire work in courses and seminars over the past 30 years was, in the main, only an interpretation of Western philosophy. The return to the historical foundations of thought, the thinking through of those questions that since Greek philosophy still go unasked—this is no abandonment of the tradition. What I do say is this: the manner of thinking of traditional metaphysics that reached its term with Nietzsche offers no further possibility of experiencing in thought the fundamental thrust of the age of technicity that is just beginning.

SPIEGEL: About two years ago in an exchange with a Buddhist monk, you spoke of "a completely new method of thinking" and said that this new method of thinking is, "at first, possible for but few men to achieve." Did you mean to say by this that only very few people can have the insights that in your opinion are possible and necessary?

Heidegger: [Yes, if you take] "have" in the completely original sense that they are able in a certain way to give utterance to [these insights].

SPIEGEL: Fine, but the transmission [of these insights] into actualization you did not make apparent even in this dialogue with the Buddhist.

Heidegger: And I cannot make it apparent. I know nothing about how this thought has an "effect." It may be, too, that the way of thought today may lead one to remain silent in order to protect this thought from becoming cheapened within a year. It may also be that it needs 300 years in order to have an "effect."

SPIEGEL: We understand very well. However, since we do not live 300 years hence but here and now, silence is denied us. The rest of us—politicians, half-politicians, citizens, journalists, etc.—must constantly make decisions. We must adapt ourselves to the system in which we live, must seek to change it, must scout out the narrow openings that may lead to reform, and the still narrower openings that may lead to revolution. We expect help from philosophers, even if only indirect help—help in roundabout ways. And now we hear only: I cannot help you.

Heidegger: Well, I can't.

SPIEGEL: That must discourage the nonphilosopher.

Heidegger: I cannot [help you], because the questions are so difficult that it would run counter to the sense of this task of thinking to suddenly step out in public in order to preach and dispense moral censures. Perhaps we may venture to put it this way: to the mystery of the planetary domination of the unthought esssence of technicity corresponds the tentative, unassuming character of thought that strives to ponder this unthought [essence].

SPIEGEL: You do not count yourself among those who, if they would only be heard, could point out a way?

Heidegger: No! I know of no way to change the present state of the world immediately, [even] assuming that such a thing be at all humanly possible. But it seems to me that the thinking that I attempt might be able to awaken, clarify, and confirm [a] readiness [for the appearance of a god] that I have mentioned already

SPIEGEL: A clear answer! But can—and may—a thinker say: [214] just wait—we will think of something within 300 years?

Heidegger: It is not simply a matter of just waiting until something occurs to man within 300 years, but rather to think forward without prophetic claims into the coming time in terms of the fundamental thrust of our present age that has hardly been thought through [at all]. Thinking is not inactivity, but is itself by its very nature an engagement that stands in dialogue with the epochal moment of the world. It seems to me that the distinction between theory and practice comes from metaphysics, and the conception of a transmission between these two blocks the way to insight into what I understand by thinking. Perhaps I may refer to my lectures under the title, *"What is Called Thinking?"*

that appeared in 1954.³³ Maybe this, too, is a sign of our time, that of all my publications, this is the least read.

SPIEGEL: Let us return to where we began. Would it not be thinkable that we see National Socialism, on the one hand, as the actualization of this "planetary encounter" and, on the other, as the last, worst, strongest and, at the same time, weakest protest against this encounter between "planetary technicity" and modern man? Obviously you have in your person a [certain] polarity that brings it about that many by-products of your activity are to be explained properly only by the fact that different sides of your nature (that do not touch your philosophical core) cling to many things that as a philosopher you know have no firm base — for example, concepts such as "home," "rootedness" and the like. How do these things go together: planetary technicity and home?

Heidegger: I do not agree. It seems to me that you take technicity in much too absolute [a sense]. I see the situation of man in the world of planetary technicity not as an inextricable and inescapable destiny, but I see the task of thought precisely in this, that within its own limits it helps man as such achieve a satisfactory relationship to the essence of technicity. National Socialism did indeed go in this direction. Those people, however, were far too poorly equipped for thought to arrive at a really explicit relationship to what is happening today and has been underway for the past 300 years.

SPIEGEL: Do the Americans today have this explicit relationship?

Heidegger: They do not have it either. They are still caught up in a thought that, under the guise of pragmatism, facilitates the technical operation and manipulation [of things], but at the same time blocks the way to reflection upon the genuine nature of modern technicity. At the same time, here and there in the USA attempts are being made to become free from pragmatic-positivistic thinking. And who of us would be in a position to decide whether or not one day in Russia or China very old traditions of "thought" may awaken that will help make possible for man a free relationship to the technical world?

SPIEGEL: [But], if none of them has this relationship [now], and the philosopher is unable to give it to them. . . .

Heidegger: How far I come with my own effort at thought and in what way it will be received in the future and fruitfully transformed — this is not for me to decide. In a special lecture on the occasion of the jubilee of the University of Freiburg in 1957, under the title, "The Principle of Identity,"³⁴ I finally ventured to show in a few steps of thought to what extent there is opened up for man in the age of technicity (insofar as we thoughtfully experience what the genuine nature of technicity is based upon) the possibility of experiencing a relationship to an appeal to which he is not only able to attend but of which he is much rather himself an attendant. My thought stands in an unavoidable relationship to the poetry of Hölderlin. I consider Hölderlin not [just] one poet among others whose work the historians of literature may take as a theme [for study]. For me, Hölderlin is the poet who points into the future, who waits for a god, and who, consequently, should not remain merely an object of research according to the canons of literary history.

SPIEGEL: Apropos of Hölderlin—we apologize for having to quote again: in your Nietzsche courses you said that "the varied conflict we know between the Dionysian and the Apollonian, between holy passion and sober exposition, is a hidden law of style of the historical determination of the German [people], and one day must find us ready and prepared for it to take its form. This antithesis is not [just] a formula with the help of which we may only describe [our] 'culture.' With this conflict, Hölderlin and Nietzsche have set a question mark in front of the task of Germans to find their essence in an historical way. Will we understand the [question] mark? One thing is certain, history will take its revenge upon us if we do not understand it." We do not know in which year you wrote that, but we guess that it was in 1935.

Heidegger: Probably the citation belongs to the Nietzsche course, "The Will-to-Power as Art," 1936-37.[35] It could date, however, from the following years.

SPIEGEL: Well, could you please explain it? It leads us from the pathway of the general to a concrete determination of the German [people].

Heidegger: The drift of the citation I could also put this way: my conviction is that only in the same place where the modern technical world took its origin can we also prepare a conversion (*Umkehr*) of it. In other words, this cannot happen by taking over Zen-Buddhism or other Eastern experiences of the world. [217] For this conversion of thought we need the help of the European tradition and a new appropriation of it. Thought will be transformed only through thought that has the same origin and determination.

SPIEGEL: You mean, in the same place where the technical world took its origin it also must. . . .

Heidegger: . . .be sublated (*aufgehoben*) in the Hegelian sense—not set aside but sublated, though not through man alone.[36]

SPIEGEL: You attribute to the Germans a special task?

Heidegger: Yes, in the sense explained in the dialogues with Hölderlin.

SPIEGEL: Do you believe that Germans have a special qualification for this conversion?

Heidegger: I am thinking of the special inner kinship between the German language and the language of the Greeks and their thought. This is something that the French confirm for me again and again today. When they begin to think, they speak German. They assure [me] that they do not succeed with their own language.

SPIEGEL: Is that how you explain the fact that in the countries of romance languages, especially among the French, you have had such a strong influence?

Heidegger: [It is] because they see that despite all of their great rationality they no longer make a go of it in today's world when it comes to an issue of understanding this world in the origin of its essence. One can no more translate thought than one can translate a poem. At best, one can paraphrase it. As soon as one attempts a literal translation, everything is transformed.

SPIEGEL: A disturbing thought.

Heidegger: It would be good if this disturbance were taken seriously in good measure, and people finally gave some thought to what a portentious transformation Greek thought underwent by translation into the Latin of Rome, an event that even today prevents an adequate reflection upon the fundamental words of Greek thought.

SPIEGEL: Professor, for our part we would like to maintain our optimism that something can be communicated and even translated, for if we should cease to hope that the content of thought can be communicated, even beyond language barriers, then we are left with the threat of provincialism.

Heidegger: Would you characterize Greek thought in distinction from the conceptual style of the Roman Empire as "provincial?" Business letters can be translated into all languages. The sciences, i.e., even for us today the natural sciences (with mathematical physics as the fundamental science), are translatable into all the languages of the world—or, to be exact, they are not translated but the same mathematical language is spoken [universally]. [But] we touch here a broad field that is difficult to cover.

SPIEGEL: Perhaps this is another version of the same theme: at the moment it is no exaggeration [to say that] we have a crisis of the democratic-parliamentary system. We have had it for a long time. We have it especially in Germany, but not in Germany alone. We have it also in the classical lands of democracy like England and America. In France, it is hardly any longer a crisis. The question, then, is this: isn't it possible, after all, that suggestions come from the thinkers (if only as a by-product) either as to how this system may be replaced by a new one and what a new one would look like, or that reform must be possible—together with some indication as to how this reform could be possible. Otherwise, we are left in a situation where the man who is philosophically untutored—and normally this will be one who holds things in his hands (though he does not determine them) and who is himself in the hands of things—we are left in a situation [I say] where such a man arrives at false conclusions, perhaps at frightful short-circuits [of thought]. Therefore, ought not the philosopher be ready [219] to formulate thoughts as to how men may arrange their relations with other men in this world that they themselves have technologized, that perhaps has overwhelmed them? And does he not betray a part, albeit a small part, of his profession and his vocation if he has nothing to say to his fellow men?

Heidegger: As far as I can see, an individual [thinker] is not in a position by reason of his thought to see through the world as a whole in such fashion as to be able to offer practical advice, and this, indeed, in view of the fact that his first task is to find a basis for thinking itself. For as long as thought takes itself seriously in terms of the great tradition, it is asking too much of thought for it to be committed to offering advice in this way. By what authority could this come about? In the domain of thinking there are no authoritative statements. The only measure for thought comes from the thing itself to be thought. But this is, above all, the [eminently] Questionable. In order to give some insight into the "content" of such thought, it would be necessary to analyze the relationship between philosophy and the sciences, whose technical-practical accomplishments make thought in the philosophical sense seem more and more superfluous. Thus it happens that corresponding to the predicament that thought faces by reason of its own proper task there is an estrangement with regard to thought nourished by the powerful place of the sciences [in our culture]. [That is why] thought is forced to renounce an answer to questions of the day concerning practical matters of *Weltanschauung*. . . .

SPIEGEL: Professor, in the domain of thought there are no authoritative statements. Likewise, it is surely not surprising that modern art, too, has difficulty in making authoritative statements. And yet you call it "destructive." Modern art understands itself often as experimental art. Its works are attempts. . . .

Heidegger: I am glad to be instructed.

SPIEGEL: . . .Attempts within a situation where man and the artist are isolated, and [yet] among a hundred efforts every now and again one succeeds.

Heidegger: This is indeed the question: where does art stand? What place does it have?

SPIEGEL: All right, but there you demand something from art that you no longer demand from thought.

Heidegger: I demand nothing from art. I say only that it is a question as to what place it occupies.

SPIEGEL: If art does not know its place, is it therefore destructive?

Heidegger: All right, cross the word out. I would like to observe, however, that I do not see anything about modern art that points out a way [for us]. Moreover, it remains obscure as to how art sees the specific character of art, or at least looks for it.

SPIEGEL: The artist, too, finds nothing in what is handed down to bind him. He can find it beautiful and say: Yes, this is the way someone could paint 600 years ago, or even 30 years ago, but he himself can do it no longer. Even if he wanted to, he could not do it. [If that were possible,] then the greatest artist would be an ingenius imposter [like] Hans van Meegeren, who could paint "better" than [his contemporaries]. But this sort of thing does not work anymore. Thus the artist, the writer, the poet are in a situation similar to that of the thinker. How often must we then say: close your eyes.

Heidegger: If we take as framework for the correlation of art, poetry and philosophy the "culture business"—then the comparison you make is valid. But if not only the "business" character is open to question but also the meaning of "culture," then reflection upon such questionable matters falls, too, within the area of responsibility of thought, whose own distressed condition is not easily thought through. But the greatest need of thought consists in this, that today, so far as I can see, there is still no thinker speaking who is "great" enough to bring thought immediately and in clearly defined form before the heart of the matter [*seine Sache*] and thereby [set it] on its way. For us today, the greatness of what is to be thought is [all] too great. Perhaps the best we can do is strive to break a passage through it—along narrow paths that do not stretch too far.

SPIEGEL: Professor Heidegger, thank you for this interview.

Translated by William J. Richardson, S.J.

Notes

William J. Richardson, S.J., is Professor of Philosophy at Fordham University and author of *Heidegger: Through Phenomenology to Thought,* 3rd. edition (The Hague: Nijhoff, 1974).

1. The Nazis came to power January 30, 1933. Heidegger was elected Rector of the University of Freiburg in May, 1933. At issue, therefore, is his relation to Nazism before, during and after his tenure as Rector.
2. Heidegger's favorite retreat was a small wooden hut at Todtnauberg in the Black Forest, not far from Freiburg.
3. In the German universities at that time, the summer semester began in late April and lasted until late July. The winter semester began in early November and lasted until early February.
4. Presumably one of the many forms of the Jewish boycott (e.g., *Juden unerwünscht*; "Jews unwelcome here!") already underway 3 months after Hitler's assumption of power.
5. The Social Democrats were one of the oldest of Germany's political parties and one of the most influential during the Weimar Republic.
6. The S.A. (*Sturmabteilung*) were the "Stormtroopers" or "Brownshirts."
7. Translated by David Farrell Krell in Martin Heidegger, *Basic Writings*, ed. D.F. Krell (New York: Harper and Row, 1977), pp. 91-112, at p. 96 (my translation).
8. The new Rector followed the time-honored custom of making a formal public address when he took office. Entitling his address "The Self-Assertion of the German University" (Breslau: Korn, 1933), Heidegger urged the academic community to assume its responsibility before the nation in the service of science—"service by labor," "service under arms," "service through knowledge." Some found a parallel for this conception of "service" in Plato's *Republic*. Others found it to be a complete

capitulation to the Nazis. Hence, the pursuit here of the apparently Nazist implications of the address.

9. *Spiegel* note: The passage appeared in the review, *Die Erziehung*, edited by A. Fischer, W. Flitner, Th. Litt, H. Nohl and E. Spranger (1933), p. 401.

10. Translated by John Macquarrie and Edward Robinson (New York: Harper and Row, 1962.) This was Heidegger's first major — and still most important — work. In it he raised the question that has pervaded all of his subsequent efforts: what is the meaning of Being?

11. The allusion is obscure. Perhaps the interviewer means: "after the manner of the oracle at Delphi," i.e., in a manner that was deliberately enigmatic and evasive — so that the hearer could interpret what was said in whatever way he wished. But the the word should be *Delphicae*, and the phrase as it stands would be simply a pedantic malapropism. Other possible explanations of the phrase are less probable and even more esoteric.

12. I.e., the specialized reference library in the seminar rooms of the Philosophy Department.

13. Erich Mühsam, 1874-1934, was a German poet, playwright and anarchist, who died in a concentration camp in 1934.

14. Translated by Peter D. Hertz (New York: Harper and Row, 1971), p. 199. The dedication in question has been restored in subsequent editions.

15. Publisher of the German editions of *Being and Time*.

16. Bernhard Rust had been a Nazi Party member and friend of Hitler since the early 'twenties and was named Reich Minister of Science, Education and Popular Culture shortly after Hitler assumed office.

17. Albert Leo Schlageter (1894-1923) was shot by the French for his role in the resistance to the French occupation of the Ruhr.

18. In his "Logic" course, Heidegger addressed the fundamental nature of thought, particularly in terms of its relationship to language. In meditating on Hölderlin, he reflected on the nature of language as it appears in poetry. The Nietzsche courses dealt with Nietzsche's thought as the dénouement of metaphysics in the West.

19. Translated by John Barlow, in *Philosophy in the Twentieth Century*, edited by William Barrett and H.D. Aiken (New York: Random House, 1962). Vol. II, pp. 251-270.

20. "Hölderlin and the Essence of Poetry," translated by Douglas Scott, in *Existence and Being*, edited by Werner Brock (Chicago: Regnery-Gateway, 1969), pp. 270-291.

21. Translated by John Sallis in *Basic Writings*, pp. 117-141.

22. Gerhard Ritter was at that time Professor of Modern History at the University of Freiburg and, on November 1, 1944, was arrested in connection with the attempt on Hitler's life, July 20, 1944. He was imprisoned, and released by the Allied forces, April 25, 1945.

23. Translated by Ralph Manheim (Garden City, N.Y.: Doubleday Anchor, 1961). By "technicity," Heidegger means more than just "technology." He uses the term to characterize *the manner in which Being manifests itself* in the present epoch of the world, acccording to which man experiences the beings around him as objects that can be submitted to his control. It is as a consequence of this experience that "technology" becomes possible. Technicity for Heidegger is "planetary" in the sense that this revelation of Being is planet-wide and affects every aspect of man's relationship to, and on, the planet where he finds himself.

24. By 1953, when *Introduction to Metaphysics* was first published, Heidegger had already begun to describe technicity in terms of its essence (i.e., as a manner in which Being is revealed — and concealed) by the neologism, *Ge-stell*. Although the word *Gestell* ("frame," "stand," "chassis") is found in ordinary German, Heidegger is using

it in completely idiosyncratic fashion to signify the collective way (suggested by the prefix, *Ge-*) in which beings are experienced by man as in one way or another "posed" (various forms of *-stellen*) to, by and for man (e.g., "com-posed," "contra-posed," "pro-posed," etc.), and thus conceivably subject to his control. The original usage by Heidegger is enigmatic for all but initiated Germans. It is untranslatable by any single English word — "pos-ure" here is at best an equally neologistic — and probably futile — approximation. See "Die Frage nach der Technik," *Vorträge und Aufsätze* (Pfullingen: Neske, 1954), pp. 13-44. An English translation by William Lovitt has come forth under the title *"The Question concerning Technology" and other Essays* (New York: Harper and Row, 1977).

25. Since technicity for Heidegger is in its essence the manner in which Being reveals itself through beings to man, man does not control it (i.e., master it by his own power) but at best can do no more than respond to it appropriately.

26. "Thinking" for Heidegger means more than merely intellectual activity — it involves an authentic response of the whole man to the revelation of Being. As such, it is non-conceptual and non-representational — a total, accepting openness to Being. Likewise, "poetizing" means more than simply writing "poetry" or the "poetic arts" in any ordinary sense — it means bringing the revelation of Being into appropriate language.

27. In all probability, Heidegger is not using the word "god" here in any personal sense but in the sense that he gives to the word (often in the expression, "god or the gods") in his interpretations of Hölderlin, i.e., as the concrete manifestation of Being as "the Holy."

28. See note 23.

29. I.e., the tendency to become absorbed in beings to the disregard of Being that reveals itself in and through them.

30. Heidegger is using the word "philosophy" here to designate the metaphysical tradition of the West that he sees as beginning with Plato and ending with Nietzsche. He sees it as interrogating the nature of beings (either in general or in terms of their ultimate ground in a "supreme" being). His own interest is in interrogating the meaning of Being itself, which he experiences as the source of light by which beings are illumined as what they are and which therefore lies at the foundation of metaphysics. Hence, he calls his effort at various times "foundational," or "re-collective," or "interrogative," or simply (as below) "another" kind of thinking. It would be the task of such a thought to interrogate the essence of technicity as a manner in which Being manifests itself in the present epoch of the world.

31. The allusion is to the way Heidegger concluded one of his essays, "The Question of Technicity," with a phrase that since then has become famous: "Questioning is the piety of thought." (*Vorträge und Augsätze*, Pfullingen: Neske, 1954), p. 44. Cf. *The Question Concerning Technology. . . ,*p. 34.

32. I.e., in the sense of the traditional metaphysics of the West.

33. Translated by Fred D. Wieck and J. Glenn Gray (New York: Harper and Row, 1968).

34. Translated by Joan Stambaugh (New York: Harper and Row, 1969).

35. *Nietzsche* (Pfullingen: Neske, 1961). Vol. I, pp. 11-254.

36. I.e., assumed and integrated on a higher level.

The Pathway
(1947-1948)

Martin Heidegger

It runs through the park gate and out towards Ehnried. The old linden trees in the castle garden gaze after it from behind the wall, whether at Easter when the path shines bright between growing crops and waking meadows, or at Christmas when it disappears in snowdrifts behind the nearest hill. At the wayside crucifix it turns off towards the woods. Along its edge it greets a tall oak beneath which stands a roughly hewn bench.

On the bench there occasionally lay one or another of the great thinkers' writings which youthful clumsiness was trying to decipher. When the puzzles crowded into each other and there seemed no way out, the pathway was a help. It quietly escorts one's steps along the winding trail through the expanse of untilled land.

Time and again when my thinking is caught in these same writings or in my own attempts, I go back to the trail traced by the pathway through the fields. It remains just as ready for the thinker's steps as for those of the farmer who goes out to mow in the early morning.

More frequently through the years, the oak by the wayside carries me off to memories of childhood games and early choices. When deep in the forest an oak would occasionally fall under the axe's blow, my father would immediately go looking throughout the woods [12] and sunny clearings for the cord allotted him for his workshop. There he labored thoughtfully during pauses from his job of keeping the tower clock and the bells, both of which maintain their own relation to time and temporality.

From the bark of the oak tree little boys carved their boats which, fitted with rowers' benches and tillers, floated in Metten Brook or in the school fountain. On these journeys of play you could still easily get to your destination and return home again. The dream-element in such voyages remained held in a then hardly perceptible luster which lay over everything. The area of these journeys was circumscribed by the hand and eye of my mother. It was as if her unspoken care watched over everything. Those play voyages still knew nothing of wanderings when all shores would be left behind. Meanwhile, the hardness and scent of the oakwood began to speak more clearly of the slowness and constancy with which the tree grew. The oaktree itself spoke: only in such growth is there grounded what lasts and fructifies; to grow means to open oneself up to the expanse of heaven and at the same time to sink roots into the darkness of earth; everything genuine thrives only if it is, in right measure, both ready for the appeal of highest heaven and preserved in the protection of sustaining earth.

Again and again the oaktree says this to the pathway which passes by sure of its course. The pathway gathers in whatever has its Being around it; to all who pass this way it gives what is theirs. The same fields and meadows, ever changing but ever near, accompany the pathway through each season. Whether the Alps above the forests are sinking into twilight, or a lark is climbing into the summer morning where the pathway winds over the rolling hill, or [13] the eastwind is blowing up a storm out of the region where mother's home village lies; whether, as night draws near, a woodsman drags his bundle of brushwood to the hearth, or a harvesting wagon sways homeward in the pathway's tracks, or children are gathering the first primroses at the meadow's edge, or the fog is pushing its gloomy burden over the fields for days on end—always and everywhere the call [*Zuspruch*]¹ of the pathway is the same:

The simple preserves the enigma of what abides and is great. It comes to men suddenly but then requires a long time to mature. It conceals its blessings in the modesty of what is always the same. The wide expanse of everything that grows and abides along the pathway is what bestows world. In what its language does not say, there—says Eckhardt, old master of letter and life—God is truly God.

But the call of the pathway speaks only as long as there are men, born in its atmosphere, who can hear it. They are servants of their origin, not slaves of machination. Man's attempts to bring order to the world by his plans will remain futile as long as he is not ordered to the call of the pathway. The danger looms that men today cannot hear its language. The only thing they hear is the noise of the media, which they almost take for the voice of God. So man becomes disoriented and loses his way. To the disoriented, the simple seems monotonous. The monotonous brings weariness, and the weary and bored find only what is uniform. The simple has fled. Its quiet power is exhausted.

Certainly the company of those who still recognize the simple as their hard-earned possession is quickly diminishing. But everywhere these few will be the ones who abide. Through the gentle force of the pathway they will one day have the strength to outlast the gigantic energies of atomic power, which [14] human calculation has artificed for itself and made into fetters of its own action.

The call of the pathway awakens a sense which loves the free and open and, at the propitious place, leaps over sadness and into a final serenity. This serenity resists the senselessness of merely working, which, when done for itself, promotes only emptiness.

In the pathway's seasonally changing breeze thrives this wise serenity whose mien often seems melancholy. This serene wisdom is at once "playful and sad, ironic and shy."[2] Someone who doesn't have it already can never acquire it. Those who have it get it from the pathway. Along its trail the winter storm encounters the harvest day, the lively excitement of spring meets the peaceful dying of autumn, the child's game and the elder's wisdom catch each other's eye. And all is serene in a singular harmony whose echo is silently carried here and there by the pathway.

Such wise serenity is a gateway to the eternal. Its door turns on hinges once forged by a skilled smith out of the enigmas of human existence.

From Ehnried the way turns back towards the park gate. Its narrow ribbon rises over the last hill and runs through some low ground until it reaches the town wall. It shines dimly in the starlight. There, behind the castle, rises the tower of St. Martin's Church. Slowly, almost hesitantly, eleven strokes of the hour sound in the night. The old bell, on whose ropes boys' hands were rubbed hot, shudders under the blows of the hammer of Time, whose dark-droll face no one forgets.

With the last stroke the stillness becomes yet more still. It reaches out even to those who were sacrificed before their time in two world wars. The simple has become simpler. [15] The ever-same astonishes and liberates. The call of the pathway is now quite clear. Is it the soul speaking? or the world? or God?

Everything speaks of renunciation unto the same. Renunciation does not take away, it gives. It bestows the inexhaustible power of the simple. The call makes us at home in the arrival of a distant origin.

Translated by Thomas F. O'Meara, O.P.,
Revised by Thomas Sheehan.

Notes

Thomas Franklin O'Meara, O.P., is Professor at the Aquinas Institute of Theology and is widely published in philosophy. Most recently his bibliographical study of F.W.J. Schelling appeared in *The Review of Metaphysics*, 31 (1977). "The Pathway," a translation of "Der Feldweg," *Martin Heidegger. Zum 80. Geburtstag* (Frankfurt: Klostermann, 1969), pp. 11-15, appeared in *Listening*, 8 (1973), 32-39. Numbers in brackets refer to the German pages.

1. The German *Zuspruch* can mean address, appeal, etc. The choice of "call" is as much an interpretation as a translation. The message, appeal, or address which the pathway (Greek, *he hodos*) sends to man is a summons, hence a call, into his essential self-absence. (TS)
2. *Das "Kuinzige"*: This phrase in Upper Swabian dialect is still in use in some areas. It is a dialect form for *kein nützend*, "not useful." From its originally negative tone it developed a positive meaning allied to "serene, playful." Heidegger paraphrases: "A serene melancholy which says what it knows with veiled expressions." (T.F.O'M.)

Seeking and Finding:
The Speech at Heidegger's Burial

Bernhard Welte

Martin Heidegger's path has come to its end. What may one say at this end, over his coffin, in light of his death? Once a whole world listened to him. Perhaps at the news of his death it will listen once more. Perhaps, in face of this death which so moves us, silence would be more fitting than speech. Yet a word or two of reflection may be said, and indeed must be said. On January 14 of this year Martin Heidegger granted me a long conversation, and he asked me to say a few words at his burial. Only for that reason do I presume to speak on this occasion. And what better thing could we do at this moment than to think once more about Heidegger's path and especially about his thoughts on death?

He once came forth from this homeland, this earth of Messkirch. Since then his thought has shaken the world and the century. And he has brought new light, new questions, new meanings to bear on the whole of Western history. After Heidegger we look back on our history differently that we did before. And don't we also look differently into the future?

He was always seeking and always underway. At various times he emphatically characterized his thinking as a path. He traveled this path without ceasing. There were bends and turns along it, certainly there were stretches where he went astray. Heidegger always understood the path as one that was given to him, sent to him. He sought to understand his word as a response to an indication to which he listened without respite. For him, to think was to thank, to make grateful response to that appeal.

What did this great thinker think of death, which now has overtaken him as well? In his magnum opus, *Being and Time*, he described the anticipation of death (pp. 71ff., 279ff.). Already as a young man he was on this course of anticipation. And on May 7, 1960, at the Hebel celebration, he cited the Alemannian poet who speaks of the quiet grave: "Sei Plätzli het gheimi Tür/ un's sin no Sachen ohne dra." ("Its little place has a secret door/ And under it there still are things.")[1] Now Martin Heidegger himself has gone through that secret door. Where does it lead? In that same short speech, Heidegger once more cites Hebel's verses on this point: "Kein Wort der Sprache sagt's/ Kein Bild des Lebens malt's." ("No word in language says it/ No image in life depicts it.") That which no word says and no image depicts is the mystery. Heidegger sought it continually. He sought it on his path, and he sought it most of all in the mystery-filled destiny [Geschick] of death. What is it? The Nothing? Being? The serene and holy?

In two essays, "Building Dwelling Thinking" and "The Thing,"[2] he also spoke about that which is ever sought for and about death. In these essays there appears the "fourfold" of earth and heavens, of mortals and immortals. Here where we lay his body safely in the earth and where the expanse of heaven opens overhead, we would do well to think of the fourfold. The mortals are mortal because they are capable of death. But in that regard he writes: "Death is the shrine of the Nothing, that is, of that which in every respect is never a mere being but which nevertheless comes to presence, indeed as the mystery of Being itself. As the shrine of the Nothing, death shelters within itself the coming-to-presence of Being. As the shrine of the Nothing death is the shelter of Being [das Gebirg des Seins]."[3] The shelter of Being: therefore death shelters and conceals something. Its "Nothing" is not "just nothing." It shelters and conceals the goal of the whole path. Here that is called Being.

But what are the divinities? They are, as the essay tells us, "the beckoning messengers of the godhead."[4] They beckon out of the country of dying, of death, of the Nothing, and of Being, and the path of Heidegger's thinking went out to meet these beckonings. It was a matter of listening to them and, with these beckonings of the divinities, of anxiously awaiting the epiphany of the divine God. The entire thought of this great thinker was on the way towards this epiphany. And on this path he was directed to endure in thought the distress of a godless time and furthermore to interpret the way of time and world as a way to the epiphany. He himself read Nietzsche as an interpreter of time and world, and he asked of Nietzsche whether he had perhaps called out de produndis.[5] De Profundis, "Out of the Depths" — that is the psalm which, from out of the depths of His absence, calls to the divine God. The call which Heidegger attributed to Nietzsche was surely his own as well.

At his 80th birthday he spoke at Amriswil, Switzerland, concerning the whereabouts of man's dwelling in our age. He asked, "Does man today dwell in the abode of the self-withdrawal of the sublime [Vorenthalt des Hohen]?"[6] He saw this as the deepest which moves man today — the withdrawal of the sublime i.e., in Hölderlin's words, of the divine God, the withdrawal which awakens the call *de profundis*. This withdrawal, or as it is sometimes called, the failure of God, does not mean according to Heidegger a mere lack, but rather, as he wrote in the "Letter to a Young Student," "the presentness, which must first be appropriated, of the hidden fullness of what is already," which may be "the divine in the world of Greeks, in prophetic Judaism, in the preaching of Jesus."[7]

The path has now come to an end. Death, the shelter of Being, has carried off Martin Heidegger into the mystery of its hidden fullness. But stirred by the Gospel, we may say with hope, "He who seeks shall find, he who knocks shall have the door opened" (Matthew 7:7). "He who seeks" — that could well be the title for all of Heidegger's life and thought. "He who finds" — that could be the secret message of his death. From out of its mystery it shines forth into the world of mortals.

Is it fitting to give Martin Heidegger a Christian burial? Is it in keeping with the message of Christianity, with the path of Heidegger's thought? In any case he wanted it. Moreover, he had never broken his bond to the community of believers. To be sure, he walked his own path and had to go his own way and follow his call. And in the usual sense of the term one could not call this path Christian without some qualification. But it was the path of perhaps the greatest seeker of this century. By waiting and by harkening to the tidings, he sought the divine God and His splendor. He sought Him as well in the preaching of Jesus. Thus at the grave of this great seeker we may speak the words of consolation of the Gospel and the prayer of the psalms, especially the "De Profundis," and the greatest of prayers, the one which Jesus has taught us.

Translated by Thomas Sheehan

Notes

Prof. Dr. Bernhard Welte, a Catholic priest and a fellow townsman of Martin Heidegger, is Professor of Christian Philosophy of Religion at the University of Freiburg. Among his many writings are *Der philosophische Glaube* (1949) and *Ueber das Böse* (1959). The speech he delivered at Heidegger's burial was originally published in *Christ in der Gegenwart*, (Verlag Herder: Freiburg, Basel, Vienna), Nr. 24, 28. Jahrgang, June 13, 1976, p.188, under the title "Suchen und Finden."

1. "Dank bei der Verleihung des staatlich Hebelgedenkpreises," *Hebel-Feier. Reden zum 200. Geburtststag des Dichters*, Karlsruhe, 1960, pp. 27ff.
2. "Bauen Wohnen Denken" and "Das Ding," both in *Vorträge und Aufsätze*, 3d. ed., Pfullingen: Neske, 1967, respectively pp. 145-162 and 163-185. Eng. trans., Martin Heidegger, *Poetry, Language, Thought*, trans., Albert Hofstadter, New York: Harper and Row, 1971, respectively pp. 143-163 and 163-186.
3. *Vorträge und Aufsätze*, p. 177; Eng. trans., p. 178f., here slightly revised.
4. *Ibid.*, pp. 150 and 177; Eng. trans., pp. 150 and 178.
5. *Holzwege*, 4th ed., Frankfurt: Klostermann, 1963, p. 246.
6. "Fragen nach dem Aufenthalt des Menschen," *Neue Zürcher Zeitung*, Nr. 606 (Fernausgabe Nr. 273), October 5, 1969, p. 51
7. *Vorträge und Aufsätze*, p. 182; Eng. trans., p. 184., here slightly revised.

II. BEING, DASEIN, AND SUBJECTIVITY

Heidegger's Way Through Phenomenology to the Thinking of Being

William J. Richardson, S.J.

[After three years of research into the role of "thought" in the work of Martin Heidegger, the author drew up in English a résumé of his findings that he then translated into German and offered to Professor Heidegger for his comment and criticism. In a long, wide-ranging discussion, Professor Heidegger confirmed the validity of the interpretation, recommending two minor changes of expression in the text of the résumé, which, of course, were made. On the basis of this résumé, Heidegger agreed to write a preface to the published work. The German text appeared with Professor Heidegger's approval together with his eventual preface (Philosophisches Jahrburch, *LXXII [1965], 385-402). Although the full study, with preface, has long since appeared* (Heidegger: Through Phenomenology to Thought, *3rd edition, The Hague: Martinus Nijhoff, 1974), the English version of the original résumé that first gained Heidegger's approval appears here for the first time.]*

The purpose of this research was to discern what Martin Heidegger means by the "thinking of Being" (*das Denken des Seins*). The method was to trace the development of this problematic out of the author's early work, by considering his writings according to the order in which they were composed rather than that in which they were published. In its edited form the research covers all of Heidegger's works published before 1962, and composed up to and including the university course which treated thematically the problem of thought in 1952: *What E-vokes Thought?* (*Was heisst Denken?*). The following pages sketch in some detail the essentials of the analysis and indicate briefly its conclusions.

A. THOUGHT AND METAPHYSICS

In a very general way one may say that the thinking of Being is that process by which Heidegger discerns the sense of Being and thus overcomes metaphysics (*Überwindung der Metaphysik*). For him, metaphysics meditates beings as beings, i.e., in their Being, but is oblivious to the sense of Being itself and, therefore, to the profound difference between beings and Being (the ontological difference). Strictly speaking, the word "metaphysics" dates from the post-Aristotelian schoolmen, but the sense of it is to be found in Aristotle himself. There, metaphysics is the meditation of *on hei on*, but *on* is essentially ambiguous, according as it is taken as a participle (*seiend: Sein*) or as a noun (*Seiendes*) and, if taken as a noun, meaning either the ensemble of beings in its totality (*Seiende im Ganzen*) or the ground of this ensemble, i.e., a being that is supreme within the ensemble and that may be called (sometimes) Being. The confusion between Being and beings is evident.

But the confusion itself is found more originally still in Plato, who is the first of the philosophers, Heidegger claims, to reduce Being to the state of a being. How this happened we can best understand if we recall that for Heidegger Being is essentially the process of *physis* by which beings come-to-presence as what they are, hence emerge from concealment into non-concealment (*a-letheia*). Being for Heidegger, then, is the process of *a-letheia*, i.e., of "truth." With Plato, this early Greek conception of truth as non-concealment undergoes a transformation, for although on the one hand the Ideas retain the original sense of *a-letheia,* insofar as they are conceived fundamentally as a source of light by reason of which the "beings" of experience shine forth through participation, nevertheless the Ideas become at the same time something to-be-seen (*eidos, idein*) and truth comes gradually to mean the proper viewing of the Ideas, the conformity (*orthotes*) between the being that views and the Ideas (likewise conceived as beings) that are viewed. Here the Ideas are transformed from a source of light into that-which-is-viewed. In other words, Being is reduced to a being. The confusion will mark the entire subsequent history of metaphysics. Token of the confusion will be the domination henceforth of the conception of truth as conformity and a disregard of the original sense of truth as non-concealment. Since truth as non-concealment is what Heidegger understands by Being, it is easy to see in what sense he understands metaphysics to be perennial forgetfulness of Being.

But if metaphysics begins with Plato, it reaches its term in Descartes and the entire modern period. With the liberation of man unto himself that characterizes the epoch, Descartes seeks some *fundamentum inconcussum veritatis* by which man himself can become the arbiter of his own truth. Truth, then, becomes not only conformity but the verification of this conformity, i.e., certitude. This *fundamentum* will underlie (*hypokeimenon*) all truths, hence the *funda-*

mentum veritatis becomes the sub-ject (*hypo-keimenon*) of truth, which for Descartes himself, is of course, the *cogito-sum*. The *fundamentum veritatis* becomes thus the *res* (*subjectum*) *cogitans*, where *cogitatio* is to be understood as the present-ing (*Vor-stellen*) of an object to and by a subject, in such a way that the pro-posing (*vor-stellende*) subject can itself guarantee its conformity to the object in a manner analogous to the way in which the subject guarantees to itself its own existence. Since only that is true which is certifiable, beings are "true" only insofar as they enter into the subject-object polarity, i.e., insofar as they are either subjects or objects. Hence the Being of beings becomes that by which they are subjects (hence subject-ivity) or objects (hence object-ivity). Their only presence is found not in their own non-concealment but in the order of (re)presentation by a subject.

However this may be, the subject for Descartes is the individual human ego. Leibniz, however, so extends the notion that it can apply to every being. For every monad is endowed with the power of presentation, i.e., *perceptio et appetitus*. Kant's transcendental philosophy is an attempt to discern the conditions necessary to render possible the presenting of objects to the subject. But the culmination of subjectism, hence of all metaphysics, arrives with Hegel, for it is he who explores the absolute character of the certitude in which Descartes' quest for the *fundamentum inconcussum* terminated, i.c., the certitude of self-awareness.

Culminated in Hegel, subjectist metaphysics reaches its ultimate consummation in Nietzschean nihilism. On the one hand, Nietzsche sees that the old supra-sensible, i.e., meta-physical, values have lost their meaning for nineteenth century Europe, and, to the extent that he takes God to be the symbol of these values, God is certainly dead. On the other hand, his own effort at re-valuation remains itself a metaphysics, for the Will-unto-Power (*Wille zur Macht*), posing as it does new values (truth and art), is eminently a subjectism. The only change is in the way in which the presentative subject is conceived: now it is a universal Will. Nietzsche fails, then, to overcome metaphysical nihilism. In fact, he adds to its momentum, for to the extent that superman responds to the exigencies of Being conceived as Will-unto-Power, he seeks (and must) domination over the earth. This he achieves by reducing all beings to control, by submitting them to man's disposition, even though this be achieved through the exact calculation of them in scientific research. This is the meaning of technicity (*Technik*), which crystallizes for contemporary society the forgetfulness of the Being-dimension in beings, the forgetfulness of the ontological difference. The measure of Nietzsche's failure is his inability to escape the subject-object polarity. This can be done only by a type of thinking that can transcend subjectism and meditate the essence of metaphysics by going beyond it to think that which metaphysics invariably forgets: the sense of Being itself.

What is said here of metaphysics may be said as well for the science of logic, for this formulates the rules of presentative thought, i.e., the type of thinking that only forms and expresses judgments "about something" (*über etwas*), i.e., about beings. Like metaphysics, logic, too, is chained to the conception of truth as conformity. In similar fashion, Heidegger interprets the traditional conception of humanism. Interpreting the essence of man as a rational animal, all traditional humanisms, he claims, either spring from a metaphysics or found one.

B. THOUGHT IN HEIDEGGER II.

It is by the thinking of Being that Heidegger proposes to overcome metaphysics, technicity, logic, humanism — not to destroy them but to found them. What he means by thought, then, may be understood first in a negative way as a process that is non-subjective (better: pre-subjective), non-presentative (better: pre-presentative). By the same token it is non-logical (better: pre-logical), and as long as we remain in the perspectives of logic and metaphysics we will be able to think of Being only as Non-being (*Nichts*). If "rational" (*ratio*) be identified with "logical" (*logos*), then this thought must be called non-rational: not irrational but pre-rational. As opposed to the tendency to dominate the objects of thought the attitude of foundational thinking (*das wesentliche Denken*), i.e., the thought that founds metaphysics by thinking Being, will be simply to let beings be, hence to render them free unto themselves.

More positively, foundational thinking tries to meditate Being: as the process of truth, i.e., non-concealment, by reason of which all beings are manifest in themselves and to each other; as the domain of openness "between" subject and object, within which the subject-object relationship may first rise; as that horizon of encounter nearer to the thinker than the beings with which he deals (because the Source out of which they and he are first made possible), yet farther from him than all else (because in itself unseizable as a being).

What is the fundamental structure of this thought? It is brought-to-pass by the nature of man conceived as ek-sistence, i.e., as endowed with the prerogative, unique among beings, of an ecstatic open-ness unto the lighting-process of Being. Ek-sistence thus understood may be called the There (*Da*) of Being, because it is that domain among beings where the lighting-process takes place. Since the There comes-to-pass in a being, this privileged being is the There-being (*Dasein*), and, conversely, There-being must be understood always as the There of Being among beings, nothing more.

To understand thought, then, we must first see more precisely the relationship between Being and its There. It is, in fact, a cor-relation. For on the one hand Being maintains a primacy over its There, throwing it forth and dominating it at all times, revealing itself and concealing itself according to its own nature. Yet on the other hand, Being needs its There in order to be itself (the coming-to-pass of non-concealment), for unless non-concealment comes-to-pass in a There that is found among beings, it does not come-to-pass at all. We understand in what sense, then, the There is "for the sake of" Being, the "shepherd," the "watchman" of Being: Being is its unique concern (*Sorge*). To think Being will be to think the truth of Being in which There-being is ek-sistent.

Being discloses itself to and in its There, but since it is Being that holds the primacy, Being is conceived as sending itself (*sich schickt*) unto its There. We may speak of this self-sending of Being as proceeding from Being and call it a "self-emitting" or, if we may be permitted a neologism to designate a new concept, a "mittence" (*Geschick*) of Being. We may speak of it, too, as terminating in There and therefore call it a "com-mitting" or "com-mitment" (*Schicksal*) of There to its privileged destiny as the shepherd of Being. In any case, one thing is certain: intrinsic to the mittence of Being is a certain negativity, by reason of which Being withdraws even as it bestows itself, conceals itself even in its revealment. The reason is that even though Being reveals itself in revealing beings, it can never be seized for itself and by itself (since it is not a being), hence conceals itself in the very beings to which it gives rise. To think Being, then, will be to think it as a mittence, not only in its positivity but in its negativity.

We must go one step further. Since the mittence of Being is intrinsically negatived, no single mittence exhausts the power of Being to reveal itself. Hence Being discloses itself to the nature of man by a plurality of mittences (*Geschicke*) which one may call "inter-mittence"(*Ge-Schick-te*), and it is this plurality that constitutes history (*Geschichte*), a single mittence constituting an epoch of history. This epoch may be understood: in a large sense as including many phases of development (e.g., the mittence/epoch of metaphysics); in a narrower sense as referring to a single phase within such a scope (e.g., the perennial essence-existence problematic); in a strict sense as referring to an individual thinker who characterises an epoch (e.g., Anaximander, Parmenides, Hegel). In any case, the thinking of Being must think Being-as-history and is therefore a profoundly historical thought.

But all this describes the relation between Being and its There. What is the precise role of thought in the process? It brings this relationship "to fulfillment." If we consider this "fulfillment" with reference to Being, thought completes the process of non-concealment by bringing Being into that form of manifestation that is most proper to the nature of man: language. If we consider this "fulfillment" in terms of the There, thought is that process by which ek-sistence assumes, i.e., achieves, its self as the There of Being. From either point of view, the fundamental attitude of thought will be one of acquiescence to Being, of responding *(Entsprechung)* to its appeal *(Anspruch)* of letting Being be itself.

The structure of this process will take the form of a re-collection *(Andenken)*: the tri-dimensional process by which Being comes (the future) to the thinker in and through beings that already are (the past) and is rendered manifest (the present) by the words that the thinker himself formulates. Such, too, is the structure of the thoughtful dialogue. Profoundly a temporal process (future-past-present), foundational thought is by this very fact historical, i.e., it thinks Being-as-history in continual ad-vent to thought through a dialogue with the past. Furthermore, thought thinks not only Being-as-history, i.e., inter-mittence, but thinks every mittence of Being in its negativity as well as its positivity, endeavoring to comprehend and express not what another thinker thought/said, but what he did not think/say, could not think/say, and why he could not think/say it.

But when all is said and done, the function of foundational thought is to help Being be itself, to dwell in Being as in its element, just as a fish dwells in water. Thought, as the fulfillment of the There, proceeds from Being and belongs *(gehört)* to Being, for the There is thrown forth by Being. On the other hand, thought attends *(hört)* to Being inasmuch as by it the There assumes itself as the guardian of Being. This thought that belongs to Being and attends to Being is what the later Heidegger (let us call him "Heidegger II") means by the "thinking of Being" *(das Denken des Seins)*. Briefly: foundational thinking is the process by which human ek-sistence responds to Being, not only in its positivity but in its negativity, as the continual process of truth-as-history.

C. THOUGHT IN HEIDEGGER I.

By "Heidegger I" we understand the Heidegger principally of *Being and Time* *(Sein und Zeit: SZ)* and of the perspectives which characterize this work. Here, too, the author's unique purpose was to try to think the sense of Being in order to lay the groundwork for (found) metaphysics, i.e., to construct a fundamental ontology. His long preoccupation with Kant had underlined the importance of insisting on the finitude of man in founding metaphysics. The *status quaestionis*, then: For Kant, what are the conditions which render possible the ontological synthesis (transcendence) of finite reason? For Heidegger, what is the relation between the radical finitude of man and the comprehension of Being as such?

Heidegger approached the problem by examining closely this comprehension of being with which finite man is endowed, for There-being is the only being which has this privileged access to Being. The basic sense of Being is that which renders it possible for beings to be manifest, and therefore accessible, to one another. The method is "phenomenological." This term is to be understood in its most radical sense as *legein ta phainomena* where *legein* has the sense of *deloun* (to make clear) or, more precisely, *apophainesthai* (to permit something to appear of itself), and *phainomena* means that which shows itself as it is. Thus the radical sense of phenomenology means *apophainesthai ta phainomena*: to permit that which of its own accord manifests itself to reveal itself as it is. Now since the phenomenon to be examined is There-being, the whole sense of the existential analysis of SZ becomes: to let There-being reveal itself in what and how it is, i.e., to *be* (manifest as) its self. What does the phenomenological interpretation of There-being reveal? That it is the process of finite transcendence whose ultimate meaning is time.

1. *The Process of Finite Transcendence.*

By calling There-being a "process," Heidegger wishes to insist that it is not an entity (*Vorhandenes*), enclosed and already achieved, but rather a dynamic process already begun but still-to-be-achieved. This process is called "transcendence," because by the comprehension of Being Heidegger understands the process by which There-being passes beyond (*trans-scendere*) beings, itself included, unto Being, i.e., seizes all beings (*com-prehendere*) in their Being. To the extent that the analysis of There-being begins with the everyday condition in which There-being first of all and for the most part finds itself, transcendence is called "to-be-in-the-World" (*In-der-Welt-sein*), where the World is understood as the horizon within which There-being encounters other beings (therefore Being), and "-in-" means the point or moment when World becomes disclosed inasmuch as There-being renders manifest the Being of beings. Again, this transcendence is also called "existence," a term which permits us now to distinguish the "existentiell" (*"ontic"*) and "existential" (*"ontological"*) dimensions of There-being: "existentiell" referring to There-being as a being among others, "existential" to There-being in its own Being, i.e., in that structure by which it is the luminous comprehension of Being. The components of this ontic-ontological/existentiell-existential structure are called "existentials," and phenomenology will endeavor to let these existentials be (manifest), first in their plurality, then in their unity, finally in the ground of this unity.

This process is finite inasmuch as it is profoundly negatived: There-being is not master over its own origin but simply finds itself among beings (*Geworfenheit*): it is not independent of the beings among which it is found, but is one of them and must deal with them, must remain referentially dependent upon them; it is not impervious to the fascination of these beings but contains within itself the tendency ("fallenness": *Verfallen*) to lose itself among them, to live only on the ontic level, to forget its own ontological dimension; it is not capable of discerning the World/Being as anything more than Non-being; it is not destined to continue forever but is a process-unto-end, an end which is (since we are dealing with the nature of man) death. This complex of negativity is designated by the term "guilt" (*Schuld*), which is not to be understood in any moral sense but simply as the "ground of a negativity" (*Grundsein einer Nichtigkeit*).

The structure of finite transcendence is composed of three components: Comprehension (*Verstehen*), ontological disposition(*Befindlichkeit*), logos (*Rede*): they are mutually complementary and equally original in There-being as the disclosedness of Being/World. By comprehension is understood that component which projects (*Entwurf*), i.e., lights up the horizon of, the World. By the ontological disposition is understood that component through which is disclosed There-being's thrown-ness, its fallen-ness, and the World itself as Non-being. Comprehension may be interpreted (although Heidegger himself does not make this explication) as constituting the intrinsically finite disclosure of World/Being in its positivity, the ontological disposition as constituting this disclosure in its negativity—both mutually complementary in the coming-to-pass of *finite* transcendence. Finally, by logos is understood that radical power, equally original with the others, by reason of which There-being can let-be-seen, i.e., can express in human fashion, what comprehension and the ontological disposition disclose. The actual coming-to-expression is the articulation of language.

If such are the components of finite transcendence in their plurality, how understand their unity? Heidegger fuses them into the conception of concern (*Sorge*), which he defines as "the anticipatory drive-towards-Being, thrown-forth as still-to-be-achieved, and fallen upon the beings of experience." When this unity is considered as a totality, it is understood as always coming-to-an-end/death. The definition suggests clearly the components of positivity (anticipatory drive-towards-Being) and negativity (thrown-down...fallen). But what of the third component of There-being, i.e., logos, equally original with the other two? Logos as such is not mentioned explicitly in the formula that describes concern. But that which gives There-being to understand what it is, not only in its positivity (transcendence) but in its negativity (finitude, i.e., guilt), and thus calls There-being to achieve its self is the voice of conscience. It is in the mode of conscience that logos plays its role in concern.

But the unity of comprehension, the ontological disposition and logos (conscience) is not sufficient to constitute a fully achieved There-being. In order to achieve itself, There-being must heed the voice of conscience, must let its self be called. This is the fullness of freedom, not simply because it is a choice that could be refused but because of its own accord There-being lets-be (manifest) that which logos has already let-be (seen). There-being thereby endorses its self as the process of finite transcendence and, in assuming its charge, achieves authenticity. This act of supreme freedom is called re-solve (*Entschlossenheit*). It is the culmination of existential phenomenology.

2. *Ultimate Meaning: Time.*

What renders possible, therefore grounds, concern? Time! for the structure of concern implies future-past-present. There-being is a dynamic drive-towards-Being, hence is continually coming-to-Being, i.e., Being is continually coming to the self which is There-being (future). But the self to which Being thus comes already is as having-been-thrown-forth (past). Furthermore it exists in the ontic as well as ontological dimension and, by reason of its comprehension of the Being that continually comes to it, renders manifest (present) these beings with which it deals. It is the unity of future-past-present in the single process of time that renders possible the unity of concern. Explicitated further, the temporality of There-being constitutes also its historicity.

How translate the process of re-solve, which achieves concern, into terms of time which founds it? Heidegger here introduces the new term, "re-trieve" (*Wiederholung*). Re-solve lets-be the process of finite transcendence; re-trieve lets-be this process as historical. For There-being to let-be its self means to "fetch" (*-holt*) its self all over again (*wieder-*), and this re-fetching, i.e., re-trieving, is the achieving of There-being's authentic self in terms of its past (of what-is-as-having-been). But There-being's self still *is*-as-having-been, insofar as Being is *still* coming to it through this past, so that re-trieve is the achieving of There-being's authentic self in terms of its future as well. It is by re-trieve, then, that There-being assumes itself, hands over to itself its own heritage, re-assumes a potentiality that has been exploited already and thereby comes to comprehend more profoundly the sense of Being in continual arrival. We understand re-trieve best when we see it at work, e.g., in the Kant-analysis, where Heidegger re-trieves the problem of founding metaphysics. Concretely, this means saying what Kant did not say and *could not* say but nevertheless made accessible to us by the words that he used. To bring to expression what another did not say, this is the meaning of re-trieve, by which the historical There-being achieves authenticity.

3. *Corollaries.*

a. *Truth*

The process of finite transcendence, grounded in the unity of time, is more than the disclosure of Being in beings. It is the coming-to-pass of truth. For truth in the sense of conformity supposes the discovery of the being which manifests itself to the knower as to-be-judged in such and such a way. The discovering of beings, therefore, is a more radical truth than the truth of conformity, and it is just such a discovering, a letting-be-manifest of beings, that is meant by the process of transcendence. The process of transcendence, then, is the process of truth. Since transcendence is finite, i.e., negatived, so, too, is truth. By this is meant that every project of a potentiality of Being is inevitably askew; every apprehension *(ergreifen)* is simultaneously a misapprehension *(vergreifen)*; what is once discovered slips back into oblivion *(Verborgenheit)*; to un-cover *(ent-decken)* is simultaneously to cover-up *(verdecken)*; to dis-close *(erschliessen)* is to close-over *(verschliessen)*. It is to discern the truth of beings in its positivity *and* in its negativity that phenomenology is necessary. Heidegger calls the negativity of truth "un-truth." If the eminent mode of disclosedness is that free choice (re-solve) of There-being to accept itself as finite transcendence, then re-solve is likewise the eminent mode of truth (and un-truth), by which There-being makes truth — and un-truth — its own *(eignet sich . . . eigentlich zu).*

b. Subjectism

Such a conception of truth makes all truth dependent on There-being. Is this a subjectivism? It would be, if There-being were a subject. But this is what There-being is not. There-being is transcendence. To conceive There-being as a subject would be to think of it as a mere entity *(Vorhandenes)*, i.e., to consider its ontic dimension and forget completely its ontological dimension. For by reason of this ontological dimension There-being transcends all beings (even itself), therefore all subject-object relationship, unto the Being which founds this relationship. As to-be-in-the-World, then, There-being is not opposed to the World as a subject opposed to an object, but is simply the luminosity of the World/Being because it is the coming-to-pass of truth. With such a conception, the entire Idealism-Realism problematic, and with it such things as the critical problem, dissolves.

D. The Breakthrough

If at this point we compare Heidegger I and Heidegger II, we see clearly: that the same problem preoccupies both (the effort to overcome/ground/found metaphysics by endeavoring to think the sense of Being, i.e., Being-as-truth); that in both cases Heidegger's effort is to overcome the subject-object polarity by letting come-to-pass the negatived process of non-concealment (truth); that the method characteristic of Heidegger II is the process of thought, of Heidegger I the process of phenomenology; that when the methods are compared in detail we notice the following:

The nature of the being that executes the method in Heidegger I is characterized as transcendence (to-be-in-the-World, existence, even ek-sistence), in Heidegger II as ek-sistence: in both cases it is that being among other beings whose distinctive prerogative is to be open unto Being. The process in both cases is profoundly marked by negativity (finitude): in Heidegger I by the finitude of transcendence; in Heidegger II by the finitude of the mit-tence of Being. In both cases the process is temporo-historical: in Heidegger I, it is the process of There-being that is fundamentally temporal and historical;

in Heidegger II it is Being that is the fundamental history. The structure of the process, however, is the same in both: Being comes (future) as having been in what already is (past) and is rendered manifest through the co-operation of man (present). In both cases the process comes to its fulfillment only when man endorses it with his liberty: in Heidegger I the process is called re-solve, the culmination of phenomenology; in Heidegger II it is called thought.

The parallelism between phenomenology in Heidegger I, when brought to a fullness in re-solve, and thought in Heidegger II is evident. It remains to ask if the parallel is merely an external one, or if the relation is so internal and necessary that we may say that phenomenology is *transformed* into thought. Let us signalize two major moments of the transition.

1. *On the Essence of Truth (1930)*

Heidegger's preoccupation with the problem of truth after the publication of SZ might have been inferred from the minor works that followed and ex-plicitated the major work: *On the Essence of Ground* becomes a meditation on transcendence because the problem of ground is fundamentally the problem of truth; *What is Metaphysics?*, insofar as it meditates Non-being as that which renders possible the open-ness of beings as such, is always dealing implicitly with the problem of ontological truth.

On the Essence of Truth (WW) meditates truth both in its positivity (nos. 1-4) and negativity (nos. 5-7). The analysis begins with an examination of the traditional notion of truth as conformity and moves slowly to the conception of truth as ek-sistent freedom (no. 4). In meditating the negativity of truth, the author achieves an important shift of perspective, for the focus changes from There-being to Being, which is conceived now as the process of truth which comports its own negativity. This negativity is of two modes, the second com-pounding the first: in the first place, truth in revealing itself conceals itself and even conceals its own concealment (mystery); secondly the mystery itself becomes forgotten (errance: *Irre*) and thereby the domain of all possible ways in which man can go astray is established. Taken together, mystery and er-rance constitute the complete negativity of truth. This negativity, taken with the corresponding positivity, constitutes the complete essence of truth, which is at the same time the truth of Essence, where Essence must now be understood in a verbal sense as the process of coming-to-presence.

In WW Heidegger mentions thought twice. In the first case at the end of Section 7 we are given to understand that thought takes place in the moment of re-solve. But there is a difference from the use of this term in SZ. There, There-being by re-solve assumes *its self* in its finitude; here, There-being by re-solve accepts the *negatived ensemble* of beings-as-such (*as* itself, i.e., in their Being and as negatived.) Common to both is the basic intuition: There-being must accept in a moment of re-solve the fact that Being in its truth is filtered through finitude (negativity). The difference: only one of focus, i.e., from There-being to Being.

The second reference to thought in WW comes immediately after the first (at the beginning of Section 8) but is separated by a sectional division. It reads: "In the Thinking of Being, that liberation of ek-sistence which is the foundation of history is uttered in Word. . . . " Upon analysis the phrase "of Being" may be given the sense of a "subjective" genitive as well as an "objective" one, and the intimate correlation of thought and language is affirmed for the first time. The whole text suggests Heidegger II rather than Heidegger I. By reason of the immediate proximity of these two references to thought, we are led to infer that the thinking of Being is the process of re-solve. The difference between the two problematics? It is the difference between Heidegger I and Heidegger II, i.e., the shift of focus from There-being to Being.

2. Introduction to Metaphysics (1935)

If in WW Heidegger I becomes Heidegger II, it is in the lecture course of the summer semester, 1935, that the main lines of the new position are firmly drawn. Here, amid changing terminology and a burgeoning problematic, the author remains faithful to his initial intentions to ground metaphysics by posing the question of Being. For the question, "Why are there beings at all and not much rather Non-being?", is the ground-question of metaphysics (i.e., interrogates the ground of metaphysics) because it asks about the ontological difference. Such an interrogation presupposes a preliminary question about the sense of Being itself.

One way to discern the sense of Being is to distinguish it from certain modalities that have always been associated with it: becoming, seeming-to-be, obliging, thinking. The most significant of these is thinking. Throughout the analysis, Being is understood as the Being of beings and interpreted in the sense of *physis*, emergent-abiding Power, whose nature is to come-to-presence in beings as non-concealment (truth). But as such, Being has need of a place where this non-concealment comes-to-pass. This is its There, which, though opposed (*Gegenüber*) to Being, is dominated by it and grounded in it. The coming-to-pass of non-concealment, however, is essentially finite (permeated by negativity), which means that all beings, including There-being itself, are revealed and simultaneously not-revealed (concealed), and thereby fall under the law of seeming-to-be which is intrinsic to Being. The consummation of the finitude of There, however, is not simply the de-cadence (*Verderb*) by which it falls prey to seeming-to-be, but the fact that from the beginning and at every moment it is a process-unto-an-end/death.

The There, though opposed to Being, is not separated from it in subject-object fashion. Rather, the There is the process which gathers together into concentration (*logos*) the overwhelming Power of Being and thus contains (*noein*) its dynamic advance to such an extent as to force it (*Gewalt-tätigkeit*) into disclosure. It is this initial correlation between Being and its There that is the coming-to-pass of truth. Being therefore needs its There in order to be itself as emergent truth, yet retains its primacy over the There insofar as this can never master Being to such an extent that the non-concealment is complete, i.e., without shadow of negativity. The There remains finite.

Since the There is not substance but process, it is essentially historical and always to-be-achieved. This achievement takes place when the There assumes itself for what it is, i.e., as the There of Being. The assumption of the self consists in re-trieving in all its freshness and with a new depth (*ursprünglicher*) the initial wonderment about the Being of beings with which the process (i.e., both philosophy and history) began.

The re-trieve of primal wonderment involves de-cision (*Entscheidung*), whereby There-being, although immersed in the welter of seeming-to-be, nevertheless comprehends this seeming-to-be and accepts its consequences. What de-cision implies may be discerned by an analysis of Parmenides' description (Fig. 4, 6) of the three ways that the thinker must follow, and by an analysis of There-being's necessary consent to its own dissolution. Briefly: There-being comprehends that seeming-to-be is the inevitable correlate of Being as finite; that it is the There of intrinsically finite Being, therefore subservient itself to the law of seeming-to-be; that the consummation of its own finitude consists in the fact that its end/death is already immanent within it; that despite this finitude it remains the There of Being, unique in its awesome prerogative (*Unheimlichkeit*). De-cision means to comprehend and to accept to be a There that is finite. It corresponds exactly to that which SZ called "re-solve."

It is the bringing-to-pass of de-cision/resolve that is the original process of thought (*logos-noein*). By thought, then, There-being wills its own (finite) openness to Being, and this is the primal sense of "to know" (*Wissen: techne*). To will-to-know is to ask, hence the fundamental method of thought is to interrogate the Being of beings, i.e., to pose the Being-question. This is done by re-trieve. Since language takes its origin when *logos* first gathers Being into non-concealment and preserves in itself this non-concealment, then the meditation upon language, whether by word-analysis or by the interpretation of authentic thinkers who have articulated Being in words (poets, therefore, as well as philosophers), will be a valuable mode of re-trieve.

If thought for the philosophers is no longer understood as the process of de-cision but a function of the intellect, separated from Being, and a tribunal which passes definitive judgment on Being's determinations, the fundamental reason is that philosophy has fallen away from the initial conception of truth as a process of non-concealment that comes-to-pass in There-being. Ultimately this is due to the forgottenness of Being. To overcome this deficiency, we must re-collect Being by posing the Being-question, as Heidegger himself has tried to do.

E. CONSEQUENCES

1. If the analysis is valid, it would seem that the Thinking of Being is more than the *terminus-ad-quem* of an odyssey that began with phenomenology. It is the transformation of phenomenology according to the exigencies imposed by the transfer of focus from There-being to Being.

2. To the extent that this shift (*Kehre*) of focus was always envisioned, as certain signs both in SZ and the Kant-analysis indicate, and as the "Letter on Humanism" in retrospect explicitly claims, we may say that it was imposed by the dynamism of Heidegger's original experience of Being and executed out of fidelity to this experience. By the same token, we may argue that SZ II, never published, comes to us in substance perhaps as the entire *corpus* of Heidegger II. To give credence to such a hypothesis, one might surmise that the "destruction of metaphysics" may have been articulated in the polemic vs. subjectism, while the problematic of "Time and Being" may well have been elaborated in terms of the primacy of Being as discerned in the problematic of thought.

3. If SZ II as such was never published, the reason is that the necessary language failed. This need not be attributed to a debility on Heidegger's part, but simply to the fact the the language of metaphysics was not capable of articulating a pre-metaphysical thought. The efforts of Heidegger II to reinterpret Heidegger I may be understood perhaps as an effort to say now what he did not and *could not* say then. We may consider Heidegger II, then, as making in his own way a re-trieve of Heidegger I. This would permit us to admit with those who claim that there is a complete dichotomy between the two periods that the later Heidegger says what the earlier Heidegger did *not* say, yet maintain with those who insist on an absolute identity that there is a profound continuity between the two, a necessary passage from one to the other.

4. The analysis enables us to explain the apparent inconsistency which speaks of the forgottenness of Being as due sometimes to the self-concealment of Being in its mittence, sometimes to the negligence of man. The solution lies in recognizing the full importance of the problem of finitude in Heidegger. Because Being is intrinsically finite, every mittence is negatived. That is why Being necessarily reveals itself under the guise of mystery and errance. In Being itself, then, is to be found the ground of the "forgetfulness" of Being. On the other hand, There-Being is the There of intrinsically finite Being, hence is itself permeated by negativity. One form of this negativity of There-being is its non-resistance to the beguilement of beings, which we have called "fallenness." To the extent that There-being freely accedes to this inherent tendency and forgets its ontological prerogative, forgottenness of Being is due to the

negligence of man. But even this negligence must be understood as rooted ultimately in Being itself, which throws-forth the There.

5. There is absolutely no point to criticising Heidegger on grounds of "scientific history," even when this becomes the history of philosophy, for it is essential to his experience that he say what others did not and *could not* say. The dialogue with his predecessors is clearly a method of re-trieve, hence a manner of articulating his own experience of Being. Essential to the experience is the conception of Beings as a *logos* (letting-be-seen) that is intrinsically finite, i.e., negatived, whose dynamism constitues the process of time. There is no evidence to "justify" the experience beyond the experience itself. It is as impossible to break the hermeneutic circle in 1962 as in 1927. In this sense, Heidegger even in the second period remains always on the phenomenological level where Being alone bears testimony to itself, and indeed, in a finite way. When all is said and done, we have only to meditate the experience itself and see if it is such that we can share it.

Note

William J. Richardson, S. J., is Professor of Philosophy at Fordham University. He is the author of *Heidegger: Through Phenomenology to Thought*, 3rd edition (The Hague: Nijhoff, 1974) and numerous articles on philosophy and psychology.

Towards the Topology of Dasein

Theodore Kisiel

It has long become a commonplace to observe that Heidegger is a thinker of one thought: being. And yet, after several decades of exegesis of his attempt to revive this time-honored question, one is often still tempted to turn his own opening gambit, the quote from Plato's *Sophist*, back upon him and his spokesmen, and remark: "You obviously have always understood what you meant when you use the word 'being.' We, however, who once thought we understood, have now fallen into perplexity" (*SZ* 1).[1]

The confusion is compounded for the reader of English, in which infinitives are not used as nouns as a matter of course. Accordingly, in order to distinguish between *Seiendes* ("being" in the substantive sense of "entity") and *Sein* ("being" understood verbally as "to be"), translators have, among other tactics, resorted to such ugly neologisms as "essent" or clumsy phrases as "that-which-is," or have sought to maintain the identity of the infinitive-noun by capitalizing it. The latter convention not only calls excessive attention to "being" as a concept but also promotes a mystique of the capital B, which thereby becomes the key shibboleth of a latter-day gnostic cultism that drowns urgent issues in an ocean of technical esotericism. Page upon page dotted with capitalized nouns strikes the knowledgeable reader of philosophy as an atavism from the days in which Hegelian idealism held forth in the English-speaking world. As an antidote to the justifiable ontophobia brought on by this overdose of Teutonic English, one can only second the discretion of the aging Heidegger, who makes sparing use of the term and at times drops it entirely in favor of a number of surrogate stratagems. More so today than a half-century ago, the very word "being" still seems curiously out of tune with the times.

Yet it remains Heidegger's central concern, not as a word or a concept but as the most basic issue every human being must face. It remains the one thought which has obsessed him from beginning to end, drawing him again and again to the effort of thought, and gathering all of these efforts together. Thus as he neared the end of these efforts, Heidegger pointed to the *question* of being and said: "It is this question — and it alone — that determines the way of my thought and its limits."[2] Accordingly, he directs his commentators to judge him and assess his place in Western philosophy solely in terms of this question, its possibility or impossibility, its limits and its potential for further development.[3]

Which makes all the more urgent the demand for some guides to direct the nagging question of the beginner: "What could Heidegger possibly mean by 'being'?" Even the experienced reader of philosophy at times may well pause and ask himself the same question. In either case, this would not at all be surprising, in view of the inertia of tradition and habit which comes into play and the confusions which inevitably arise when one attempts to ask an old question in a new way.

If it is not surprising, it is at least ironic that Heidegger's conception of "being" as it is elaborated in exegeses often still has all the appearance of something quite abstruse and academic. For this is precisely Heidegger's own complaint against 2,500 years of philosophizing about being. That "being" has over the centuries come to be considered logically indefinable, self-evident, the most general and therefore the emptiest of concepts is for Heidegger a history weighty with consequences for the West, where the question of being first stirred and saw the light of day. Nietzsche seems to toll the death-knell when he sees in this "highest concept" an empty world, full of vapor and smoke, which names the gigantic and fateful fallacy of the Occident and now seems to us like a hollow word-idol that "dissolves like a tatter of cloud in the sunlight" and disappears as "the last streak of evaporating reality."[4]

Heidegger's efforts to revive the question accepts this epochal characterization of being as the distinctive and now obsolescent question of the West. His revision first of all attempts to reverse the speculative flight of philosophy over what it considers the most general of generalities by taking the issue of being back to its most concrete manifestation and expression. For the question of what it means to be for the human *being*, far from being so abstract and academic, can pose itself in his unique existence as the first and most pressing of all questions. As it confronts us in the concrete human situation, being is not the metaphysical *ens commune*, but the very thrust and context of our temporal and historical existence. Even the blandness of "common being" finds its experiential locus in the matter-of-fact way in which one may unthinkingly utter "Here I am" or "There it is" without sensing the full problematic charge pent up in diminutives like "am" and "is." The secrets of the commonplace tend to surface into the open only in the more exclamatory forms of the experience of *being-here (Da-sein)*, which throw the "matter-of-fact" into question and unleash the "thousand natural shocks which flesh is heir to." "Here I am" can express not only the most mundane and mildest of disclosures but also the event of a major epiphany whose full implications may inspire an entire lifetime. With "Dasein" now firmly established as a technical term left untranslated in the English literature on Heidegger, it is all the easier to forget that the term expresses the mind-boggling simplicity of the human situation, articulating itself in a gamut of revelations ranging from the most routine and commonplace to the extraordinary and uncommon shock of self-recognition in which one is taken aback by all that it means *to be here.*

The experience of "Da-sein" comprehends not only varying experiential intensities and degrees of disclosure but also, in strict correspondence with these variations, a variant emphasis upon the network of relationships which it draws into a unity. If at first, for the sake of maximum concreteness, attention is called to the "I am" in its variant relations to the "here," this by no means excludes extension of the term "Dasein" to experiences in which perhaps "you are," "we are" or "it is" come to the fore. But Heidegger is not so much concerned with the variations on the theme of Dasein as he is with the unity which manifests itself in and through these variations. In grammatical terms, it is the unity of being which expresses itself in and through its various temporal tenses, with the one proviso that, in each case, these tenses are to bear reference to their context, to the "here" in which they take place. In short, the verb *sein* is to be declined in its *Da* to the point where *Sein* and *Dasein* come to be considered as the same. The "qualifying" adverb "here" is to become a *sine qua non* of the verb "to be." Being cannot be abstracted from its context, it is always subject to modulation by the manners and mores of the situation. This simply expresses one of the consequences for the grammar of a thought oriented to "this side," which cannot merely be a formal-logical grammar abstracted from its context. Being human means being situated; accordingly, man's being is mediated by his situation. "Here" thus becomes the bridge and passage between man and being.

If, as in *Being and Time,* the experience of "Here I am" is taken as rudimentary, it serves to underscore the indivisible coherence of these three terms. Ultimately, at this rudimentary level, one cannot speak of the self apart from the field in which it is situated and the temporal process of being in which it is implicated. Transposed into a philosophical context, each one of these simple words — among the most bandied in our language — warrants a lifetime of meditation. In explicit opposition to Descartes, Heidegger insists that they be thought together, each in relation to the others. The term "Dasein" applies equally ("equiprimordially" Heidegger would say) to the human situation (world), the self, and its being, so that a consideration of each at once implies the other two.

It is within this concrete contexture of relations that Heidegger seeks to rekindle the question of being and develop it in new and fruitful ways. The somewhat artificial term "Dasein" (which in ordinary German means "existence") is used in a technical way for the express purpose of renewing the question through such a relocation—bringing it back down to earth, as it were—and only this. It is first introduced (SZ, 7, 12) to name the ontological structure of ontic man, the being whose being is a vital issue and can therefore become a burning question, in lieu of more anthropological equivalents in vogue at the time (SZ, 46-7), such as "life" (Dilthey), "existence" (Kierkegaard) and "person" (Scheler). The term proclaims, on the one hand, that the question of what it means to be is to be approached through the human being, or better, through the human situation, through the place in which the question first arises and in the ways in which it arises, as a very human kind of question. On the other hand, in its explicit reference to a place rather than an entity and to the verbal rather than the substantive sense of being, it hints at a movement which goes beyond man toward the being in which he is implicated. For Dasein is more than man; it refers at once to the experiential process of disclosure and the field of relations in which man is implicated; it is both the occurrence of revelation and its frame of reference. In other words, the turn from man to being, the movement characteristic of the later Heidegger, is already operative in the very first steps of *Being and Time*, in the very projection of the term "Dasein." In the end, the term is stripped of all ontic vestiges and becomes simply the overture and clearing of being itself and, as such, the dimension that enables man to be man (which is what Heidegger means by the "essence" of man). As a result of this development, the "I" in the "Here I am" recedes into the background in order that the situation of being, "being here" pure and simple, may be made to stand forth. In the end, Dasein is no longer identified as the entity who understands being but as being itself. "Here I am" implies the proximity of being in human experience, the "here of being," and Heidegger insists that it is only for the sake of the latter, more ontological considerations that he investigates the former, more existential concerns. At the same time, he observes that the existential and the ontological are inextricably intertwined, so that various strategies of emphasis may serve to bring forth the ever-present background experience of being which is so much a part of our experience that we tend to overlook it and take it for granted. "Being here" should thus be taken literally to refer to the nearness of being itself. In his later sorties into this neighborhood, the sense of being stands so boldly in the forefront that Heidegger himself is forced at times to remind the reader of the "to-and-fro relatedness" (SZ, 7) still in effect between the existential and ontological. "But—as soon as I thoughtfully say man's essence, I have already said relatedness to being. Likewise, as soon as I say thoughtfully: being of beings, the relatedness of man's essence has been named."[5]

It is within the compass of this most central of relations, the relationship of being-here, that all phases of Heidegger's thought find their place.

SITUATING THE QUESTION

Beginnings are always difficult and full of risk. Initial decisions are made, the outcome of which cannot be known until their full implications have been drawn. A small error in the beginning can, through amplification, become a great error in the end. Clarification in the course of development will undoubtedly prompt corrections in the course, but, short of total abandonment of a line of investigation, the starting point would still exercise its influence on the direction of elaboration.

In the face of a tradition which had come to consider the issue of being as fruitless, remote, and unnecessary and had deigned to let the question lapse quietly into oblivion, Heidegger seeks to salvage the question from its millennial embarrassment and to launch it upon another beginning. In view of the obscurity and confusion in which the issue now finds itself, to the point where even the terms of the *question* of what it *means to be* had become unclear, Heidegger first proposes to "work out" the question itself. In fact, *Being and Time* concludes with the issue of a "secure horizon for the question and answer" (*SZ*, 437) still very much in suspense. The problem of situating the very question will in effect dominate Heidegger's thought far beyond *Being and Time*, which is concerned primarily with situating the question in relation to the question of personal existence. Later, concern will shift to situating the question in relation to other questions, not only personal but also scientific and philosophical. In regard to the latter, the question is to be situated in relation to the tradition to the point where the reasons for its demise and its neglect by that tradition are to be exposed. Moreover, the basis and possibility for starting anew may well be found in the very same tradition, in the form of long-forgotten resources still operative in it.

So central is the question which Heidegger seeks to work out that it lies at the very source of the questions of science and philosophy as well as the basic personal decisions of existence. As the "flaming center of all questioning,"[6] it is the question of all questions, i.e., the question of the very possibility of questioning. Accordingly, even without the historical neglect and confusion into which the question had fallen, to ask this question would still call for turning the interrogative mood back upon itself and inquiring into the conditions of emergence and the dynamics of its own questioning as well as of all other questions.

Small wonder then that so much of Heidegger's thought takes place under the sway of the question mark. The titles of his books and lectures alone serve to signal this: *What is Metaphysics?*, *What is a Thing?*, *The Question of Being*, *What is Philosophy?*, *What does Thinking Mean?* Likewise, the themes which he selects for detailed investigation hark back to fundamentally interrogative experiences: anxiety, concern, guilt, death, finitude, Nothing. The essence of man is found to reside in the passion for questioning; man's dwelling place is in the aporia of existence. The locus of truth is shifted from the assertion to the question. And the movement of questioning becomes one with the movement of time at the heart of being. So central is questioning that even the terms of the *question* of the *meaning* of *being* upon examination soon begin to dovetail and converge to the point of becoming identified with each other.

But let us begin at the beginning. In the opening pages of *Being and Time*, Heidegger finds that the situation of the question had become so obscure and remote from the real concerns of our age that even the terms of the question were wholly unclear. Accordingly, the question itself must once again be "worked out;" it must once again be adequately posed or positioned (*SZ*, 4,5). It must be taken back to its natural habitat where it is a genuine and vital question, and not just an idle question conjured by pedants absorbed in pointless academic pursuits. Working out the question of the meaning of being therefore calls for the exposition of the concrete context shaping its interrogative moment and impelling and sustaining the process of inquiry. If a radically new start is to be made, then one must get at the very roots of the question by returning to the point of incipience where it first arises and takes hold of us. Accordingly, the questioner himself is to be questioned in terms of how he is in fact questioned in *his* being. How otherwise to raise the question concretely and to "breathe life into the questioning"[7] than to show how the question is indigenous to life itself and so to place philosophical questioning in continuity with the most basic of human questions? To bring the question home means to bring it back to its question-provoking source in existence and to trace the seminal interrogative relation latent to it.

The task of *Being and Time*, accordingly, is to probe more deeply into the interrogative relationship that man has with his being in order to bring this relationship to fuller conceptualization. In a move which is decisive for the concept formation of all of Heidegger's thought, the opening pages of *Being and Time* unravel the interrogative relationship into two interrelated axes of the comprehensive relation of Dasein. If man questions what it means to be, then 1) he must already have some understanding of what it means to be and 2) he must have a tendency or capacity to question what it means to be. These two dimensions of the interrogative relation to being are designated by the terms *understanding* and *existence*. The terms hark back to their respective precedents in hermeneutic and existential philosophy but, in being brought together in the task of situating the question of being, they undergo a profound ontological transformation. To overlook this is to misunderstand completely the way in which Heidegger employs these terms. Both bear etymological reference to a specific situational stance which makes the more complex interrogative stance possible: One stands *under* the sway of a certain interpretation of what it means to be and, on this basis, stands *forward* in going about his being. Understanding and existence thus establish, respectively, the context and the direction of the question, provide it with its contextual and vectorial determinants, its *stasis* and its *dynamis*. The unity in tension of the two relations is reflected in the very term Dasein, where "da" in German means both "here" and "there," and suggests at once the proximity and the distance of a sense of being which, on the one hand, initiates the question and, on the other, provides it with its goal.

The understanding relationship: Man understands being. The formula "understanding of being" might easily be misconstrued to mean that we already have a grasp of the concept of being. But it is intended to suggest a more matter-of-fact understanding of what it means to be that comes from living a life rather than knowing about it. We go about our being before we know about it. We in fact do not know what "being" means conceptually but are familiar with its sense preconceptually in and through the activities of living. We conduct all of our activities within the compass of a comprehension of being, by which we are already seized and governed without being particularly aware of it. If the term "knowledge" still applies to the understanding of life, it is more the immediate "know-how" or "savvy" of existence, a knack or feel for what it means to be and what we can do that comes from experience. From a long familiarity with the world, we already know how to "get along" with people and "deal" with the things of the world in "going about our business." In short, we already know our way "about" the world and its manners and customs, we already know how to live, and this skill in the ways of being is a "knowledge" *in actu exercito* which expresses itself through our attitudes and styles of action.

But all this is understood "as a matter of course," without reflection, where the appearance of obviousness harbors the basic paradox of understanding, namely, the elusiveness of our most familiar experiences and the difficulty of the simplest things of life. Augustine's classic lines on time are exemplary here: "What then is time? If no one asks me, I know. If I wish to explain it to one that asketh, I know not." It is above all to such basic experiences, so difficult in their simplicity, that we might apply Michael Polanyi's maxim, "We know more than we can tell."

But if familiarity shelters the mysteries of the world, self, time, truth and being, it also blocks access to them by generating a conspiracy of silence about them. For one thing, what is most familiar to us can in its unobtrusiveness be what is most likely to be overlooked. It is so near, and yet so far. For another, the very variety of life militates against its simplicity. Life is so daily, and in our concern for the particularities of daily existence, the more comprehensive sense that we have of what it means to be can easily lapse into oblivion. One might even say that there is a natural attitude which obliterates the difference between particular beings and their being.

Heidegger goes so far as to impute the entire philosophical tradition of succumbing to this natural tendency, insofar as it has established the thing or substance as the paradigm for being. In fact, Heidegger already found himself in a sustained tradition which for at least a century had criticized the reifying tendencies of the human mind as the major obstacle and primary source of distortion to a more comprehensive idea of being. The researches of Dilthey, Yorck, Bergson, Husserl and Scheler directly shape the counter-chosistic idea of being which guides all of *Being and Time*, in providing the distinction between the historical and the ontic, between the "existence" of Dasein and the "reality" of things. Here is one of the major historical sources which prompted the necessity of repeating the question of being as signaled in the opening lines of *Being and Time*.

Despite the impediments raised by the vague and average understanding we have of being, it is also a source and possibility of a fresh new understanding of what it means to be. Its very latency invites and even demands exposition. Its familiarity with being, if not knowledge, is at least a precedent to knowledge and hence a potential source of knowledge. Our understanding of being thus orients the direction of interrogation of being, indicates something of how the question is to be answered, and provides resources from which to draw in answering it.

The basic problem is to find the proper concepts to articulate the content of this familiarity precedent to knowledge. "For we understand being but lack the concept. This preconceptual understanding of being is, for all its constancy and scope, by and large completely indeterminate. The specific kind of being of, for example, material things, plants, animals, men and numbers is familiar to us, but what is familiar is as such not known."[8] Ontology accordingly cannot situate itself in any known conceptualization of being, but must place itself at the limit of such conceptualization, precisely at the boundary between the conceptual and the non-conceptual, and look to the preconceptual for fresh new concepts. Can we assume that our understanding of being is entirely tractable to conceptualization? At least the effort must be made. What can be said at this point is that answering the question of being develops into the conceptual labor of making our preconceptual understanding of being explicit. It is a matter of letting experience come to a natural conceptual blossoming in "home-grown" concepts, as it were, without resorting to concepts originating in alien soil.

But how do we come to make this effort? Latency alone is insufficient motivation for the question of being. The preconceptual understanding of being *per se* is so obvious and self-evident that it raises no question, calls no attention to itself and so is "assumed" without question. Our understanding of being is an intimate experience, so intimate that the cognitive correlation of subject and object appears to be inadequate to express it. So ensconced are we in this situation, in any immediacy which is more of being than of knowledge, that Heidegger considers this understanding which is one with life itself not as a property of man but a seizure of being itself, a state of being possessed by it, a comprehension *of* being, as it were. As things stand here, we stand in too close even to have occasion to question it, unless perchance we have occasion to depart from our ensconcement and to stand up to our being.

The existential relation: Man "ex-sists" his being, i.e., he stands out toward it. To articulate this more tensed axis of experience, Heidegger introduces the "formal idea" of *existence*. Man does not simply understand being; it is also an issue for him. To be for man is at once a having to be. The apparently somnolent state of standing in a familiar network of relations articulated by the habit of life is traversed by the tendency to stand out and forward from this initial state. If understanding at first is meant to suggest a proximity of being to man, existence is intended to open up distances within its context, especially the kind of distance which permits questions. It suggests a transcending movement within the context toward its horizons, disclosing a leeway of operating room therein. The latent proximity of being is also a clearing, the later Heidegger will say, a temporal playing field of possibility.

The idea of existence accordingly serves to specify and delimit the phenomenon of understanding being by evoking the range and scope of possibilities latent within it. As a guiding idea, existence directs the task of articulating the categories which conceptualize the ontological structures of being human, which Heidegger accordingly names the *existentialia*: the disowned ("inauthentic") possibilities of everyday commonplaces and the owned possibilities of the unique person, the limits to these possibilities and the ways of being these possibilities. In contrast to the traditional metaphysical categories, the existentials highlight the "how" of the execution of life rather than the "what" of its contents. They aim to conceptualize the human being in the performance of his being as it is lived forward rather than after the fact.

Considerations of existence thus transpose the discussion from the contextual statics to the temporal dynamics of being. Existence, which brings out the dimension of possibility latent in understanding, is the first conceptual step toward deepening our sense of understanding being in the direction of time; it is the bridge between being "and" time. The sense of existence, which, far more than understanding, overtly parades across the pages of *Being and Time*, is repeatedly proclaimed as the bold provisional assumption guiding the entire endeavor and examined again and again for its potential for yielding an "idea of being" which is temporal and free from reifying tendencies. For "existence," like "life," is a concept which is intended to counter any and every sense of rigid substantive being.

Like understanding, existence is assumed to be the very being of human be-ing. If understanding at first suggests the initial state in which man finds himself, existence stresses the projected activity of being. Just as understand-ing is more an understanding that man is rather than has, so likewise, in ex-istence, man *is* his possibility. Accordingly, as a way of existence rather than a mode of knowing, our understanding of what it means to be is never a mere staring at a fixed meaning but the living out of a possibility. In other words, meaning is first "performed" before it is conceptually formed. The question of being is first articulated in an inchoate concern for being before it is the ex-pression of an explicit desire to know. The motivating interrogative mood of anxiety itself manifests the travail and tensile character of human temporality and thus yields some sense of the interplay of nearness and distance operative in the self-explication of time.

Existence emphasizes the future and freedom of understanding. As with other crafts, the "know-how" of understanding life is basically a "can-do," or better, the "can be" for the sake of which man exists. Thrown forward into what he is not but can be, the human being is challenged to work out the im-plications of his existence, unlocking its deeper structures and coming to terms with it in its entirety. Explication here is more than just the passage from obscure to explicit knowledge. It assumes the character of a personal drama charged with historical destiny. Being takes on an urgent and pressing sense as it is intensified and deepened in the effort to be, of which one of the highest manifestations is the effort of questioning.

Against the background of understanding, Heidegger's "existentialism" assumes a hermeneutic flavor, insofar as the questioning and free decisions of existence are explications of facticitous possibilities which, in turn, are themselves "cleared" by the more basic self-explication of time. Moreover, such a hermeneutics of existence is explicitly employed for ontological ends, and this assumes, at this stage in Heidegger's development, a transcendental flavor, which however does not refer to the subjective consciousness, but rather is to be defined in terms of the temporal structures of existence. Never-theless, like any transcendental philosophy, it is aloof to any ambition to being a concrete philosophy of life; it is interested in questions of fact only insofar as they elucidate questions of essence. The essence of man is not actually man himself, but the conditions which enable man to be man. What such an on-tology seeks are the comprehensive existential structures which make the par-ticularities of human existence possible. The existenti*ell* themes of dread, guilt, conscience, resolve and death are investigated only to the extent that they articulate the existenti*al* structures of human existence, which in turn are of interest only to the extent that they articulate the basic temporal conditions surrounding the emergence and development of the question of being. The objection that not everyone, brain-damaged children, for example, will in reality face the decision between authenticity and inauthenticity as it is outlined in *Being and Time* is accordingly no argument against this structure as an essential possibility of human existence. In a transcendental framework, facts must be preceded by the conditions which make them possible. Being is essentially possibility rather than reality. But what sort of possibility is this, Heidegger now asks, if it is silhouetted against the very horizon of time and not beyond time, as in all previous transcendental philosophies? This perhaps is the most basic question which ensues from the quest for an idea of being in the existence which understands.

Notes

Theodore Kisiel is Professor of Philosophy at Northern Illinois University, De Kalb, Illinois, co-author of *Phenomenology and the Natural Sciences* (Northwestern U.P., 1970) and translator of Werner Marx's *Heidegger and the Tradition* (Northwestern U.P., 1971). This essay is an excerpt from a book in progress on Heidegger.

1. References in parentheses refer to the pagination of *Sein und Zeit*, Tuebingen, 1967.
2. "A Letter from Heidegger" (dated October 20, 1966), Manfred S. Frings (ed.), *Heidegger and the Quest for Truth* (Chicago: Quadrangle Books, 1968) p. 17.
3. "A Letter from Martin Heidegger" (dated September 20, 1966), John Sallis (ed.) *Heidegger and the Path of Thinking* (Pittsburgh: Duquesne U.P., 1970) pp. 9-11.
4. *An Introduction to Metaphysics*, pp. 33, 29.
5. Martin Heidegger, *What is Called Thinking?*, Translated by Fred D. Wieck and J. Glenn Gray (New York, Evanston, and London: Harper & Row, 1968) p. 79.
6. *An Introduction to Metaphysics*, p. 35.
7. *Ibid.*, p. 17.
8. Cf. Martin Heidegger, *Kant and the Problem of Metaphysics,* translated by James S. Churchill (Bloomington: Indiana U.P., 1962) p. 205. *My own translation here.*

Into the Clearing

John Sallis

Today we are perhaps beginning, belatedly, to understand what an immanent critique of *Being and Time*[1] might require—belatedly, for Heidegger himself, having undertaken again and again since 1930 "to subject the *Ansatz* of the question in *Being and Time* to an immanent critique," finally indicated in the mid-1960's that through this undertaking "the name of the task of *Being and Time* gets changed." Changed into what? Heidegger answers the question with a question, these two questions serving to enframe "The End of Philosophy and the Task of Thinking": "Does the title for the task of thinking then read instead of 'Being and Time': clearing and presence [*Lichtung und Anwesenheit*]?"[2] But here it is a matter not simply of a change *from* the text *Being and Time*, but rather of an immanent, i.e. radicalizing critique set upon bringing into the open something already in play, inconspicuously, perhaps even concealedly, in *Being and Time* itself. Let us focus on a moment of the text in which such first stirrings are unobtrusively inscribed.

I.

A circling within the text is completed at that juncture where the analysis of Dasein comes to be directed specifically to "Being-in" (Div. I, Ch. 5). For, the "preliminary sketch" (*Vorzeichnung*) of the constitution of Dasein as Being-in-the-world was drawn by way of a preliminary, orientational characterization of this moment (SZ, 12); and following the preliminary sketch, a rigorous (though of course only "preparatory") analysis was provided for the other two moments, world and self, leading finally back to Being-in as a theme for rigorous analysis. It is at the point of return to "Being-in" that the word "clearing" comes decisively into play (SZ, §28).

For what purpose? As an interpretive name for Being-in itself, as interpretively synonymous with the names "there" ("*Da*") and "disclosedness" ("*Erschlossenheit*"). That Being-in is a constituent of the Being of Dasein means: Dasein is always its "there," Dasein is its disclosedness, Dasein is a clearing. Later another synonym will be added: Dasein is its truth. The first connection, however, is more immediate: a clearing (the paradigm: a clearing in a forest) is a place that can be lighted up whenever the sun's rays, the light, shine down through the opening above — or, more pointedly, a clearing must always be there already in order that the light break through so as to light up whatever stands there in the clearing. In *Being and Time* the difference between light (*Licht*) and clearing (*Lichtung*), manifestly in play metaphorically, is still precarious because of the attachment of the issue of clearing to "the ontically figurative [*bildlich*] talk about the *lumen naturale* in man" (SZ, 133). Explicitly, to say that Dasein "is 'illuminated' ['*erleuchtet*'] is to say: cleared [*gelichtet*] in itself *as* Being-in-the-world, not through another being, but rather in such a way that it *is* itself the clearing."[3] The text is unequivocal here: rather than confounding light (illumination) and clearing, it is a matter of recovering for the issue of clearing what is really at issue in that ontically figurative (and traditional) way of talking about the *lumen naturale*, of detaching the issue from the metaphor of light, placing it on the other side. And so, immediately following, the difference is openly traced: "Only for a being that is existentially cleared in this way does what is on hand [*Vorhandenes*] become accessible in the light, hidden in the dark" (SZ, 133).

With the return to the analysis of Being-in, it is, then, a matter of exhibiting those moments, those "existentials," by which Dasein is itself the clearing — that is, of analyzing the existential constitution of the "there," of the clearing. This return, it turns out, completes another circle, one at a deeper stratum of the text — or rather, at this deeper stratum, several circles. For in the analysis of the existential constitution of the clearing, it turns out that a major constituent is understanding and that understanding is fulfilled in interpretation; it suffices then to recall that at the outset (SZ, §7) interpretation was already identified as the specific procedure of the analysis to come: the analysis (interpretation) has become an analysis (interpretation) of interpretation, and in this interpretation of interpretation it circles in a new way, back upon itself, reflexively. Even though the analysis is limited to inauthentic interpretation — this limitation being prescribed by the horizon of the entire preparatory analysis, everydayness — the reflexivity reaches far enough to allow that "preliminary sketch" of Being-in-the-world to be recognized as a moment of that specific fore-structure which belongs to the existential interpretation; and thus the previous, merely procedural circle is attached to the circle reflected from the matter itself.

The reflexivity intrinsic to the interpretation of interpretation is not, however, the only kind that breaks out in the return to "Being-in." Another is exhibited in the analysis (SZ, §29) of disposition (*Befindlichkeit*). The relevant characteristic of disposition is that according to which it discloses Dasein in its thrownness—that is, in the "facticity of its being delivered over" (SZ, 135). To what is Dasein delivered over? It is delivered over to the Being which, in existing, it has to be" (SZ, 134); it is 'delivered over to the 'there'" (SZ, 135). Dasein's thrownness is a thrownness into the "there," into the clearing which it has to be, into disclosedness. Accordingly, disposition is such that in it "Dasein is brought before its Being as 'there'" (SZ, 134)—that is, Dasein's thrownness into disclosedness is disclosed—that is, disposition is that mode of disclosedness in which is disclosed Dasein's character as disclosedness. This reflexivity within disposition, that it is disclosive of disclosedness, is the source of that primordial disclosive power which, intensified in anxiety, will later be exploited for the sake of a more primordial access to the Being of Dasein. How can the existential analysis exploit the reflexivity of disposition? How can it avail itself of the disclosive power of moods without thereby abandoning itself to them and disclaiming itself as a theoretical affair? There is only one way: taking its "distance" from the dispositional disclosure, it must with appropriate reticence attend to that disclosure, accompanying it "only in order existentially to raise to a conceptual level the phenomenal content of what has been disclosed" (SZ, 140).

The reflexivity of disposition points beyond the preparatory analysis (Division I) to the development of a more primordial access to Dasein (Division II); a third reflexivity points to Division III, to its question, the question of the entire work, the question of the meaning of Being. For the analysis of interpretation leads to a determination of the concept of meaning, and the text explicitly reflects this determination back upon the question of the meaning of Being. Granted the determination of meaning as that from which something becomes understandable, the question of the meaning of Being is correspondingly determined as a question about that from which Being becomes understandable to Dasein.

Thus, in the return of the analysis to "Being-in," a threefold reflexivity breaks out—reflexivity of such extent as to reach out to the entirety of *Being and Time*. It is little wonder that this return is announced by that word which, when the name of *Being and Time* eventually gets changed, displaces "Being": "clearing."

II.

We narrow our range, focusing now on one constituent of the clearing: understanding (*Verstehen*). A retracing of the existential analysis of understanding (SZ, §31) will provide an opening onto those first stirrings in behalf of "clearing"and "presence."

As Dasein is no subject, so understanding is no immanent representational activity of a subject. Rather, understanding is to be taken up existentially, i.e., in connection with Dasein's comportment to its Being, a comportment which, distinct from blind relatedness between mere things, is fundamentally a matter of disclosure. The analysis begins by indicating the major terms in the relevant disclosive structure:

> In the for-the-sake-of-which [*Worumwillen*], existing Being-in-the-world is disclosed as such, and this disclosedness we have called understanding. [Reference is made to §18.] In the understanding of the for-the-sake-of-which, the significance which is grounded therein is disclosed along with it (SZ, 143).

This says: The structure of understanding, as a kind of disclosedness, is such that in and through something, something else gets disclosed. Two items get disclosed: existing Being-in-the-world and significance. In and through what? The "for-the-sake-of-which" — identified in the analysis of worldhood (SZ §18) as a potentiality-for-Being (*Seinkönnen*), a possible way to be, a possibility in that sense which, not yet positively delimited, is to be distinguished from mere logical possibility, from the contingency of things on-hand, and from "free-floating" possibility in the sense of the "liberty of indifference." "Significance," determined in that same earlier analysis, is identical with the worldhood of the world, i.e., the referential totality by which a concrete world is structured. "Existing Being-in-the-world": This says simply "Dasein," with emphasis on its comportment to possibilities.

So, on the one side, the for-the-sake-of-which discloses existing Being-in-the-world — that is, those possibilities to which Dasein comports itself serve to disclose Dasein. But how is it that Dasein can be disclosed by possibilities?

> Dasein is not something on-hand which possesses its potentiality for something by way of an extra; it is primarily Being-possible. Dasein is in every instance that which it can be, and in the way in which it is its possibility (SZ, 143).

Dasein is not something at hand which then, as a supplement, has a comportment to possibility; rather, its comportment to possibility determines what it is and how it is in any given instance. Even further: "Possibility as an existential is the most primordial and ultimate positive ontological determination of Dasein" (SZ, 143f.). Dasein is disclosed in and through its possibilities, *from* those possibilities, because it is determined by its comportment to those possibilites, because "it is in every case what it can be" (SZ, 143).

On the other side of the disclosive structure, the for-the-sake-of-which discloses significance — that is, a possibility prescribes what must be done to actualize it (an "in-order-to"), this, in turn, requiring that something be done (a "towards-this"), etc.; and in each case what is to be done prescribes that with which it can be done. The possibility of providing oneself with adequate shelter prescribes securing the shingles against wind and rain; this, in turn, prescribes nailing them down properly; and this one does with a hammer. Within a given context a possibility delineates with a certain degree of determinacy a referential totality; it structures a world.

The analysis becomes more precise through the thematizing of understanding as projection (*Entwurf*). What does Dasein project in understanding? Does it project possibilities? Not primarily. What does it project primarily? It projects itself upon possibilities.

> Dasein has, as Dasein, always already projected itself; and as long as it is, it is projecting. As long as it is, Dasein always has understood itself and always will understand itself from possibilities (SZ, 145).

The primary sense of projection is Dasein's self-projection, its projection of itself upon possibilities. *From* those possibilities Dasein is, in turn, given back to itself, disclosed to itself. Dasein does not disclose the possibilities (by projecting upon them) so much as the possibilties, being projected upon, disclose Dasein. Yet there is a sense in which Dasein may be said to project possibilities:

> Furthermore, the character of understanding as projection is such that understanding does not grasp thematically that upon which it projects — that is, possibilities. Grasping in such a manner would take away from what is projected its very character as a possibility and would reduce it to the given contents which we have in mind [*zieht es herab zu einem gegebenen, gemeinten Bestand*]; whereas projection, in throwing, throws before itself the possibility as possibility, and lets it *be* as such. As projecting, understanding is the kind of Being of Dasein in which it *is* its possibilities as possibilities (SZ 145).

This says: in projecting (in the primary sense: projecting itself), Dasein projects possibilities *as* possibilities. It does not create or invent them but lets them be as possibilities.

Another side has now to be added. For Dasein's self-projection is not a projection *only* upon possibilities:

> With equal primordiality it projects Dasein's Being both upon its for-the-sake-of-which and upon significance as the worldhood of its current world (SZ, 145).

Dasein's projection is two-sided, a projection upon possibilities and upon significance (worldhood). Because this two-sidedness belongs to it, "projection always pertains to the full disclosedness of Being-in-the-world" (SZ, 146). But how can one and the same projection have these two sides? Where is the unity? It lies in the connection between those two items on which Dasein projects: a possibility opens up significance, i.e. prescribes, delineates a referential totality; and significance opens onto possibility, for, in engaging oneself in a world, one tacitly submits himself to a certain range of possibilities connected with the structure of that world. The unity of possibility and significance gives unity to the projection: one and the same projection is a projection upon both.

In turn, there is a certain analogous doubling of that self-disclosure that is correlative to Dasein's self-projection. Dasein is to some degree disclosed to itself, not only from possibilities, but also from significance. And thus, globally considered, projective understanding can assume two forms:

> Understanding *can* devote itself primarily to the disclosedness of the world; that is, Dasein can, proximally and for the most part, understand itself from its world. Or else understanding throws itself primarily into the for-the-sake-of-which; that is, Dasein exists as itself. Understanding is either authentic, arising out of one's own self as such, or inauthentic (SZ, 146).

These two forms, authentic and inauthentic understanding, derive from the fact that one or the other side can be dominant.

A final moment of the disclosive structure constitutive of understanding is added in §32. It involves extending to beings other than Dasein a disclosive connection analogous to that of Dasein: They too get projected upon possibilities and significance, though of course they do not project themselves:

> In the projecting of understanding, beings are disclosed in their possibility. . . .Beings within-the-world generally are projected upon the world—that is, upon a whole of significance. . . (SZ, 151).

As Dasein is projected upon possibilities and significance and thus disclosed, so beings other than Dasein get projected, generally upon significance, and disclosed therefrom. When such beings have been thus disclosed, they may then be said to have meaning.

What is meaning? Its determination is grounded on the analysis of understanding:

> Meaning [*Sinn*] is that wherein the understandableness [*Verständlichkeit*] of something maintains itself. . . .*Meaning is the upon-which* [Woraufhin] *of a projection from which something becomes understandable as something*. . .(SZ, 151).

Meaning is that upon which something is projected and from which it becomes understandable: possibility or significance, as the case may be—in any case, an item entwined in that total disclosive structure that constitutes understanding. But understanding is one of the major constituents of the "there," of the clearing, and its structure is accordingly entwined in that total structure by which the clearing itself is delimited. Meaning has been brought into the clearing. And, setting the relevant reflexivity into play, the question of the meaning of Being is likewise brought into the clearing. The analysis of understanding, by grounding the determination of "meaning," inscribes the question of the meaning of Being within the sphere of the clearing, gathers the issue of Being and time into the *alētheiē eukuklēs* (cf. Parmenides, Fr. 1).

III.

But how does the analysis of understanding bring also into play the issue of presence? Within the text there is only one indication, an indirect one: a reference appended to the analysis, almost as though it were a passing remark, a reference to traditional ontology. The reference follows a more extended passage devoted to Dasein's "sight" (*Sicht*). Understanding is identified as what makes up Dasein's sight, and the passage serves to extend the analysis of understanding, just completed, back to the earlier analyses of Dasein's various modes of sight: circumspection (*Umsicht*), that sight with which Dasein in its concernful dealings with equipment holds the equipmental totality in view; and considerateness (*Rücksicht*) and forbearance (*Nachsicht*), those modes of sight which serve analogously in Dasein's solicitous dealings with others. To this appropriation of the issue of sight to that of understanding is then added the reference to traditional ontology:

> By showing how all sight is grounded primarily in understanding..., we have deprived pure intuition [*puren Anschauen*] of its priority, which corresponds noetically to the priority accorded beings-on-hand [*Vorhandene*] in traditional ontology (SZ, 147).

The reference is far-reaching and decisive.

Intuition is deprived of its priority. What priority? A text of lectures contemporaneous with the redaction of *Being and Time* is explicit: Intuition is accorded priority in the sense that knowledge is taken to be primarily intuition. By whom is it accorded such priority? The lecture text answers: by the entire tradition. And that same text exhibits the ways in which that priority was granted by Hegel, Kant, Leibniz, Descartes, Aquinas.[4] Throughout the tradition, knowledge is taken as primarily intuition—that is, intuition is the paradigm in such fashion that all knowledge, to the extent that it is not simply intuition, is charged with compensating for what it lacks in intuition. Knowledge is ideally the sheer beholding of what is present, of what is merely there on hand present to one's gaze. Thus it is that the priority of intuition is correlative to the priority of beings-on-hand, a priority equally accorded by the tradition, a priority called into question almost from the outset of *Being and Time*.

The analysis of understanding culminates in a destruction of the priority heretofore accorded sheer intuitive presence to what is openly present to one's gaze. It constitutes thus a radical break with the tradition. But the text of *Being and Time* signals another break too: "Even the phenomenological 'intuition of essences' [*Wesensschau*] is grounded in existential understanding" (SZ, 147). The lecture text marks the break unmistakably, citing Husserl's "principle of all principles" (from *Ideas* §24): "that whatever presents itself originarily to us in intuition (in its bodily actuality, as it were) is simply to be accepted as that as which it gives itself but only within the limits in which it there gives itself." The principle enjoins one to attend to things as they show themselves *in intuition*. And thus it attests to Husserl's solidarity with the tradition: Taking over the traditional priority of intuition, Husserl elevates it to the rank of an explicit methodological principle.

How is intuition to be deprived of its priority? By showing that all sight is grounded in understanding. How does the grounding of sight in understanding serve to deprive intuition of its priority? Because intuition is itself a kind of sight which, if grounded in understanding, relinquishes its priority to the latter. Actually, this priority is already relinquished in the earlier analyses of sight to which that of understanding gets referred back, most notably in that of circumspection (*Umsicht*): Since an item of equipment can show itself (as what it is in itself) only from out of an equipmental totality, that "sight" to which it is "given" is grounded in the sight by which the totality is held in sight—that is, Dasein's concernful dealing with an item is grounded in a prior, holistic sighting (cf. SZ §15).

Correlatively, that same earlier analysis also deprives being-on-hand (*Vorhandensein*) of its traditional priority by exhibiting its subordination to being-at-hand (*Zuhandensein*)—a subordination that gets confirmed in the development initiated by the analysis of understanding (cf. SZ §33). This subordination bears decisively on the issue of presence. How? By displacing presence—that is, by replacing the sheerly present thing with a thing for which absence is constitutive. Under ordinary circumstances an item of equipment is not sheerly present in a self-contained positivity. On the contrary, it is extended beyond itself into the referential totality by which it is essentially determined; it is "elsewhere," beyond itself, not sheer self-contained presence. Furthermore, such an item is of such a character that when it shows itself most primordially as what it is (e.g., a hammer in hammering), it is never grasped thematically (i.e., as sheerly present) but rather remains withdrawn, holds itself back in a certain inconspicuousness in favor of the work for which it is in use. An item of equipment is "in itself" by withdrawing into itself, by being absent (cf. SZ §15). Drawn back into itself, drawn forth beyond itself—both modes of absence serve to determine the characteristic presence of equipment, a presence which, thus determined by absence, is distinct from the sheer presence which, as the correlate of intuition, is accorded priority by metaphysics and phenomenology.

The grounding of sight in understanding completes what the earlier analyses initiated. It refers intuition, displaced into concern, grounded already in circumspection, back to understanding itself. In understanding, Dasein projects itself upon possibilities. It *is* its possibilities—that is, it too is extended, extends itself, beyond itself so as to escape all self-contained positivity. And by its manner of projecting upon them, Dasein lets its possibilities be *as* possibilities, granting them that reserve of absence which prevents their crystallizing into the sheer presence of a given content. Possibilities disclose significance; and Dasein, projecting upon possibilities, projects also upon significance in such a way as to let it be as such, to let a referential totality take hold, to let a world take shape. But this shape is still more withdrawn than those items of equipment that come to presence within it. Something exceptional, some disruption, is required for it to become even minimally thematic (cf. SZ §16); its peculiar presence is even less the sheer presence correlative to intuition, is even more a presence essentially determined by absence. It is little wonder that traditonal ontology, according priority to the sheer presence of intuition, completely passes over the phenomenon of world.

The grounding of sight in understanding gathers the entire analysis of Being-in-the-world into the issue of clearing. More decisively, it gathers into that issue the destruction of sheer presence accomplished by that analysis, the collapse of sheer presence into the play of presence and absence. In the gathering of this play into the clearing we hear the first stirrings within the *Sache* of *Being and Time.*

Notes

John Sallis is Chairman and Professor in the Department of Philosophy at Duquesne University. He is editor of the journal *Research in Phenomenology*, and has published several books including *Being and Logos* and *Phenomenology and the Return to Beginnings*.

1. *Sein und Zeit* (Tübingen: Max Niemeyer Verlag, 1960⁹). Hereafter, "SZ."
2. *Zur Sache des Denkens* (Tübingen: Max Niemeyer Verlag, 1969), pp. 61, 80.
3. The *Hüttenexemplar* of SZ contains two notes pertaining to this passage. The first, keyed to "gelichtet" reads: "*Aletheia*—Offenheit—Lichtung, Licht, Leuchten." The other, keyed to the final "ist" reads: "aber nicht produziert." Heidegger, *Gesamtausgabe* (Frankfurt a.M.: Vittorio Klostermann), Band 2, p. 177.
4. *Logik: Die Frage nach der Wahrheit* (Frankfurt: Klostermann, 1976), pp. 114-25.

Heidegger's Model of Subjectivity:
A Polanyian Critique

Robert E. Innis

In the preface to the Harper Torchbook edition of his *Personal Knowledge* (hereafter: PK),[1] a book which had the same place in his work as *Sein und Zeit* did in Heidegger's, Michael Polanyi wrote:

> Things which we can tell, we know by observing them; those that we cannot tell, we know by dwelling in them. All understanding is based on indwelling in the particulars of that which we comprehend. Such indwelling is a participation of ours in the existence of that which we comprehend; it is Heidegger's *being-in-the-world* (p. x).

A little further on we read:

> Indwelling is being-in-the-world. Every act of tacit knowing shifts our existence, re-directing it, contracting our participation in the world. Existentialism and phenomenology have studied such processes under other names. We must re-interpret such observations now in terms of the more concrete structure of tacit knowing (p. xi).

What, more exactly, is the correlation between these notions of indwelling and tacit knowing and Heidegger's root notion in *Sein und Zeit* and other works of being-in-the-world? What would be involved in re-interpreting Heidegger's analyses in Polanyi's terms? I think that a reflection upon parallels between central ideas in the projects of these two men will light up the lack of radicality of certain of Heidegger's positions and at the same time allow the very real power of some of the Heideggerian analyses to be retained.

I.

The central theorem of Polanyi's thought can be put as follows: "acts of consciousness are . . . not only conscious *of* something, but also conscious *from* certain things which include our body."[2] This statement is clarified in the preface to his little book, *The Tacit Dimension*:

> All thought contains components of which we are subsidiarily aware in the focal content of our thinking, and all thought dwells in its particulars, as if they were parts of our body. Hence thinking is not only necessarily intentional, as Brentano has taught; it is also necessarily fraught with the roots it embodies. It has a *from-to* structure (p. x).[3]

This from-to structure is one of the interpretative keys to Polanyi's philosophical anthropology of knowledge. What does he mean by it and how does it reveal the essential structure of tacit knowing?

In a motoric skill, involving a co-ordination of bodily movements and their integration into a unified performance, the skill is an entity constructed out of a set of movements without our explicitly focusing on the individual movements themselves. When we are learning the skill, however, one of our greatest difficulties is not to focus or concentrate on the individual items (i.e., movements, positions, weights, etc.) that, *in conjunction*, constitute the skill as a coherent entity. If we do, as is well known, we paralyze the action. Playing the piano involves not focusing on our fingers nor on the explicit series of movements that succeed one another with such rapidity. Making them into objects of explicit consciousness brings the process to a halt. We have to *rely* on the particulars without focusing on them. We have to use the particulars as instruments or as subsidiaries, depending on their intrinsic orientation to the action as a whole. The *focus* of our attention is the task itself: driving in the nail, hitting the ball, avoiding the child running into the street, sewing the wound, and so forth. In such cases as these we have a form of "understanding" or "comprehension" that seems to be primordial and paradigmatic.

In a feat of visual perception, as well as auditory perception, the same structure obtains. It is well known that we can spot friends and other familiar objects without being able to give an account of the criteria by which we recognize them.

> We may instantly recognize a familiar writing or voice, or a person's gait, or a well-cooked omelette, while being unable to tell—except quite vaguely—by what particulars we recognize these things. The same is true of the recognition of pathological symptoms, of the diagnosis of diseases and the identification of specimens. In all these instances we learn to comprehend an entity without ever getting to know, or to know clearly, the particulars that are *unspecifiable because they are unknown.*
>
> But a particular pointing beyond itself may be fully visible or audible and

yet be unspecifiable in the sense that if attention is directed on it focally—so that it is now known in itself—it ceases to function as a clue or a sign and loses its meaning as such.[4]

There are, it is clear, criteria, but we are not in explicit control of them and we have to rely on them in order to achieve the feat of recognition. A face or physiognomy is constituted by a set of individual items functioning as clues—shadow, light, angle, and so forth—which we have to construe by a process of *merging* them into a unity. The clues, functioning as subsidiary particulars, present a situation as intrinsically problematic, as puzzling, and the object itself is the solution to the puzzle or the meaning toward which the clues are pointing.

The whole visual or auditory form lies at the focus of our attention while we are subsidiarily aware of the particulars, functioning as vectors, pointing toward it as their integrating center of unity or meaning. Further, Polanyi contended that there is a *tacit relation* existing between the particulars and the wholes toward which they point. The particulars and the wholes themselves are separated by a *logical gap*, which can be crossed only by the tacit integrative act/power of consciousness.

There arises from a generalization of such considerations a *universal triadic structure* that applies to all the *meaningful* uses of consciousness.[5] In the chapter on "Skills" in *Personal Knowledge* Polanyi identifies *wholes* and *meanings* (PK 57f.). *Any* unity in the experiential field either *is* a meaning or *has* a meaning, and this interpretation applies to affective, perceptual, linguistic-symbolic, or motoric unities. As Polanyi puts it:

> Anything that functions effectively within an accredited context has meaning in that context and. . .any such context will be appreciated as meaningful. We may describe the kind of meaning which a context possesses in itself as *existential*, to distinguish it especially from *denotative*, or, more generally, *representative* meaning. In this sense pure mathematics has an existential meaning, while a mathematical theory in physics has a denotative meaning. The meaning of music is mainly existential, that of a portrait more or less representative, and so on. All kinds of order, whether contrived or natural, have existential meaning; but contrived order also conveys a message (PK 58).

Contexts are, therefore, *ordered wholes* and, as we shall see, they closely parallel Heidegger's notion of referential totalities (*Bewandtnisganzheiten*) though without their restriction to the world of implements.

Relying on a generalization of Gestalt theory and its thesis concerning the holistic character of the experiential field, Polanyi both in PK and in his last published work *Meaning* tried to chart the genesis and structure of comprehensive unities, starting from the integration of our own bodies in skilful movement and coordination all the way up to the highest realms of symbolic and creative integration in the sciences, arts, and religions. In all these cases his innermost intention was to show that the "ideal of strict objectivism is absurd" (PK x) and that on the basis of such considerations as these he could build a comprehensive and analogous model of knowing.

I would like to cite a long passage in which Polanyi encapsulates most clearly his whole procedure and its connection with the critique of objectivism:

> I want to establish an alternative ideal of knowledge, quite generally...by modifying the conception of knowing.
>
> I have used the findings of Gestalt psychology as my first clues to this conceptual reform. Scientists have run away from the philosophic implications of Gestalt; I want to countenance them uncompromisingly. I regard knowing as an active comprehension of the things known, an action that requires skill. Skilful knowing and doing is performed by subordinating a set of particulars, as clues or tools, to the shaping of a skilful achievement, whether practical or theoretical. We may then be said to become 'subsidiarily aware' of these particulars within our 'focal awareness' of the coherent entity that we achieve. Clues and tools are things used as such and not observed in themselves. They are made to function as extensions of our bodily equipment and this involves a certain change in our own being. Acts of comprehension are to this extent irreversible, and also non-critical. For we cannot possess any fixed framework within which the reshaping of our hitherto fixed framework could be critically tested (PK xiii).

In the final analysis, Polanyi wanted to establish the primacy of tacit knowing without denigrating or minimizing the critical power that man has due to his power of articulation.[6] Thus, just as there are two fundamentally different structures of consciousness—the focal and the subsidiary—so there are two forms or kinds of knowing: *tacit and explicit*. "The essential *logical* difference between the two kinds of knowledge lies in the fact that we can critically reflect on something explicitly stated, in a way in which we cannot reflect upon our *tacit awareness of an experience*."[7] Tacit knowing is "such as we have of something we are in the act of doing....[W]e may say that we always know tacitly that we are holding our explicit knowledge to be true."[8]

II.

The analyses of the fundamental forms of world disclosure or encounter that we find in *Sein und Zeit* (hereafter: SZ)[9] and in Heidegger's other early works involved a transposition in both form and language away from terms which referred directly to consciousness and to epistemological issues and their replacement by another set which constituted, in effect, a non-subjectivistic and non-psychological frame of reference. As Heidegger put it, "subject and object do not coincide with Dasein and world" (SZ 60). While, to be sure, in

Husserlian phenomenology subjects and objects are indissolubly connected by an irreducible intentionality, Heidegger wanted to insist that first and foremost Dasein does not "confront" the world objectively in the way a thematizing, epistemological subject would confront an object, (that is, by standing over against it (SZ, §§13-15). "Being-in-the-world is not first of all the relation between subject and object but what first makes such a relation possible in so far as transcendence accomplishes the project of the Being of being."[10] As is well known, the replacement of language referring to subjectivity is meant to avoid a surreptitious intrusion of "substantiality" into one's conception of the self.

> *Ontologically*, every idea of a 'subject' — unless refined by a previous ontological determination of its basic character — still posits the *subjectum* (*hypokeimenon*) along with it, no matter how vigorous one's ontical protestations against the 'soul substance' or the 'reification of consciousness.' The Thinghood itself which such reification implies must have its ontological origin demonstrated if we are to be in a position to ask what we are to understand *positively* when we think of the unreified *Being* of the subject, the soul, the consciousness, the spirit, the person. All these terms refer to definite phenomenal domains which can be given form ["*ausformbare*"]: but they are never used without a notable failure to see the need for inquiring about the Being of the entities thus designated (SZ, 46).

It is one of the great and lasting merits of Heidegger's work to have struggled continuously with this temptation to reify consciousness and subjectivity in a naive realist fashion and with the temptation of taking an objectifying subjectivity as the paradigm of human world-disclosure.

More specifically, though, how does the Dasein-world correlation stand to the subject-object correlation? As Heidegger saw it, the conceptual framework of the subject-object correlation necessarily fell into conceiving the relationship as one between two substances or two independent entities existing in the modality of simpler presence (*Vorhandenheit*). On the contrary, as we read in *Die Grundprobleme der Phänomenologie* (hereafter: GP), Heidegger thought that "...the monad, because it is essentially re-presenting, that is, a mirroring of a world, is transcendence and not simply present substance-like thing or a windowless receptacle" (p. 427).[11] In Heidegger's original schematization there were two radically different modes of givenness of those beings with which Dasein has to deal — including itself — which in SZ were called being-useful (*Zuhandenheit*) and mere presence, or presence-at-hand (*Vorhandenheit*). Things are classified as merely present if they fall into a framework of observation where they are considered, in objectifying fashion, as *objects* present to and standing before a subject who is explicitly dealing with them. A being, however, is constituted as useful, or ready-to-hand, if it belongs to a framework not of observation but of use (SZ §§15-16).

In Heidegger's analysis of being-in-the-world the primacy of readiness-to-hand is crucial, for he wants to establish that this is the primordial mode of enconter of things in a world. Implements (*Zeuge*), the paradigmatic instances of the modality of being useful or ready-to-hand, are defined by their insertion into a referential totality (*Bewandtnisganzheit*) (SZ, 83-88). The whole world of implements is characterized by its "in-order-to. . ." structure. As we read in GP, "the tool is 'in-order-to'; we are conscious of the 'what-for' [*des Wozu*] of the tool in the use of it" (415). As such, then, the tool or implement does not stand over against us as an object to be observed but is something that we use, something we rely on, something that we "know" and are familiar with, but in a non-objectifying and non-thematizing fashion. Now the referential totality of a set of tools or implements, considered as a unity, makes up what Heidegger means by the *world*. All implements as ready-to-hand, have meaning and use, only when they have an order and orientation within this world.

> Circumspective concern includes the understanding of a referential totality, and this understanding is based upon a prior understanding of the relationships of the 'in-order-to,' the 'what-for,' the 'for-this,' and the 'for-the-sake-of.' The interconnection of these relationships has been exhibited. . .as 'significance.' Their unity makes up what we call the 'world.' The question arises of how anything like the world in its unity with Dasein is ontologically possible (SZ, 364).

The world itself cannot be reduced to the totality of implements or objects, but is the (transendental) condition of the possibility of their appearing at all (SZ, 75). While the world lets them appear as what they are, it itself does not thematically appear, for "the world in general is not something objectively present or ready-to-hand" (GP, 420). It can be thematized, however, or itself appear if there occurs a breakdown or rupture within the totality of relationships that makes up the structure of significance or meaningfulness within which Dasein lives and moves. *In the reflective mode*, thematization of the world and of worlds would occur in philosophical reflection—foundational reflection—wherein we no longer *live in* the worlds thematized at the time of analysis. Thus the significance of the Husserlian reductions even for SZ (cf. GP 29). *In the direct mode* the world in which one is factically moving would appear when the structural totality itself shifts because the lines of relations undergo a transformation, generally from the outside. This occurs in the experience of anxiety (SZ §40). In such a case, as also in the former, we move from one world to another, but in no sense do we move *out* of the world altogether. At the same time we also do not encounter any absolute standpoint or pivot upon which we can rely. Rather, in line with the *projective* character of understanding, as delineated in SZ, we find ourselves embedded in a *set* of worlds and, in a sense, carried along with them, for they are temporal through and through.

III.

My first question is this: Just how fundamental is this distinction between objective presence-at-hand and readiness-to-hand, and is such a schematization necessary in order to avoid the reification of the subject and an objectifying subjectivity?

On Heidegger's interpretation of the matter, subjectivism and objectivism go together. Consequently, the proper way to criticize objectivism is to strike at its root, the *model of the subject* and its intercourse with the world.[12] The early work of Heidegger, with the centrality of its notions of world and of concernful, non-objectifying and non-thematizing dealings with things, already struck a mighty blow at the idea of an isolated monadic consciousness trying to bridge a gap between its inner sphere of consciousness and the so-called "outside" world, whose ontological status would have to be *secured*. Dasein as being-in-the-world is already "outside" among beings, already dwelling in a realm of sense, understanding itself out of the possibilities already projected as its world.

> The world is therefore something 'wherein' Dasein as a being already *was*, and if in any manner it explicitly comes away from anything, it can never do more than come back to the world.
>
> Being-in-the-world, according to our interpretation, amounts to a non-thematic circumspective absorption in references or assignments constitutive for the readiness-to-hand of a totality of implements (SZ 76).

Now, on the Polanyian model, the subject precisely as conscious is also already ahead of itself and outside of itself (in-the-world) because tacit knowing as source of all meaningful unities within the field of consciousness manifests the twofold irreducible distinction between subsidiary and focal awareness. In fact, it is this crucial distinction which lights up how, in Heidegger's conception of the world, implements or tools can be "apprehended" as *ordered to* a larger whole or context. The *gap* between the manifold relations and the whole or totality toward which they are oriented manifests the need for an integrative synthetic *power* instantiated in acts and sets of acts. The whole or totality, as a unified structure of meaningfulness which lets beings appear in their equipmental nature, then itself functions as a pre-determining framework of disclosure in which we dwell. The framework is assimilated to our bodies, used *subsidiarily* as an instrument, whether preconceptual or conceptual, as we focus upon ('view') or bring into a unity the things we encounter in our concernful dealings *within* the world.

Consequently, the manifold relations parallel Polanyi's subsidiary particulars. But these particulars only have meaning when merged into a unity, no matter how complex. Indeed, since the world of implements generally arises within an articulate matrix and involves the use of signs, symbols, and other referential devices (cf. SZ §17), the world is also intrinsically constituted by language, though it is, of course, not reducible to it. The principal difference here between Heidegger and Polanyi is that the distinction between focal and subsidiary awareness seems to undercut the distinction between *presence-at-hand* and *readiness-to-hand*. *Every* act of tacit knowing manifests this distinction between the two forms of consciousness. Every act involves a pouring of ourselves into subsidiarily intended particulars, expanding or contracting our existence, shifting and re-directing it. The original and paradigmatic genesis of sense and familiarity with the world involves a hermeneutical act in the sense in which Heidegger discusses it at SZ §32.

In acts of tacit knowing in which pre-articulate as well as articulate wholes and systems of wholes arise, something is grasped *as* something even if we may not be able to fully or adequately *say* it (*apophantic "as"*) (cf. SZ 154), as in our comprehension of the space in which we move or of a complex three-dimensional organic topography. Indeed, the expert pianist or agile athlete or wine connoisseur are in just this situation. In fact, more generally, we may be familiar with a complicated whole — visual, auditory, conceptual, aesthetic — without being able to specify focally or know explicitly all the manifold particulars upon which we are relying or which we are integrating, or being integrated into.[13] In other words, our understanding here is ultimately *tacit* (or rooted in the tacit), preconceptual, akin to Ryle's "knowing how" and to Heidegger's own original conception of understanding not as a mere form of "knowing," but as a primordial mode of being of Dasein, as the fundamental determination of existing (cf. GP 393). Here also are the tacit roots of Heidegger's "familiarity with the world in concernful dealings" (GP 428).

IV.

There are even more extensive parallels, as well as crucial differences, between the Heideggerian and Polanyian operations. First of all, the roots with which thinking is fraught — Polanyi's subsidiary particulars, inarticulate as well as articulate — correspond to the thrown character of Dasein's being-in-the-world and further to its facticity, historicity, and finitude. To the degree that these roots are embodied in language and other articulate systems that we take over a-critically and are taken over by, they pre-define as *premises* what Heidegger delineates and develops in SZ as the *fore-structure* of understanding and its necessarily *circular* character. Dwelling in an interpretative framework and matrix of significant relationships which we have not thematically generated (*Vorhabe*), our heuristic imagination thrusts itself forward, or is drawn forward, toward a realm of sense which it intimates beforehand (*Vorsicht*), and which allows us by means of a prior system of concepts (*Vorgriff*) to articulate (*Gliederung*) the world into which we are projected or toward which we are thrown (cf. SZ §§31-34). These premises shift and change radically in the history of man's dealings with the world and with himself. Here one might fruitfully study what Heidegger discusses as the fundamental project of modern science in "The Age of the World Picture" and "Science and Reflection" in light of Polanyi's rather different characterization and evaluation in *Science, Faith and Society* and PK.[14] While both see the history of western science as a series of ruptures, the inner dynamics of these ruptures are not the same. Copernicus, Kepler, Galileo, Newton, Einstein stand for radically different events for the two men, for they understand differently the significance of the shifts in systems of intellectual values that are associated with them.[15]

Secondly, being-in-the-world as comprehending involves a "mastery" of the possibilities and sense-implications of *dealing* with things, but the precondition of dealing with things or sense-ful unities is their ultimate *emergence* in the world of Dasein. The emergence of unities in the experiential field is a tacit achievement and is something primordial. On Polanyi's position it is not a feat of explicit, operative action but resembles more a spontaneous event.[16] In fact, Polanyi's discussion of the oft-remarked spontaneous character of the event of understanding, which he finds verified in the grammar of discovery in both the arts and the sciences and which is rooted in the analogous structure of skills,[17] parallels the Heideggerian contention — and its extension by Gadamer — that understanding is a happening in which we are caught up, or to which we are *appropriated*.[18] Indeed, the dynamic character of the processes of tacit integration, rooted in the thrusting movement of the imagination and driven on by intellectual passions, would lead us to experience ourselves, in our comprehending being, as being in constant intentional motion. Does this not parallel Heidegger's notion of the being of Dasein as being-moved (SZ 374f)?

Thirdly, Heidegger argued that in order to grasp a being as present-at-hand or merely present, a shift (*Umschlag*) is necessary that breaks our direct involvement in the world (SZ §69b). Thus, "pure" perception is already incipient objectification and thematization, continued in purest forms in science and metaphysics. But, on Polanyi's position, perception is never just "pure" or "disinterested," not even in the highest realms of scientific abstractions.[19] The model of perception — integration of particulars into wholes — can be extended to all forms of our indwelling in sets of dynamic and subsidiarily intended vectors. In no sense are we involved in a vacant "staring" or "gaping" at the world, considered as an object, when we are perceiving. There is a commitment and participation present in the original recognition of perceptual types.[20] Symbolic apprehension, too, involves the pouring of ourselves into systems of linguistic and symbolic elements and bringing them to bear (and letting ourselves be brought to bear by them) on experience, but the whole process is one of *concretion* and *application* and not merely one of external conceptual subsumption.[21]

Fourthly, in SZ and other early works Heidegger traced, we know, the being of consciousness back to the ecstatic unity of time and the temporalizing process (cf. also KM §§32-34; §44). We are conscious of time by *being* it, not by standing over against it, just as we do not stand over against ourselves when, in our selfhood unified by care, we and our worlds are lighted up in the experience of anxiety. We are the anxiety-ridden and care-unified existence. Now, for Polanyi, self-experience likewise makes no reference to self-objectification or to a self-intuiting relation to one's self. The power of tacit syntheses, paradigmatically illustrated in the ways we are conscious of our bodies, corresponds to the Heideggerian temporalizing of time. Ultimately *we* are the irreducible *from-pole* in the process of tacit knowing, and it is this insight which grounds Polanyi's calling of his own philosophical project "post-critical" and which allows him to ground human existence in the "ubiquitous controlling position of unformalizable mental skills."[22] There is no way, for Polanyi (as well as, incidentally, for Husserl), that the field of self-experience in which selfhood is ultimately rooted can be present-at-hand; and our tacit, subsidiary awareness of ourselves and of our articulate instruments takes on the function of a final ground which finds itself and is aware of its calling.[23]

Fifthly, both Heidegger and Polanyi share an opposition to Cartesianism, but for rather different reasons and with rather different results. Heidegger connects Cartesianism and the rise of the subject with the beginning of the culmination of Western metaphysics in the universalization of science and technology and the "mathematization" of the whole world, the result of which is the reduction of the world to the status of a "standing reserve." Polanyi is in agreement with Heidegger that there are other equally valid and equally important methods and forms of world disclosure which are not reducible to an intuiting consciousness operating according to a monolithic totalization of the criteria of clarity, distinctness, and mathematical-geometrical rigor. But while there is with Heidegger a tendency to ascribe the pejorative aspects of these qualities to science as such, Polanyi wanted to show that they belonged to a false self-conception of science, to an ideology, and could not and did not correspond to the way in which science is *actually practiced* and to the constitutive conditions, rooted in the structure of tacit knowing, to which it is subject. The so-called methodical canons and criteria are in actuality embedded in scientific praxis as maxims and only have sense for the researcher who is in possession of the requisite skills.[24] Moreover, in no sense, on Polanyi's interpretation, does science want to, nor can it, "dominate" the world, "reduce" it to a posit of human subjectivity. Nor does it lead ineluctably toward a totalization of technology, the axiomatization of whose rules plays a central role in part 4 of PK. As we read in *Science, Faith, and Society*:

> The advancement of science consists in discerning Gestalten that are aspects of reality. We know that perception selects, shapes, and assimilates clues by a

process not explicitly controlled by the perceiver. Since the powers of scientific discerning are the same kind as those of perception, they too operate by selecting, shaping and assimilating clues without focally attending to them (p. 11).

Sixthly, by reverting once again to the crucial aspect of the vectorial character of subsidiary particulars and their internal differentiations, it is possible, I think, though I can only hint at it here, to handle the issues raised by Heidegger's discussion of "The Thing."[25] These particulars have directions and their own intrinsic qualities. The *unifying center* that comes to presence in a complex set of particulars gives us the Polanyian analogue of what Heidegger calls a thing.[26] This is so also when the unity arises through the merging or integration of experiential and linguistic-symbolic particulars combined, as happens in most cases of articulate knowing. What concretely a particular thing is will depend on these subsidiaries and the matrix of consciousness in which they are "brought to a stand" by our assimilating the particulars to ourselves. The problem is to specify, therefore, in rigorous phenomenological fashion, the modes and varieties of indwelling as so many intentionality structures. They would be so many ways of being-in. The same observation would apply to the problematic of world, which I think is the richest in the Heideggerian corpus.

Polanyi would discuss such a notion under the rubric of a *framework*. Just as for Heidegger the world is not the sum of thematically intended objects but the transcendental condition for objects of all sorts appearing, and just as it functions as the ultimate horizon of comportment with its various aspects, so a framework is something, on Polanyian principles, that we indwell and use subsidiarily. It is something we participate in and are embodied in. We expand or contract as it expands and contracts. In this way the self would not be experienced as a point, a transcendental ego, but would grasp itself by reflecting upon and living in the various frameworks of meaning and by grasping their principles of formation (cf. SZ 146). Here, I think, Polanyi's position coincides with Cassirer's, and I find myself in agreement with the objections made by Cassirer to Heidegger's project in the Davos discussion.[27]

V.

In conclusion, since Polanyi's analyses of the *from-to* structure of tacit knowing are meant to be totally general and to apply to *all* forms and contexts of sense-giving and sense-reading—that is, to all types of wholes, whether perceptual, linguistic–symbolic, affective, or motoric—on its basis would be made possible an outline of possible autonomous, yet analogically unified forms of world-disclosure or forms of constitution of sense based on the foundations of tacit syntheses. The proximity of the Husserlian project is especially clear here. In some aspects, Polanyi's tacit knowing, rooted in the pre-articulate structure of skillful achievements, parallels the root meaning of Heidegger's notion of understanding as the fundamental mode of being-in and being-among beings. To be sure, the primary relation to the world is not thematizing and objectifying in the Heideggerian sense, and Heidegger is right to attack the Cartesian intuitional model with its consequent contention that knowing involves a sort of looking at what is present before one's mental gaze. Polanyi, too, attacks this model and its viability even for "derivative" forms of knowing; and his notion of subsidiary awareness and of indwelling, precisely yet flexibly defined, give us the keys to many of Heidegger's analyses even though they do not duplicate or replace certain aspects of the existential analytic in SZ such as the analyses of temporality, care, and historicity.

Thus the confrontation model of knowing, even as a possibility, cannot be sustained on the basis of a radical examination of knowing itself.[28] The pivotal set of oppositions upon which Heidegger based his movement away from the principle of subjectivity and which have persisted throughout his later work are not phenomenologically ultimate and involve an overlooking of just how the tacit character of consciousness and the tacit foundations of knowing are to be conceived. Just what, more extensively, the consequences would be for later Heideggerian reflections upon non-objectifying thinking, and especially for the vagaries of the Being-question, I leave to others and to other times.

Notes

Robert E. Innis is Professor of Philosophy and Chairman of the Department at the University of Lowell, Massachusetts. His articles have appeared in *Inquiry, International Philosophical Quarterly, The Thomist, Philosophy Today, Zeitschrift für Allgemeine Wissenschaftstheorie* and elsewhere.

1. (New York: Harper and Row, 1964 [reprint]).
2. "The Structure of Consciousness," in *Knowing and Being*, ed. Marjorie Grene (Chicago: University of Chicago Press, 1969), p. 214.
3. (Garden City: Doubleday Anchor, 1967).
4. *The Study of Man* (Chicago: University of Chicago Press, 1963), p. 45.
5. Cf. the paper "Logic and Psychology," *American Psychologist*, 23 (1968) where this topic is first discussed at length. One may also refer to my article, "The Triadic Structure of Religious Consciousness in Polanyi," *The Thomist*, XL, 3, July, 1976, for an extended discussion and presentation of this notion. Cf. especially part I, "Meanings, Wholes, and Tacit Triads," pp. 394-400.
6. Cf. the chapter on "Articulation" in PK, the article, "Sense-Giving and Sense-Reading," in *Knowing and Being*, and chapter 4 of *Meaning* (Chicago: University of Chicago Press, 1975). One may also refer to my paper, "Meaning, Thought and Language in Polanyi's Epistemology," *Philosophy Today*, 18 (1974), pp. 47-67, and my lecture "Polanyi's Epistemology and the Philosophy of Language," given at the Skidmore College Conference on the relevance of Polanyi's thought to the various disciplines, June, 1977.
7. *The Study of Man*, p. 14.
8. *Ibid.*, p. 12.

9. (Tübingen: Max Niemeyer Verlag, 1963), zehnte, unveränderte Auflage. I have not always used the Macquarrie-Robinson translation, and where I have done so, I have often modified it.

10. *Kant und das Problem der Metaphysik* (hereafter: KM), dritte Auflage (Frankfurt am Main: Vittorio Klostermann), p. 212.

11. Ed. F.W. von Herrmann, Gesamtausgabe II, 24 (Frankfurt am Main: Vittorio Klostermann, 1975).

12. For another, and very perceptive discussion of this cf. Paul Ricoeur, "Heidegger and the Question of the Subject," in *The Conflict of Interpretations*, ed. Don Ihde (Evanston: Northwestern University Press, 1974), pp. 223-235.

13. A treatment of cognate issues from another standpoint will be found in Anton Ehrenzweig, *The Psycho-Analysis of Artistic Vision and Hearing* (New York: George Braziller, 1965).

14. Polanyi discusses the problematic of premises in chapter six of PK and in an important appendix to his *Science, Faith and Society* (Chicago: University of Chicago Press, 1964).

15. The remarkable book by Gerald Holton, *Thematic Origins of Scientific Thought* (Cambridge, MA: Harvard University Press, 1973) contains important historical discussions of many of these issues under the rubric of *themata*.

16. *Science, Faith and Society*, p. 33.

17. Cf. sections 10-12 of chapter 5 of PK and the extensive discussions in *Meaning* of discursive and non-discursive modes.

18. Gadamer's notion of a *Wirkungsgeschichte* comes to mind as well as the extension of the model of "play" (*Spiel*) into a general model of understanding. I am preparing a study, "Play as Cognitional Model," where its viability will be discussed in detail. Cf. also my review article on Gadamer's *Truth and Method* in *The Thomist*, 40 (1976), pp. 311-321. Further indications will be found in my article, "Art, Symbol, Consciousness," *International Philosophical Quarterly*, 17, 4 (1977).

19. Cf. the extensive discussion in the chapter on "Intellectual Passions" in PK.

20. The same is true of the recognition of order and patterns. Chapters 2 and 3 of PK attempt to show the tacit, participatory elements involved in the foundations of the most exact sciences.

21. The whole linguistic problematic has not been thematically treated in this paper, but the reference here is to Gadamer's linguistic ontology of human understanding. I would also like to note the extreme relevance of a remarkable book by Johannes Lohmann, *Philosophie und Sprachwissenschaft* (Berlin: Duncker and Humboldt, 1965), and of his review of Gadamer's *Truth and Method* in *Gnomon*, 37 (1965), pp. 709-18.

22. "The Unaccountable Element in Science," *Knowing and Being*, p. 106.

23. The notion of a calling is developed throughout PK and especially in chapter 10. It is a crucial component in Polanyi's own interpretation of the finitude and historicity of human existence.

24. Cf. my article, "In Memoriam Michael Polanyi," in *Zeitschrift für Allgemeine Wissenschaftstheorie*, VIII/I (1977), pp. 22-29 and my "Agassi on Rationality," *Inquiry*, 18, 97-102.

25. Heidegger's essays "The Origin of the Work of Art" and "The Thing" in Martin Heidegger, *Poetry, Language, Thought*, trans. Albert Hofstadter (New York: Harper and Row, 1971) are full of provocative insights but are highly unsystematic. Nevertheless, along with *Die Frage nach dem Ding* they remain the chief Heideggerian statements on the problem.

26. Although the notion of a unifying center is the critical one, different centers come to presence as different "carriers" are brought into a unity. While I think that the

substantive position of Heidegger can be reconstituted outside of the manneristic matrix of his later thought, I cannot demonstrate that here.

27. This discussion is now found in English in Nino Langiulli, *The Existentialist Tradition* (Garden City: Doubleday Anchor, 1971). The definitive German text (more definitive than that translated) may now be found in *Kant und das Problem der Metaphysik*, 4th expanded edition, 1973, pp. 243-268.

28. This theme lies at the center of the masterwork of Bernard Lonergan, *Insight* (London: Longmans, 1957), which is remarkably similar in substance and method to *Personal Knowledge*. I would also like to note that Merleau-Ponty's *Phenomenology of Perception* arrives at conclusions essentially identical with those of Polanyi in many places, but this work combines phenomenology and Gestalt theory rather than Gestalt theory and reflection upon scientific practice, as does Polanyi's chief work.

III. IN DIALOGUE WITH MAX SCHELER

Reality and Resistance:
On *Being and Time*, Section 43

Max Scheler

[*Immediately after* Being and Time *was published in February of 1927, Heidegger sent a copy to Max Scheler, who in September of that year composed a forty-page fragment on the book. Only recently published, that document represents the first serious discussion of that work by a major thinker. In a letter of August 6, 1964, Heidegger wrote to Manfred Frings: "Scheler was one of the very few, if not the only one, who at that time immediately recognized the formulation of the question in* Being and Time. *He interpreted it as the highest level and conclusion of metaphysics, whereas I conceived it as the beginning of a new [kind of] thinking. Above all it was the thematic of Dasein, temporality and death which occupied Max Scheler. He planned a fully detailed discussion of my work. The matter occupied him until his early and unexpected death in Frankfurt, May [19], 1928. I later learned from Max Scheler's wife, Maria, that his copy of* Being and Time *was covered with notes. . . . During the winter semester of 1927–28 Max Scheler invited me to Cologne for a lecture at the Kant Society, of which he was the head. I spoke about the chapter on schematism in Kant's* Critique of Pure Reason (cf. the Preface to the first edition of my book, Kant and the Problem of Metaphysics, 1929). *During that visit — I stayed at Scheler's house for three days — we spoke together for the last time and discussed in detail how the formulation of the question in* Being and Time *was related to metaphysics and to his conception of phenomenology. . . ." Shortly after Scheler's death Heidegger wrote that Scheler was "the strongest philosophical force in Germany, nay, in all of Europe — in fact, in all of present-day philosophy."*

The excerpt below is taken from "Idealismus und Realismus, V: Das emotionale Realitätsproblem" in Max Scheler, *Späte Schriften, ed. Manfred S. Frings*

Bern: Francke, 1976, pp. 259-269. Scheler's marginal notes which Heidegger mentions above appear ibidem, pp. 305-340. (Tr. note)]

In his unusual and far-reaching book, *Sein und Zeit*, vol. I [= SZ], Heidegger is the first person to get to the heart of the matter. It is not my intention here to characterize in detail, let alone as a whole, the significance and original depths of these investigations. Here I will consider closely only some points in Heidegger's statements about the specific problem of the being of "being-real" ["*Realsein*"]. He deals with this in section 43 of his work. To begin with, Heidegger makes a very valuable distinction—which I too have made— between four questions: "(1) whether any entities which supposedly 'transcend our consciousness' *are* at all; (2) whether this reality of the 'external world' can be adequately *proved*; (3) how far this entity, if it is real, is to be known in its being-in-itself; (4) what the meaning of this entity, reality, signifies in general" (SZ, 201). Here too the very primitive neo-Kantian confusion of questions is surpassed.

The first methodological objection which he makes against the treatment of the problem (and he directs it against me and Nicolai Hartmann among others) is stated in the sentence: "The possibility of an adequate ontological analysis of reality depends upon how far *that from which* the real is to be thus independent—how far *that which* is to be transcended—has *itself* [first of all] been clarified with regard to its *being*. Only thus can even the kind of being which belongs to transcendence be ontologically grasped. And finally we must make sure what kind of primary access we have to the real, by deciding the question of whether cognition can take over this function at all" (SZ, 202). The first sentence states very correctly: If being-real is defined in terms of being-conscious or being-an-ego (whether being-real also be defined by "independence" from these or by being-in-itself) or if, as in my doctrine, it be defined in terms of life and drives [*Trieb*] and so forth, then first of all we have to secure the *mode of being* of all of these. Here I completely agree with Heidegger—quite apart from his use of the expression "first of all," which is a consequence of the fact that he begins ontology with what he calls "Dasein," which he equates with the existence that for each person is always his own and which he then defines more precisely as "being-in-the-world." *That in relation to which [woraufhin] being-real is a kind of being cannot itself be real*: it must have another mode of being although (as Hartmann says) being-real cannot be "explained" by real things and the causal relations between them, as all "critical realism" so naively tries to do. But I would like to add immediately that [Heidegger's] propositions here do not affect *my position* (cf. above[1]). Knowledge, consciousness, the ego [*260*] are derived long *before* the problem of reality sets in. Moreover, being-real pertains to objectifiable being, to which I oppose non-objectifiable being-in-act and being-a-self (being enacted) and being that is gathered into itself and, further, being self-sustained as the manner of being a person. And I further oppose to objectifiable being the kind of being of "life," which in the immediacy of its being is constantly (1) in the state of becoming [*Werde-sein*] (which is not the same as "to become something" [*Sein-werden*], which can also be found in the sphere of the real); (2) non-objectifiable being, which can be found only in the state of "inwardness"; (3) being in *absolute time* in distinction to everything that is "really there." And when in a real-ontological sense I define being-real as image posited through vital urge [*Drang*], I do not mean to further impose *realitas* on the state of becoming of the vital urge itself. The "desire" ["*Sucht*"], the "thirst" for being-real is itself not at all real, precisely because it is not objectifiable but first of all "seeks" realization [*Realsein*]. I entirely agree with Heidegger that it is high time to finally stop transporting the categories and modes of being found in the *narrow* sphere of physical being over into life, consciousness, the ego, and so forth. Heidegger has done an admirable job in showing how Descartes' doctrine of the soul as a thinking thing ("*res*" *cogitans*) and his doctrine of the *res extensa* have arisen in this way. But whereas *this* reproach may fit other people, it does not fit me.

However, what I reject in Heidegger is the solipsism of existence which he takes as his *point of departure*. It represents a pure *reversal* of the Cartesian "cogito ergo sum" into a "sum *ergo cogito*." But even in Heidegger there *persists* the fundamental error of Descartes, namely, that that which, in the order of the being of entities, is in fact the *farthest off of all* (one's own ego; and basically this also holds in Heidegger's own doctrine of Dasein's "loss of the world") is held to be given as primary. What is Dasein and "being-in-the-world" supposed to mean? Here he introduces the word "world" which is not only very ambiguous (and world is actually not primarily given; according to Kant it is in fact only an "idea" of the progress of the understanding) but also pregnant with the whole theistic theology of the past, because world possesses a definite meaning only in opposition to "God." Furthermore what does it mean for the *solus ipse* [oneself alone] that its kind of being is Dasein and that Dasein is "being-in-the-world"? Here the "in" is not supposed to mean anything like "enclosed." According to Heidegger "world" itself *precedes* in being all spatiality and temporality. Here "being-in" is supposed to mean something like "being caught up in something" or "being involved in something." Can this idea have any meaning at all unless the "*solus ipse*" also experiences itself as independent from the world—something Heidegger cannot admit? Aren't these the gloomy old theologoumena of Calvinist origin (cf. also "thrownness"), which are here translated into an apparently pure ontological language?

[*261*] No, we maintain that the first absolute wonder is the wonder about the state of affairs "that there is something at all and not nothing" (Cf. "Vom Wesen der Philosophie"[2]), rather than about the existence of the *solus ipse*. It

may be a supreme goal for us "to come back to the being of the *solus ipse*" — or as *I* put it, to *gather* oneself unto oneself — from out of the "they" and "idle chatter" which Heidegger paints so magnificently with Pascalian colors, and from out of "fallenness" into what is immanent in the world. But why should this kind of being, which is the *most difficult* of all to elucidate, serve as the starting point for ontology? Exactly why is it called "existence," when existence first of all certainly means the mode of being of a temporally and spatially determined X and surely not the personhood of a human being? Today don't we know almost certainly that man as an individual being *is given to himself last of all*; that first of all he is immersed entirely ecstatically into the *we*, the *thou*, into inner-worldly being;[3] that he has to laboriously wrest every step towards his selfhood from a concatanation of deceptive identifications with the men, the living beings, the animals, plants and things which he himself is not?

And yet another objection: If being-in-the-world is supposed to constitute the being of the *solus ipse*, indeed in such way that being-real is disclosed only within the limits of the world-immanent but not beforehand (as the "presence-at-hand" of the primarily "ready-to-hand"), then how does Heidegger know that there is only *one* world, that corresponding to actuality there are not as "many worlds" as you like (*multiversa*, not an "*universum*"), as many as there are *soli ipsi* (whose essence is this kind of being, viz., Dasein), just as in antiquity Democritus accepted this position as a consequence of his (impossible) assumption of an infinite "existing" void with a plurality of enclosed totalities of causal connections and spaces in between — or as William James has recently held in his book, *A Pluralistic Universe*?

There is the priorly given kind of being which I call being-real. Furthermore there is the *unity* of the nexus of effects [*Wirkkonnex*] within it, which alone grants us the right to hold that only one instance of worldhood exists and which, as I have shown,[4] also first guarantees the unity of an objective space and time. Heidegger and I agree that the existence in general of the we and the thou is an *a priori* proposition, but according to Heidegger's statement, the being-with-each-other of more than one *solus ipse in no way* guarantees the unity of the world of worldly being. For if existence is to be called "being-in" in the world and not, as in Democritus' assertion, "the enclosedness" of a world, then we have to ask: Being-in in *which* world, in which instance of worldhood? There could just as well still be being-with-each-other if every *solus ipse* lived in his world and his alone.

On the other hand Heidegger answers the third of the aforementioned questions — whether cognition is at all what yields reality — exactly as I do. [*262*] Although Heidegger could have rather used the word "knowledge"[*Wissen*], his results are nonetheless the same as ours. In no way do knowledge and cognition yield the being-real of the real. He says: "Cognition is a *founded* mode of access to the real" (SZ, 202), but, according to Heidegger, not founded by the unity of resistance against the unity of the vital center [*Triebzentrum*] but rather founded by dread and care as the kind of being of "Dasein." When Heidegger says: "But even the real can be discovered only on the basis of a world which has already been disclosed" (SZ, 203), I too certainly hold that the structure of the spheres is given prior to being-real. But the fact that this structure of the spheres in general forms a unity of the world presupposes the unity of being-real and its unified origin in the vital desire [*Sucht*] which posits *being-real*.

I agree fully with Heidegger that Kant's "Refutation of Idealism" quite sufficiently divides one and *only one* objective time from the subjective time-sequence but that it doesn't prove "the existence of things outside of me"; and that Kant's approach to the problem presupposes the false assumption of the immanence of consciousness. I also maintain that Heidegger is correct when he says: "*The presence-together-at-hand of the physical and the psychical is completely different ontically and ontologically from the phenomenon of being-in-the-world*" (SZ, 204). But this same lack of difference holds as well for the problem of reality, which, as I have shown,[5] is one and the same for the physical and psychical. Also to the point is this sentence: "If Dasein is understood correctly, it defies such proofs, because in its being, it already *is* what subsequent proofs deem necessary to demonstrate for it" (SZ, 205). The being of being-real is a being of self-assertion, and not only all proofs but also all knowledge and cognition presuppose it from the start. And equally to the point is what Heidegger says against people like Jakobi or Wilhelm Stern or Theodore Lipps who want to take the reality of the external world on "faith." The need for proof and also the possibility of proof in itself are thereby presupposed—in order then to be broken down by such a silly thing as an act of mere belief (cf. also the following[6]). The sentence which disputes the false proposition of the primacy of immanence in consciousness also seems correct to me: "Our task in not to prove that an 'external world' is present-at-hand or to show how it is present-at-hand, but to point out why Dasein, as being-in-the-world, has the tendency to bury the 'external world' in nullity 'epistemologically' before going on to prove it" (SZ, 206). But what has to bear the *burden* of proof in certain cases is the irreality or existential relativity, or further, the subjectivizing of a phenomenon into one of the inner world. Heidegger's remarks against critical realism and idealism are also essentially to the point. Concerning critical realism he writes: "Indeed realism tries to explain reality ontically by real connections of interaction between things that are real" (SZ, 207). [*263*] And concerning idealism he correctly says that it neglects to clarify the mode of being of the subject of being-consciousness, the *res cogitans*.

Then in some not very precise statements Heidegger opposes himself to Wilhelm Dilthey's thesis and my own. What he says against my own doctrine is too fragmentary to warrant my discussing it at any length.[7] To say that I have not defined the mode of being of life or that I have shored it up with some underpinnings only as an afterthought — after I have given lecture courses for years now about the mode of being of life — is, as far as I'm concerned, as false as could be. And when he then says, "The experiencing of resistance — that is, the discovery, in striving, of what resists us — is possible ontologically only by reason of the disclosedness of the world" (SZ, 210 [italicized in the original]) and: "The 'against' and the 'counter to' in their ontological possibility are supported by disclosed being-in-the-world" (*ibid.*), then I must strongly object to these propositions — as what I said earlier has shown.

But it is entirely a misunderstanding when Heidegger speaks of a "summation" of the experiences of resistance which produce the being-real of one and only one world. I teach precisely that against the *one* vital drive-center [*Trieb- und Lebenszentrum*] resistance produces the unity of a real sphere — *before* all individual realities insofar as they are indebted to such being-functions and qualities of sensation in a secondary way. What is given prior to the "discovery in striving" of external resistances is the subjective multiplicity of space as spatiality and, besides, as temporality — but in no way a "world," let alone *one* world. "Worldhood" as a phenomenon (not as an "idea") is, I am sorry to say, entirely unknown to me. The "referential totality of significance" (SZ, 210) seems to me a very vague and ill-defined concept. There simply is no proof (cf. the following) that the drive-impulse is a "modification" of a non-cognitional mode of comportment which Heidegger calls "care," and that resistance presupposes being as something we are concerned for (or the being of our fellow-man as someone for whom we have solicitude). Heidegger goes on to say that resistance is only one character of reality along with others. But if we properly distinguish the problem of the "in-itself" of the so-called "independence" or transcendence or existential relativity and so forth, and if we properly distinguish being-real as a mode of being vs. that which is real, then we see that this character is the only constitutive one for being-real. And it is equally not the case that "resistance presupposes necessarily a world which has already been disclosed" (SZ, 211). If "world" in this sentence means being which is independent of living subjectivity and all that this subjectivity holds "to exist" by virtue of this world — not just the forms of activity which well up from the life-center and, secondarily, the forms of intuition and consciousness of spatiality and temporality — then it is rather the case [*264*] that *world is disclosed* only in resistance and in the rhythmical change of a subsequent cancellation of resistance (via suspension of the drive-center's drive-impulses which yield being-real).[8] But at the same time only through ever newly initiated acts of re-flection — man's "being thrown back" upon himself[9] — is there formed what Heidegger calls "Dasein." The suffering of resistance is simultaneously the basis of the subsequent perceptive and pictorial clarification of *what* we suffer and of the self we become and, secondarily, of the self-consciousness which, as a Dasein-structure that is present as completed, is Heidegger's point of departure. The being of the world and the being of the self are strictly equiprimordial, and both of them as modes of being arise out of resistance, the cancellation of resistance, and the subsequent view of what *has come about.*

Now how does Heidegger himself proceed in order to grasp the peculiar quality of being-real? To being with, he restricts this "title" to "innerworldly entities." That which has existence in Heidegger's sense, i.e., the vital subject-hood of the *solus ipse,* has no reality. "There is" being-real only in a possible relation to the being of Dasein. Even the world—or better, the worldhood of the world—has no reality. In Heidegger, being real *presupposes* the disclosure of the world. Within innerworldly entities the nature which surrounds us sets itself off as a whole; in nature we run across two modes of being-real: readiness-to-hand and presence-at-hand. The reality of things (this is the word in its "traditional meaning") is only a modification of presence-at-hand and comprises neither nature as a sphere itself nor all the things present-at-hand in nature. Thence comes the insight: Neither does reality have a priority, nor can this kind of being adequately characterize in an ontological way something like world and Dasein (SZ, 211).

These propositions contain true and false in a curious mixture. It is annoying that the being of the givenness of reality and the being of being-real itself are not distinguished. In Heidegger that in no way leads to the idealism of consciousness. That is the superiority of his doctrine. Consciousness is not introduced as a kind of being. It also seems to me to be the sense of Heidegger's excellent insight that the pre-given world and what is immanent in it are given to us primarily as "ready-to-hand," as "implements," and that this givenness is a pre-conscious and also pre-objective one.[10] But all the more in Heidegger does nature, as well as the being-real factor in nature, become existentially relative, in *my* sense, to Dasein—that is, not to consciousness, knowledge, cognition, and the like, but rather to man as a mode of being, indeed to the *solus ipse*—to Heidegger. Let us recall that neither in Heidegger nor in Nicolai Hartmann is there any "existence in general" which would go beyond the specific and particular instances of "existence," and certainly no *intellectus "infinitus,"* no "consciousness in general." Almost with contempt all such things are dismissed [265] as fancy names for the "they" into whom and into whose "idle chatter" man's selfhood is first of all "fallen." Nonetheless, it holds for Heidegger: "When Dasein does not exist, 'independence' 'is' not either, nor 'is' the 'in-itself.' In such a case this sort of thing can be neither understood nor not understood. . . .*In such a case* it cannot be said that entities are, nor can it be said that they are not. But *now,* as long as there is an understanding of being and therefore an understanding of presence-at-hand, it can indeed be said that *in this case* entities will still continue to be" (SZ, 212). But here are we not very close to the borders of solipsism? Certainly not a solipsism of consciousness, but nonetheless we are confronted with the proposition: without "me," there is nothing. Out of instinctive caution, of course, he here uses such phrases as "cannot be *understood*" and "cannot be *said*." But for Heidegger, to every mode of being there belongs, as by essential law, a determined kind of understanding, and understanding itself, in all its modes in the being of Dasein, grounds not only readiness-to-hand but also presence-at-hand—and being real. Of course he also says, "But the fact that reality is ontologically grounded in the being of Dasein does not signify that only when and as long as Dasein exists can the real be as what it is" (SZ, 211f.). But doesn't that contradict the sentences we just cited? Or does he mean to say that the removal of Dasein does not affect that *which* is in itself, but only its being-real? Or that the real, i.e., real things, are not affected, but that the kind of being of being-real is? According to what I teach, the reversal of the first interpretation holds true. Being-real, and therefore the reality of things, are not affected by cancelling the *solus ipse*—nor is the essence of man at all affected—but precisely for this reason: because there is also a supra-singular (but not supra-individual) "Dasein" which by way of vital urge posits in its fortuitous thusness in itself, everything which is "given" to me as resistance in my striving endeavors and which, as supra-singular (but concretely individual) spirit, encloses in an indivisible act within the limits of [its] essence that which I, in and with the supra-singular Dasein, can ideate. But Heidegger doesn't want to travel this road any more than Hartmann does. But is there really any other way than mine if one rejects the critical realism of Hartmann and the impossible "theory of images" (cf. the previous) and if, on the other hand, one wants to avoid the solipsism of Heidegger?

The restriction of being-real to "inner-worldly entities" mixes the true and the false. The true consists in the fact that (1) the being of the *ens a se* is obviously *not* being-real, neither as a bare *ens a se* nor as spirit and vital urge; spirit originally has its essence only as being-in-act [*Akt-Wesensein*], whereas vital urge is a becoming which strives *towards* realization; and that (2) both the person as a spiritual individual act-center and life in man—here Heidegger is right—have no "reality," because to both of them there belongs: (a) being-in-act, which means non-objectifiable being; (b) becoming (all reality, inclusive of [266] something in process of becoming real, is completed being); and (c) non-determinedness by everything which is not itself person and life (in persons this is "freedom," in living beings it is "spontaneity"). But as correct as it is to restrict the categories of being-real to objectifiable being, to being-as-completed (*natura naturata*, history which has happened, life which has become) and to being which is clearly determined from without, it is equally inadmissible that being-real presupposes the disclosure of the world. The world itself is becoming-real from moment to moment, but it is not a presupposition of being-real, which in all its spheres occurs outside the objects created by us in experience (the *ficta*, pure and mixed). The primary givenness of the real modes of "readiness-to-hand" prior to "presence-at-hand" is a good and striking expression, in Heidegger's terminology, of my own view. Readiness-to-hand still remains even when the understanding of things and values disintegrates, when presence-at-hand falls away. Probably the mode of being of implements belongs to the animal and its environment. The real is not necessarily a thing; but it certainly is a resistance-center which presents itself in an image, while as present-at-hand it is a center of effects. Only both together deserve to be called reality. Because the condition of the world is the uniform totality of *one* causal nexus in the widest sense, and because reality and causality and, besides, vital urge and spirit, found reality as becoming-real, there can be, according to me, only *one* world.

But how do these things stand in Heidegger's doctrine? If the being of the world founds being-real (and therefore certainly causality as well) and if existence (that of the *solus ipse*) is called being-in-the-world, then how does Heidegger know at all that he and I are in one world? Certainly for Heidegger too being-with-each-other is no accidental empirical state of affairs. The "we" is ontologically contained in "Dasein." That prevents and excludes singularism, i.e., a relatedness of the world to the individual as an individual being, as we find it in Stirner's *The Ego and His Own*. But is the *solus ipse* any less a *solus ipse* for the fact that in the being of his self he also has the existence of another *solus ipse* with him? Heidegger does not admit a supra-singular "existence" in which the instances of *soli ipsi*, above and beyond their givenness, could *be* in unity as a presupposition of possible agreement—in fact, he rejects this as a form of the "they." But then nothing guarantees even the unity of the world in which they might be able "to be together." To be sure, Dasein is called "being-in-the-world" and is said to be a presupposition for reality and causality. In which world? In one of the many instances of worldhood? In my doctrine too the person is not "in" the world. The person as becoming is the act-center-correlate of a world that in each case is becoming. The person is also not part of the world. Nicolai Hartmann, who seems to recognize only objectifiable being, has sharply criticized me for this in his *Ethics*—without valid reason, as it seems.[11] But whereas I teach that the person-centers [267] are already moved into the sphere of possible understandability by their eternal ground and not first of all by the world, in Heidegger this moment of unification also is lacking. And I don't see how he intends to escape an absolute pluralism of instances of the *solus ipse*, Dasein, in which everyone has his world or is in his world as in his instance of worldhood.[12]

But how is being-real given in Heidegger's thought? I am in agreement with Heidegger on quite a number of negative issues: [Being-real is given] *not* by thinking, drawing conclusions and so forth; not by intuition and perception,

which for him are subsequent differentiations of understanding and of interpretation; also not in such a way that being-an-object would found being-real,
even if being-real must be objectifiable; also not by "synthesizing" these
separate functions as, for example, Oskar Külpe does; and also certainly not
by "*being* conscious of. . . ,*" which is a very derived mode of being; not by
knowledge or cognition, for where these begin to be, reality and its kind
already stand majestically before them; not by receiving affects from a real being, for it is ridiculous that being-real should be explained by reality (as
Husserl has already shown altogether strikingly in his *Ideas*); also not by sensation, for being-real is neither being-red nor being-sour and so forth, and a
pure sensation as "phenomenon" does not exist.[13] The psychological concept of
sensation presupposes reality, indeed, even stimulus, as something given and
as a concept. Here too I am in agreement with Heidegger: Being-real is not at
all given by a perceptual or, in the widest sense, purely intellectual act.
Nonetheless he rejects Dilthey's and my conception. He accepts something in
Dasein — indeed as a character of Dasein — which is neither striving nor
perceiving nor "a feeling of" something, which as an originally given simple
structure is analyzable into such separate acts only in a very mediated way,
but which as a structural totality always governs divisions of that kind, [name-
ly,] "*care*" and the "*dread*" that is bound up with care in a peculiar fashion. That
in which *being*-real (not reality) discloses itself is: care. Heidegger says: "Care,
as a primordial structural totality, lies 'before' every factical 'attitude' and
'situation' of Dasein, and does so existentially *a priori*; this means that it always
lies *in* them. So this phenomenon by no means expresses a priority of the
single 'practical' over the theoretical. When we ascertain something present-at-
hand by merely beholding it, this activity has the character of care just as
much as does 'political action' or taking a rest and enjoying oneself" (SZ, 193).
He says further that willing, wishing, tendency and strivings are grounded only in the structure of care (SZ, 193f.), and again, "in the order of the ways in
which things are connected in their ontological foundations. . . *reality is referred
back to the phenomenon of care*" (SZ, 211).

[*268*] But that inner-worldly readiness-to-hand and presence-at-hand which
care discovers in concern for the pre-given "world" have yet a primordial
disposition [*Urbefindlichkeit*] of "Dasein" behind them. It is *dread*. As primordial
disposition it stands behind care, and its being-correlate is "*being-in-the-world as
such*" (SZ, 186). Dasein's dread before its own "being-in-the-world" — the fact
that it is — its dread before itself, thus leads to "fallenness" into the contents of
the world and into the "they." Indeed: "Being-in-the-world (in the face of
nothing determined) discloses, primordially and directly, the world as world"
(SZ, 187). Care is thus founded on dread and for its part founds every kind of
fear. These very strange theses — less strange if one knows Pascal's *Pensées* and
Kierkegaard's thoughts on these phenomena — cannot be evaluated here in

their entire significance. Here we can only go so far as to ask whether dread and care are in fact emotional comportment-correlates for certain kinds of being, especially for *being-real*.

The dangers which lie in questions like this are clear to see. How are we to distinguish here what is essentially and ontologically meaningful for man "*as such*" from what conditions him only "characterologically"? or from what holds true, for example, only within a given cultural horizon or for a particular historical stage of man's development? or from what finally holds true only for Heidegger and me? To be sure, characterology itself takes on an entirely different ontological weight and different significance if the *solus ipse* and his kind of being become the center of reference for all types of being. I will concede that to Heidegger. But precisely because I do not share this doctrine (cf. the previous), one should not take it amiss if I pose a less banal preliminary question: Are dread and the "care" which has its source in dread actually the basic dispositions and comportment of primitive peoples (for example, the ever happy, carefree inhabitants of the island of Sumatra) or for a child? Isn't dread—for example, the dread which gave birth to the myth of original sin—an historical product which I'd say can be demonstrated very precisely in its particular cases? For my part I am convinced that ever since Judaism and Christianity defined Western man, he has lived under a disproportionately greater burden of dread that any other type of man in the world, and that this weight of dread in great measure conditions his enormous world-activity, his hunger for power and his never-resting thirst for "progress" and technological transformation of the world; and furthermore that this dread has emerged in a very peculiar and strong way in Protestantism. But it is an extremely long road from such things as these to the ontology of man. And furthermore, aren't such things as care and dread situations and relations which are much too material for indicating the *mode* of existence of man—even if one subsequently tries to formalize them as Heidegger very instructively does for "care" when he finally [269] defines it with the purely ontological concepts "*being-ahead-of-itself-already-in-a-world*" (SZ, 192)? Couldn't the being-structure which Heidegger states in these words just as well be an expression of a disposition of hope which anxiously presses forward, although without an object, a disposition of a soaring eros-anticipation of rushing into a world of exultant hope and expectation? Aren't both states of affairs, dread and hope, *isomorphic* in relation to this structure?

Translated by Thomas Sheehan

Das Sein is translated as "being," *das Seiende* as "entity," and *Dasein* as both "existence" and "Dasein." (Tr. note)

1. Scheler is referring to earlier sections of "Idealismus und Realismus." Cf. note 4.
2. Cf. Max Scheler, *Gesammelte Werke*, vol. 5, 87ff.
3. Cf. *Gesammelte Werke*, vol. 7, Part C.
4. Cf. Part Three of "Idealismus und Realismus," *Späte Schriften*, pp. 208-241; English trans. by David R. Lachterman, Max Scheler, *Selected Philosophical Essays*, Evanston: Northwestern U.P., 1973, "Idealism and Realism."
5. *Selected Philosophical Essays*, "Idealism and Realism."
6. *Späte Schriften*, 269-293.
7. *Späte Schriften*, p. 210f; also in *Selected Philosophical Essays*, "Idealism and Realism."
8. For a discussion of Scheler's phenomenological method, cf. *Späte Schriften*, "Nachwort des Herausgebers," p. 357ff.
9. *Späte Schriften*, p. 189.
10. *Späte Schriften*, p. 199 (also in *Selected Philosophical Essays*, "Idealism and Realism") and *Gesammelte Werke*, vol. 2. s.v. "Milieu" in the Sachregister.
11. Cf. *Gesammelte Werke*, vol. 2, Vorwort to 3rd edition and Part II, VI, A, 3c.
12. I am not thinking of a pluralism in Leibniz's sense, but of a vitalistic pluralism of existence, without pre-established harmony. (Scheler's note, p. 267.)
13. *Erkenntnis und Arbeit*, in *Gesammelte Werke*, vol. 8, esp. p. 323.

Heidegger on Transcendence and Intentionality: His Critique of Scheler

Parvis Emad

Even a cursory reading of Heidegger leaves one with the distinct impression that he attaches no significance to the notion of intentionality. While the intentionality of consciousness is central to both Husserl and Scheler, this term is conspicuously absent from Heidegger's major discussions of phenomenology. On what grounds, we may wonder, does Heidegger by-pass intentionality, the topic which was the major preoccupation of phenomenologists in the 'twenties? Due to the lack of textual evidence this question, until recently, would lead to all kinds of speculations. However, in Heidegger's Leibniz-Lectures of 1928, recently published as volume 26 of his *Gesamtausgabe* (edited by K. Held, Klostermann, 1978, hereafter *G.* 26), we find a detailed criticism of intentionality which once and for all renders speculations superfluous as to why he ignores this central theme of phenomenological research. The textual evidence now available makes the conclusion inevitable that intentionality is not a central concept in Heidegger because he denies its *phenomenological* originality. How are we to understand this?

Before addressing this question it should be pointed out that although Heidegger's critique of intentionality has unmistakable bearings on at least the Husserl of *Logical Investigations*, the major thrust of this critique is directed at Scheler. Therefore, to see the full thrust of Heidegger's criticism, it is necessary that we discuss first the subject of this criticism, i.e., Scheler's notion of intentionality. Only then will we be in a position to grasp Heidegger's rejection of intentionality as the primary and original field of phenomenological research.

I. INTENTIONALITY IN SCHELER

Scheler's definition of intentionality is brief and can be understood through a discussion of his notions of "act" and "spirit" (*Geist*). He designates as spirit "all things that possess the nature of act, intentionality and fulfillment of meaning."[1] As the sole representative of the spiritual mode of being (*geistige Seinsweise*), act contains the nucleus of Scheler's notion of intentionality. Therefore, to become familiar with this notion it is necessary that we briefly discuss Scheler's theory of act.

According to Scheler, act is spiritual and therefore stripped of all psycho-biological determinations. The radical separation of the spiritual from the psycho-biological mode of being as captured in the notion of act is deeply rooted in Scheler's philosophy. Indeed this separation is formulated at Scheler's earliest stage of thinking. Reviewing his own philosophical development, Scheler remarked in 1922 that his *Habilitationsschrift* contains a number of basic thoughts which subsequently came to fruition in his philosophical thinking. In particular he mentions the distinction between spirit and soul as offered for the first time in this work.[2] This distinction anticipates his later separation of act and spirit from the psycho-biological mode of being. In this earlier work Scheler emphatically demarcates the spiritual from the psychic sphere of being: "The form of reality of the specific *spiritual life* defies. . .subsumption under the concept of *psychic being*."[3] In the last work that Scheler published he refers to the distinction between spirit and soul or that of the "spiritual sphere of being" and the "psychic sphere of being" as a distinction between "spirit" and "life." Scheler insists on this distinction because any biological, psychological or anthropological determination of life depends upon processes of objectification. These are completely spiritual since

> neither in its knowing, intuiting and thinking capacity, nor in its emotional and volitional one, is spirit or *nous* an outcome or 'sublimation' of life. The modes in which cognition operates can nowhere be traced back to the bio-physical pattern found in processes of the automatic and objectively goal-seeking type.[4]

It is precisely these spiritual processes of objectification which Scheler calls acts and considers intrinsically intentional. Act must be carefully distinguished from psychic functions, because, as the manifestation of spirit, act is non-objectifiable. Whereas, for example, the ego can become an object to an act, "an *act* is never an object. No matter how much knowledge we have of an act, our reflection on its. . .execution. . .contains nothing like an objectification."[5] Strictly speaking, the impossibility of objectification underlies Scheler's entire theory of act. Intentional acts can never become objects and, accordingly, they are not functions; ". . .'functions' have nothing to do with 'acts.'"[6]

Whereas functions such as seeing, hearing, tasting, etc. are psychic, and, as representative of life, they are observable and objectifiable, acts are non-observable, non-psychic and non-objectifiable. "Functions are psychic; acts are non-psychic. Acts are executed; functions happen by themselves."

One may see and listen without explicitly knowing that one sees certain colors or hears certain sounds. It is only the objectifying act which enables one to know the object of one's own seeing and hearing, etc. That is why functions always presuppose the body and a limited environmental world. Moreover, functions are occurrences in the realm of time and can be observed and measured in temporal terms to determine their duration. By contrast, acts are strictly supra-temporal; they exercise their influence *into* time without being *extended* in it. As Scheler states: "Acts spring from the person into time; functions are facts in phenomenal time." Furthermore, functions may become objects to acts, while acts are the very condition for the possibility of objectification in general. Finally, acts are independent from the psycho-biological makeup of their carrier, while functions are not. Scheler makes this point clear when he says that

> laws of acts and their interconnections of foundations are transferable, for example, to beings of quite a different *functional* character. But it is impossible for laws of functions. . .to set limits on laws of acts, which are *a priori* in nature.

If, for example, we take perception and memory as two distinctive kinds of acts, we can see readily how both are transferable. Whether perception or memory is found in man or in an animal does not affect the *essence* of perception or memory in the least. By contrast, laws governing physiological functions differ from species to species, e.g., a great deal of what a dog smells or hears is utterly lost to humans.

Insofar as an act is an act *of* something (the act of seeing, the act of thinking, etc.) and exhibits a close and intimate connection with its object, Scheler stresses the existing essential interconnection between the two. Whatever variation a bearer of an act might undergo, the interconnection as the "phenomenological invariable" remains unchanged. This interconnection is expressed in the highest principle of Scheler's phenomenology. Briefly, this principle states a correlation "between the *nature* of the *act* and the *nature* of the object."[7] Considering, for instance, the act of seeing and its object, the color, we see this correlation clearly; the object of seeing, color, is not correlated, let us say, to the acts of hearing, thinking and so on.

Up to this point we have concentrated on the objectivizing ability of acts. In order to fully account for Scheler's theory of act, we must consider the ideative aspect of act. Although more or less discernible in all acts, this aspect can be studied in the act of ideation. Through the act of ideation the essential modes and formal structures of the world are grasped. This act can be executed when reality is tentatively suspended. Since spirit is essentially capable of suspending reality, one is able to intuit the *essence* of pain regardless of its contingent and changeable location in one's body. The act of ideation is indeed so penetrating that one does not need to experience all kinds of pain to know its essence. An experience of a single kind of pain, when subjected to the act of ideation, would reveal the essence of pain as such.

It would be profitable to conclude our exposition of Scheler's theory of act with a review of its major points. The notion of act in Scheler builds the nucleus of his theory of intentionality; acts are without exception acts *of* something. In contrast to functions they are non-objectifiable, unobservable and supra-temporal. Finally, they are capable of revealing the essential structures of the world, as we tried to show by using the example of pain. But more important than all these features is the consideration of the essential interconnection which exists between acts and their objects. It is this interconnection which makes possible the applicability of acts to various objects and contains in essence Scheler's view on transcendence. To see that Scheler's conception of transcendence is inseparable from his notion of intentionality we must take a close look at the application of act to various objects.

As unobjectifiable and supra-temporal, act signifies a certain 'distance' between itself and its objective correlate. As far as this 'distance' is concerned it matters little whether the objective correlate of an act is a concept (correlated to the act of thinking) or a color (correlated to the act of perception). What matters is the movement of transcendence from the person, an act-executing center, towards its objective correlates. This movement is what Scheler understands by "consciousness of something," which he explicitly identifies with his concept of person. For, as he says:

> one who uses the term *consciousness* to designate all "consciousness of something"...[and] who understands by "consciousness of something"...all intentionally directed acts filled with meaning...may also call the person the concrete "consciousness-of."[8]

The manner in which Scheler interprets "consciousness-of" as the person, becomes clear when he emphasizes the intentional nature of the person: "It *belongs to the essence of the person* to exist and to live solely in the *execution of intentional acts.*"[9]

As the executor of acts, however, the person is correlated to objects which are given to its acts. These objects are neither singularly nor totally identical with the person. The person keeps a certain 'distance' from these objects, because, as the person, it is *the* agent which relates to the objects through the intentional nature of act. Were it not due to the intentionality inherent in act, the person would not be in a position to relate to itself (act of self-perception), to time (acts of expectation, recollection and perception), and to the holy (the act of prayer). Therefore, it is justifiable to maintain that the correlates of the acts executed by the person are "transcendent" to these acts. This means that for the person to experience its being as the concrete unity of the execution of acts, a transcendence towards objects is necessitated by acts. Insofar as acts are intentional for Scheler, intentionality is identified with the process of going beyond and stepping over, i.e., transcendence. Scheler indeed identifies intentionality with transcendence by stating that intentionality "signifies a goal-directed movement toward something which one does not have oneself or has only partially and incompletely."[10] To be sure, one may perceive a movement of going over from the act towards its object. This movement is readily discernible in the manifold ways described by Scheler in which acts are correlated to their objects. Aging, time, and death, for example, would not have been objects of our consciousness had they not been objective correlates of the acts of immediate perception, immediate recollection, and immediate expectation. It becomes clear that Scheler basically conceives transcendence as a movement from act toward its objective correlate and thus identifies intentionality with transcendence.

It is precisely the identification of intentionality with transcendence which calls for Heidegger's most vehement protest. As he states:

> Transcendence . . . must never be identified and equated with intentionality; if this happens, as it has happened frequently, it shows only that one is still too far off from an understanding of this phenomenon (G. 26, p. 215).

Indeed it is Heidegger's contention that the movement from the act to its objective correlate is *not* the genuine movement of transcendence. For, the most profound sense of transcendence is not captured as a movement *from* an act-executing center *to* an object. Since Scheler's conception of intentionality only reflects a movement from an act-center towards an object, in Heidegger's words: "Scheler failed to grasp what transcendence actually means" (G. 26, p. 215). To see clearly why Heidegger insists that intentionality should not be identified with transcendence we must take up his detailed criticism of intentionality in Scheler.

II. HEIDEGGER'S CRITIQUE

Heidegger criticizes Scheler's conception of phenomenology two years before the appearance of, and also following the publication, of *Being and Time* (Harper & Row, 1962, hereafter *B & T*). This should be remembered because his criticism of Scheler gains precision and intensity after the appearence of his major work. Therefore, to fully account for Heidegger's critique of intentionality we should separately consider the two phases in which he takes issue with Scheler.

Two years before the publication of *B & T*, Heidegger offered a lecture course entitled "The History of the Concept of Time" in which he devoted some space to Scheler, whom he considered to be, next to Husserl, one of the leading phenomenologists of the time.[11] In this lecture course Heidegger expresses the opinion that Scheler interprets intentionality not in an original way, but in terms of the notion of person which he develops under the influence of Augustine, Calvin, Zwingli and Pascal. This prevents him from venturing a radical inquiry into the being of *intentio* and *intentum*.

It is perhaps of historical interest to note that here Heidegger is well aware of the difference between the Husserlian and Schelerian versions of phenomenology. He points out explicitly that Scheler's way of determining inner experience, act, and ego, has nothing to do with the *theoretico-rational* orientation of Husserl. However, in spite of Scheler's awareness of the inadequacy of a mere theoretico-rational orientation, he fails to gain access to a field which makes possible ways of intentionally bearing ourselves towards beings.

With the appearance of *B & T*, Heidegger's critique of intentionality gains precision as he tries to unfold a phenomenon which is more original than intentionality and unjustifiably has been identified with it. This phenomenon is nothing other than transcendence. The full import of Heidegger's rejection of the originality of intentionality is evidenced in his demarcation of the genuine field of phenomenological research in terms of transcendence. Heidegger's conception of transcendence is presented in section 69 of *B & T*, and in *Vom Wesen des Grundes*, but more extensively in volume 26 of the *Gesamtausgabe*. In order to delineate his views on transcendence we must consider Heidegger's explicit assertions on transcendence in *G.*, 26 and section 69 of *B & T*. Doing so we shall see that Heidegger defines transcendence as grounded in temporality.

There is an intimate relation between transcendence and temporality that is obscured in the English translation of *Sein und Zeit (SZ)*. In clarifying this obscurity, one can refer to a footnote of section 69 of *SZ* where Heidegger states:

> That the intentionality of 'consciousness' is *grounded* in the ecstatical temporality of Dasein and how this is the case, will be shown in the following section (*SZ*, p. 363).

In the Macquarrie and Robinson translation, this footnote reads as follows:

> That the intentionality of 'consciousness' is *grounded* in the ecstatical unity of Dasein, and how this is the case, will be shown in the following Division (*B & T*, p. 498).

To complicate the matter further the translators amended this footnote by stating that "This Division has never been published" (*B & T*, p. 498). This translation is misleading in two regards. First, the expression *ekstatische Zeitlichkeit* (i.e., ecstatical temporality) is rendered "ecstatical unity," which is incorrect and obscures Heidegger's purpose in indicating in advance a relationship between intentionality and the temporality of Dasein. Second, by taking the German term *Abschnitt* to mean "division," and by strengthening this meaning in their parenthetical explanation (according to which this division has never been published), they mislead the reader into assuming that a certain division of the unpublished Part Two of *B & T* was supposed to clarify how intentionality is grounded in the "ecstatical unity" of Dasein. In order to shed light on this mass confusion let us proceed in the following way.

It should be pointed out first that the German term *Abschnitt* used in this highly significant footnote not only means "division," but also designates a "section," a "chapter" and sometimes even a "paragraph." This is important because the term *Abschnitt* in this footnote refers directly to the following *section* 69c entitled, "The temporal problem of the transcendence of the world." The original goal of the footnote is lost in the *B & T* translation. Its purpose was to prepare the reader for understanding that intentionality is grounded in the transcendence of Dasein. Perhaps as significant, if not more so, the reader is mislead into believing that Heidegger's interpretation of intentionality is to be treated in the unpublished Part Two of the work.

A careful reading of section 69c in itself should be enough to arouse suspicion concerning the validity of the thesis that the treatment of intentionality, as grounded in temporality, is postponed to a certain division of the unpublished Part Two of *B & T*. This suspicion quickly turns into conviction when we consider the discussion in *G.* 26. There in section 11, entitled "The Transcendence of Dasein," Heidegger states that the entire analysis of Dasein has one goal, namely, to work out the temporality, i.e. the basis "upon which transcendence itself should be understood. Throughout the entirety of the investigation [carried out in *B & T*] transcendence must be considered as central to the basic state [of Dasein]" (*G.* 26, p. 214). There Heidegger emphasizes the intrinsic relationship of temporality to transcendence by characterizing the analyses leading to the temporality of Dasein as

> serving the purpose of progressively working out the notion of transcendence so that a point will be reached where, in section 69, transcendence once again and explicitly will be posed as a problem. For this reason section 69 in its entirety carries the title, "The temporality of Being-in-the-world and the problem of transcendence of the world"(*G.* 26, p. 215).

It is precisely here that the reader is again reminded of the significant footnote on p. 363 of *SZ* as directly pointing to the following section 69c, "The temporal problem of the transcendence of the world." Heidegger's claim is quite clear: in section 69c the problem of intentionality is shown to be grounded in Dasein's transcendence, i.e. its temporality. In order to show this clearly we must demonstrate that a) transcendence is made possible by temporality, and b) that intentionality is grounded in transcendence.

In contrast to section 69c, where the phenomenological analysis does not begin with an explanation of the term transcendence, volume 26 begins with a thoroughgoing analysis of this term. Here Heidegger poses the following question: "What does the general expression transcendence mean both as a concept and as a technical philosophic term?" (*G.* 26, p. 203). He begins by considering the concept transcendence (*transcendere*) as meaning to go over and to step beyond (*übersteigen*). This implies, in his words:

> 1. an activity in the broadest sense, an action; 2. formally a relation, namely, stepping over towards something, indeed from something towards something else; 3. something which is being transcended, a limit, a barrier, a gap, something which lies in between (*G.* 26, p. 204).

Subsequently he analyzes the philosophic employment of the term transcendence by stating that traditionally this term indicates:

> 1. what is transcendent as distinguished from what is *immanent*; 2. what is transcendent as differentiated from what is *contingent* (*G.* 26, p. 204).

As opposed to what is immanent, that which is considered to be transcendent implies the idea of something which is extraneous to consciousness, and consciousness is regarded as that which remains within itself. Expressions such as soul, subject and consciousness, etc. are often taken to imply a sphere inhering in itself, i.e., the mind. The idea of an inner realm subsisting within itself in turn gives rise to the idea of something which lies *outside* of this realm, i.e., existing in a realm extraneous to consciousness. Heidegger calls this philosophic employment of the term transcendence *epistemological* and states:

> Whenever explicitly or implicitly the problem of transcendence is posed as opposed to an immanent sphere, a conception of Dasein. . .is advanced as that of a capsule. For without such an incapsulated being it is absurd to pose the problem of going over a barrier and a limit (*G.* 26, p. 205).

From the epistemological employment of the term transcendence Heidegger distinguishes its *theological* one. This employment is closely tied up with the idea of contingency. We consider as contingent whatever directly concerns us, ultimately things as they may or may not be. Contingent things are those which are, in one way or another, conditioned. By contrast, that which transcends the realm of contingency "is not conditioned, and is actually beyond our reach" (*G.* 26, p. 206). In this sense, "transcendence means stepping over towards that which lies beyond conditioned entities" (*G.* 26, p. 206), i.e. towards the divine being.

In view of both its epistemological and theological employments, Heidegger maintains that neither does justice to the phenomenon of transcendence. Seen adequately, transcendence does not indicate a relation between an inner and an outer sphere, nor does the term imply a movement towards an entity which subsists beyond the realm of contingency and is therefore incomprehensible to our finite ways of knowing. Thus he asks: how does one do justice to the notion of transcendence as a phenomenon?

To answer this question it should first be pointed out that Heidegger does not deprive the term transcendence of the movement which is basic to it. Indeed he concentrates on this movement and intensifies it when he states:

> Dasein itself is the process of going beyond. This means, transcendence is not one of many ways of bearing oneself toward other entities. Rather, transcendence indicates the basic state of Dasein, a state which enables Dasein to bear itself toward entities (*G. 26*, p. 211).

By focusing on and intensifying the movement which the term transcendence implies, Heidegger invites us to pose the question as to how this movement should be conceived. To answer this question, it is necessary that we take up the problem of temporality. In Heidegger's words: "With respect to the basic phenomenon [of transcendence] it is necessary that we turn to temporality" (*G. 26*, p. 254). In volume 26 Heidegger approaches temporality in a different way than he did in *B & T*, presumably because here he is concerned with merely showing the implications which temporality has for the issue of intentionality. He defines temporality as "the unified unity of the original temporalization of awaiting, retaining and rendering present" (*G. 26*, p. 264). To understand this definition we must become familiar with the threefold distinctions: "awaiting," "retaining" and "rendering present" in their essential unity.

Volume 26 takes up the problem of temporality in terms of our reckoning with time and its measurement. Ordinarily time is understood as something which hastens away, resides in the subject (or consciousness), pertains to our sensibility and is radically different from eternity. The ways in which time is ordinarily conceived, Heidegger points out, "are not arbitrarily invented. The nature of time must be such as to call for these conceptions" (*G. 26*, p. 255).

How do we distinguish the ordinary from the original conception of time? Understood originally, time does not hasten away, does not reside in the subject and is not determined by appealing to eternity. None of these characterizations does justice to time as an original phenomenon. For, to hasten away, to reside in the subject and to be different than eternity, time must exist as the active agent which shows its activities in the described ways. However, as Heidegger states: "Time does not exist, it merely temporalizes itself" (*G. 26*, p. 264). He discusses the temporalization of time by setting out from the familiar activity of measuring time. With regard to this activity, he says:

> We do not measure time out of sheer curiosity to determine "what time it is."
> Rather we measure time because we have to reckon with it. To reckon with
> time means...that we have to use time properly, i.e., we are keen not to
> loose time (*G. 26*, p. 257).

When I measure time I am not motivated by merely knowing what time it is.
On the contrary, I am profoundly motivated by the desire to know, in Heidegger's words, "how much time do I still have?" (*G. 26*, p. 260). The unmistakable interest I take in how much time is still left to me is indicative of my
being concerned with what comes "afterwards." According to Heidegger we
make use of the expression "afterwards" only "when we *await* something that
comes towards us and requires to be settled" (*G. 26*, p. 260). Reckoning with
time and measuring it then refers us to the phenomenon of awaiting.

In awaiting we are not explicitly aware of something which approaches us
"after" such and such has been taken care of. Awaiting, as a way of our being,
primarily lacks an objective point of reference. Awaiting is not like sense
perception which is directed to a material thing. Seeing, e.g., is directed to
color, but awaiting merely to the indefinite, unspecified "afterwards." The
outstanding feature of awaiting is readily observable in the fact that awaiting is
void of any reflection upon and awareness of events. What is expected to come
"afterwards" could be anything: a desirable event, an unpleasant task or a bor-
ing situation. It is important that awaiting, as a mode of our existence, is not
identical with, and is not exhausted in, our evaluation of events according to
their desirability, undesirability, etc. For this reason Heidegger points out that
"awaiting as such and *out of itself* gives rise to an 'afterwards'" (*G. 26*, p. 260).
This "afterwards" is essentially unspecified and undetermined. The fact that,
following what I am doing right now, I may "close the book" and "go to see a
movie," etc., is not already sketched out in awaiting. Without awaiting, as
constitutive of my being, "closing the book now" and "going to see a movie
afterwards" would have required my prior access to a sequence of "nows," one
of which I would choose for "closing the book" and another for "going to see a
movie." Such a sequence of "nows" does not exist because, if it existed, I would
have been a being outside of and independent of this sequence. Were this the
case, measuring time, i.e., reckoning with it just to see "how much time is still
left to me," would have been an unnecessary undertaking. However, the
phenomenological analysis attests to the contrary, for no sooner do we say
"now" than "we are thrust away from what takes place in a now. The function
of repelling-beyond-itself (*Fortweisungsfunktion*) pertains essentially to a now"
(*G. 26*, p. 259).

Considering our presentation of the phenomenon of awaiting, we must take
note of two things. First, awaiting is the primary mode of the temporalization
of time. Second, the relation between awaiting and specific events which take
place "afterwards" shows a movement of going beyond, i.e, transcendence. In

and through awaiting, we transcend the empirically specifiable events. Already in our discussion of awaiting we see the affinity of transcendence and temporality.

When we reckon with time to see how much time is still left to us we come to awaiting as the indicator of the direction of our existence towards the future. However, awaiting is not identical with an infinite and indefinite future. Instead of conceiving the future as infinite, Heidegger articulates its limitation by pointing out that it arises out of a retaining, which is prior to a recollecting of events that took place (or could have taken place) on former occasions. Retaining, as another way of our being, is not identical with our ability to recall former events. On the contrary, retaining enables us to have a past and to recall bygone events. In this sense, retaining is not the sum total of all the past events of my life. In retaining, my past existence is not pulled behind myself as a burden. Rather than this, in retaining I retain a "future" (my future) as what has existed all along. "Retaining" is distinguished from recollecting the past through the use of the expression "*Gewesenheit*," i.e., "having been." This term refers to the movement of existence towards a future which we have already been. This movement is equally suggested by the term "awaiting" which, as he puts it, stretches itself "on the entirety of my having-been;. . .having-been temporalizes itself only out of and from a future" (*G.* 26, p. 266). Retaining is (as the way in which I have existed all along, like awaiting) void of any kind of awareness of and reflection upon events. However, to designate certain events as past is only possible on the basis of the retention of our having existed all along. Strictly speaking, it does not matter at all ". . .how far and how exactly we recall what existed on a former occasion. . ." (*G.* 26, p. 261). It may well have been the case that "we have forgotten. . ." (*G.* 26, p. 261) what happened in the past. Forgetting and remembering are both made possible on the basis of our "having been," i.e., on the basis of a future which has been "retained." When certain events are brought into light out of forgottenness and identified as past, when we remember things bygone, we do so by reflecting upon the retention of a future which "has been." Here again we see how retaining involves transcendence. An event which no longer exists is designated as a past event and is transcended (gone beyond) within the dimension of the retaining of the future.

When we reckon with, and thus determine how much time is still available to us, we are ahead of ourselves in accordance with what we have already been. This is the result of the hitherto presented discussion of "awaiting" and "retaining." The former is referred to in the ordinary conception of time as the future and the latter as the past. That dimension of time which is ordinarily referred to as present is not ignored by Heidegger in his attempt to work out the original conception of time. To see this we must recall his definition of temporality as a "unified phenomenon of an awaiting which renders present by having been." Any genuine "now" is not an isolated and indifferent instance of time, identical with any other. Rather, the "now" springs from a future (awaiting) as it has already been retained. In Heidegger's words: " 'Now' expresses our existence towards that which is present. . . . We call this mode of our existence. . .*rendering present*" (*G.* 26, p. 261). Considering this modality of time, we must note two significant points. First, the deep-rooted tendency to level off the present (taken as the current moment in a sequence of undifferentiated and identical nows) is made conceivable by the dimension of rendering present. Second, now-events may be transcended towards the genuine present only on the basis of this dimension.

To achieve our goal, namely to show that temporality makes transcendence possible, we need to recall the movement which takes place between awaiting and a future event, between retaining and past events, and finally between rendering present and "now." This movement precisely expresses the profound sense which Heidegger gives to the term transcendence. Having taken a radical stand on the meaning of transcendence, we may now turn our attention to the relationship of intentionality and transcendence.

A close reading of section 69c of *B & T* is readily conducive to an understanding of transcendence. The gist of the discussion of transcendence is here captured in two statements made by Heidegger about Dasein, world and temporalization. The first statement readily relates Dasein to world: "In so far as Dasein temporalizes itself, a world *is* too" (*B & T*, p. 417). The second statement characterizes world more specifically by setting it apart from entities other than Dasein: "The world is neither present-at-hand nor ready-to-hand, but temporalizes itself in temporality" (*B & T*, p. 417). The first statement makes the temporalization of Dasein responsible for there being a world. In the second statement the thesis is advanced that world is inaccessible, unlike existing entities (in the terminology of *B & T*, world is neither present-at-hand nor ready-to-hand). Stated briefly, the second statement merely points out that the world does not exist as entities do, but temporalizes itself in temporality.

Interestingly enough Heidegger makes quite a similar statement about time when he says, "Time does not exist, it merely temporalizes itself" (*G.* 26, p. 264). When we take these together in their interconnection, one thing stands out quite clearly: Time, Dasein and world do not exist as entities do, they merely temporalize themselves as temporality. Knowing this, do we gain a positive insight into the Dasein-world "relationship"? I believe we do if we take up again the basic statement which Heidegger makes about temporality, at the same time as we reconsider his explicit assertion about transcendence.

Let us begin with the latter. Heidegger offers a brief definition of transcendence by saying: "Dasein transcends beings, but the jump-across, which Dasein carries out, is made towards world" (*G.* 26, p. 233). The question is: how are we to conceive the world, as the *terminus ad quem* of transcendence, without reducing it to an object and thereby depriving it of its phenomenological status? The answer, it seems, is to be sought in Heidegger's basic formulation of temporality. As mentioned above, temporality is "the unified unity of the original temporalization of awaiting, retaining and rendering present." It is one thing to offer a formulation of temporality in terms of "awaiting," "retaining" and "rendering present"; it is quite another thing to draw attention to *how* this "awaiting," "retaining" and "rendering present" is concretely experiencible. The notion of the world captures the *how* of "awaiting," "retaining" and "rendering present" insofar as their experience varies from individual to individual and situation to situation. In short, world indicates a *how* which in the actual experience of temporality has a priority over Dasein. Heidegger articulates this priority when he says: "*The world is already presupposed. . .*and must already have been disclosed so that in terms of it entities. . .can be encountered" (*B & T*, p. 417). This means that the actual mode of the experience of "awaiting," "retaining" and "rendering present" is decisive for *how* entities are encountered and as *what* they are encountered. Since neither temporality nor the encounter with entities are selfsame, repetitive, and pre-established modes of experience, but are literally unpredictable and inaccessible to calculation, Heidegger can say that "the fact that entities are discovered along with Dasein's own. . .existence, is not left to Dasein's discretion" (*B & T*, p. 417).

Concluding our discussion of transcendence, we should take note of the fact that although Heidegger rejects the traditional views of transcendence, he retains and intensifies the movement which this expression indicates. Heidegger radicalizes this movement by designating Dasein as its *terminus a quo* and world as its *terminus ad quem*. By radicalizing the movement of transcendence Heidegger perceives a deeper sense in it than is captured by the notion of intentionality. To be sure, intentional manners of behavior such as hoping, fearing and expecting are indicative of our being conscious of what we hope for, are afraid of, or expect. However, these modes of intentionality "would have been impossible. . .[and] without an open direction, if Dasein which hopes, fears and expects" were prevented from "stretching itself out. . .in something like an afterwards" (*G.* 26, p. 265). The fact that in hoping, and in similar intentional modes, we are consciously directed "towards" something not yet in our possession is indicative of "what we called awaiting, which is nothing other than. . .our being *carried away* into something like an afterwards" (*G.* 26, p. 265). To be carried away into the future makes possible a consciousness of something which we do not yet have. Thus intentionality as such a consciousness is subsequent to, and does not precede, our inescapable lot to be ahead of ourselves. Since being ahead of ourselves implies "awaiting," and this is inseparably bound up with "retaining" and "rendering present," intentionality is subsequent to and does not precede our temporality. If intentionality is subsequent to temporality and the latter involves transcendence, then it is clear that intentionality is not identical with transcendence. No matter how goal-directed our consciousness may be, it is temporality and thus transcendence, and *not* intentionality, which ultimately makes intelligible our consciousness *of* something. Since Heidegger perceives a deeper sense of movement in transcendence, he inevitably disputes the originality ascribed to intentionality.

III. Conclusion

Scheler conceives intentionality as identical with transcendence. This identification is not arbitrary but is the inevitable consequence of Scheler's commitment to the idea of spirit as a supra-temporal entity. That Scheler saw no temporal implications in the problem of transcendence is no wonder; to him time is something we arrive at via execution of supra-temporal acts. This means that, like the tradition criticized by Heidegger, Scheler is unaware of the subtle, hidden and elusive role of time.

It is precisely on this account that Heidegger rejects the identification of intentionality with transcendence. The former is not supra-temporal but implicates time. Indeed without the temporalization of time no intentionality would have been possible. Thus, in the light of Heidegger's analysis of temporality, the intentionality of consciousness loses its primacy and is absent from his major discussions of phenomenology.

Notes

Parvis Emad is Professor of Philosophy at DePaul University, Chicago. The present essay draws on material from his forthcoming book, *The Question of Value: Heidegger and Scheler*.

1. M. Scheler, *Formalism in Ethics and Non-formal Ethics of Value* (hereafter *Formalism*), trans. by M.S. Frings & R. Funk, 1973, p. 389.
2. Cf. Max Scheler, *Frühe Schriften*, Bern 1971, p. 203.
3. *Ibid.*, p. 320.
4. Max Scheler, *The Nature of Sympathy*, trans. by P. Heath, 1954, p. 74.
5. *Formalism*, p. 387.
6. *Ibid.*, p. 388, for this and the following three quotations.
7. *Ibid.*, p. 78.
8. *Ibid.*, p. 392.
9. *Ibid.*, p. 390. Italics are Scheler's.
10. Max Scheler, *Selected Philosophical Essays*, trans. by D. R. Lachterman, 1973, p. 296.
11. I am grateful to Professor Walter Biemel and to Dr. Petra Jaeger for allowing me to read the text of "The History of the Concept of Time," upon which the following remarks are based.

In Memory of Max Scheler
(1928)

Martin Heidegger

Max Scheler is dead: amidst great work of wide-ranging importance, at the point of beginning anew to forge ahead into the ultimate and the whole, at the start of new teaching duties from which he expected so much.

Quite apart from the extent and variety of his productivity, Max Scheler was the strongest philosophical power in contemporary Germany, nay, in contemporary Europe — in fact, in all of present-day philosophy.

Crucial for and characteristic of his Being were: the totality of questioning; an unusual sense for all newly emerging possibilities and energies as he stood amidst the whole of what is; an unrestrainable impulse to think and interpret always in [terms of] the whole.

We recognize what only a few, to be sure, were privileged to experience with him directly in day-long, night-long discussions and struggles: a veritable state of being possessed by philosophy, something over which he was not master but yet had to follow, something which, in the raggedness of today's existence, often drove him to exhaustion and despair. But being thus possessed was his substance. Through all the changes, in ever new beginnings and struggles, he remained faithful to the inner direction of his Being.

This fidelity must have been the source of the childlike kindness he sometimes revealed. There is no one seriously engaged in philosophy today who is not indebted to him in an essential way, no one who could replace the living possibility of philosophy which disappeared with him. But this irreplaceability is the sign of his greatness.

The greatness of such an existence can be measured only with the means which it itself must provide. The greatness of this philosophical existence lay in his relentless [courage to] face things head-on — to face that which time continues to roll obscurely towards us,[1] to face that which cannot be reckoned into what has come down to us, to face mankind, which will not let itself be appeased and smoothed over into a shallow humanism which praises the past.

What Dilthey and Max Weber, each in his own way, faced up to was, in an original way and with the strongest philosophical energy, powerfully alive in Scheler.

Max Scheler is dead. We bow before his fate. Once again a path of philosophy falls back into darkness.

Translated by Thomas Sheehan

Notes

Heidegger spoke the above eulogy for Max Scheler at the beginning of his lecture on May 21, 1928, at Philipps University, Marburg. Almost fifty years later he sent Professor Manfred Frings a copy of his handwritten notes of the eulogy, which were then published in *Max Scheler im Gegenwartsgeschehen der Philosophie*, ed. Paul Good, Bern and Munich: Francke, 1975, pp. 9-10. An expanded version of the text has since been published in Martin Heidegger, *Metaphysische Anfangsgründe der Logik im Ausgang von Leibniz*, ed. Klaus Held, *Gesamtausgabe*, II, 26, Frankfurt: Klostermann, 1978, pp. 62-64, but the translation here is made from the transcription of the handwritten notes.

1. "was die Zeit erst dunkel noch heranwältz."

IV. OVERCOMING METAPHYSICS

Heidegger and Metaphysics

Walter Biemel

In speaking about a thinker we always run the risk of substituting a simplification for the rich variety of his thought, of replacing the exciting efforts of his thinking and the uncertainty of his path with some tedious review of issues which seem to have been so easily mastered. What was in flux becomes rigidified, and issues that fired the imagination and swept one up with enthusiasm seem from a distance tame and innocuous. When we talk about them, the changes, indeed the revolutions, that his thought effected appear to have come to rest and in the long run to be rendered dull and harmless.

But I have not yet mentioned the greatest danger in speaking about a thinker, viz., that we will translate his language back into a language familiar to us in order to make it understandable. But what we really do is mutilate what is proper to the thinker, because he is present and functions and lives in *his* language. His language is his thought, and if we give up his language, we give up his thought. Yet we may think we can express what he said better and more clearly and make it more accessible, so we insinuate that he intentionally expressed himself in a difficult way in order to stand out and make some kind of impression. This reproach is as old as thought itself. It was lodged against Heraclitus, who was called the "Obscure," and today it is made against Heidegger. But to talk that way is not to know what one is saying. To try to understand Heidegger by giving up or avoiding his language is like trying to swim without water. The task of speaking about a thinker cannot mean some attempt to replace his language, for that is absurd, but rather to lead oneself toward his language. It should not be a speaking *about* but a speaking *to*.

If we keep in mind all the difficulties that weigh down our attempts to speak about a thinker, what can we do at all? I will select one question and through it explain why Heidegger is the thinker who has initiated, in the first half of this century, a revolution the consequences of which we can hardly visualize even today.

Just as the nineteenth century stood under the sign of Hegel (and of course this does not mean that other important philosophers had no influence), so we may say that the twentieth century stands under the sign of Heidegger's works, without in any way meaning to deprecate the significance that belongs to phenomenology and Husserl or to a philosopher of the rank of Wittgenstein. No one can avoid confronting Heidegger, whether positively or negatively, whether the emphasis be put on *Being and Time* (1927) or on the later works with the "turn" that is connected with them. (By this phrase "the turn" we mean that Heidegger devoted himself more radically and exclusively to his basic question about "Being" in such a way that those trained in traditional philosophy and thought find it quite strange and difficult to accept.) His influence has spread to all European countries where philosophy is done, and it is especially evident in France where the so-called existentialist movement (let me mention only Sartre and Merleau-Ponty) arose out of *Being and Time*. Early on, Heidegger's influence was already felt in Japan, and in recent years translations of his work have appeared in Yugoslavia and Czechoslovakia. In the United States Heidegger stands in the center of philosophical discussion in a very significant way, and for a long time the philosophical interest of Latin America has been bound up with him. This is not the place to show how Heidegger's thinking has had influence on the most diverse sciences, from psychiatry, medicine and psychology to philology, art, history, and theology. Rather, what will let us see the uniqueness of his thought is the question: What is Heidegger's position on metaphysics? And linked with this first question there is a second: What does Heidegger mean by saying that, in the future, thinking will no longer be philosophy?

Heidegger's epoch-making work *Being and Time* appeared in 1927 in Husserl's *Jahrbuch für Philosophie und phänomenologische Forschung*, and it was dedicated to Husserl. At first it might have seemed that another important work was being published under the aegis and in support of the new movement started by Husserl. Husserl himself set about reading this work in hopes of finding in it an extension of his own doctrine to the area of history, which he himself had neglected. The marginal notes he made in his own copy, now preserved in the Husserl Archives in Louvain, show the consternation this book caused him. He did not find what he was looking for. What had happened? A new way of questioning, searching, and investigation came to light. The phenomenological reduction was not mentioned, the transcendental ego, the final ground of the phenomenological search, was nowhere to be found, and the word "phenomenology" took on an interpretation that was tied into Aristotle more than Husserl. At the very center stood the question which, in this form, had remained foreign to Husserl: the question about the meaning of Being.

Already in secondary school Heidegger had come upon this question when he was given Brentano's work *On the Several Senses of Being in Aristotle.*[1] But at that time no one, not even the man who gave him the book (he later became Archbishop Gröber of Freiburg) could imagine how this question would lead to an upheaval in twentieth century philosophy. What happened here was not simply the influence of a certain book on a philosopher, but an encounter with a question that has no equal in its radicalness. That does not mean that Heidegger threw overboard all philosophy heretofore and began to do philosophy from the ground up, that he saw his philosophizing as an absolute beginning. That is what Husserl did, and that is why he ended up with what is fundamentally a very narrow knowledge of the history of philosophy. Husserl wanted to establish philosophy anew, and that is why the Cartesian doubt was for him the model, but one which had not yet been carried through radically enough.

For Heidegger it was entirely different. (We shall return presently to his position on Descartes.) He did not jettison the tradition like excess ballast but rooted himself in the tradition and conceived of it as what had to be mastered. Someone who has not read Heidegger can hardly imagine how thorough is his knowledge of the history of metaphysics, and only when the unpublished lectures come out (I am thinking especially of his lectures on Aristotle and on Schelling)[2] will it be possible to form an approximate idea of how much Heidegger has stood in constant dialogue with the tradition. But even the works already published on Plato, Aristotle, Leibniz, Kant, Hegel, and Nietzsche and his interpretations of the early Greek thinkers show how his thought spans the arch from the beginning of Western thinking up to the fulfillment of metaphysics. I do not mean to say that Heidegger has simply accumulated a vast quantity of knowledge such as we might expect from an historian of philosophy. No, Heidegger is not concerned with a history of philosophy. What he has attempted is unique in its kind: a new understanding of metaphysics in its totality.

Heretofore the history of metaphysics had been seen as a succession of different theories and systems where each new system or doctrine hoped to render the previous ones superfluous, and where in the long run the decisive factor in this history seemed to be accident or caprice. But Heidegger has sketched out a new plan with a new clue, a new horizon of understanding which suddenly reveals the inner sense of this history and transforms it from a chaos of mutually contradictory opinions and views into a coherent self-unfolding. What made it possible for Heidegger to offer this new interpretation of the whole of metaphysics from Plato to Nietzsche was the understanding which opened up to him along with the question about Being. The passage from Plato's *Sophist* with which *Being and Time* begins shows what the book is about: "It is obvious that you have long known what you really mean when you use the expression 'being' [*seiend*]. But whereas we once thought we understood it, we now find ourselves in difficulty" (*Sophist*, 244a). This difficulty did not pertain only to Plato. It is just as distressing in the present age, even though we may not care to admit it. Heidegger takes it seriously as the fundamental difficulty of all metaphysical thinkers—that is, in each of the great projects of philosophy he sees an answer to the question, What does 'being' (*seiend*) mean? Metaphysics then becomes the arena in which, up to our own time, we have played out possibilities for answering this question.

In this way the unifying horizon of metaphysics is staked out. But Heidegger's project does not stop there. The next task is to show whether the series of answers is haphazard or forms a meaningful whole. To anticipate his general solution we may say: the several answers to the question of the meaning of 'being' form the horizon for a possible history made up of corresponding epochs. This history is not a matter of some obscure theories but rather of a fundamental sustaining insight which defines the structure of an historical epoch. To avoid the danger of hazy generality into which such assertions can dissolve, let us discuss the modern period as a concrete example of what all this means.

What happened in the modern era was shaped by the change in the meaning of beings as contrasted with the medieval understanding of beings as created. The immediate expression of this change was the new conception of the essence of truth. In Husserl's and Heidegger's explanations of Descartes we can see clearly the difference between respectively the phenomenological interpretation and the interpretation in terms of the history of Being. For Husserl Descartes was the exemplar, the forerunner, the liberator, because he dared to question everything and to put his methodical doubt at the center of his philosophizing. But in Heidegger's contrasting interpretation we see that with Descartes man comes on the scene with the claim of becoming sure and certain of his Being amidst the totality of beings. The holy no longer lies in the beyond, but "in man's free self-unfolding of all his creative powers."[3] The reason why method acquires such significance is that it is grasped "as the way to determining the essence of truth, which is grounded exclusively by the powers of man."[4] The basic question now becomes: "By what means can man, of and for himself, attain a first and unshakable truth, and what is this truth?"[5]

At the same time the question about beings is tied up with the question about truth. Man himself becomes the real *subjectum*, the "that-which-underlies," for he alone is capable of reaching a guaranteed truth, i.e., he alone can provide the guarantee for truth. This change in the meaning of truth, whereby truth no long has anything to do with the Greek *aletheia*, unconcealment, nor with revealed truth, but simply is truth-become-certitude—this change is in turn the presupposition for the exact sciences' investigation into the given. Only at this moment can there be exact natural sciences because, with this new conception of truth and of the subject as that-which-underlies, all beings which are not subjects become objects of a pro-posing thinking and must be able to be fixed and defined in an unequivocal way. Only this scheme of beings creates the arena for the exact sciences of nature, which could not have existed among the Greeks or in the Middle Ages because these two conceptions of truth could have no room for nor interest in such sciences.

This transformation of truth into certitude is so familiar to us that we have difficulty bringing about another possibility of interpreting truth (although that is precisely what Heidegger does). And with the transformation of truth there occurs another basic change whose clearest expression is found in the fact that modern history is a history of power. Let us cite Heidegger again: "This freedom [of modern man] everywhere entails his own domination over the determination of the proper essence of man, and in a profound and explicit sense this domination requires power. Therefore in the history of the modern period for the first time power takes on essential authority and is capable of becoming fundamental reality. This in fact is what modern history is."[6] Con-sequently there is power as Will to Power only in that epoch of history where man as subject makes himself the center of beings and refers all other beings to himself and measures them in relation to himself.

In such a moment and situation the preconditions are created for the emergence of technology, which Heidegger reads as one of the most visible forms of the Will to Power. His concept of technology is so broad that it en-compasses "objectified nature, the business of culture, manufactured politics, and the gloss of ideals overlying everything."[7] To understand this situation more clearly, let us again let Heidegger speak for himself:

> The need to secure the supreme and unconditioned self-development of all the powers of mankind towards the unconditioned domination of the whole earth is the hidden spur that goads modern man on to ever new convulsive changes, and forces him into binds which guarantee for him that his pro-cedures are secure and his goals safe. These scientifically established binds appear in many forms and guises. The bind can be human reason and its law (the Enlightenment) or the realities and facts that such reason arranges and organizes (Positivism). The bind can be humanity with all its structures har-moniously integrated and shaped into beautiful form (the *humanitas* of classical thought). The bind can be the unfolding of the powers of a nation dependent only on itself, or it can be the "proletariat of all lands," or it can be individual peoples and races. The bind can be the development of mankind in the sense of the progress of world-wide rationality. . . .[8]

Descartes' metaphysics is the decisive beginning in laying the foundations for the metaphysics of the modern age. He conceives one being as subject and all the rest as objects, viz., as what can be pro-posed or put in front of a pro-posing thinking, hence as what can be posited and furthermore disposed over. Therefore in Descartes the seed is already planted for the prospect of the interpretation of beings in terms of will. In the sequel this interpretation is carried on by Leibniz, with his conception of the monad which is determined by strivings and represented as a center of power. And it is continued by Kant, who through the transcendental turn or Copernican Revolution conceives of the subject as in fact totally open as that which makes experience possible, so that if we want to make *a priori* assertions, those whose validity cannot be put in doubt, we must know the conditions of the possibility of experience. We can get to these conditions only by investigating the subject and its powers of knowing. Descartes already made a start in that direction when he demanded in the first rule of *Rules for the Direction of the Mind* (Regulae ad directionem ingenii) that knowledge must begin with a knowledge of the power of the subject.[9]

Kant still posited the subject as finite, and for him finitude was the basic presupposition. In German Idealism, however, it was abandoned. Now a metaphysics of the absolute was to be created, first in Fichte, then in Schelling and finally in Hegel. Fichte started out from the absolute ego, Schelling took nature as unconscious Spirit, and Hegel thought the absolute as absolute Idea, as absolute Spirit coming to itself. The moment of the will always remained operative. Finally in Nietzsche, the last phase of modern metaphysics, the will itself became the foundation. "With Nietzsche's metaphysics," Heidegger writes, "philosophy reaches its fulfillment, that is, it has completed the circle of its prescribed possibilities."[10] Nietzsche thought of himself as the adversary of Plato. Whereas Plato had located true Being in the Ideas, in reason, Nietzsche wanted to take it back into life, conceived as the Will to Power.

This excursus should have shown, if only by way of intimation, how Heidegger conceives and lays out the development of metaphysics. He is the first and only person to carry out such a project up to the present. But so far we have explained only one side of the question about Heidegger and metaphysics, namely, how he interprets the history of metaphysics comprehensively as a unified development. But Heidegger does not rest content with that much, as a quotation will immediately illustrate: 'Metaphysics is in all its forms and historical stages a unique, but perhaps necessary, fate of the West and the presupposition of its planetary dominance."[11] In order to understand this claim we have to back up a bit. So that he might be able to interpret the whole course of metaphysics, Heidegger had to find a place which was no longer located within metaphysics, he had to stand at once within metaphysics and outside it. But we should not misunderstand this "outside." It cannot mean a dismissal of metaphysics, for to do that is to be lacking in any understanding of metaphysics. There are positions, especially in Anglo-American philosophy, in which metaphysics is rejected out of hand as nonsense. Here there is no possible appreciation for the power of metaphysics in shaping history, and it is dismissed as a mistake and a dead end.

But Heidegger—and this is decisive for his procedure—seeks the ground of metaphysics. In "The Way Back into the Ground of Metaphysics" he recalls a letter in which Descartes compared philosophy to a tree whose roots are metaphysics, whose trunk is physics, and the branches which stem from the trunk are the other sciences. Heidegger comments: "Sticking to this image, we ask: In what soil do the roots of the tree of philosophy have their hold? Out of what ground do the roots—and through them the whole tree—receive their nourishing juices and strength? What element, concealed in the ground, enters and lives in the roots that support and nourish the tree?"[12] In order to experience this ground he goes back to the beginning of metaphysics, to Plato and further back to the thinkers we usually call the "Pre-Socratics." But this title is already an evaluation which usually suggests that these early thinkers did not get as far as Socrates, Plato and Aristotle. Heidegger overturns this evaluation. In these primordial and original thinkers, Anaximander, Parmenides, Heraclitus, the question of Being broke out for the first time. So decisive is this event that with it the historicity of man properly begins. As he says in "On the Essence of Truth": "History begins only when beings themselves are expressly drawn up into their unconcealment and conserved in it, only when this conservation is conceived on the basis of questioning regarding beings as such."[13] The Greek word *aletheia* is usually translated as "truth," but the translation that gets to the essence of *aletheia* is "unconcealment" or "unhiddenness." Heidegger has shown that it is not legitimate to always use the same term for what the Greeks thought of as *aletheia*, the Romans as *veritas* and moderns as "truth" or *verité* or *Wahrheit*. "Truth originally means something wrested from a state of concealment."[14] That is the Greek experience of truth, and it is an illusion to think that concepts have always had the same meaning in the various periods of history, as if they were an expression of a trans-worldly truth. That is an ahistorical, inadequate conception of truth, one which overlooks the historical character of human being.

But what happens in Plato, the philosopher with whom metaphysics begins? In his interpretation of Plato Heidegger has shown how the meaning of truth as unhiddenness gets transformed. Plato defines true being as the Idea and thinks of the Idea as what invests things with appearance and form, and so the Idea is already properly related to possible, indeed to correct, perception. Plato still retains the character of truth as unconcealment, but at the same time he also introduces the transformation of truth into correctness. There is a similar ambivalence in Aristotle, who on the one hand thinks of truth as unhiddenness, and on the other says, "True and false are not in things but in the understanding."[15]

These references mean to suggest that the original conception of truth in the

Greeks — as uncovering, as snatching something from the hidden — is changed. For Heidegger this change means that something fundamental happens which may be briefly sketched as follows. What was at stake in the original thinkers was the experience, for the first time, of what Being means. This got lost in the metaphysics which followed, because metaphysics no longer asked the question about Being (*das Sein*), but only about beings as a whole (*das Seiende im Ganzen*). The return into the ground of metaphysics is for Heidegger likewise the return to Being. The further he got with his own thinking, the clearer it became to him that metaphysics was not capable of thinking of Being itself. Metaphysics gives various interpretations of beings: as *idea*, as *energeia*, as created being, as subject or power or spirit or Will to Power, but it is incapable of thinking back into its own ground and asking where these interpretations get their authority and what they are grounded on. So we touch on one of the most difficult points in Heidegger's thinking, namely, that the history of metaphysics as a whole corresponds to the forgottenness of Being. Metaphysics constantly speaks of beings without questioning back into what supports and happens in these interpretations. That is why Heidegger says, "Metaphysics is in all its forms and historical stages a unique, but perhaps necessary, fate of the West and the presupposition of its planetary dominance."[16]

Through his interpretation of metaphysics Heidegger wants to lead us back to the original thinkers and their experience of Being, and this he understands as the overcoming of metaphysics. Metaphysics is not to be surmounted or transcended by a meta-metaphysics; rather, by thinking through metaphysics we should be brought to the point of thinking upon Being. Hegel demanded that philosophy give up its title: "*love* of wisdom" in order to become *actual* wisdom and knowledge. Heidegger does not demand this change but rather that philosophy itself should be transformed and become "thinking." And that means no less than preparing a new relation to Being itself, a relation which no longer allows beings as a whole to become objects and no longer understands the pro-posing subject as all-powerful and able to get everything into its grasp, but rather sees man as the open place for Being. Being itself is thought, by way of suggestion, as the clearing which man stands into and must guard and tend. When Heidegger says that, and when he surveys the development of metaphysics from a unified viewpoint, he also envisages a period whose time of arrival no one can predict. We see then that Heidegger does not just face what already was, but that he also looks ahead into what will and can be. Such a look into the future may appear to be audacious, but no philosopher of our century has so much perceived and understood and branded audacity as the sign of the growing power of subjectivity as has Heidegger. He likes to cite the saying of Heraclitus that hubris is more to be extinguished than a conflagration.[17]

We who stand within the era when metaphysics is fulfilling itself must feel like strangers when faced with Heidegger's vision. Even if we have not gotten indefinitely far, it was not long ago that the hardly imaginable event actually happened: that man landed on the moon and photos were transmitted from Mars. But all these undoubtedly magnificent achievements of technology only show that all is well with technical knowledge and control — one of the consequences of modern metaphysics. They cannot give rise to reflection on how it is going with man himself, understood as the one who sustains the openness of Being. That is why it is only natural that there are so many opponents of Heidegger's thought, although at the same time it must be added that such opposition is incapable of touching what Heidegger's thought has striven to open up. Until now there has not yet been a true dialogue or discussion with Heidegger's thinking, because the partner for such a dialogue is lacking. One could say of Heidegger what Kant once said of his own philosophy: I have arrived 150 years too early.

But early and late meet in Heidegger's thought. As we saw, his return to the pre-metaphysical thinkers of the origin at the same time gives access to metaphysics and shows the destiny which, in metaphysics, has been allotted to Western man. For this metaphysics is not just *any* achievement; in it Being shows itself, although as forgotten.

In contrast with Hegel, who intended to reveal the movement of Absolute Spirit, Heidegger was no prophet. He did not see himself as the peak of a development, as its fulfillment or end, but on the contrary as a possible beginning, a possible shift in direction. His admiration and concern for the poetry of Hölderlin had their foundation in the parallelism of the experiences of both men. Hölderlin brought his era into poetry as the time of the flight of the gods, the time of need, and likewise the time of awaiting the God who was to come. Poetry and thinking stand in an essential nearness to each other, and this consists in the fact that in the final analysis both are related to and show Being itself. To show this referral to Being, to make man attentive to it — that was the one concern which moved Heidegger in everything he said and did.

Translated by Thomas Sheehan

Notes

Walter Biemel, formerly a student of Heidegger's, is currently Professor of Philosophy at the Staatliche Kunstakademie in Düsseldorf, West Germany. He has edited various volumes of the *Husserliana* series, and most recently a volume in Heidegger's *Gesamtausgabe* (cf. note 2 below). Besides numerous articles, his publications include *Le concept du monde chez Heidegger* (Louvain: Nauwelaerts, 1950) and *Martin Heidegger: An Illustrated Study*, trans. J.L. Mehta (New York: Harcourt Brace Jovanovich,

1976). The present article first appeared as "Heidegger und die Metaphysik" in *Symposium Heidegger: Omagiu românesc lui Martin Heidegger*, ed. George Uscatescu (Madrid: Destin, 1971), pp. 42–55.

1. *Von der mannigfachen Bedeutung des Seienden nach Aristoteles* (Freiburg: Herder, 1862; reprinted Darmstadt: Wissenschaftliche Buchgesellschaft, 1960). Eng. trans. *On the Several Senses of Being in Aristotle* by Rolf George (Berkeley: University of California Press, 1975).
2. Heidegger's lecture course from the summer of 1936 has been edited by Hildegard Feick as *Schellings Abhandlung Ueber das Wesen der menschlichen Freiheit (1809)*, (Tuebingen: Niemeyer, 1971). His 1925–26 course which treats of Aristotle is published as *Logik. Die Frage nach der Wahrheit*, ed. Walter Biemel (Frankfurt/Main: Klostermann, 1976), *Gesamtausgabe*, II, vol. 21.
3. Heidegger, *Nietzsche*, vol. II (Pfullingen: Neske, 1961), p. 133.
4. *Ibid.*
5. *Ibid.*, p. 134.
6. *Ibid.*, p. 144.
7. Heidegger, *Vorträge und Aufsätze*, 3d. ed. (Pfullingen: Neske, 1967), "Ueberwindung der Metaphysik," p. 80. English trans., "Overcoming Metaphysics" in *The End of Philosophy*, trans. Joan Stambaugh (New York: Harper & Row, 1973), p. 93.
8. *Nietzsche*, II, 145.
9. René Descartes, *Rules for the Direction of the Mind*, trans., Laurence J. Lafleur (Indianapolis: Bobbs-Merrill, 1961), pp. 3–5.
10. *Vorträge und Aufsätze* as above, p. 83; English trans., p. 95, here slightly revised.
11. *Ibid.*, p. 77; English trans. p. 90.
12. "Einleitung zu: 'Was ist Metaphysik?'" *Wegmarken* (Frankfurt/Main: Klostermann, 1967), p. 195; 2d ed., p. 365. English trans. "The Way Back into the Ground of Metaphysics" in *Existentialism from Dostoevsky to Sartre*, ed. and trans. Walter Kaufmann (New York: World Publishing, Meridian Books, 1956), p. 207.
13. "Vom Wesen der Wahrheit" in *Wegmarken*, 1st ed., p. 85; 2d ed., p. 190 . English trans. "On the Essence of Truth" by John Sallis in Martin Heidegger, *Basic Writings*, ed. David Farrell Krell (New York: Harper & Row, 1977), p. 129.
14. "Platons Lehre von der Wahrheit" in *Wegmarken*, 1st ed., p. 129, 2d ed., p. 223. English trans. "Plato's Doctrine of Truth," trans. John Barlow in *Philosophy in the Twentieth Century*, ed. William Barrett and Henry D. Aiken (New York: Random House, 1962), vol. III, 261; here slightly revised. In the second edition of *Wegmarken* Heidegger glosses "Wahrheit" ("truth") with "im Sinne des Wahren" ("in the sense of the true") and glosses "Verborgenheit" ("state of concealment") with "Verbergung" ("concealing").
15. *Metaphysics* E, 4, 1027 b 25 f.
16. Cf. note 11 above.
17. Diels, Fragment 43.

Metaphysics and the Topology of Being in Heidegger

Otto Pöggeler

When it comes to so controversial a matter as the thought of Martin Heidegger, we cannot go wrong in drawing upon new titles to interpret it. Yet, the more the titles, the more the misunderstanding, even if each title may shed certain light on the matter. Regarding the title of the present essay, it cannot be denied that metaphysics has been the subject matter of Heidegger's thought even though he turns away from traditional metaphysics. But what allows us to speak of a "topology of Being" [*Seinstopik*] in Heidegger? Indeed, what does this expression mean? Is it supposed to be a characterization of Heidegger's thought, or only a preliminary indication of certain facts within his thought? And what is the relationship between the topology of Being and metaphysics?

If such titles as metaphysics and topology of Being are not to be attached to Heidegger's thought like external labels, then we have to ask how this thought understands itself. In this way maybe we can clarify the meaning of both terms, for if they are not external labels, then their relationship must be shown from out of this thinking itself.

Heidegger's thinking begins with a question which has remained uniquely and exclusively the guiding question of Western metaphysics. It is the question which Aristotle formulated at the beginning of the classical Greek philosophy: *ti to on*? What is a being in its Being? The "first" science in philosophy has the task of grasping beings *as* beings, thus of determining their Being. For this primary science the Aristotelian thesis holds true: "A being is stated in many ways." For instance, I can say *what* this being in front of me is (a lecturn) and *that* it is (it is at hand, is presently here, or however else we might express it). Thus a being in its Being is comprised of what-it-is and that-it-is. Furthermore, as Scholastic philosophy says, a being can be grasped as *res* (thing), *unum* (one), *aliquid* (something), *bonum* (good, worth aspiring after), *verum* (true, i.e., manifest in its Being). These terms are ultimate and supreme determinations which, like *ens* itself, transcend any other determinations and therefore are convertible with *ens*. These supreme determinations are called transcendentals.

Heidegger did not take up the doctrine of the manifold ways of stating being as something one might run across in the history of thought. Rather, he encountered it as a problem in the course of his own philosophical research. In his dissertation, *The Doctrine of Judgment in Psychologism*, he inquired into the kind of Being or actuality of the logical phenomenon and of the sense which pertains to an object and lets it become known and thereby "true." Thus he was asking about *ens tamquam verum* (a being as true). Following neo-Kantian lines of thought, and above all Husserl's *Logical Investigations*, he sharply differentiated between the Being of the logical phenomenon (the *verum*) and that of psychical phenomena. Each of these have their own kind of Being; but by attempting to understand the judgment with its forms (and the logical phenomenon) as originating in the psychical realm, psychologism fundamentally misconstrues the kind of Being of the logical and remains ignorant of it as an independent kind of Being. Can this independent and irreducible mode of Being be proved to psychologism?

Heidegger says it cannot be proved, but it can be exhibited. In the realm of the transcendentals there can be no more proof insofar as these, as their name implies, lie above and beyond all determinations and have no genus above them from which they could be deduced via application of the specific difference. In his dissertation Heidegger states: "Here perhaps we confront what is ultimate and irreducible, what excludes further clarification and brings any further inquiry to a standstill" (p. 95). The task of metaphysics is to *exhibit* these ultimately and mutually irreducible characteristics of Being. For Heidegger it is not these transmitted metaphysical ideas that are crucial, but rather the question which he heard in them. If a being can be stated in many ways, must we not ask about the unity from out of which the multiplicity of meanings of Being is articulated? Can we evade such a question by maintaining that "Being" is the most general and indefinable concept? Must the answer to the Being-question be a definition? The question about the unity of Being in the multiplicity of its meanings is the spur which has driven Heidegger's thinking forward. This question alone — and not simply the question about the Being *of beings* — is the "Being-question" in Heidegger.

The Being-question is again silenced in his *Habilitationsschrift*. There Heidegger strives to reach a "metaphysical settlement" on such issues as how sense could be valid for objects, how *verum* could be convertible with *ens*, and how the many meanings of Being could come together into a unity. As a metaphysical and teleological interpretation would have to show, a being can be known, sense can hold true of an object, and consciousness can reach an object simply because sense is to be ascribed to consciousness as that which is most proper to it. A knowing consciousness, moreover, is related to its metaphysical origin; as finite and temporal, it is grounded in absolute Spirit which is conceived as eternal and opposed to the "world" as the realm of the temporal and transient. A valid meaning participates in the eternity of the Absolute and thus remains static in itself, separate from temporal actuality and above all from the course which psychical phenomena take. Here Heidegger makes several presuppositions. For one thing, he presumes that philosophy must have a metaphysico-teleological, and ultimately a theological, closure. For another, he assumes that the eternity of the Absolute, as unchangeable, must be opposed to the temporality or changeability of the world, and that meaning or being-true is intrinsically bound up with an eternal, unchangeable, immutable, constant and self-subsisting being.

In his Freiburg lectures after the First World War Heidegger abandons these metaphysical and speculative presuppositions. In keeping with the basic dictate of phenomenology, he tries in these lectures to gain a "natural concept of the world." As being-in-the-world, life must be understood within itself; philosophizing must presuppose no Transcendence which would explain whatever is, especially once one suspects that the Transcendent, the God of philosophy, is not the God of faith. Life in its facticity always understands itself in some way; meaning belongs to it. Meaning in its kind of Being is no longer thought in terms of a schema where unchangeable eternity, residing statically in itself, is placed over against temporality as the changeable. Rather, meaning is to be conceived as the very movement of factical life which, in its originality, is history.

This facticity and historicity of life was experienced in original Christian faith, and so Heidegger in one of his earlier lectures quotes a statement from St. Paul's First Letter to the Thessalonians in which, concerning the return of Christ, he says that "the Day of the Lord will come like a thief in the night." The return of Christ cannot be dated chronologically nor grasped with reference to a particular content. St. Paul speaks only of its suddenness. The return of Christ belongs to the historical enactment [Vollzugsgeschichte] of life which cannot be objectified. Anyone who tries to render controllable, by means of chronological calculation and content-oriented definitions, the uncontrollable Day of the Lord only deceives himself about the facticity of life. As Paul writes, "When they say, 'Peace! No danger!' then destruction will come quickly like pain in a pregnant woman, and no one will be able to flee it." Heidegger's thought was sustained by the opinion that any thinking which obscures its relations to the uncontrollable future by calculating time and appealing to controllable, rational, "objective" content does not thereby escape the "doom."

But isn't it the very nature of thought to objectify? Metaphysical thinking, born among the Greeks, renders beings present in their Being. Such thinking is a "seeing" whereby a being in its Being is placed in view. The Being of beings is posited as a possible constant-being-in-view, a Being which stands in constant presentness. But in going beyond beings to a constantly present Being, does not thought miss life in its facticity, which, in its originality, is historicity? Heidegger thinks so. In one of his early Freiburg lecture courses entitled "Augustine and Neoplatonism" he shows how Augustine falsified the original Christian experience of God by interpreting it with the aid of Neoplatonic, metaphysical concepts such as *fruitio Dei*. The *frui* in *fruitio Dei* as *beatitudo hominis* is a *praesto habere* [The "enjoying" in the "enjoyment of God" as the "beatitude of man" is a matter of "having present"] which means an interior having-in-view. Thus the Being of God is conceived as a Being that can be constantly in view. In this way God can be enjoyed as peace and as tranquillity of heart, but He is likewise all too easily forced out of the tumult of factical historical life and robbed of His most proper vitality.

For metaphysics, thinking is a "seeing," and Being is a Being-in-view which stands in constant presentness. Doesn't metaphysics thereby miss the realm in which beings may show themselves in their Being, the realm of facticity and historicity? Does this realm belong to metaphysical thought as that which it has forgotten? Once we know that metaphysics understands Being as continuous presentness, must we not ask the crucial question: Doesn't metaphysics grasp Being thoughtlessly in terms of a certain mode of time, the present? Doesn't constant presentness mean being-present-*now*? And therefore doesn't metaphysics unthematically understand Being within the horizon of time? Once we ask *these* questions, the Being-question is radically changed, for we must now raise the following issues: Could it be that the unity of Being (unfolded into the multiple meanings of Being) has not been thought about because the horizon of time (within which Being is always already understood) has not come up for discussion? indeed, that this horizon could not be questioned because of the unquestioned equation of Being with constant presentness?

If we wish to understand Being *as* Being and in its multiple meanings, then the unity which unfolds into this multiplicity must become a problem. We must ask explicitly about the sense [*Sinn*] of Being which makes the multiplicity of its meanings [*Bedeutung*] intelligible. The sense of Being is the *ground* whence alone the multiple meanings unfold. Because Being is the *transcendens* beyond any specification, its sense is to be understood as the *transcendental horizon* for determining Being as Being. If metaphysics understands Being as constant presentness and thus in terms of the present, if it unthematically understands Being in the light of time, then metaphysics of itself leads us to ask whether time belongs essentially to the unity, sense or transcendental horizon of Being, to the ground of its manifold meanings.

Thus the question about the sense of Being becomes the question about Being and time. On the first page of *Being and Time* Heidegger quotes the question raised in Plato's *Sophist*: What do we really mean when we use the word "being" [*seiend*]? What do we Western, i.e., essentially metaphysical, thinkers mean when we say "is"? The point is whether we understand Being all too obviously as constant presentness while forgetting "time," which alone renders it thinkable. Since our thinking is ontological, i.e., concerned with the Being *of beings*, doesn't it forget the ground on which it stands, the sense of Being to which time belongs? And so doesn't it require a fundamental ontology which would put ontology on its proper ground? In Part One, Divisions One and Two of *Being and Time* (the only published portions of the work), Heidegger interprets, in terms of its temporality, that being which is distinguished by the understanding of Being: man as Dasein. From the temporality [*Zeitlichkeit*] and historicity of Dasein who understands Being, Heidegger wanted to bring up for thought the time [*Zeit*] which belongs to the sense of Being. In the unpublished Division Three, he was going to determine the time character of the transcendental horizon in which Being unfolds into its multiple meanings. But the attempt failed, and the third Division went unpublished. The investigation did not reach its goal.

After the failure of *Being and Time*, Heidegger tried to inquire into the transcendental horizon independently of the problem of temporality. That which is transcendental about this horizon as the "*transcendens* pure and simple" is Being which, as such, lies beyond the manifold Being of the various regions of beings as well as beyond all transcendental modes of Being. This Being is understood in Dasein as the one who transcends beings and carries out the differentiation of Being and beings. This *ontological* difference, and with it the transcending of beings to Being, is the very center of metaphysical thinking, its *meta*. But Heidegger does not simply ratify this metaphysical transcending of beings to Being. He goes further by asking about the "essence" of the domain where such transcending is accomplished.

In thinking beings as beings, metaphysics conceives a being in its Being or truth. When a being is understood as a being (e.g., a man as a man), this being comes into its Being and thus into the openness of its truth. Without examining its assumption, metaphysics takes Being itself as what is present in selfsame constant presence. But for Heidegger, the assumption that Being is the same for all eternity and that man, at least in his Being and essence, has no history is very questionable. Therefore, he must ask: How should we think Being as Being if it is not simply and entirely constant presence? If we may put it this way, what is Being itself in its "Being" or "essence"? In reference to *what* do we understand Being "as Being"? How are we to think the sense — or as he now puts it, the truth — of Being?

We must differentiate precisely between the question of Being as concerned with the truth *of beings,* and the question of the truth of Being itself.... Heidegger's question does not concern simply Being as the truth of beings, but concentrates entirely on the question of the truth of Being itself. Prior to the question which guides metaphysics (What is a being in its Being or truth?), he puts the fundamental question: What is Being itself in its truth? He tries to reveal the ground, never articulated as such, on which the metaphysical question already stands. In this way his question about the truth of Being itself is the return to the heretofore hidden ground of metaphysics.

To be able to articulate the truth of Being as the ground of metaphysics, Heidegger asks about the essence of truth. The existential analytic in *Being and Time* had already shown that truth is disclosed when Dasein brings himself into his utmost resolve. There Dasein must experience himself as fraught with a twofold negativity. First, the fact that he is and that truth happens is beyond Dasein's power. Second, Dasein finds himself always in a situation, and allows in truth only a limited place for its openness. However, by releasing himself into this negativity, Dasein learns that it belongs to the essence of truth. Dasein's double negativity recurs as a twofold nothing in the essence of truth. A twofold non-presence and concealing belongs to presencing, the opening up of truth: first, it remains hidden why truth opens up at all; and then, truth always gives itself into a limited openness. Truth, therefore, is a matter of the co-presence of revealing and concealing, of grounding and denying ground. As ground, it is the absence of ground, the non-ground; as the history of revealing and concealing, it is the mystery of un-concealment, *aletheia.*

Heidegger believes that the nothing in non-being—truth as concealing and as non-ground—must be thought as belonging to Being. The nothing which belongs to Being is not, of course, the absolute nothing which can only be an *ens rationis.* Rather, it is a no-thing in relation to beings; that is, the Being to which nothing belongs is not a being, nor a property of beings, nor controllable by any being. Being is the truth of beings only as a ground which is their non-ground. As this twofold negativity, Being is not at all controllable; it is the history over which we do not dispose. Being is indeed the truth *of beings,* but in *its own* truth, it is the uncontrollable and temporal history, the event of Appropriation, *Ereignis.* In the event of Appropriation, the temporal and "giving"-character of the truth of Being shows itself.

Since the years 1936–38, when Heidegger wrote the so-called "Contributions to Philosophy" (*Beiträge zur Philosophie,* the actual title of which is "On Appropriation," *Vom Ereignis*), he has thought the truth of Being as Appropriation. The truth of Being needs Dasein as its momentary abode. It appropriates itself to man in that it claims [*aneignet*] his comprehension of Being as the "there" of Being. In Dasein's being-appropriated to the truth of Being, the ontological difference which is eventuated between Being and beings lets beings be placed into their Being. Being and man (as the understanding of Being) belong together in the "there" or truth of Being in such a way that Dasein can never dispose of this truth but must adapt himself to its history. The truth of Being is no ground which can be determined and secured; it is uncontrollable non-ground which grounds only historically.

Let us now take another look at the course of Heidegger's thinking by focusing on the question: In what sense does the path of thought constitute a "way" which would be Heidegger's "method"? At the beginning of his path of thought Heidegger took up the metaphysical problem of the Being of beings and sought the unity of Being which unfolds into its multiple meanings. The inquiry into the unity of the multiplicity of Being underwent a radical change when he asked whether the metaphysical doctrine of Being satisfies the activity and historicity of life. By thinking of Being as constant presence without reflecting on the horizon of time within which presence and presentness is thought, metaphysics carries the realm of facticity and historicity within itself—but as that which it has forgotten. *Being and Time* failed in its attempt to think out the horizon of time as the sense of Being, but why this work *had* to fail could be shown only after the sense or truth of Being had been articulated.

In its whole approach, *Being and Time* is a divided endeavor which, for *that* reason and no other, had to fail. On the one hand it moves towards thinking the truth of Being, but on the other, it still speaks an inadequate "metaphysical" language. In a metaphysical and "modern" manner it sets out from transcendental subjectivity as "unshakable foundation of truth" and calls the Being of this subjectivity "existence," an expression drawn from the modern metaphysics of will. To be sure, *Being and Time* thinks against modern transcendental philosophy and metaphysics insofar as the Being of existence is thought out in terms of finite temporality. But because existence was not yet satisfactorily differentiated from modern subjectivity by historical reflection, Heidegger did not find the transition from the temporality of existence to the time-character of the sense of Being. By its very nature, modern subjectivity closes itself off from the truth of Being. It seeks to be its own sustenance and therefore cannot adapt itself to the happening of truth over which it cannot dispose. Modern subjectivity is not Dasein as the "there" of Being, as Being's momentary abode. Furthermore, *Being and Time* still takes Being as the ground on which everything should be placed. To be sure, the "Destruction of the History of Ontology" would bring out the historicity of thought. This destruction does not allow thought to adapt itself to the uncontrollable history of truth, but only seeks to get at its ultimate basis which has been covered over. By seeking to prepare foundations for all ontology as the question of Being, *Being and Time* still follows the metaphysical thrust towards a final ground. But how could the truth of Being, once it is known as Appropriation, as the history which always happens suddenly, be a firm foundation brought forth as ultimate ground? At most it could be called a non-ground, but taken in its own right it cannot be called "ground" at all.

After the failure of *Being and Time* Heidegger's thought sought to enter the non-ground of the truth of Being. This entering-in [*Einkehren*] has also been called the turn [*Kehre*] from Dasein to Being. But this talk about the turn would misconstrue everything so long as one did not see that this turn has not been and could not be accomplished as planned in *Being and Time*, namely, as the systematic transition from the analysis of existence to the sense of Being. The turn can be achieved only as a reversal [*Umkehr*] through which Dasein gives up on supplying a final ground and positing himself on his own powers. This reversal must undo the history of metaphysics, and in *this* sense it is the way back into the ground of metaphysics. For Heidegger, the road *back* was the road *through* the history of metaphysics, one which retraces the major decisions for the self-assertion of man and the search for ground. Recall that in his 1933 Rectoral Address Heidegger called Prometeus the first philosopher, the one who asserted himself by *stealing* the fire from heaven. The metaphysical thrust towards final ground is maintained in the fundamental ontology which, with Kant's words, Heidegger called "a metaphysics of metaphysics." This phrase gives the impression that the inquiry into man's essence as questioner could "outbid" and justify the metaphysical inquiry into the Being of beings. To state it in terms other than those of modern and transcendental philosophy, the phrase gives the impression that we could ask about the "Being" of Being (the essence of metaphysics) by turning the metaphysical question of the Being of beings back upon itself. But metaphysics cannot be grounded and "overcome" by reaching out for something higher than metaphysics. Rather, thought must fit itself into the truth of Being and give up the metaphysical will to elicit and secure an ultimate ground. Thought cannot overcome [*überwindern*] metaphysics; it must try to incorporate [*verwinden*] it.

In *The Question of Being* (1956; E.T., p. 94), Heidegger says that the question (What is metaphysics?) "stabs itself in the heart," not so as to terminate the life of thought but so that it may live transformed. When concerned with a "what" or "essence," the question is still being asked in a metaphysical way which must be given up if the truth of Being is to be experienced as the history which even metaphysics bears without knowing it. Heidegger passes sentence on metaphysics as history so that it can become that history which leads to new life. . . .

In Heidegger's words, the fundamental movement of his thought is the "step backwards." He takes up the metaphysical question so as to articulate its unspoken core, the truth of Being, and thereby to step back into this truth. The question about the truth of Being must do away with the impression that it is a metaphysical question even potentially. Locating the place [*Erörterung*] of Being with respect to its truth (I call this a "discussion" of the *topos* of Being) is no longer metaphysical. Insofar as this "discussion" of the *topos* of Being locates the truth of Being as the unthought of metaphysics, it leaves the place of metaphysics, where the truth of Being fails to appear, in favor of a place where this truth can become Appropriation. In this novel sense, locating the *topos* [*Erörterung*, usually "discussion"] is a *path*, not in the sense of abandoning one position for another, but rather as a "localization" which returns to and articulates the unthought in what has already been thought and thus goes from one place to another and fits itself, in its place, into the history of truth. The path of this localization is not just Heidegger's path but should be nothing else than a retracing of the course of Western thought, the step back to the origin of our history whereby this origin is located in terms of its unthought and returned to its originality so that it can become "another origin."

By a localization or topology of Being, Heidegger pulls back from metaphysical thinking and articulates its unthought, thus placing this thinking back into its place and its limits. I will now add a few remarks towards clarifying what "localization" means. First let us distinguish between explanation, clarification, and "localization" [*Erklären, Erläutern, Erörtern*]. Explanation means leading a being back to another being or to "Being" as its ground. "Nothing is without reason or ground" is the great principle which makes possible the explaining and thus the controlling of beings. In the nineteenth century explanation became the method of the sciences, dominating not only the sciences of nature but the human sciences as well. Religion, for example, was rationalistically and positivistically reduced to such psychological conditions as man's fear and was thereby considered explained. In a less coarse explanation, religion was traced back to the history of the psyche, the history of the individual and the people. "Extension" and "consciousness" were the ultimate principles at which explanation arrived, and this reference to the two Cartesian substances perhaps indicates that behind explanation as a method there stands the metaphysical thrust towards ultimate ground. Not that we should label the ontological grounding of metaphysics as ontic explanation; but we must ask whether such ontological grounding has adequately distinguished itself from ontical explanation so that all misunderstanding is excluded, and whether its approximation to ontic explanation might not be due to the fact that it does not think the truth of Being itself.

It was a liberation for thought when, at the beginning of this century, ontology and phenomenology opposed explanation by pointing out, for example, that nothing is decided by interpreting religion as an expression of historical humanity or explaining it in terms of something else. There is a different kind of thinking from explanation, one whose essential feature can be designated as clarification. To clarify means to let something be in the purity of its essence and to refrain from hasty explanations. The demand, "Back to the things themselves" means, for example, not to explain logic by psychology, not to hastily take religion or poetry as an explanation of a people's mind, but by means of an unprejudiced description of things, to let them be seen in their own essence as what they are. But the danger of clarification is that the purity of the essence will be taken as *constant* presence and placed in some supercelestial realm, that a domain of logical laws "in themselves," values "in themselves," and generally essences in themselves will be posited. To use a modern expression, the danger is that everything will be led back to a transcendental ego which lies beyond any demonstrable ego. Then the problem would remain: How can concrete history be related to values, religion, and poetry as things "in themselves"?

Heidegger seeks to show that no relation need be established here at all, so long as we do not forget that the Being of beings or the essence of things only happens in the realm of the truth of Being itself, for which historical man is "used." In the beginning Heidegger pointed to the domain of the truth of Being via man's historical understanding of Being. But "understanding" as a guiding-term remained ambiguous: it seemed as if understanding in an "historical" sense might be the same as the self-understanding *of* humanity, used as a ground for explaining things. But the word "localization" perhaps articulates more adequately what is actually the issue in Heidegger's thought: the truth of Being itself which, as Appropriation, gives our question about the Being of beings its *place*. Being, when thought from the truth of Being, is itself a "localized" Being to which finitude and historicity belong from the start, even if, within limited areas, there may be a Being or essence which always endures and to which we could return from all historical places.

Erörterung is the *logos* of Heidegger's thinking. Perhaps we use language "authentically" when we use it as a means for *Erörterung*. Of course, language makes possible different ways of speaking, and Heidegger has differentiated poetical speaking from the speaking proper to thinking in his brief formula: the poet names the Holy, the thinker utters Being. What the poet does, namely, responding to the claim of the Holy and, as Heidegger says with Hölderlin, "naming" the Holy and the divine, is something the thinker cannot pretend to do. The thinker utters Being, i.e., he "locates" the utterence of the Being of beings into the history of truth. In this truth and in the world as its structure there is no ultimate ground to be grasped ontotheologically. Granted the claim of the divine, there is always a measure given, but the thinker cannot possess this measure as an ultimate. That is why he has no right to construct an all-encompassing metaphysical system: not only does this or that system become questionable, but the very idea of system at all. Since thought possesses no ultimate measure, it cannot ground, legitimize, or correct the "world" as physics and biology put it forth. Of course, thought can "discuss" again and again the unexamined presuppositions that have gone into physics or biology. For example, Heidegger has tried to "place" classical physics by showing that, on account of its conception of time which is limited to a particular image of the world, a number of assumptions have entered this physics even though they do not belong to it as a pure science. And this view has been substantiated in its own way by modern physics. A "discussion" of the statements made by individual philosophical disciplines or certain sciences must begin at the point where unexamined assumptions, philosophical or otherwise, are thoughtlessly taken over, such as the concept of infinity in mathematics, the basic concepts of aesthetics, ultimately the conception of aesthetics itself, and so on.

The crucial question is not whether discussions like these are in fact carried out, but how discussion as *Erörterung* can be legitimized as a basic method of thought. In its primordiality, is truth an event which needs "localization"? Is it a way leading to various regions? If so, can this be demonstrated? But if we could demonstrate that this is so, we would have already transcended "localization," because it fits itself, in its place, into the happening of truth without ever being able to encompass this truth as the way to various regions. But if we experience this "way" only in its place and in differentiation from another place without being able to demonstrate it as a whole, then doesn't "localization" lack authentic legitimization? Or is this question about legitimization a false one? Surely we can show that Heidegger's thought arrives at such "localization" as an uttering of the truth of Being because he experiences the end of metaphysics as grounding and clarifying, such that metaphysics itself points towards thought as "localization." Only one who ventures such a thinking can find out what other kinds of unexamined presuppositions determine the course of such thinking. *Erörterung* cannot be "legitimized" as an "absolute method."

But why do we use the old name of "topics" [*Topik*] for this "localization" or utterance of the truth of Being? It has been said that Heidegger's early thought followed a "hermeneutical logic" oriented not to things always at hand but to self-interpretative historical life and above.all to its praxis. Praxis, of course, has become the magic word and the focus of lively questioning ever since Hegel. But in viewing our praxis we view ourselves, and in viewing ourselves we are easily prevented from experiencing the uncontrollable history of truth. In his later period Heidegger situates his thinking close to poetizing and to the aphoristic thinking of the "pre-Socratics." If we seek to correspond to "localization" within a thinking that consciously reflects on the paths it takes, then we arrive at "topics," even if Heidegger himself has not expressly posed this relation.

Topics is the *ars inveniendi*, the art of finding arguments and basic concepts for a dialogue about an issue. It serves dialogue and its art, "dialectic." Topical and dialectical thinking does not offer truth as something convertible with constantly present Being; it offers only what is probable, *endoxon*, or *verisimile*. If we grant that appearance and concealment belong essentially to truth and that truth in its primordially is what appears as true [*Wahr-Schein*], then we must not devalue topical, dialectical thinking because it "only" imparts what is probable. Topical thinking was once regarded as significant. In the tradition of Aristotle-interpretation, for example, his writings called *Topica* were put together with those on the categories, since the latter are first discovered through some kind of topology of Being [*Seinstopik*]. But for the most part topical-dialectical thinking was forced out of the "first science" and pushed into rhetoric, humanism (which opposed Scholasticism), jurisprudence and theology. For the sake of man's historicity, Giambattista Vico, whose own background was in rhetoric, tried to justify the "old" topical method against the "new critical" and strictly systematic method of Cartesianism. And for the jurist "topics" was inevitable. From his own practise he distrusted the strictly systematic method. He knew that "every definition in civil law is dangerous." He had to interpret the written law, which is to say that he had to adjust it to historical change. Likewise "systematic" theology, insofar as it has to articulate a unique historical claim, is opposed to rigorous systematization. Far into the modern era dogmatics was treated topically and put under the title *"Loci communes."*

It seems the tradition gives clues for working out a topical "localizing" kind of thought at the very heart of metaphysics, one which has always been sidetracked and never articulated originally. Be that as it may, our question is how to characterize Heidegger's latest publications, his numerous talks, lectures, essays, papers, and letters. These efforts at thought are a single great "localization" which makes it possible to speak from that other and authentic place. In such "discussion" Heidegger's procedure is to concentrate on individual guiding-terms and propositions, on *topoi* as I should like to call them within the terminology of "topics." Therefore perhaps we may call this thoughtful localization a "topology" in the sense of a saying (*legein*) of the place (*topos*) in European thought, and in this way a self-gathering unto the basic terms of thinking as such. *Topoi* are guiding-terms such as *aletheia* or *idea*, and guiding-propositions such as the "principle of ground," "poetically man dwells," as well as grammatical forms like the sentential subject-object relation which has so decisively determined our thinking. Each of these *topoi* points towards one place of truth.

Topological thinking attempts something very simple. It calls attention to presumptions hidden in the concepts we use; it seeks to speak language in a different way, to reflect on the fact that we fit into one place in the history of truth when we speak as we usually do. As a topology of Being, this thinking is a reflection on what we Westerners really mean when we say "is." After the failure of *Being and Time*, Heidegger devoted his thought more decisively to the simplicity of such a meditation.

At the conclusion to *The Question of Being*, an essay which added a topology — or indication of the place whence one speaks and describes — to

Ernst Jünger's descriptive topography of nihilism, Heidegger quotes a saying of Goethe which we may apply to his own reflections. Goethe writes: "If a man regards words as sacred testimonials and does not put them into quick and immediate circulation like small change or paper money but wants to see them exchanged for their true value in intellectual trade and barter, then he should not be blamed for pointing out that traditional expressions, at which no one takes offense, nonetheless exert damaging influence, obscure the view, distort understanding, and give a false direction to whole fields of research."

Translated by Parvis Emad

Note

Otto Pöggeler is Professor of Philosophy and Director of the Hegel Archives at the Ruhr University, Bochum, West Germany. His books include *Der Denkweg Martin Heideggers* (Pfullingen, 1963), *Philosophie und Politik bei Heidegger* (Freiburg, 1972), and the edited collection, *Heidegger: Perspektiven zur Deutung seines Werks* (Cologne, 1969). This translation presents the text of a lecture given in 1961 before the Goerresgesellschaft and subsequently published in *Philosophisches Jahrbuch*, vol. 70/71, 1962, pp. 118–138, under the title "Metaphysik und Seinstopik bei Heidegger." Professor Emad's translation of this text first appeared in *Man and World* 8 (February, 1975), 3–27, and we thank the editors of that journal for permission to reprint it here. The ellipses indicate passages omitted from the full translation on pp. 9, 11–18, and 20–21 (German, pp. 123, 124–130, and 132–133). Throughout the original, Pöggeler mentions his sources parenthetically or not at all, and the translator has followed this practise. In a footnote to the first publication of his translation, Professor Emad notes: To understand more fully what Pöggeler has in mind when focusing on *Erörterung*, it may be helpful to recall Heidegger's own treatment of the term. In his essay on the poetry of G. Trakl he calls *Erörterung* "pointing toward a place, showing a place and heeding it" (*Unterwegs zur Sprache*, p. 37, Neske, 1960; English translation, *On the Way to Language*, p. 159).

Finitude and the Absolute:
Remarks on Hegel and Heidegger

Jacques Taminiaux

German Idealism, as we all know, consisted in a certain development of the thought of Kant. Indeed, Hegel's first philosophical publications—the writings whereby he entered the philosophical scene—were focused in a special way on Kant. On the other hand we know that Martin Heidegger, by taking up the question of the meaning of Being as the proper task of thought and by linking this question to the deconstruction of metaphysics, was led, from the period of his first writings, into debate with Kant.

In the most general terms, the present essay intends to ask how Heidegger's thought about the ontological difference and Hegel's dialectical thought differ from each other. And I will seek to answer this question by confronting Heidegger's retrieve of Kant as carried out in *Kant and the Problem of Metaphysics* with Hegel's retrieve of Kant as carried out in *Faith and Knowledge*. Since Kant's *Critique of Pure Reason* (hereafter CPR) is the primary object of both retrieves, it is the text that will command our attention.

A. INTERPRETATIONS OF KANT

1. *Heidegger*

In contrast with the positivist and neo-Kantian readings which were dominant at the time, Heidegger asserted that to explain CPR is to delineate the intrinsic possibility of metaphysics both as pure and rational knowledge of beings in general *(metaphysica generalis)* and as knowledge of the totality of the principle regions of beings *(metaphysica specialis)*. In keeping with the spirit of Christian metaphysics, Kant considered this *metaphysica specialis*, the science of God, the soul, and the world, to be metaphysics in the strict sense. The point, then, is to determine the essence or intrinsic possibility of this *metaphysica specialis* which makes claim to being knowledge of suprasensible beings. But the question of the possibility of this knowledge leads back to the more general question of the possibility of rendering beings manifest as such, i.e., to the question of the possibility of a relation to beings whereby they manifest themselves *as* beings. And Kant found a clue to the possibility of such a relation in the method of physics. This science had come to understand that reason knows physical beings as manifest only on the basis of a plan that the science itself projects beforehand. The knowing relation to physical beings presupposes prior comprehension of the Being of those beings. The Kantian problem of the intrinsic possibility of metaphysics focuses on the question of the essence of this prior comprehension. In Heidegger's language the problem is stated as follows: Knowledge of beings—ontic knowledge—is possible only by means of a knowledge of the Being-structure of beings, i.e., ontological knowledge. Or in other terms: "The manifestation of beings, i.e., ontic truth, depends on disclosure of the Being-structure of beings, i.e., ontological truth." The Kantian problem is that of the intrinsic possibility of ontological knowledge, or more succinctly, of ontology. This is the problem that is announced in the famous question: "How are synthetic *a priori* judgments possible?" That is to say: Insofar as, for Kant, to know is to judge, how can knowledge, prior to all ontic cognition, *a priori* bring Being to beings in such a way as to allow beings to show themselves as they are? Such knowledge does not come from experience, for experience presupposes it. Rather, it consists in an activity of judging according to *a priori* principles. The faculty of this activity is pure reason, conceived as a pure prior relation to beings which determines the Being of beings. Kant gives the name "transcendental" to the inquiry into the possibility or essence of the *a priori* synthesis, i.e., the inquiry into the essence of the pure prior relation to beings. Heidegger calls this pure prior relation "transcendence." Transcendental inquiry, therefore, is the search for the origin or foundation of transcendence.

According to Heidegger, the dimension (or "domain of origin") within which the regress to the foundations takes place is characterized by one word: finitude. CPR is a critique of pure finite reason. This characteristic of reason as finite is essential to and the presupposition for the problematic of laying the foundations. This finitude stands out by the fact that, from the very beginning of CPR, finite intuition is what characterizes the essence of knowledge. According to Kant, human knowledge is at once intuition and thought; but thought, in order to *be* thought, must first of all hold to the finitude of the intuition that is proper to it. Intuition, Kant says, is "derived" in the sense of being ordered to beings which it does not itself produce, which are there of and by themselves and which intuition can only "consent to" or receive. In order to make this being to which it is immediately ordered accessible to others, finite intuition requires a mediation which alone can universalize the immediate contact and transform it into knowledge. This is the role of the understanding. The understanding, therefore, is intrinsically finite at the very core of the universalizing function which it guarantees, for it is entirely subordinated to intuition. And it is even more finite than intuition insofar as it lacks the immediacy of the latter.

Not only does finitude essentially characterize the domain of origin within which the regress to the foundation of transcendence is carried out; it also radically characterizes the very foundation towards which the regress moves. The crux of this return to the origin of the transcendental synthesis is, as Kant himself says, the transcendental deduction. Now, from the way Kant's successive analysis, first in the transcendental aesthetic and then in the transcendental logic, in effect cuts intuition and thought off from each other by envisaging each of them in its purity and independence, we might be led to think that the deduction merely relates *extrinsically* two elements which are not intrinsically referred to each other. But, says Heidegger, this is not the meaning of Kant's procedure. Indeed, we can understand nothing of the transcendental deduction if we fail to see his discovery of a unifying power which, far from reuniting intuition and understanding after they have been cut off from each other, consists in making their togetherness structurally possible. This newly discovered power makes both faculties emerge as belonging together. It is the transcendental imagination. Kant says, "We have a pure imagination as the fundamental faculty of the human soul, which *a priori* serves as the foundation of all knowledge." It is the imagination, Heidegger emphasizes, that is the very happening of the transcendental synthesis, the very occurrence of transcendence.

In what, then, does the proper essence of transcendence as transcendental imagination consist? And how can it be the root of the two stems of knowledge: intuition and understanding? The proper essence of the transcendental imagination can be seen already in the structure of the empirical imagination, which consists in the ability to intuit in the absence of the object. The empirical imagination is intuitive and as such receives a view or image. But insofar as it is not bound to the presence of this or that being, it spontaneously gives itself the views it receives. It is therefore at once receptive and spontaneous or productive. And in a pre-eminent way this is the structure of the transcendental imagination. As contrasted with empirical imagination, transcendental imagination does not give itself over to intuiting this or that ontic view or image. Rather, it forms the field of manifestness within which every ontic view can enter and become manifest: the horizon of objectivity within which every object can emerge. In this sense it is productive or spontaneous. But this spontaneity is intrinsically receptive; the opening that it forms is nothing other than the openness towards that-which-is. And just as empirical imagination is not bound to the presence of this or that being, so even more radically the transcendental imagination is tied not to beings, to that-which-is, but to something which, in comparison with beings, is a "nothing." And yet this no-thing is the passing-beyond (transcendence) by virtue of which beings can be present and can manifest themselves.

The transcendental imagination — this transcending of beings which makes possible the receiving of beings — is intrinsically time. As such it is the root of the two stems of knowledge, intuition and understanding — if it is true that intuition has time as its fundamental form and that understanding is a cognitive relation to all possible objects only by virtue of certain transcendental determinations of time, the schemata treated in Kant's doctrine of schematism.

As the original conjunction of receptivity and spontaneity, the transcendental imagination, as time, attests that the ontological knowledge or transcendence of which it forms the foundation is intrinsically bound up with the finitude of man.

According to Heidegger's terminology of that period, this interpretation was a "retrieve," which means the same as the word "dialogue" which appears only later in his career. As a retrieve, this interpretation does not just stick to what Kant explicitly said, but moves into the unsaid of CPR. Heidegger expresses this move as follows: "The problem of laying the foundation of metaphysics is rooted in the question of the Dasein in man, i.e., in the question of the ultimate foundation of man, who is, as essentially eksistent finitude, the understanding of Being."[1] But Kant pulled back from this move into the question of finitude, as is shown by the fact that the second edition of CPR attributed to the understanding what the first edition had attributed to the imagination. Thereby in one stroke the dominating priority of the "I think" and of logic over fundamental ontology was established, with the result that the understanding of Being, as the finitude of Dasein, was relegated to forgottenness. By that same stroke Kant opened the way to Hegel's absolute metaphysics defined as logic, the specter of the most profound oblivion of the fact that the essence of metaphysics must be maintained by deepening the "problem of finitude."

2. Hegel

At first glance, the retrieve of Kant which Hegel carried out in his work *Faith and Knowledge* seems to move in a direction diametrically opposed to that taken by Heidegger's retrieve. Both see Kant as "pulling back," but whereas Heidegger's interpretation shows Kant's move to be a recoil before finitude, indeed a blindness to it, so as to guarantee the luminous force of pure reason, Hegel's interpretation on the contrary shows Kant's move to be a recoil before the luminous power of reason so as to hold fast to finitude. Heidegger holds that the driving question of CPR is that of ontological knowledge or the comprehension of Being, and that one cannot take CPR as a theory of knowledge except by backsliding and failing to hold the work at the high level of its motivating question. By way of contrast, Hegel holds that CPR is entirely imprisoned within the limits of the goal which Locke had already proposed: to consider finite understanding, to come to a knowledge of the knowing faculty. Whereas Heidegger maintains that CPR, to the degree it is faithful to its intention, reveals the one and only topic of philosophy, Hegel maintains to the contrary that only in spite of its intention does CPR reveal that topic.

The opposition in these viewpoints would seem to put an end to the confrontation we would like to carry out. And all the more so when we read what Hegel takes to be the one and only topic of philosophy:

> We must not . . . regard it as the problem of the true philosophy to resolve at [the Kantian] terminus the antitheses that are met with and formulated perchance as spirit and world, or soul and body, or self and nature, etc. On the contrary, the sole Idea that has reality and true objectivity for philosophy, is the absolute suspendedness of the antithesis. This absolute identity is not a universal subjective postulate never to be realized. It is the only authentic reality. Nor is the cognition of it a faith, that is, something beyond all knowledge; it is, rather, philosophy's sole knowledge.[2]

It would seem that we are miles away from Heidegger. Whereas *Kant and the Problem of Metaphysics* ended by keeping open the questions which were met along the way of the retrieve — the questions of Being, truth, finitude — Hegel's interpretation of Kant begins with the solid and unquestioned assurance of a knowledge of the Absolute. Any comparison of these two retrieves, therefore, would seem to be arbitrary.

Yet it would be hasty and erroneous to conclude that the comparison ends up in two mutually closed positions. For within the opposition of the two retrieves there is the paradoxical fact that both of them see eye to eye on the same point in Kant. Recall that Heidegger says that the problematic of the transcendental deduction can be understood as the root of the foundation, that is, as the unifying element which by nature lets emerge the elements to be unified: intuition and understanding.[3] Heidegger shows that the imagination, understood as the root of the foundation, is quite different from a *tertium quid*, one faculty among others. Rather, it is originary. Now Hegel: "The whole transcendental deduction both of the forms of intuition and of the categories in general cannot be understood . . . [if we] take the faculty of [productive] imagination as the middle term that gets inserted between an existing absolute subject and an absolute existing world. The productive imagination must rather be recognized as what is primary and original . . . ."[4] And further:

[T]he Kantian forms of intuition and the forms of thought cannot be kept apart at all as the particular, isolated faculties as which they are usually represented. One and the same synthetic unity . . . is the principle of intuition and of the intellect . . . .

[This must be understood by] those who, when they hear talk of the power of imagination, do not even think of the intellect, still less of Reason, but only of unlawfulness, whim and fiction; they cannot free themselves from the idea of a qualitative manifold of faculties and capacities of the spirit.[5]

Such is the paradox. As they retrieve Kant, Heidegger and Hegel both recognize, each in his own way, that the transcendental imagination is the topic for thought. One might immediately object that this coincidence is of no great import since, despite the analogy, neither understands the transcendental imagination in the same way. But let us be careful about being too hasty here. How does Hegel understand Kant's doctrine of transcendental imagination? What merit does he see in it? It is, he says, a truly speculative idea. "Speculative" and "speculation" come from the Latin *speculum*, mirror, a movement towards something other than oneself which nonetheless restores one to oneself. If the transcendental imagination, understood as the originary root, can be called a speculative idea, that is because it is not some kind of collecting which unites opposing elements after they have been divided, but rather a restoration of sameness through division, a synthesis in and by which the opposed become one, and through which "identity is identical to difference." On this point Hegel's retrieve of Kant rejoins Heidegger's: the original synthetic unity of the transcendental imagination founds the syntheses of the understanding and of the intuition. What is at stake here is precisely the central topic of Heidegger's retrieve, namely, the original and bivalent unity of receptivity and spontaneity. The transcendental imagination, Heidegger shows, is the original synthesis insofar as it is essentially "spontaneous receptivity and receptive spontaneity." Hegel says the same when he emphasizes that, by contrast with ancient conceptions of sensibility defined simply as receptivity, Kant's merit is to have understood intuition as spontaneous receptivity, just as he understands understanding as receptive spontaneity. Of course the text itself of *Faith and Knowledge* hardly insists on the intrinsically temporal character of the imagination. Yet this aspect of the imagination did not go unnoticed by Hegel, as is evidenced by the fact that two years later his Jena lectures very closely associated the imagination and what he then called "the universal time of consciousness."

One will doubtless object that while there is indeed a striking similarity, the two retrieves do not at all have the same issue at stake. On the one hand it is a matter of finitude, on the other of the Absolute. But what matters here is not the verbal antithesis which these two words suggest, but rather what they offer for thought. And it may well be that, in a very particular sense, Heidegger's denunciation of Kant's blindness to finitude and Hegel's denunciation of his blindness to the Absolute bear equally on the same point. What Heidegger condemns in neo-Kantian interpretations (which themselves are made possible by Kant's own blindness to what he had discovered) is the reduction of the transcendental problematic to a theory of experiential knowledge at the expense of ontological knowledge. What Hegel denounces is the reduction of the problematic to that of the understanding so that "knowledge of appearances is dogmatically regarded as the only kind of knowledge there is . . . . "[6] This is what Hegel understands by finitude: the priority accorded to representation limited to phenomena.

Therefore, despite the seeming contradiction, Heidegger and Hegel condemn the same reductionism. Could it then be that despite their verbal antithesis, Heidegger's word "finitude" and Hegel's word "the Absolute" come together in a common meaning? What do these two words refer to?

First we ask: What is Heidegger's retrieve looking for under the title of finitude? As Beaufret emphasizes, when Heidegger retrieves Kant's thought, he elevates that thought to the plateau of "a difference that distinguishes Being and beings and holds them separate from each other only in order to unify them both in an original disclosure." In short, it is the ontological difference. According to Heidegger this is the subject matter (Sache) of thought. The difference is what calls forth the enduring power of thought. In *Identity and Difference* Heidegger has given us perhaps the most explicit discussion of the difference. He writes:

> Being passes beyond and above—it comes over to—that which it discloses, that which arrives as self-disclosive only by virtue of this coming-over. "To arrive" means to take shelter in unhiddenness; thus sheltered, to perdure in presence; to be a being . . . .
>
> Being in the sense of this disclosive coming-over, and beings as such in the sense of the arrival which hides itself, are present as differentiated by the Same, the difference, which alone provides and holds apart the "between" in which coming-over and arrival are maintained in relation, at once separated from and turned toward each other. The difference of Being and beings, taken as the difference of coming-over and arrival, is the revealing-concealing emergence of the two.[7]

The question now is to find out whether this may not be exactly what Hegel envisages under the title of "the Absolute."

In the Conclusion of *Faith and Knowledge*[8] Hegel pulls together in the most concise manner what he understands by this Absolute which Kant had the merit of approaching and the fault of missing. Now, the process which Hegel describes here has a structure which is strikingly similar to the process which Heidegger describes. We can draw the parallel point by point.

According to Heidegger, Being passes beyond and above that which it discloses. It transcends beings, it is the no-thing. According to Hegel, the Absolute is "pure nullification . . . of finitude," i.e., of that which has the status of the finite and upon which phenomenal representation is exclusively focused. By this "transcending coming-over," says Heidegger, beings emerge. The Absolute, says Hegel, at the same time as it is pure nullification, is the source of finitude.

Heidegger holds that what arrives, the being which shows itself, takes shelter in the coming-over, it withdraws. Hegel holds that finitude is "non-finite," i.e., it does not cease to negate itself, to reabsorb itself into this bottomless depth, *Abgrund.* This process of coming-over and arrival, Heidegger declares, is the process of truth in the sense of a showing which holds itself back in that which shows itself. Regarding the nothing, Hegel writes: "Out of this nothing and pure night of infinity, as out of the secret abyss that is its birthplace, the truth lifts itself upward." Finally, for Heidegger, if Being in the sense of the coming-over and beings in the sense of the arrival are present as different, they are so by virtue of the Same, the difference, the *Austrag,* understood as conciliation. It is precisely as conciliation that Hegel thinks the process of negation and emergence to which he gives the name of the Absolute.

B. Finitude and the Absolute

Up to this point in our investigation, the common structure which we have discovered is only a skeleton. Let us flesh it out with thought. Within this structure three topics command our attention: the nothing, truth, and the circle or reciprocity. Now, since all three topics inhere in one and the same structure which is the very subject matter of thought, it would be wrong to think of them as if each carved out a separate and closed area of investigation. Rather, they are intersecting axes which lead us to one and the same area. Having stated this caution, let us begin by taking up the theme of the *circle,* for the question of reciprocity (or overlapping intersection) presses to the fore.

1. *The Circle*

Turning to Heidegger we can say that from *Being and Time* on, his whole procedure has consisted in a deliberate effort at entering the circle. In *Being and Time* the point was to ask the question of the meaning of Being, which, although it had engaged all of Western philosophy since its Greek origins, had since fallen into oblivion. The elaboration of this question in *Being and Time* takes the form of a circle. To pose explicitly the question of the meaning of Being requires a prior explanation of the being who questions. It is the nature of this question to rebound back upon the questioner. More precisely, Being, as that which is asked about, that towards which one questions, is intrinsically related back to the question itself as a mode of the Being of the very being which we are. But reciprocally the question, as a mode of interrogative Being which we ourselves are, is essentially affected by Being. In other words, Being itself is problematic, astonishing and worthy of question only in relation to the Dasein who questions. But insofar as questioning is constitutive of man's Being, the Dasein who questions is intrinsically referred to Being insofar as Being is that which is worthy of questioning. There is, says Heidegger, a remarkable relation both forward and backward between what is questioned (Being) and the questioning itself as a mode of Being of a being (Dasein). Heidegger sharpens the point in "The Way Back into the Ground of Metaphysics": "To characterize with a single term both the involvement of Being in human nature and the essential relation of man to the openness ('there') of Being as such, the name of 'being there' *[Dasein]* was chosen for that sphere of Being in which man as man stands."[9]

The whole effort of *Being and Time* consists in unfolding the interplay and vectors of this twofold reference, at once anticipatory and retrospective. First we have the forward reference of the projection which grounds the understanding in which Dasein maintains itself, insofar as the movement of the projection is a transcendence or going-beyond which does not aim at this or that being but at the horizon or depth from which these beings can emerge: the world, Being. But likewise there is the backward reference of the same projection, since it is defined as a *thrown* projection. Understanding and disposition *(Befindlichkeit)*, Heidegger says, are equiprimordial, and far from transcendence producing the world of Being, it is itself always and already called forward by the world. Thus we have the forward reference of Being: it is the prior horizon by virtue of which beings can bring themselves forth or appear. And as well there is the backward reference of Being, for although Being is always prior to beings, it also always falls back upon — and is nothing without — those beings. As Heidegger says: The Being which we ask about is always the Being *of beings*. Thus the further consequence of a forward reference from beings to Being (beings obscure Being, ontic knowledge does not concern itself with Being) and a backward reference of beings toward Being (beings highlight Being, and ontic knowledge would be nothing without ontological knowledge).

By working out the question of the meaning of Being in this circular fashion, Heidegger's procedure is shown to be caught up in a strange and surprising back-and-forth, an "in-between." And what brings about this circular elaboration of the question is the emergence of the ontological difference. This is said right from the beginning of *Being and Time* (§7) in a text which reveals the circular structure of the question: "What is *asked about* in the question to be elaborated is Being, that which determines beings as beings, that in terms of which beings have always been understood no matter how they are discussed. The Being of beings 'is' itself not a being."[10]

One might question that this association of the circular character of the question and the emergence of the ontological difference remains within the first stage of Heidegger's thought where this difference is not really formulated and where the circularity of the inquiry is bound up with the priority accorded to man as the primary object of philosophical inquiry. But this is not the case. We might even say that the association of the two becomes closer and closer as Heidegger goes along.

As proof consider this fact: At the point where the apparent priority of Dasein (which had led to the existentialist interpretations of *Being and Time*) begins to fade and where for the first time Heidegger explicitly inquires into the ontological difference—I refer to the texts from the period of *Introduction to Metaphysics*—he locates this inquiry within a circular procedure. This is seen sufficiently in "The Origin of the Artwork." From the very beginning of the essay, the reflection is guided by a circle. We might answer the question, "In virtue of what is the artwork an artwork?" by saying that the origin of the artwork is the artist; but this answer is obviously too quick, since the artist is an artist only by virtue of the artwork. And if we say that this reciprocity perhaps points to a third term—art itself—which would be the origin of both artist and artwork, how can we ask about art itself? Without the art*work,* art is only an empty idea. Yet we could not recognize an artwork if the essence of art had not already claimed us in some way. Heidegger writes: "Thus we are compelled to follow the circle. This is neither a makeshift nor a defect. To enter upon this path is the strength of thought, to continue on it is the feast of thought . . . ."[11]

Here again it is the emergence of the ontological difference that reveals the circularity of the reflection. The essence or artwork-ness of the artwork is the happening of a disclosure. But this is not the offering of an object to a subject who dominates it or delights in it, since this disclosure provides no information, guarantees no mastery, permits no definition: it is there for nothing and as nothing. Pure appearance, pure effulgence, the disclosure itself, is entirely hidden. What shines forth in it is the "betwixt and between" of the manifest and its manifestation, the being and its Being, in such a way that the origin of the artwork is the putting-into-work of that origin or initial leap *(Ur-sprung)* which is at once older and younger that all things and which is the transcendence of Being over and beyond beings and the abiding of beings in Being.

The circularity of the procedure is therefore connected with the topic or subject matter of thought, which is indicated by the term "ontological difference." And here we may note that by virtue of its circularity and because of the difference which calls it forth, the procedure avoids the properly modern relation of subject and object—not only avoids it but undercuts it in such a way that this relation can no longer be considered radical.

As early as *Being and Time,* the fact that the circularity of the method entails overturning the modern relation of subject and object was clear throughout and especially from the texts in which Heidegger says that Descartes, in taking the discovery of the *cogito* as radical, necessarily had "to omit both the question of Being and the question of the meaning of the Being of the being" which he defined as the *cogito*. The plan of *Being and Time* included, among its proposed tasks, a phenomenological destruction of the Cartesian *cogito-sum*. Although this destruction was not carried out, we may assume that its essential elements are provided in such writings as "The Age of the World View" and the remarks gathered under the title "The Overcoming of Metaphysics." In these texts Heidegger shows how the establishment of the modern subject-object relation is connected with the most thorough elimination of the ontological difference or (to stay with the language of *Being and Time*) of the backward and forward relation of Being and beings, Being and Dasein, and of each of these with regard to the other. The thoroughness with which the subject-object relation eliminates the ontological difference consists in the fact that it attempts to eradicate difference in general and in all senses of the term. It might seem that this relation presupposes at the very least a difference between subject and object, but such is not the case. From the beginning, this relation happens by means of reducing one of the terms to the other. As Heidegger says, "In the order of the transcendental genesis of the object *[Gegenstand]*, the subject is the first object *[Objekt]* of ontological representation."[12] In the framework of Descartes' thought, the object, that which is "placed there," *ob-jectum*, is conceived as a stable and sure base. But as regards their foundation, the stability and surity of this placing go back to a positing, a *Vor-stellung*, a re-presentation which itself is defined as the deepest stability and surity — the *cogito* itself — and in such a way that the object has nothing peculiar or original about it that might be different from the subject. The peculiarity of the object is its object-ness — which is the *cogito* itself, already stretched out in front of itself as that which (in a way seemingly distinct from the object) merely offers itself to itself, places itself before itself, re-presents itself.

Just as Heidegger's analysis underlines the disproportionate weight given to the ego, so too it emphasizes a kind of rigidification. The words which are typical of this analysis of the subject-object relation, i.e., of representation, are: fixing, stabilizing, securing, constantly preserving. To represent is to fix. And in *Being and Time* the hermeneutical discussion of the Cartesian ontology of the world had already emphasized this stabilization when it showed that the ontological foundations of Descartes' definition of the world as *res extensa* are summed up in the idea of substantiality, which implicitly rests on a certain idea of Being as subsistence in permanence. Under the weight of this pure fix-edness and this uniform stability which defines both *cogito* and *cogitatum*, the difference lies deeply buried.

Let us now turn to the theme of the circle in Hegel. The evidence that this theme is intimately connected with Hegel's thought is so overwhelming as to be a truism, for without a doubt Hegel is the thinker who most strongly emphasizes that thought proceeds not by avoiding a so-called circle but by placing itself decisively within the circle. The famous formula of the Preface of *The Phenomenology of Spirit* is well known: The true is the becoming of itself, the circle which presupposes and has, at the beginning, its proper end as its goal and which is actually real only by mediating both its developed actualization and its end. Equally well known is the circular presentation of the system in the *Encyclopaedia*. Each of the parts of philosophy forms a circle, and the ensemble is a "circle of circles" which, in its dizzying development, articulates a whole gamut of backward and forward references between logic, nature and spirit, each one following and at the same time preceding the other. But since this theme of the circle in Hegel first comes to us in a text from the Jena period, we must investigate that period of his thought in order to find some solid guidelines for a dialogue with Heidegger.

During this period Hegel wrote a sentence of which Jean Hypollite was particularly fond: "The task is to think life." In assuming that task, Hegel's procedure appears for the first time as circular. I suggest that this very meditation on life, sketched during the Frankfurt period and bound up with a circular thematic, entails a reflection on the difference, while simultaneously undercutting the modern subject-object relation in such a way that this relation is divested of its claim to radicality.

We have to say from the start that by the word "life" Hegel does not at all mean a delimited area of reality, an ontic domain situated alongside other domains. This reflection does not have to do with beings but with Being. To inquire into the relation of life and the living is to inquire into the relation of Being and beings.

The circularity of this reflection consists in the fact that it reveals a simultaneously backward and forward relation between life and the living, the living and life, while at the same time emphasizing man's involvement in the interplay of this twofold reference. There is the forward relation of life towards the living, for life is the element by means of which the living can reveal itself as living. But there is also the backward reference of life with regard to the living, for without the living, life would be only a fleeting abstraction. Thus: a forward reference of the living towards life, in the sense that the living reveals life, and a backward reference of the living with regard to life, in the sense that the living cannot reveal life except by not being life, that is, by hiding it. Therefore Hegel calls life a circle *(Kreis)*. But to reflect on this circle is to meditate on an original difference, since life cannot be except by separating itself from itself: it unites only by dividing itself and is a joining only by being a non-joining, "a joining of the joining and the non-joining." And just as Heidegger in *Being and Time* placed Da-sein into the intersection of the forward and backward reference of Being to beings and of beings to Being, so Hegel places man within the interplay of the reciprocal encroachment of life and the living. The priority which Hegel at this time gives to Greek religion over modern religion consists precisely in the fact that Greek religion, according to him, bears witness to man's involvement in this unifying and dividing process of life. For Hegel Greek religion is the religion of beauty, and beauty is nothing but the manifestation of the unifying process which defines life. During this period Hölderlin wrote: "The great saying of Heraclitus, *Hen diapheron heautoi,* could only have been uttered by a Greek, for here is the essence of beauty." Hegel thought the same. In his *Fragment of a System* he shows that the religion of beauty is the one which corresponds to the joining of joining and non-joining. But he also says that this religion of beauty is the only one which can be profoundly human. In other words, man's essence lies in corresponding to this unifying-dividing process which is life.

Here is where Hegel's reflection undercuts the modern subject-object relation. One might object that, from this point on, the words "object" and "subject" are found all over Hegel's text and, moreover, that Hegel defines Greek religion as subjective in contrast to modern religion as objective. Certainly. But in fact Hegel attempts to divest these words of their modern meanings. Or better: The priority which he gives to so-called subjective religion implies a polemic against the modern subject-object relation insofar as the latter is connected with the elimination of the originary process of the joining and non-joining, the difference between life and the living. In fact the whole critique which Hegel directs first against Judaism and then against Christian religion consists in denouncing the monopoly of the understanding, i.e., that relation to beings which consists in dominating them. He says: "To conceptualize (and this is precisely the business of the understanding) is to dominate. When the subject has the form of subject and the object has the form of the object, the subject is the all-powerful reality and the object is the dominated."[13] Of course this criticism is anachronistic as regards the religious forms it examines, for it slips a specifically modern mode of thinking back into Judaism and original Christianity. But the important thing is that the reflection of the difference is bound up with calling the subject-object relation into question. Behind the fact that man is conceived as subject *qua* all-powerful reality and that the world is conceived as object in the sense of the dominated, there lies hidden something more profound. "To situate the unity of the real in man," writes the young Hegel, "is to raise man to the rank of a being who makes all the rest of reality a thought; that is to say: he kills it, dominates it." Blindness to life, to what Hegel calls "the originally free Being of life," is inherent in the process of conceptualization, the understanding. As such, the understanding has nothing of the origin about it. By contrast the imagination is originary since its business is not objects but "modifications of life." It entirely escapes the dilemma of domination and servitude, for it is not even a faculty but is man's being seized by the unifying-dividing process of life. As the religion of beauty which puts the imagination into play, Greek religion is called subjective religion by Hegel. But in that case the word "subject" no longer means what it does for modern man: the fixed and dominating position of the ego. Rather it takes on the ancient Greek meaning of *hypokeimenon,* the collection of things, the unifying in-gathering. If Greek religion is subjective, it is because in it man gathers in and accepts the free manifestation of life as a unifying-dividing process.

And just as Heidegger's description of the constitution of the priority of ego emphasized a kind of rigidity, so too Hegel denounces a fixedness within the monopoly of the understanding. "The business of the understanding," he writes, "is to fixate objectivity." And further: the understanding is related to the "inert"; it "crystallizes."

2. *Truth*

As we have mentioned above, the topic of truth does not consist in a defined area of research which would be accessible to a regional discipline like epistemology. Neither Hegel nor Heidegger will allow that epistemology could have the status of radicality, because this discipline refuses to recognize that the question of truth is inherent in the circle which we just discussed.

In Heidegger we notice that the question of truth involves a circular process. This can be seen from the famous paragraph 44 of *Being and Time,* which, as Tugendhat has clearly shown, starts off the whole Heideggerian problematic of truth. The question of truth demands a circular process in the same way that the question of the meaning of Being does. In fact, Being and truth have been linked together ever since the beginnings of philosophy in Greece. Aristotle defined first philosophy equally as the science of truth and as the science which investigates beings *qua* beings, i.e., with regard to their Being. Since this association of Being and truth is the heritage of the whole of Western philosophy, the destruction of the tradition, which Heidegger undertakes so as to clarify the meaning of Being, is aimed at placing truth within the arena of the problematic of fundamental ontology. And since this very problematic involves circularity (insofar as that which is questioned reflects back upon the questioning as Dasein's mode of Being), the same goes for the problematic of truth.

Recall how Heidegger proceeds in §44 of *Being and Time.* Step one (§44a) examines the traditional concept of truth so as to seek out its ontological foundations. Step two (§44b) shows how the foundations reveal an original phenomenon of truth whence the traditional concept of truth is derived. Step three (§44c) inquires into the mode of Being of truth and the presupposition of truth. Only in this third stage do we see that the question of truth is involved in this interplay of forward and backward references which we mentioned earlier with regard to the question of Being.

The traditional concept of the essence of truth brings two themes together: the locus of truth is the assertion, and the essence of truth consists in the correspondence of the assertion with its object. Because the two theses give major importance to the assertion, the search for the ontological foundations of the traditional concept of truth passes through the question about the relation of the assertion to what is asserted insofar as the assertion is confirmed to be true. In what does that relation consist? The answer is that this confirmation happens on the basis of a self-manifestation of the being: the being shows itself as such. And as regards its ontological meaning, the assertion which proves to be true *is disclosive* of the being itself. To assert is to make known, to wrest the being from hiddenness and to let it be seen in its unhiddenness.

The second step of the analysis, by saying that "true" in the primary sense is to-be-disclosive, seems to put the whole weight of this revealing upon Dasein, the one who makes the assertion. Since to disclose is a mode of Being of Dasein, Dasein is therefore true in the primary sense. Being-disclosed is true only in a secondary sense. With the openness of Dasein, who is always ahead of himself, we reach the most original phenomenon of truth. In fact the text says that the disclosedness of innerworldly beings "belongs" to this openness. If we were to stop here, we might think that the reciprocity which we discussed a moment ago is no longer found here and that, on the contrary, the referential movement is unilateral: it goes from Dasein to the beings which are disclosed. But that is not the case, and this fact brings us to the third step of the analysis.

Paragraph 44c does not consider Dasein as the foundation of truth but rather as "being-in-the-truth." Dasein is enmeshed in the presupposition of truth. In other words, Dasein is not constitutive of its own openness; rather, this openness, the very openness of the world or of Being, is what destines Dasein to himself. Truth is one with, and cannot be without, the disclosive projection; yet this very projection presupposes truth, for it is, as Heidegger says, a "thrown" projection. That is why he says that "Being-true, like Being-disclosive, is ontologically possible only on the basis of Being-in-the-world." The anticipation of the being (which is the whole disclosive process) is itself anticipated by the opening or truth of Being. This projective process itself is not what originally gives truth, but goes back to a more original bestowal. That is why it is again said in this third step of the analysis: "There is *(Es gibt)* Being only as long as there is truth. Being and truth are of the same origin."

Here again the reflection's circularity points towards an original difference, that between Being and beings, for as a whole the sentence says, "There is Being — *and not beings* — only as long as there is truth." This means that original truth itself is the difference. Just as Being is the Being of the beings which it is not, so truth is the truth of the beings which it is not. But the phrase "just as" is incorrect since we do not have Being on the one hand and truth on the other.

Heidegger's whole effort after *Being and Time* is to insist that, in order to ask the question of the essence of truth in its radicality, we have to ask it as the question of the truth of "essence" in the verbal sense of *Wesen*, "Being." It is one and the same thing to say that the subject matter of thought is Being and that it is *aletheia*. *Aletheia* is the very name for Being, and the twofoldness which the Greek word expresses with the alpha-privative designates the difference which is Being, the presence of what is present. This is not a super-presence behind or beyond the thing which is present, but is the very coming-forth of what is present, an emergence which holds itself back precisely while giving itself, the manifestation (of what is manifest) which itself is not manifest, which reveals only by withdrawing itself.

It goes without saying that in this reflection all representational intentions are out of the picture. It is not a question of thought moving towards a correspondence or coincidence (for that could only conceal the difference) but rather of accepting the withdrawal of the origin and, with regard to such acceptance, exercising a kind of vigilance.

Now let us turn to Hegel. It might seem rash to presume the possibility of a confrontation between Hegel and Heidegger on this pont. Moreover, Heidegger himself seems to preclude such a confrontation when he shows in his essay "Hegel and the Greeks" that, according to Hegel, the level which Spirit attains in Greek philosophy is not the level of truth, and that among the basic words of Greek philosophy which Hegel interprets in his *Lectures on the History of Philosophy*, the word *aletheia* does not appear. And Heidegger asks: "But doesn't *Aletheia*, truth, dominate the beginning of the path of philosophy in Parmenides?" And more precisely: "The speculative-dialectical definition of history entails the consequence that Hegel was precluded from really seeing *Aletheia* and its power as *the subject matter of thought*."[14] But another essay, "Hegel's Concept of Experience," does speak (if elusively and obscurely) about a "decisive change" which might have intervened at a certain moment in Hegel's thought in such a way as to open it up. "The change concerns the content of the system. It begins soon after the publication of the *Science of the Phenomenology of Spirit*, and probably was occasioned and strengthened by his transfer to the teaching position at the Nuremberg gymnasium."[15] Up to this point I have relied on texts prior to this period of teaching. Recall *Faith and Knowledge:* "Out of this nothing and pure night of infinity, as out of the secret abyss that is its birthplace, the truth lifts itself upward." This text, which suggests an un-truth, a night, a withdrawal, at the heart of truth, sends us back to the older texts which unite the theme of truth with that of the circle of life. These texts, in fact, call the circle of life in its unifying-dividing process a mystery.[16] "The bond of the finite and the infinite is assuredly a sacred mystery, because it is life and consequently the secret of life." And again: "This bond is such that one should speak only in mystic language of the relation it sets up between terms."

And Hegel gives the name "truth" to this secret circle of life. The locus of such truth is not the assertion, and its essence is not the correspondence of subject with object. Such correspondence is only what is envisaged by the reflective understanding which divides up life and crystallizes it in objectivity. Rather, truth is the very light of life, its emergence, its blossoming forth. Hegel writes: Life is *phos*, light. And just as in Heidegger Dasein's mode of Being as disclosive is itself appropriated by the openness of Being, so too Hegel thinks the relation of man to truth as an appropriation by light. "For in every man there is light and life; man is the property of light." And if it is true, as Hegel writes, that "beings are living" and that "Being is pure Life," then we must say that for Hegel too Being and truth are of the same origin and that this origin is intrinsically difference.

In a text which is entitled *"Aletheia"* and which is a commentary on Heraclitus, Heidegger attempts to hear the resonances of Heraclitus' word *zen*, "to live." He writes in this regard:

> The verb "to live" speaks in the largest, uttermost, and inmost significance, which Nietzsche too in his note from 1885/86 was thinking when he said: "'Being' — we have no conception of it other than as 'life.' How can something dead 'be'?"[17]

And later in the text: "The verb *zen* means: emergence into the light." Indeed, *"Zoe* and *physis* mean the same thing." Both words designate emergence from concealment, the original difference.

It is precisely in this area — where the hidden difference makes its approach — that Hegel's thought on truth is grounded. And again the echo of this difference resounds in the famous passage from the Preface of the *Phenomenology* regarding truth:

> Appearance is the process of coming-to-be and passing away, a process that itself does not come to be and pass away, but is *per se,* and constitutes reality and the movement of the life of truth. The truth is thus the bacchanalian revel, where not a member is sober; and because every member no sooner becomes detached than it *eo ipso* collapses straightaway, the revel is just as much a state of transparent unbroken calm.[18]

3. The Nothing

We come to our last topic, the nothing, and here we may be more brief since this theme is implicit in what we have already seen.

In Heidegger the theme of the nothing is bound up with that of the circle. The nothing does not define man's way of Being by contrasting it with that of the *en-soi* as it does, for example, in Sartre's dualistic approach. Rather, as

Heidegger writes in "What is Metaphysics," transcendence or Da-sein as man's way of Being, maintains itself properly in the nothing. But the nothing is not reduced to subjectivity's power to posit itself. Rather, it is inseparable from the double reference which we have mentioned above. Projection, the self-exceeding which constitutes existence as transcendence, *is* nihilation (i.e., passing beyond all that is, a leap beyond beings) *only* insofar as it is itself called forth by the more original leap *(Ur-sprung)* of Being beyond beings. In this regard Heidegger writes in "Letter on Humanism": "Dasein in no way nihilates as a human subject who carries out nihilation in the sense of denial; rather, Da-sein nihilates inasmuch as it belongs to the essence of Being as that essence in which man ek-sists. Being nihilates—as Being."[19]

Now Hegel: here too the topic of the nothing is bound up with the motif of the circle. In opposition to the anthropological emphasis which existentialist interpretations have given to Hegel's texts—an emphasis which consists in investing man exclusively with the performance of the nihilation—we must affirm that Hegel described man's way of Being as a passing-beyond which is carried out in the nothing. However, he referred this passing-beyond to a nihilation of which man is not the source but which takes place originally in Being itself—in Hegel's terms: in the Absolute. Being is the "labor of the negative." Recall the conclusion of *Faith and Knowledge:* The Absolute is pure nihilation of finitude, it is the nothing, and from this nothing truth arises as from a mysterious abyss.

Far from being ignorant of all this, Heidegger insists on it. Indeed, the paragraph which we just cited from "Letter on Humanism" goes on: "Being nihilates—as Being. Therefore, the 'not' appears in the absolute Idealism of Hegel and Schelling as the negativity of negation in the essence of Being." And again: "Nihilation comes to the fore through this dialectic...."

C. CONCLUSION

We located this study within the perspective of the question, "How is Heidegger's thought about difference distinct from Hegel's dialectic thought?" Our investigation led to the conclusion that it is not their respective themes which separate them, for their subject matter is the same. And in this regard we were careful not to force any affinity which Heidegger would reject.

Not only does Heidegger write that nihilation comes to the fore in and through the dialectic, but he himself recognizes and points out the affinity of the themes of truth and circle. He even writes that *aletheia* is present in the *Phenomenology of Spirit.* And with regard to the theme of the circle as it is implied in the short and famous sentence at the beginning of the *Phenomenology*—"The Absolute is already in and for itself with us and wishes to be with us"—Heidegger writes, "Without this being-with-us the Absolute could not emerge in its unconcealment *(Unverborgenheit).* Without this emergence *(physis)* the Absolute would not be in life *(zoe)*."[20] And further along he adds: "...There can be no introduction to the *Phenomenology.* The phenomenology of Spirit is the parousia of the Absolute. The parousia is the Being of beings. There can be no introduction or leading [of man] to the Being of beings, for man's essence is led and accompanied by Being and *is* this very leading and accompanying."[21] In other words, the *Phenomenology* is embedded in a circle which it mediates. And what is at stake in this circle—in the specifically Hegelian modality of confronting natural consciousness and absolute self-consciousness—is the difference of ontic and ontological consciousness, the ontico-ontological difference.

The objection might be made that the three themes we have mentioned may indeed touch the heart of Heidegger's thought about the difference, but that they are insufficient to encompass what is specific to dialectical thought. On this point let me simply mention that Merleau-Ponty (who never spoke or wrote lightly), in an attempt to delimit the essentials of dialectical thought in one of his courses at the Collège de France (1955/56), defined it by the following themes: the labor of the negative, revision of the ordinary notions of subject and object, and circularity.

But if both Heidegger and Hegel call upon the same themes, what separates them?

It might seem that the distinction comes down to Hegel's gradual distantiation from the initial themes of his writings during the Frankfurt and Jena periods. This idea of gradual distancing is doubtlessly at work in Heidegger's debate with Hegel. In fact, when Heidegger wants to emphasize Hegel's blindness to the ontological difference, he refers to texts later than the *Phenomenology,* i.e., the texts of the systematic teaching. That is the case with his essay "Hegel and the Greeks," which refers to the Berlin *Lectures on the History of Philosophy.* It is also the case with his essay "The Onto-theo-logical Constitution of Metaphysics," which refers to the *Science of Logic.* On the other hand, when he wants to emphasize that there is thought about the difference in Hegel, Heidegger appeals to the *Phenomenology,* as he does in his essay "Hegel's Concept of Experience."

This notion of gradual distantiation is perhaps not to be excluded from consideration, but I think we should use it with great caution. For it seems to me unquestionable that, on the one hand, the Jena writings anticipate the systematic structure of the *Encyclopaedia* and the *Logic* and that, on the other, the writings from the period of the system are open to an interpretation which can bring out the theme of the difference.

In other words, even though I admit, as Heidegger suggests, that the systematization entails a kind of rigidification, I am inclined to think that right from the beginning, from the moment Hegel takes up the philosophical project, the proper subject matter of his thought lies in the theme of the difference, but that the way in which he relates to it entails the elimination of the difference.

The key term which reveals how Hegel's involvement with the theme of the difference is, at one and the same time, the emergence and the elimination of the difference is: the Absolute. In attempting to bring out what this word means, we uncovered a structure similar to that which is meant by the word "finitude" in Heidegger. And then, in attempting to lay out the three themes which this structure implies, we recognized at the center of each theme the topic of the difference. It is not immaterial that this structure, these themes, and these motifs are intended by the word "Absolute."

The task of thought as envisaged and taken up in this word is indeed the difference, but when seen as the Absolute, the difference and the whole interplay of references connected with it are condemned to elimination. By definition the Absolute is that which absolves itself from all reference, that which, in the very difference and in the interplay of references which it implies, makes itself equal to itself, coincides with itself. As a result, at the very moment when the difference is recognized as radical, it is no longer radical but derived—or, what amounts to the same thing, is uprooted. It follows that at the very moment when the notion of coincidence seems discredited, it actually is expanded, and words like "concordance, equivalence, equality" take over the whole of Hegel's text. Again: At the very point when the circle is recognized as an unavoidable and integral element, it is wrenched from its inherent role so as to be placed completely in view in the form of a totality accessible to intellectual insight. And further: Just when truth is recognized as arising from a mysterious abyss, it loses all mystery and is declared to be logical, since, as Hegel says, it is only "one moment of the supreme Idea and no more." And as a final result, even when the nothing is associated with this mysterious abyss, it too finds itself circumscribed and defined as "[one] side of the absolute Idea."[22] The difference, therefore, is absorbed into a conciliation in which it is eliminated and swallowed up in the indivisible unity of self-consciousness.

Yet the fact remains that Heidegger, in a note to "Identity and Difference," uses the word "reconciliation" (Versöhnung), so charged with Hegelianism, to name the unifying-dividing process of the coming-over and the arrival, the very process of the difference. Perhaps this is an index of two things: on the one hand, that the dialectical and speculative fulfillment of metaphysics, in the very movement by which it covers over the origin, bears special witness to that origin; and, on the other, that there is no possible language for the difference and that the destruction of metaphysics cannot be completed.[23]

Translated by Thomas Sheehan

Notes

Jacques Taminiaux is Professor of Philosophy at the University of Louvain and Director of the French section of the Husserl Archives there, and an editor of the *Phaenomenologica* series (Nijhoff). He is the author of *La nostalgie de la Grèce à l'aube de l'idéalisme allemand* (The Hague: Nijhoff, 1967) and the editor and translator of G. W. F. Hegel, *Système de la vie étique* (Paris: Payot, 1976). His numerous articles have appeared in Europe and America. The present article is a translation of "Finitude et Absolu. Remarques sur Hegel et Heidegger, interprètes de Kant," *Revue Philosophique de Louvain*, 69 (May, 1971), 190-215.

1. Martin Heidegger, *Kant and the Problem of Metaphysics,* trans. James S. Churchill (Bloomington: Indiana University Press, 1962), p. 238; translation slightly revised here.
2. G. W. F. Hegel, *Faith and Knowledge,* trans. Walter Cerf and H. S. Harris (Albany: State University of New York Press, 1967), p. 67 f.
3. Cf. *Kant and the Problem,* "The Transcendental Imagination as the Root of Both Stems," pp. 144 ff.
4. *Faith and Knowledge,* p. 72f.
5. *Ibid.,* pp. 70 and 73.
6. *Ibid.,* p. 77; translation slightly revised here.
7. Martin Heidegger, *Identity and Difference,* trans. Joan Stambaugh (New York: Harper and Row, 1969), p. 65; translation revised here.
8. *Faith and Knowledge,* pp.189-191.
9. Martin Heidegger, "The Way Back into the Ground of Metaphysics," trans. Walter Kaufmann in *Existentialism from Dostoevsky to Sartre,* ed. Walter Kaufmann (New York: World-Meridian, 1956), p. 213; translation slightly revised here.
10. Martin Heidegger, *Being and Time,* trans. Joan Stambaugh, in Martin Heidegger, *Basic Writings,* ed. David Farrell Krell (New York: Harper and Row, 1977), p. 46.
11. Martin Heidegger, "The Origin of the Work of Art," trans. Albert Hofstadter, in *Basic Writings,* p. 150.
12. Martin Heidegger, *Vorträge und Aufsätze* (third edition, Pfullingen: Neske, 1967), I, 66.
13. For this and what follows: G. W. F. Hegel, "The Spirit of Christianity and Its Fate," trans. T. M. Knox, in Hegel, *Early Theological Writings,* ed. and trans. T. M. Knox and Richard Kroner (Chicago: University of Chicago Press, 1948), pp. 182-301.
14. Martin Heidegger, "Hegel und die Griechen," in Heidegger, *Wegmarken* (Frankfurt: Klostermann, 1967), p. 267 and 269.
15. Martin Heidegger, *Holzwege* (fourth edition, Frankfurt: Klostermann, 1963) p. 183.
16. Cf. "The Spirit of Christianity and its Fate."
17. For this and the following sentence: Martin Heidegger, *Early Greek Thinking,* trans. D. F. Krell and F. A. Capuzzi (New York: Harper and Row, 1975), p. 115f.
18. G. W. F. Hegel, *The Phenomenology of Mind,* trans. J. B. Baillie (revised second edition, New York: Humanities Press, 1949), p. 105; translation slightly amended here.

19. Martin Heidegger, "Letter on Humanism," trans. F. A. Capuzzi, in *Basic Writings*, p. 238.
20. *Holzwege*, p. 187f.
21. *Ibid.*, p. 189.
22. *Faith and Knowledge*, p. 189-191.
23. Cf. Jacques Taminiaux, "Dialectique et différence," in *Durchblicke. Martin Heidegger zum 80. Geburtstag*, ed. Vittorio Klostermann (Frankfurt: Klostermann, 1970), pp. 318-330.

The Poverty of Thought:
A Reflection on Heidegger and Eckhart

John D. Caputo

As a tribute to the achievement of Martin Heidegger, I wish to offer a brief reflection on the "poverty of thought." To speak of the "poverty" of thought is to evoke all that is strange — and at the same time compelling — in what Heidegger calls "thought." For unlike the metaphysical interpretation of thinking, Heidegger demands that the thinker divest himself of the pretension that he can give a rational account of things, that he somehow achieves mastery over objects. The thinker must recognize that Being, which is the matter to be thought, holds sway over thought and that thought occurs only as the gift of Being.

To speak of the poverty of thought is also to recognize the enigmatic alliance that exists between Heidegger and the mystical and religious tradition. For the mystic and religious authors have from of old insisted upon what is called in the New Testament "poverty of spirit." In the Sermon on the Mount we read: "Blessed are the poor in spirit for theirs is the kingdom of heaven." The poverty of which the Scripture speaks does not consist in being divested of physical possessions, but more radically in having freed one's heart from attachment to things. According to Meister Eckhart of Hochheim (1269-1327/9), the great Dominican preacher and Rhineland mystic, to be poor in spirit means to be empty of creatures in order to be full of God. Hence, to speak of the poverty of thought is to raise the question of the relationship of thought to mysticism, and in particular, of Heidegger to Meister Eckhart. What do these two towers at opposite ends of the German tradition, this thinker and this mystic, have in common? I should like to suggest here, in a much more adumbrated way than I have done elsewhere,[1] something of the richness of this kinship. Then, by way of conclusion, I will try to differentiate Heidegger from the mystical and religious tradition, and thereby indicate how, in remaining faithful to the chosen path, Heidegger has remained his own man, neither mystic nor metaphysician, but rather, as he puts it himself so simply, a thinker.

One of the most daring and paradoxical sermons which Eckhart composed was dedicated to the theme of poverty of spirit. In that sermon, which took its point of departure from the passage from the New Testament which we have just cited, Eckhart wrote: "He is a poor man who *wills* nothing and *knows* nothing and *has* nothing." I should like to reflect on what each of these things means for the mystic and on how each also applies in its own way to thought.[2]

(1) He who is poor in spirit *wills* nothing. The will-lessness which Eckhart has in mind does not refer to an effortless passivity, to lassitude, but to a suspension of all teleological attitudes. He who is poor in spirit does not will to have this virtue or that, or even to do the will of God. While all who have such a will are good people, they do not possess true spiritual poverty, for they are not poor of willing itself. Eckhart expresses the particular kind of suspension of the teleological which he has in mind by saying that the will-less soul lives "without why." The soul does not love God for the gifts that God can give him, for that is not to love God but God's gifts. He loves God purely, without any hope or expectations of a reward. Loving God, Eckhart says, is like living: it needs no why. I live for the sake of living; I love God for the sake of God.

True poverty consists in having no will. One does not will to do the will of God, or will to be united with God. One does not will at all. Rather, the soul simply *lets* the life of God flow freely through itself. It is in connection with this will-less letting-be that Meister Eckhart uses the word *"Gelassenheit"* (letting-be, releasement), a word familiar today to every reader of Heidegger. The soul with true poverty, the soul which lives in *Gelassenheit,* has moved totally beyond the sphere of willing into a will-lessness which lets God be God in the soul. The soul does not attempt to storm God with a gigantic moral effort; rather, it quietly opens itself to God who rushes in upon it and fills it with His life.

The poverty of thought is also a non-willing. For thought does not desire to produce results; it is not efficacious. In the midst of productivity, thought produces nothing. In the midst of control, thought is lord over nothing. In the midst of mastering the earth, thought is earth-bound and mortal. The task of thought is not to acquire the power with which to travel to the moon and back; it is to learn to dwell on the earth. It does not desire to harness the earth's energy but to receive the earth's gifts. In the midst of political activity, the poverty of thought can give no concrete instructions about the reform of human institutions. The task of thought is to think in response to the destiny which is unfolding in Western history *(das Seinsgeschick),* not to assume mastery over it.

The poverty of thought means that thought, as Heidegger conceives it, is less than technology and political action. But its nobility is that in virtue of this very impotence thought is responsive to a higher power. For according to Heidegger no merely human action can save humanity. Humanity's fate rests on a higher destiny, the destiny of Being itself. And if the poverty of the thinker is that he cannot master beings, his nobility lies in his responsiveness to Being. For the thinker stays ready for the new dispensation. His is a preparatory poverty. He prepares for the possibility of a new advent of Being, a new beginning. For Being cannot turn towards man if man does not open himself to Being.

Both Heidegger and Eckhart have understood the poverty of human willing, and that there is in will-lessness a higher action, an action which prepares the way for a power which surpasses every human force.

(2) Meister Eckhart said that the poor in spirit *knows* nothing. For the wisdom of men is foolishness in the eyes of God. The highest knowledge (*Wissen*) of all is to know nothing, to divest oneself of knowledge, to be pure and free of knowledge. Knowing nothing: that means "unknowing" (*Unwissen*), a holy unknowing which Nicholas of Cusa, following Eckhart's lead, called a learned unknowing (*docta ignorantia*), for it is an unknowing which is learned in the ways of God. The poor in spirit know that no concept can grasp God. The concept is man-made, a creature, an idol. It is not the God whom we have devised with our thoughts whom we should seek, Meister Eckhart said, but the essential God, God in His very Being.

Now just as will-lessness is not lassitude, so the unknowing of which Eckhart speaks is not mere lack of understanding. On the contrary, he says, human passivity is oriented towards God's activity, for it is the condition of God's activity in us. The soul which ceases to know with its own knowledge makes a clearing for a knowledge which comes from God. God cannot speak His Word in the soul, Eckhart insists, if the soul is filled with its own discourse. Hence the soul must clear itself of all "noise," that is, it must suspend all concepts and images, all spoken and written words. Then alone can the Eternal Word be spoken. Then the soul comes to participate in God's own self-knowledge. In a text that would later attract the attention of Hegel, Eckhart writes that the soul comes to see God with the same eye in which God sees Himself. That is why Cusanus would call this ignorance "learned."

The poverty of thought, for Heidegger, is to be divested of representations (*Vorstellungen*). Thinking does not force what-is into a system of "concepts" which frame it out and circumscribe it. Representations bring the being into human horizons and subject it to human determinations. Representations posit (*stellen*) beings as they stand (*stehen*) over and against (*gegen*) the thinking subject. The being itself disappears and is replaced by the "object" (*Gegenstand*). In representational thinking things do not rise up before us and emerge in the fullness of their presence, of their own Being. Rather, an "object" appears which has been predelineated by human thought. The object is a structure projected by subjectivity, a structure constituted within a framework laid down by representational thought.

Consider, for example, the rose which blossoms in the spring. The rose opens itself up, it rises up and unfolds. It radiates its color and its fragrance. The rose addresses us and speaks to us of life and birth. Why does it blossom? How is that possible? Such questions never arise. It is not that we lack the answers to these questions; rather we have suspended the questions. For the rose suffices unto itself. It does not lack an explanation for itself which human thinking must rush to supply. The rose rises up and stands forth on its own grounds and from out of its own Being, which is in accord with Heidegger's famous interpretation of the Greek word *physis*. The botanist's "object," the genus *rosa,* however, has a determinate structure. It has five leafy petals, e.g., and it responds to particular environmental stimuli. It blossoms because of certain determinable conditions in the air and in the soil. It fits into a system of causes and effects; it takes its place in "nature" conceived of as a spatio-temporal-causal system.

The rose blossoms because it blossoms. In order to experience its blossoming we need only let it be the thing which it is, let it rise up before us and address us. But the object of the botanist is projected on a human screen, framed within a set of human explanatory principles. The rose blossoms without such explanations. It is like life itself, without why. I live because I live, for no other purpose and from no other grounds than my own life. So too the rose blossoms from out of its own grounds and for the sheer sake of its own blossoming. It rises up and radiates of itself, for that is its very beauty *(Schönheit),* viz., its rising up and shining *(scheinen).* There are no causes here, no environmental factors, for all such structures are projected by representational thought, by subjectivity.

The poverty of thought is that for it there are no objects and no subjects. Thought is therefore less than philosophy and less than science. The thinker cannot develop a new crossbreed of the genus *rosa,* nor develop a repellent to combat insect blight. Compared to science, thought is unknowing. Thought possesses no representations with which to interpret and predict physical and psychical phenomena. It offers no proofs, lays down no axioms, predicts no results, possesses no criteria, has no methodology. It cannot be introduced or summarized in a manual. It offers no world view, no overview of man and the world. It lacks the exactness of the natural sciences and the systematic rationality of philosophy.

But the poverty of thought, by which it lacks all representations, is the condition of its openness to a higher address. The thinker, in the silence of his representationless thought, hears an address which would be drowned out by the noise of science and philosophy. The thinker *lets* a power speak in him which is not merely a human voice. He hears a speaking which is not man's but that of language itself, that is, of Being. In the sacrifice which surrenders representations he receives a gift of Being itself. He experiences the thing in its Being, in its innermost rising up, in the upsurge by which the thing itself emerges into presence and comes towards us. We do not project the rose, we release it. We do not frame it about with human determinations, we let it rise up and come to us, over-come us. The thinker surpasses "objects" for the sake of "things," things as they "are." And the silence and representationlessness of the thinker is the condition of his experience of Being.

Heidegger and Eckhart have experienced that in the poverty of unknowing, in the surrender of science *(Wissenschaft),* there lies the gift of an entirely different kind of knowing and thought.

(3) Meister Eckhart concludes his sermon on mystical poverty by taking up the third kind of poverty: "But the third poverty, of which I now wish to speak, is the most extreme: it is that a man *have* nothing." Not only must the soul surrender its knowing and its willing, but also its very being; it must not only surrender what it does, but what it is. But in giving up what it is the soul finds its truest being. Meister Eckhart held that the creature is a pure nothing. By this he meant that the creature *as* a creature, insofar as it is something *other* than God, is nothing at all. To the extent that the creature "is" it has borrowed its Being from God. The creature has Being the way the air has light, that is, only so long as and in complete dependence upon the fact that the sun shines. The air does not have light of itself but only in a continuous process of borrowing light. If the creature is to any extent at all, it is through Being itself. For as white things are white by whiteness itself, so beings exist through Being itself. But Being is God. The creature does not "have" Being, it borrows it. Of itself it is nothing at all.

The poor in spirit, those who have spiritual poverty, are those who have acknowledged their nothingness. The highest poverty of all is to effect a return out of its created nothingness into pure Being itself. The poor in spirit are those who have entered into the movement of *exitus* and *reditus.* For from Being itself (God) there flows out the whole created world, a world which in proportion to its distance from Being itself approaches nothingness. But then there is the opposite movement undertaken by the soul in its spiritual poverty. This is the movement of detachment from everything created and back into Being. The *reditus,* which terminates in God (Being), is higher than the *exitus,* which terminates in creatures (nothingness). Thus the poverty of the spiritually poor culminates in the riches of pure Being, in the return to union with Being, which is God. "Blessed are the poor in spirit, for theirs is the kingdom of heaven."

The poverty of thought is that of itself it cannot think. Thought is not something that man undertakes; it is not an achievement resulting from an effort which man exerts. Rather, thought is a response which man makes when Being is visited upon him. Being is not something which man dreams up in thought. Rather thought is what takes place in man when Being calls upon him. Thought is always the thought of Being—"of" Being insofar as thought thinks Being, but also "of" Being insofar as Being brings itself to thought in man; it is Being's own thought. Of himself man is thoughtless. Of itself thought drifts towards beings, calculating, manipulating, accumulating beings. Left to its own resources thought tends to fall amidst beings. And so thought stands in need of a grace which will lift it up and bring it back from its fall. The *exitus* into beings can be reversed only by a *reditus* which is initiated and effected by Being itself. Thought is nothing that man has succeeded in doing; it is Being's doing in man.

Thought and Being subsist in a relationship to one another. But this is a relationship which is sustained by Being. Like the relationship of the air to light, thought is sustained as thought only so long as Being gives itself to thought, gives itself to be thought. Being "sustains" thought; it "holds" (*tenere*) it there. Man does not "attain" thought; rather thought is sustained and maintained in man by Being. Being gives itself to thought, lends itself to thought. Thought is the response to the gift, the giving of thanks.

Heidegger and Eckhart have understood the poverty of purely human resources. What does man have which he has not received? What can man do without the grace of a gift, without the gift of grace? The poverty of man is that of himself he has nothing. But the nobility of this poverty is the gift which is bestowed upon those who are poor.

The works that Heidegger has left behind for us to meditate upon are not the newest thing in philosophy. For not only are they spoken at the end of philosophy, but beyond that they remind us of very old words in the old master of thought, Meister Eckhart. Thinking abides not only in the nearness of poetry, but also, I believe, in the nearness of mysticism. This is not to say that Heidegger is a mystic and that Being is to be understood as a cryptic way of speaking of God. Being is God (*esse est deus*) in Meister Eckhart, but it would be a serious misunderstanding to suggest that the same thing is true of Heidegger. For the meditation which Heidegger undertakes is a meditation upon a presence which makes its presence felt in the *history* of the West. Being is the emergent power (*physis*) by which beings emerge into manifestness, abide there and then fall into concealment (*a-letheia*). Being is above all an *historical* power in the radical sense of the power from which what Heidegger calls the "missions of Being" (*Seinsgeschicke*) have issued. Heidegger's eye is turned towards time, not eternity. He is preoccupied with the fate of the West and, in particular, in these times of need, with the outcome of the current technologization of the earth. Being is not God, nor is thinking a prayer, although it has its own "piety." Being is the sending and withdrawing power from which the Western tradition originates, and thinking is the attempt to meditate that tradition, to experience that tradition in the radical upsurge in which it takes its origin. There is a kind of mystical and religious "element" in Heidegger's thought, but this is not to be confused with the essence of his thought.

We are not saying, however, that there is no room at all for God in Heidegger's thought. Being is not God, but neither does it exclude God. On the contrary, the appearance of God, the manifestation of God, is itself dependent on the historical clearing which is made for Him. The progressive rationalization of the world, which has passed into its most extreme form in the age of *Technik*, makes the revelation of God all but impossible. The task of thought is to make the way clear for a new dispensation, a new age of the Holy, in which God and the gods may once again address mortals. The task of thought is to help prepare for a new advent of God.

It is instructive to liken thinking to mysticism. For like mysticism thinking is a released unknowing, a will-less letting be. Like the mystic the thinker understands the poverty of human resources; he knows that in the end the supreme dignity for man is to be the shepherd of a higher presence. But thinking is neither mysticism nor philosophy. It is a *singulare tantum*. It does not reach its fulfillment in a *unio* in which time is transcended. It does not seek the eternal now, of which Eckhart speaks, in which a man does not grow older. On the contrary thinking is in its deepest dimension radically committed to time and the historical. Thinking thinks in terms of the historical dispensations which originate in Being itself. Heidegger is a world-ly thinker, thinking through the world-ing of the world, retrieving the historical origin of our world and thinking forth to the possibilities which lie concealed in these origins. While there is an unmistakable likeness between Eckhart and Heidegger, while they are both great masters of *Gelassenheit*, still they have in the end differing "concerns" *(Sachen)*. They are each masters of separate realms.

Notes

John D. Caputo is a Professor of Philosophy and Chairman of the Department at Villanova University (Pa.). He is author of a book on Heidegger, of which the present article is an adumbration: *The Mystical Element in Heidegger's Thought* (Ohio University Press, 1978). He is currently engaged in a study of Heidegger and Scholasticism.

1. For a more detailed study of Heidegger and Eckhart see my "Meister Eckhart and the Later Heidegger," which appears in two parts in *The Journal of the History of Philosophy* XII, 4 (October, 1974), 479-94 and XIII, 1 (January, 1975), 61-80, and my book *The Mystical Element in Heidegger's Thought*, (Ohio University Press, 1978.) Also see my "Phenomenology, Mysticism, and the *Grammatica Speculativa:* A Study of Heidegger's *Habiltationsschrift*," *The Journal of the British Society for Phenomenology*, V, 2 (May, 1974), 101-17.

2. The remarks that follow on Meister Eckhart are inspired in particular by Eckhart's sermon *"Beati pauperes spiritu"* which is to be found in modernized German in *Meister Eckhart: Deutsche Predigten und Traktate,* hrag. u. übers. v. Josef Quint (München: Carl Hanser Verlag, 1963), Serm. 32, pp. 303 ff. An inadequate English translation of this sermon is to be found in *Meister Eckhart: A Modern Translation* by Robert Blakney (New York: Harper and Row, 1941), pp. 227 ff. The remarks that follow on Martin Heidegger are inspired in particular by two texts from Heidegger. (1) Martin Heidegger, *Was ist Metaphysik?* 9. Aufl. (Frankfurt: Klostermann, 1965), pp. 47–51. Engl. trans. R. Hull and A. Crick, in *Existence and Being,* ed. W. Brock (Chicago: Regnery, 1949), Gateway Books, pp. 355-61. (2) Martin Heidegger, "Das Ende der Philosophie und die Aufgabe des Denkens," *Zur Sache des Denkens* (Tübingen: Niemeyer, 1969), pp. 61 ff. Engl. trans. Joan Stambaugh (New York: Harper and Row, 1972), pp. 55–73.

V. TECHNOLOGY, POLITICS AND ART

Beyond "Humanism": Heidegger's Understanding of Technology

Michael E. Zimmerman

Not too many years ago, discussions about technology were generally limited to rosy predictions about the application of scientific discoveries to nature, and technology itself was heralded as the key to man's conquest of the natural world. Whereas the Western ideal of unlimited progress continues to guide the thinking of many people, events during the past several years have begun to convince others that the essence of technology has been concealed, that it presents dangers to man and his world which have hitherto been unsuspected. Certainly the successes of technology have convinced many that it is the embodiment of reason. But this conclusion has been forcefully challenged recently, not only by *thinkers*, such as Herbert Marcuse (who claims that technology is no handmaiden to man, but an autonomous system which controls man), but also by *events*. The on-going ecological crisis, the horror of technological weaponry, the growing sense of helplessness felt by those who are victimized by gigantic corporations and bureaucracies all contribute to the growing awareness that much more needs to be understood about the nature of the technology which has made these things possible. Martin Heidegger devoted a large portion of the last forty years of his career to the contemplation of this topic. This essay will provide an introduction to his thinking in this area.[1]

It is important to remember that Heidegger did not think like a late twentieth-century American. He was a philosopher, and a German. Americans, reared as they are in a culture which prizes the practical and which thus puts little faith in "mere speculation," often have difficulty in seeing Heidegger's perspective. As a German schooled in theology as well as philosophy, Heidegger never accepted the view that man is a merely "natural" being or that history is a series of accidental events. He saw man as uniquely endowed with the capacity to disclose the sense of the world about him, and he took history as the process by which the beings of the world become manifest in different ways. For those who refuse to believe that history has any direction, Heidegger is inaccessible. But those who believe that it is no mere accident that only Western man came to interpret nature as a mathematical field manipulable by devices designed by calculating intelligence will find that Heidegger has something important to say. Briefly put, Heidegger claims that the "essence" of technology is not technological devices, but the disclosure to man of all beings whatsoever as objective, calculable, quantifiable, disposable raw material which is of value only insofar as it contributes to the enhancement of human power. Heidegger says that the revelation of all beings as raw material for man is the culmination of the history of Western culture and philosophy and at the same time it is the triumph of nihilism. It is this complex interrelationship of philosophy, technology, and nihilism that we must now explain.

Heidegger always claimed that genuine philosophy is not some reflection on trivial matters by thinkers locked in ivory towers. He always condemned those who allowed philosophy to degenerate into just such meaningless hairsplitting. Heidegger says that the authentic task of philosophy is to ask about the sense of Being, and he devoted his entire professional life to this task. The sense of Being, he said, has been forgotten for the past 2500 years, and this "oblivion" of Being has led to the technological age. He defines Being *not* as the "supreme being," or "ground" of beings, but instead as that which makes the beings of the world accessible and intelligible to us.

The objection might arise that such talk is meaningless, for things are accessible to us insofar as we perceive them with our sense organs. But Heidegger counters with the claim that we can perceive beings *as* beings, i.e., that we can know the objects of the world around us *as* objects within the world, only insofar as we have some understanding in advance of their Being. For Heidegger, there is a difference between Being (that which reveals beings to man) and beings (things of any kind). The essence of man is such that he alone has been granted this ability to stand *within* the world of beings, because he alone can understand the Being of beings. Heidegger's technical term for the essence of man is *"Da-sein,"* which is ordinarily used in German to mean "existence," but which is literally translated as "to be there."[2] Man is the "there," the location or place in which other beings, and he himself, can stand revealed. Heidegger's claim sounds less foreign if we reflect on the fact that without a being such as man the universe would be shrouded in darkness—in the sense that awareness would be lacking. Man allows the universe to come into awareness, but he is able to do this only insofar as Being acts through him to illuminate that universe. Being, then, is transcendental in the sense that (1) an understanding of it is necessary for any of our dealings with beings, and (2) it is beyond man's power to control or dominate. Man is man insofar as he is granted this ability to understand the Being of beings. But Being does not always reveal beings in the same way. History, in fact, is the history of the different ways in which beings are disclosed to man. But man is not responsible for these fundamental changes in the way things appear to him. It is Being itself, usually without man being thematically aware of it, which illuminates beings in novel ways. Sound common sense, of course, wants to reject all such talk as idle chatter. A tree is a tree for the ancient Greeks as well as for modern man, is it not? Does it not stand "revealed" to both in the same way? Heidegger answers: No.

For the Greeks, the Being of the tree was *physis* (we unthinkingly translate this as "nature"), the power of a being to emerge from the darkness of non-presence, to grow and develop and maintain its presence in the face of the possibility of lapsing again into non-presence. For a modern botanist, however, the tree might be seen as a specific complex of cellulose which, by modern scientific methods, can be turned into any number of useful products. In fact, modern man views the whole of the universe in terms of its value for the promotion of human power. For the Greeks, the "reality" (Being) of the tree was its power to keep itself in stable presence; for modern man, the reality of the tree is its use-value as a commodity. The "reality of the real" or the "Being of beings" for use is the *value* of objects in man's quest for world mastery. The history of Western culture is the history of how the Being of beings gets reduced to the value they have for man. But let us retrace our steps for a moment.

At the beginning of Western history, the Greeks determined that the Being of beings was their "constant presence." To really be was to be *present*: stable, permanent, unchanging in the midst of flux. The Greeks did not just think up this idea of Being. Instead, they gave expression to the way they actually experienced the Being or reality of beings. Put in another way, the Greeks were granted power to see things in a new light and to understand the Being of beings in this unique way. The history of philosophy involves the gradual transformation of this understanding.[3] But philosophy has tended to overlook the strange event of Being—the clearing of an open place of sense, what Heidegger calls "Being itself"—and instead has concentrated on investigating those objects in the world opened up by Being. The uncanny fact *that* there is something rather than nothing, *that* beings are somehow accessible to man, this was neglected.

Western history changed decisively when Descartes called upon man to leave behind his childish dependence on authority, tradition, and revelation for the determination of truth and reality, and instead to take upon himself—as a *free,* autonomous adult—the responsibility for that determination.[4] Thus man decided to "give himself the law" about the truth of reality. Although Copernicus had only recently shattered man's illusions about being the center of the physical universe, Descartes established man as the *ontological* center: henceforth, the reality of the real was what *man* asserted it to be. Recall that, for the Greeks, the reality of the real was constant presence. For medieval man, too, presence was determinative for reality: God's absolute presence maintained the existence of all His creatures. With Descartes, the reality of the entire cosmos was also revealed as presence, but as something present *for* the self-certain subject (man). "To be" meant to be conceived by and through the subject and held over against the subject. Everything got determined and evaluated from the *standpoint of man.* Put in another way: Western man here assumes divine prerogatives; he tries to make himself "God." Because his own self-consciousness is the standard by which he judges the truth of everything else, what is true is what human rationality determines to be true. That the truth gained by this kind of method (exact science) is agreed upon by all rational men in no way invalidates Heidegger's claim that such truth is inherently subjectivistic. It is so because it is valid within the context of the revelation of the universe as a mere object able to be calculated by the human subject.

Man no longer needs divine revelation to guide him to truth; he has the power to gain absolutely certain truth on his own. The world now presents itself to him in a new way. Instead of a realm of beings ordered in a great chain and sustained in their presence by the absolute presence of God, the universe now stands revealed as a mathematically quantifiable field of energy present as an object for the subject. Why is it mathematical? Because if the subject is the standard for determining the reality and truth of what is present, and if what can be presented-as-certain to the self-certain subject is only what is able to be *measured* precisely and exactly, and since only the mathematical is so precise, then only extended (mathematically measurable) beings are taken as "real" by the subject, i.e., able to be known with certainty. The queen of the sciences immediately becomes mathematical physics, and all other fields of research strive to emulate physics as closely as possible. Anything not able to be known precisely and exactly by such sciences is deemed "unreal," or the "object of superstition" (e.g., God). This is the dawn of the age of technology. The essence of technology, it should be clear, is nothing technical. Instead, its essence is the fact that the Being or reality of things is disclosed as calculable, wholly "rational" (mathematical), and thus *controllable.*

Heidegger's critics have often noted that he does not make an adequate distinction between pure science and technology, especially if the latter is defined as having to do with the drive to master nature. Heidegger indeed refuses to make such a distinction, at least a hard and fast one. While he certainly recognizes that the sciences have uncovered astonishing facts about the world around us, he nevertheless asserts that one of the principal motives of science has always been power. Descartes himself pointed this out when he claimed that man can and should become "master and possessor of nature." Francis Bacon, another important midwife in the birth of modern science, also says that the quest for scientific knowledge aims to bring man power over nature. As Marcuse and Heidegger have noted, the "logic" of Western history is the "logic of domination."[5] In the course of Western history, *logos* changes from the event of the manifestation of beings to an instrument by which man gains control over the forces of nature.

But the rise of technology is also connected with the alliance between Western philosophy and Christian theology. According to Heidegger, Plato and Aristotle diverted man's attention away from Being-as-such (that which enables us to understand beings) and focused his interest instead on the question of the "ground" of reality. They initiated the leading philosophical question: why is there something rather than nothing? Thinkers, such as St. Augustine, answered this question much as did Aristotle, by saying that God is the reason why there is something rather than nothing. God, the Creator, is not only the "ground" of or "reason" for the existence of all created beings; He himself is the highest being. Western man's logic depends upon the notion that there must be a *ground* for everything.[6] But with Descartes modern man decided that he himself was ready to be the ground of reality. Although man never claimed that he had *created* the universe, he nevertheless asserted his right to be the standard and measure for determining the reality and truth of everything *in* that universe. Moreover, he gave himself limitless rights to exploit the universe in any way he saw fit. (Of course, insofar as the Christian God was allowed to become identical with the God of metaphysics—the "ground" of reality—the Christian God "died" when metaphysics collapsed at the end of the nineteenth century. Heidegger has always viewed as a tragedy the alliance of theology and Western philosophy.)[7]

Technological devices, then, can only have arisen as a result of the fact that our understanding of Being changes, or that Being illuminates beings in a new way. The *essence* of technology, i.e., the new way in which beings are "present" to us in technology is called *das Gestell*, i.e., the "disclosive framework," by Heidegger. This "disclosive framework" lets the universe be understood primarily in terms of how it can be represented (*vorgestellt*), arranged, positioned, transformed, organized, or mobilized for the realization of some human goal.[8] Thus the Rhine River is no longer seen as the home of the Rhine Maidens, nor as something of instrinsic worth, but as something able to be "framed" or arranged so as to produce hydroelectric energy. Everything is now able to be interpreted as part of the stockpile which stands over against us as an object manipulable by the human subject. Whole rivers, forests, landscapes, and animal species are destroyed or rearranged for the benefit of some human project. To be capable of transforming a forest into packaging for cheeseburgers, man must see the forest *not* as a display of the miracle of life, but as raw material, pure and simple.

Of course, insofar as man is no longer seen as having any connection with the transcendent and is thus a "natural" being, man himself can be taken as raw material, and in fact as the most important one. Heidegger warns us against being naive about the condition of the contemporary world. Writing during the dark days around World War II, he points out that someday we shall have to reckon with factories which produce human beings.[9] In technological culture, "moral" distinctions lose their meaning; expediency becomes all important. Language gets debased and becomes mere "communication," which gains ease of transmission at the expense of depth. That man himself is threatened with being ground up by technological devices means at least that man himself is not really in charge of technology. Indeed, the view of reality necessary for the emergence of such devices is something *given* to man. Descartes was merely the particular man who first gave expression to this new appearance of things. Thus technology is no mere subservient system of mechanical devices, but a new view of reality, a view which tends to draw man into the same process of "framing" which allows us to dominate the rest of nature. The essence of technology includes the will to power, which is never satisfied with any achieved state of power, but always demands more and more power. This is the "dialectic of civilization" so deplored by Marcuse. Western rationality has brought us to the point where we could control nature sufficiently to alleviate human want. But the will to power continues to drive us far beyond the point where such alleviation is achieved. Apparently, man can only be freed from this world-mobilizing will to power if he can somehow cease to view reality as something which is his to control as he sees fit.

Heidegger claims that the real threat of technology for man is not atomic weaponry or other destructive devices. These can destroy us physically, but to live as human beings under the sway of the technological view of reality might well destroy the spiritual essence of man. To see what Heidegger means by this requires that the reader open himself up to a new way of understanding the relations between man, nature, and Being. Heidegger asserts that the history of the modern world is the history of the quest for more and more power. World War II, for example, is said to have arisen not merely because of the deeds of a power-hungry dictator, but because the world had been revealed as a stockpile of raw materials available for the aggrandizement of human power. Modern history includes the development of power-machinery, the rise of industry, the objectification of the natural world, the rape of the environment, the treatment of a man as a commodity ("the most important raw material"), the terrifying, world-wide wars. The destructiveness arises in large measure because — according to Heidegger — man has disconnected himself from that realm of presence in which he dwells but which also transcends him, and has thus made himself the measure of all things. Heidegger calls this nihilism.

For Heidegger, the technological view of reality goes hand in hand with nihilism, for technology is possible only insofar as man makes himself the ground for all truth, reality, and value. Nihilism is precisely the assertion of man as absolute, and the negation of all transcendent, eternal standards. Once man has made his own existence the only value in the cosmos, then he is free to do anything which he is powerful enough to defend as valuable. One only has to reflect upon the result of the nationalisms of the twentieth century to see to what extremes human beings will go on the basis of culturally and historically limited systems of value, especially when these value-systems are linked up with technological powers. At the end of the nineteenth century, Nietzsche, Freud and others became aware of the danger behind the collapse of the old values which had placed some restraint upon the appetites of men. But they were unable to provide an adequate replacement for those values. Heidegger tells us that it is beyond man's power to bring about the change in the apprehension of reality that is necessary to end the reign of technology and nihilism. Thus he takes current ideologies such as socialism, Marxism, or capitalism as ineffective; indeed, he says that they even serve to strengthen the current problem, since all of them are basically formed around the subjectivistic way of understanding reality. Although Marxism, for example, can be said to have pointed out the serious problem of human alienation in technological culture, it still looks upon nature primarily as "stuff" useful for the material enhancement of human life.

Herbert Marcuse, the former student of Heidegger, tries to show how man can bring about changes in himself through *praxis* or action, changes needed to overcome the repressiveness of technological culture.[10] But even Marcuse, whose ontology is similar to Heidegger's, in the end can find no effective action which can lead us out of the current predicament. Heidegger affirms time and time again that man's task is to prepare himself for a new disclosure of the presence of things, and Marcuse himself admits that if we are to move into a new age beyond the "performance principle," we shall have to gain a new understanding of the Being of what is. For Heidegger, the new disclosure of Being will involve the "releasement" of the human being from the will to power. Such releasement (a term which Heidegger borrows from Meister Eckhart) would allow man to dwell within the world, *not* as its master, but as its servant endowed with the gift of letting the beings of the world display themselves in all their glory. Instead of seeing the world as a manipulative object thrown and held over against us as subjects, we would cultivate the world by letting beings *be* what they are and how they are, and not as they are according to the power-oriented viewpoint of the subject.

The recent rise of "ecological consciousness" might be a harbinger of such a change in our apprehension of the Being of beings. This movement arose in large measure as a result of the growing awareness that man was about to destroy himself because of his destruction of the environment. Heidegger would certainly agree with many of the aims of this new consciousness, including its desire to halt the senseless pillaging of nature for profit. But he was more radical than most ecological thinkers, who continue to look upon man as the "husbander" of nature who has the "right" to manipulate nature as long as he does not cause too much damage in the process. For this still fails to see that the most important threat of the technological view is not a physical one, but a spiritual one.[11] Because man is man only insofar as he is the "place" where the Being of beings can be exhibited and because technological man concentrates wholly upon the domination of beings (including himself!) without any recollection of Being as such, the danger is that man will cease to be man, that the understanding of Being will disappear. Thus man might learn to come to terms with most ecological problems by better technical devices and better understanding of the workings of nature, but if the technological view of reality continues to prevail, mere physical survival might not be instrinsically worthwhile, especially if man continues to think of himself more and more as a particular kind of *thing*. Without awareness of our participation in the revelation of beings, without awareness of the fact that we are *not* our own ground, man might continue to live, but without any genuine insight into who he is.

Yet Heidegger did not call for the breaking up of technical devices and equipment. In fact, he said more than once that what poses the threat also contains the possibility of rescue within itself.[12] To exist in an authentic way, he tells us, involves the re-appropriation of one's heritage in light of future possibilities. But our heritage is in large measure technology and the understanding of Being which makes it possible. To be authentic would require a new appropriation of technology in such a way that technological devices and their products would not completely seize our awareness of what is. We must be able to walk away from the technological, to free ourselves from it in order to become aware of the transcendent dimension within which we exist. Heidegger said that we live in a "needy age." We are in need of a kind of conversion which would grant us a new vision of reality, free us from the drive to power, from the tendency to look at all things as commodities, and open us to our most authentic possibility, which is to allow beings in the world to manifest their own intrinsic worth. It should be clear just how far such a notion is from the current offerings of our political parties and thinkers. Heidegger does not give us much by way of a political program for change. He looks for hope beyond the present categories. If his analysis of the nature of technology is accurate, and certainly much of it is, then we would serve the world well by opening ourselves up to new possibilities for understanding reality and our place *in* it.

Notes

Michael E. Zimmerman is Associate Professor of Philosophy at Tulane University, New Orleans, and author of *The Eclipse of the Self* (Ohio U. P., 1980) and of numerous articles on Heidegger. He was Secretary-Convenor of the Eleventh Heidegger Conference (New Orleans, 1977).

1. Two of the most important essays by Heidegger concerning technology are "Die Frage nach der Technik" and "Wissenschaft und Besinnung," *Vorträge und Aufsätze* (Pfullingen: Günter Neske, 1967), translated by W. Lovitt in Martin Heidegger, *The Question Concerning Technology* (New York: Harper & Row, 1977). Other relevant texts already in English are: *What is Called Thinking?* trans. Fred D. Wieck and J. Glenn Gray (New York: Harper & Row, 1968); *The End of Philosophy*, trans. Joan Stambaugh (New York: Harper & Row, 1973); "What are Poets For?" in *Poetry, Language, Thought*, trans. Albert Hofstadter (New York: Harper & Row, 1971), and *Discourse on Thinking*, trans. John M. Anderson and E. Hans Freund (New York: Harper & Row, 1966).
2. The German *"da,"* like the French, *"là,"* may mean both "there" and "here." We here follow Richarson's translation of it as "there," although Theodore Kisiel's article in this collection is equally correct in rendering it as "here."
3. Cf. Otto Pöggeler's very helpful essay, "Being as Appropriation" *("Sein als Ereignis"),* trans. Ruediger Hermann Grimm in *Philosophy Today,* XIX (1975), 152-178.
4. For elaboration of Heidegger's interpretation of Descartes, compare the essays by Walter Biemel and William J. Richardson in this volume.
5. Cf. Herbert Marcuse, *One-Dimensional Man* (Boston: Beacon Press, 1964), especially the second part, "One Dimensional Thought."
6. Cf. Martin Heidegger, *Der Satz vom Grund* (Pfullingen: Günter Neske, 1971). Part of this volume has been translated by Keith Hoeller as "The Principle of Ground" in *Man and World,* VII (1974), 207-222.
7. Cf. Martin Heidegger, *Identity and Difference,* trans. Joan Stambaugh (New York: Harper & Row, 1969), especially the essay "The Onto-Theo-Logical Constitution of Metaphysics."
8. Cf. "Die Frage nach der Technik," *op. cit.*
9. Martin Heidegger, *The End of Philosophy*, p. 106.
10. Cf. Herbert Marcuse, *Eros and Civilization* (Boston: Beacon Press, 1966).
11. On this issue and other related topics concerning technology and man's future, cf. the excellent essay by Hwa Yol Jung, "The Paradox of Man and Nature: Reflections on Man's Ecological Predicament," in *The Centennial Review,* XVIII (1974), 1-28.
12. "What Are Poets For?" *op cit.*

Heidegger and Marx:
A Framework for Dialogue

David Schweickart

The Marxist encounter with Heidegger has not been overly felicitous. Herbert Marcuse spent four years (1928–1932) studying with Heidegger, for, as he says, "I believed, like all the others, that there could be some combination between existentialism and Marxism."[1] Looking back, he does not consider his engagement fruitful:

> [Being and Time] gives a picture which plays well on the fears and frustrations of men and women in a repressive society — a joyless existence, overshadowed by death and anxiety; human material for the authoritarian personality.... I see now in this philosophy, ex post, a very powerful devaluation of life, a derogation of joy, of sensuousness, of fulfillment.[2]

Georg Lukács makes a similar charge:

> As a confession of a citizen of the 1920's Heidegger's way of thinking is not without interest. Sein und Zeit is at least as absorbing reading as Celine's novel, Journey to the End of Night. But the former, like the latter, is merely a document of the day showing how a certain class felt and thought, and not an "ontological" disclosure of ultimate truth. It is only because this book is so well suited to the emotional world of today's intellectuals that the arbitrariness of its pseudo-argumentation is not exposed.[3]

Heideggerians obviously have difficulties in evaluating these and similar Marxist critiques. First of all, the standards operative in these criticisms (which come from outside the Heideggerian project) are not made clear, and to that degree the grounds for response and exchange are indefinite. Second, Heideggerians may well suspect that the effort to understand Heidegger has been less than wholehearted. There seems to be a truth in Sartre's acid reply to Lukács:

> Yes, Lukács has the instruments to understand Heidegger, but he will not understand him; for Lukács would have to *read* him, to grasp the meaning of the sentences one by one. And there is no longer any Marxist, to my knowledge, who is still capable of doing this.[4] [He adds in a footnote:] This is because they insist on standing in their own light. They reject the hostile sentence (out of fear or hate or laziness) at the very moment that they want to open themselves to it. This contradiction blocks them. They literally do not understand a word of what they read. And I blame them for this lack of comprehension, not in the name of some sort of bourgeois objectivity, but in the name of Marxism itself.[5]

It is "in the name of Marxism itself" that I shall attempt to discuss Heidegger in a manner less vulnerable to Sartre's criticism — though not invulnerable, for I will insist on standing in the Marxian light. If one wanted to do full justice to Heidegger, the Sartrean "progressive-regressive method" might well be appropriate: analysis of the work, the man, his family, the class structure of his society, and the dynamic evolution of the underlying economic forces, followed by a "reinvention" of the unitary project which culminated in an original event, the philosophy of Martin Heidegger.[6] But obviously such an endeavor is beyond the scope of a single essay. Instead, I will sketch a less ambitious approach which I hope will shed some fresh light on the confrontation of Marx and Heidegger. To begin with, I will specify the general truth-criterion which Marxism brings to bear in evaluating philosophical (and other) positions. In the second and third parts of the essay I will recast certain Heideggerian positions — those related to his critique of Marxism — in such a way that they may be tested by this criterion. If we can formulate the criterion broadly enough to be acceptable to at least some Heideggerians, a groundwork for dialogue might be established.

LIBERATORY PRAXIS AND THE QUESTION OF TRUTH

Because Marxism itself is fiercely divided today, a truth-criterion acceptable even to most Marxists must necessarily be general. Even limiting ourselves to "Western Marxism," i.e., the tradition that has dissociated itself from the orthodox "Diamat" of the Third International, we find structuralist, existentialist, phenomenologist, and other Marxisms contending for intellectual hegemony. However, almost all of them share a commitment to at least one basic tenet of Marx's thought, his Eleventh Thesis on Feuerbach: "The philosophers have only *interpreted* the world in various ways; the point is to *change* it."[7] It is to this thesis that almost all factions appeal, implicitly or explicitly, when confronting one another. I shall call a commitment to this thesis a commitment to *liberatory praxis*. *Liberatory praxis* is, for Marxism, at once a value and a truth-criterion. Commitment to *liberatory praxis* as a value presupposes the judgment that human life ought to be richer and more meaningful than it is for the vast majority of people, and that certain concrete social, political, economic and cultural structures existing today cut people off from leading such lives. *Liberatory praxis* recognizes as good whatever contributes positively toward that fundamental restructuring of society which opens up the realm of authentic possibilities latent in the present order.

This definition lacks precision, as it must at this historical juncture. Contemporary Marxists are far from unanimous as to the more specific features of *liberatory praxis*. Debates rage as to which structures are oppressive and in which ways, how they might be changed and to what, and which possibilities truly exist and which are illusory. But this lack of precision does not imply a lack of content. Dialogue within the framework of *liberatory praxis* differs markedly from argument that tries to convince that there *is* oppression, that things *could* be better, that real possibilities exist which are blocked by real societal forces. Commitment to *liberatory praxis* as a value is not the exclusive prerogative of Marxism, of course. This commitment is shared by a broad spectrum of individuals from radical feminists to liberation theologians. It is also shared no doubt by certain Heideggerians. The attempt at dialogue initiated in this essay is directed especially at such Heideggerians.

Marxism involves a commitment to *liberatory praxis* not only as a value but also as a truth-criterion. In Marxism the fact-value distinction dissolves, for *liberatory praxis* grounds not only its axiology but also its epistemology. As Lukács states, "The criterion of truth is provided by relevance to reality. This reality is by no means identical with empirical existence. This reality is not, it becomes."[8] For a Marxist, the point is to change the world. To change it, one must understand it, not only as it is, but also as it might become. But to understand it, one must bring to bear a conceptual apparatus: a science, a philosophy, a set of categories which comprehend the given and point to the future. Which set? The set which is *true*, i.e., the set which *works*. Marxism, in short, asserts a pragmatic theory of truth with *liberatory praxis* as its *telos*.

As such, Marxism is, or at least should be, the antithesis of dogmatism. To the extent that certain conceptions, no matter how sacred, interfere with *liberatory praxis* they must be rejected. Again Lukács' formulation is apt:

> Let us assume for the sake of argument that recent research had disproved once and for all every one of Marx's individual theses. Even if this were to be proved, every serious "orthodox" Marxist would be able to accept all such modern findings without reservation and hence discard all of Marx's theses *in toto* — without having to renounce his orthodoxy for a moment. Orthodox

Marxism, therefore, does not imply the uncritical acceptance of the results of Marx's investigations. It is not a "belief" in this or that thesis, nor the exegesis of a "sacred" book. On the contrary, orthodoxy refers exclusively to *method*.[9]

Despite its non-dogmatism, the Marxist conception of truth seems far removed from the Heideggerian doctrine of truth as "uncovering." I will not investigate here how the two conceptions might be related, but let me briefly examine several of Heidegger's remarks which might seem to stand sharply opposed to the Marxian conception. We shall see that the opposition is not so stark as it first appears.

In *An Introduction to Metaphysics* Heidegger writes,

> It is said, for example: Because metaphysics did nothing to pave the way for the revolution, it should be rejected. This is no cleverer than saying that because the carpenter's bench is useless for flying it should be abolished. Philosophy can never *directly* supply the energies and create the opportunities and methods that bring about historical change; for one thing, because philosophy is always the concern of the few. Which few? The creators, those who initiate profound transformations. It spreads only indirectly, by devious paths that can never be laid out in advance, until at last, at some future date, it sinks to the level of a commonplace; but by then it has long been forgotten as original philosophy.[10]

The tone here, with its hint of elitism, is not that of a Marxist, but Marxists need not dispute Heidegger's basic claim. Original philosophy is no doubt the creation of a few. An extended series of mediations intervenes before the theoretical work of a major thinker objectifies itself in mass consciousness, and it is no doubt true that the lines of influence cannot be laid out precisely in advance. Of course we would insist that the lines of influence between theory and practice extend in both directions. Marxism, in its aspiration to be the consciousness of a rising class, seeks to draw its energy, at least in part, from the unarticulated hopes, fears and struggles of that class and to relate its theoretical efforts back to that concrete reality. Original philosophy has often served as a weapon in the hands of a rising class. (Enlightenment philosophy comes at once to mind.) It may well be the case that original philosophy sinks to the level of a commonplace once the decisive battles have been won, but its doing so in no way negates philosophy's practical importance in the interim. Heideggerians need not disagree.

In *An Introduction to Metaphysics* Heidegger addresses what he takes to be another misconception concerning the nature of philosophy, the view that philosophy is "an overall systematic view of what is, supplying a useful chart by which we may find our way amid the various possible things and realms of things . . . . Philosophy is expected to promote and even to accelerate—to make easier, as it were—the practical and technical business of culture." This view is false, he asserts, because "it is the very nature of philosophy never to make things easier but only more difficult."[11]

Marxism does not see itself as facilitating the "practical and technical business of culture," but it does aim at "supplying a useful chart" with which to comprehend that which is, so as to promote the liberatory struggle. Marxism does aim at making things "easier." Nevertheless, the practical experience of Western Marxism reveals the partial truth of Heidegger's claim. Theory which makes things "easier" does not always enhance the liberatory project. It is easier, for example, to make the proletariat a Platonic idea than to investigate the concrete, shifting realities of class under advanced capitalism—but this Marxist idealism has been disastrous for praxis. It is easier to identify socialism with the absence of private property than to probe the nature of "liberation" at the heart of *liberatory praxis*. However, this easy approach prevented many Marxists from recognizing in time the abortive, horrifyingly distorted nature of Soviet "communism." I disagree that philosophy should *never* make things easier, for Marxism seeks a society wherein life is as free as possible from toil, dependence and ugliness; but I do not dispute that "the authentic function of philosophy [is] to challenge historical existence."[12]

I have articulated the framework from within which I will approach Heidegger, the "light" in which I wish to stand. Specifically, I have argued that Marxism insists on judging philosophical projects in light of liberatory praxis, its fundamental truth-criterion. I have suggested that a Heideggerian *need not* rule out this criterion immediately. In my view he *should not* rule it out, particularly if he is sympathetic to *liberatory praxis* as a value. Of course if he is not at all sympathetic, there is little likelihood of fruitful dialogue. To demonstrate more concretely the function of *liberatory praxis* in the Marxian project, I now turn my attention to a position of Heidegger's of particular interest to Marxists, his critique of Marxism.

MARXISM AS A HUMANISM

Heidegger indicts Marxism as a "humanism." Before trying to render this charge intelligible to *liberatory praxis*, let me examine Heidegger's formulation. Marxism is a humanism, says Heidegger in his "Letter on Humanism," and like all humanisms it is metaphysical:

> But if one understands humanism in general as a concern that man become free for his humanity and find his worth in it, then humanism differs according to one's conception of the "freedom" and "nature" of man....However different these forms of humanism may be in purpose and in principle, in the mode and meaning of their respective realizations, and in the form of their teaching, they nonetheless all agree in this, that the *humanitas* of *homo humanus* is determined with regard to an already established interpretation of nature, history, world, and the ground of the world, that is, of beings as a whole.[13]

He continues:

> Every humanism is either grounded in a metaphysics or is itself made to be
> the ground of one. Every determination of the essence of man that already
> presupposes an interpretation of beings without asking about the truth of Be-
> ing, whether knowingly or not, is metaphysical.... In defining the humanity
> of man, humanism not only does not ask about the relation of Being to the
> essence of man; because of its metaphysical origin humanism even impedes
> the question by neither recognizing nor understanding it.[14]

The first paragraph quoted above charges that Marxism begins with "an
already established interpretation of beings as a whole," i.e., a metaphysics.
Marx, we note, emphatically denies that he begins with any kind of fixed,
dogmatic abstraction:

> The premises from which we begin are not arbitrary ones, not dogmas, but
> real premises from which abstractions can be made only in imagination. They
> are the real individuals, their activity and the material conditions under
> which they live, both those already existing and those produced by their ac-
> tivity.[15]

Heidegger would no doubt dispute the claim that beginning with "real individuals" is necessarily non-metaphysical. Marxism is metaphysics, he would
insist, because it has not "asked about the truth of Being." This charge is for-
mally correct. No Marxist to my knowledge has ever addressed this question.
But I must inquire as to the significance of the question. What precisely is the
nature of the alleged defect? What is this "Being"? How does Marxism (or any
humanism) overlook its truth? In what sense does humanism ignore the relation of man's essence to this truth? Heidegger's answer is not reassuring:

> Yet Being—what is Being? It is It itself. The thinking that is to come must
> learn to experience that and say it. "Being"—that is not God and not a cosmic
> ground. Being is farther than all beings and is yet nearer to man than every
> being, be it a rock, a beast, a work of art, a machine, be it an angel or God.
> Being is the nearest. Yet the near remains farthest from man.[16]

And what about man and his relation to Being?

> What man is—or as it is called in the traditional language of metaphysics, the
> "essence of man"—lies in his ek-sistence.... Man occurs essentially in such a
> way that he is the "there" [das "Da"], that is, the lighting of Being. The "Being"
> of the Da, and only it, has the fundamental character of ek-sistence, that is, of
> an ecstatic inherence in the truth of Being.... Man is..."thrown" from Be-
> ing itself into the truth of Being, so that ek-sisting in this fashion he might
> ground the truth of Being, in order that beings might appear in the light of
> Being as the beings they are.[17]

The language here is disturbing, but let us resist the temptation to see only disguised theology or overt mysticism. To be sure, Heidegger is *not* talking about God in these passages. About what, then, is he talking? What is "Being"? Heidegger prefers to read "Being" as the "presence" of beings, not in the entitative or substantialist sense of "just-being-there" (this is a derived mode of Being, viz., as "presence-at-hand") but rather in the sense of their "meaningful accessibility"; that is, in the broadest terms, their "meaning" or "intelligibility," their "significance" *(Bedeutsamkeit)*.[18] Heidegger is saying, then, that meanings *appear* to human beings, hence that the Being of beings is their *appearance*: Heidegger's program is neither metaphysical nor theological but phenomenological. We are "thrown" into a world of significant and intelligible beings whose significance and intelligibility appear to us because of the specific character of our nature, our "ek-sistence" or "self-exceeding" (transcendence, temporality) which is the "openness" of our Being which allows us to think, to talk, and to see things as they are. Whereas metaphysics does ask about the meaningfulness and intelligibility *of beings,* it neglects to ask about the very happening or emergence of meaningfulness or intelligibility itself. To do that would require a return to man as self-exceeding, as transcending himself into "nothingness," thus a reflection on the dimension of absence (which happens in and with man) whence comes the presence of beings. This interplay of absence and presence is called the "revealing" *(aletheia)* or truth of Being. This is the question metaphysics ignores.

Interpreting Heidegger in this manner reduces a Marxist's immediate negative reaction, but it does not yet establish the force of Heidegger's criticism. What of importance has been overlooked in not inquiring into the "truth of Being"? Heidegger's answer seems to be this: humanism fails to see that Being is *prior to* man. "Man does not decide," he writes, "whether and how beings appear, whether and how God and the gods or history and nature come forward into the light of Being, come to presence and depart. The advent of beings lies in the destiny of Being."[19] Further on he notes: "[Man's] projection is essentially a thrown projection. What throws in projection is not man but Being itself."[20]

If we discount the theological overtones of the language and read "meaning" for Being, can we make sense of these assertions? One thing is clear. Heidegger is insisting that man does not *create* meaning. "Being is illuminated for man in the ecstatic projection. But this projection does not create Being."[21] It is precisely the error of humanism to subjectivize meaning. This thought underlies his critique of "values":

It is important finally to realize that precisely through the characterization of something as "a value" what is so valued is robbed of its worth. That is to say, by the assessment of something as a value what is valued is admitted only as an object for man's estimation. But what a thing is in its Being is not exhausted by its being an object, particularly when objectivity takes the form of value. Every valuing, even where it values positively, is a subjectivizing. It does not let beings: be.[22]

Heidegger thus stakes out a position sharply at odds with Sartre's — to whose "Existentialism is a Humanism" his own "Letter on Humanism" is in large measure a response. For Sartre, if God does not exist, man must acknowledge all significance as his own creation. To the objection, "Your values are not serious, since you choose them yourselves," Sartre replies: "To that I can only say that I am very sorry that it should be so; but if I have excluded God the Father, there must be somebody to invent values."[23] Heidegger refuses this dichotomy. He insists that his thought is neither atheistic nor theisic nor indifferent; he claims to be asking the more primordial question, the one that must be considered before the question of God's existence can even be meaningfully posed. He is asking, that is, about meaning itself. But the answer he gives to this question seems to negate Sartre's claim. Without committing himself to either atheism or theism, Heidegger maintains that "meaning" is prior to man.

In trying to clarify Heidegger's critique of Marxism (and humanism in general), I have counterposed Heidegger to Sartre. Sartre wants to say that man creates meaning; Heidegger denies that this is so. But if such is the substance of Heidegger's critique of humanism, a Marxist is inclined to see himself as exempt, for on this issue Marxism seems closer to Heidegger than to Sartre. Suspicious of both "bourgeois individualism" and Hegelian (and religious) idealism, Marxism has tried to chart an alternative course. Marxism agrees with Heidegger that "man does not decide whether and how beings appear." That beings appear differently in different historical epochs is a fundamental tenet of historical materialism; values in particular are regarded as dialectically determined by class structure and the concrete material conditions of the era.

It is not clear, however, that Marxism can so easily avoid "humanism." Sartre's challenge to Marxism seems compelling: "If we refuse to see the original dialectical movement in the individual and in his enterprise of producing his life, of objectifying himself, then we should have to give up dialectics or else make of it the immanent law of History."[24] Marx rejects both mechanistic determinism and Hegelian idealism; he insists that his premises are real individuals. If history is intelligible and yet not the product of blind physical forces or a restless Spirit, then its intelligibility must reside, it would seem, in the fact that human individuals are intentional beings reacting dialectically to economic, class, political and cultural forces. Lukács, it is true, attempted to retain dialectics, rooting it in neither the individual nor a World Spirit but rather making class (the proletariat) the "identical subject-object" of history.[25] But he himself later admitted (and rejected) the idealism of such a solution.[26]

Sartre makes his case not only by arguing that his position is the only one compatible with Marx's own views, but also by appealing to *liberatory praxis*. He indicts contemporary Marxism for having forgotten the concrete individual. Marxism has developed a "practical anemia" and will "degenerate into a non-human anthropology if it does not reintegrate man into itself as its foundation."[27] Sartre thus insists on the humanism of Marxism, stressing the active, non-determined character of the real individual in order to revitalize what he considers to be the only philosophy of our time, a philosophy whose "sclerosis does not correspond to normal aging."[28]

If Sartre is correct that Marxism is at root a humanism, how stands Heidegger's critique? We drew from his critique the claim that meaning precedes man, that man is not the source of all significance. But such a charge remains too abstract for a Marxist. What are the implications for *liberatory praxis?* If it can be shown that humanism has detrimental implications, then Marxism must take the charge seriously, and perhaps re-evaluate its own foundations. But does Heidegger's criticism of humanism point to any feature of Marxism which might have such implications, any feature which might stand in the way of genuine liberation? We cannot dismiss this question too lightly, for there is a Heideggerian argument to be made which merits our attention.

The Logic of Domination

Heidegger himself is not thinking in terms of *liberatory praxis* when he makes his indictment of humanism. However, it is possible to construct an argument from those of his remarks which fall within our horizon. Heidegger's "Letter on Humanism" questions Marx's materialism: Even if materialism is not taken to mean that everything is simply matter, it remains "a metaphysical determination according to which every being appears as the material of labor."[29] Materialism is thus a form of *technology*, where "technology" signifies "a mode of *aletheuein*, a mode, that is, of rendering things manifest,"[30] rather than an assemblage of scientific-technical equipment. His later essay — "The Question Concerning Technology" — explicates more fully the difficulty with this "mode of revealing." The essence of modern technology, Heidegger says, is a "challenging [*Herausfordern*] which puts to nature the unreasonable demand that it supply energy which can be extracted and stored as such."[31] This way of revealing which "challenges forth in the frenziedness of ordering" represents a supreme danger for man:

> The danger attests itself to us in two ways. As soon as what is unconcealed no longer concerns man even as object, but exclusively as standing-reserve, and man in the midst of objectlessness is nothing but the orderer of the standing-reserve, then he comes to the very brink of a precipitous fall, that is, he comes to the very point where he himself will have to be taken as standing-reserve. Meanwhile, man, precisely as the one so threatened, exalts himself to the

posture of lord of the earth. In this way the illusion comes to prevail that everything man encounters exists only insofar as it is his construct. This illusion gives rise in turn to one final delusion: it seems as though man everywhere and always encounters only himself.[32]

Marx, of course, is well aware of the phenomenon of man as a "standing-reserve." *Capital* documents the historical transformation of the peasants and craftsmen of precapitalistic societies into interchangeable elements of "abstract labor" who serve as mere appendages to modern machinery. He is less concerned, to say the least, with what Heidegger terms the second manifestation of the technological attitude: the fact that man always and everywhere encounters only himself. Marx and Engels write in *The German Ideology*:

> Communism differs from all previous movements in that it... for the first time consciously treats all natural premises as creatures of hitherto existing men, strips them of their natural characteristics and subjugates them to the power of the united individuals.[33]

Thus it would seem that Marx and Engels envision a society wherein united individuals are indeed "lords of the earth" who encounter only themselves. But Marx sees this self-encounter not as a final delusion but as liberation. For Marx, a basic feature of capitalist society is the "reification" of human relations so that they appear as relations among things.[34] The structures of domination that permeate capitalist society are thus rendered invisible, and the irrationality of the system is made to appear "natural." The struggle for liberation requires making the human relations of existing societies manifest; the goal of authentic communism is to structure society so that the real relations among human beings become rational and transparent. If Heidegger should reply: "Well and good, but such a restructuring is not enough," the Marxist must pause and take stock. *Why* is it not enough? One cannot simply say that there is more to reality than just man. No Marxist denies the literal truth of such a statement; Marx does not regard human creativity as proceeding *ex nihilo*.

To the Marxist question, "Why is a restructured society not enough?" Heidegger might well respond as follows:[35] the Marxist (humanist) conception of man as an active, laboring, creative being *blocks* the path to genuine liberation. For such a conception which views man as a "lord of beings" rather than as he really is, the "shepherd of Being," implies a challenging dominating attitude toward *nature*. Nature is regarded as the mere "stuff" upon which to exercise human will. Such an attitude leads not only to the ecological disruptions we perceive today, but also to a truncation of human experience. The basic realm of *poiesis*, the artistic realm where beings show themselves as they really are, recedes.

> There was a time when it was not technology alone that bore the name *techne*. Once that revealing which brings forth truth into the splendor of radiant appearance was also called *techne*. The *poiesis* of the fine arts was also called *techne*.[36]

How should I evaluate this charge? It has idealistic overtones; it suggests that the *fundamental* problem facing us today is the way we *think* about the world. Nonetheless, Marxism admits the base-superstructure connection to be dialectical. Concrete material conditions profoundly shape one's conception of the world. But it is also true that our conception of reality influences human *praxis* and the structures which result from *praxis*. Since Marxism itself has emerged from an oppressive society permeated with structures of domination, it might well be the case that the Marxist vision has been less than complete in negating these structures. It might be true that Marxism implicitly projects man as the arrogant "lord over nature."

The charge is worthy of investigation, but we need not plead guilty too quickly—for there are elements in Marx's thought which suggest an alternative account of this "logic of domination."[37] To Heidegger the roots of the technological attitude and of contemporary humanism trace back to Descartes, where man, liberating himself from revelation-based certainty "decided, by himself and for himself, what, for him, should be 'knowable' and what knowing and the making secure of the known, i.e., certainty, should mean."[38] Marx, on the other hand, locates the whole problematic of domination in the division of labor. The specific form of domination under consideration—the domination of nature—is traced to the primitive cleavage between mental and manual labor structurally established with the emergence of chiefs and priests. At this juncture consciousness sets itself up as something independent of nature. "From now on consciousness is in a position to emancipate itself from the world and to proceed to the formation of 'pure' theory, theology, philosophy, ethics, etc."[39] To be sure, a decisive shift in attitude takes place with the rise of capitalism, a shift which Marx too notes in Descartes. "Descartes, in defining animals as mere machines, saw with the eyes of the manufacturing period, while to the eyes of the middle ages, animals were the assistants to men."[40]

Marx conceives the relation between man and nature to be dialectical. He emphatically affirms that man is a natural being, but humanity, though a part of nature, is estranged from nature. Thus man conceptualizes nature as alien, as other, and the more so the more intense the alienation. This antagonism, however, is not seen as an irreducible element of the human condition, but as a condition which true communism can and will resolve. "Thus communism as completed naturalism is humanism; as completed humanism, it is naturalism. It is the true resolution of the antagonism between man and nature and between man and man."[41] What can this mean, the overcoming of the antagonism between man and nature? A Heideggerian might well suspect that it is an overcoming by means of *conquest*. But Marx suggests something rather different in his celebrated passage concerning the relationship of man and woman:

> The immediate, natural, necessary relationship of human being to human being is the *relationship* of *man* to *woman* . . . . In this relationship the extent to which the human essence has become nature for man or nature has become the human essence of man is *sensuously manifested*, reduced to a perceptible *fact*. From this relationship one can thus judge the entire level of mankind's development . . . . The relationship of man to woman is the *most natural* relationship of human being to human being. It thus indicates the extent to which his human essence has become a natural essence for him, the extent to which his human nature has become nature to him.[42]

It is no accident that Marx articulates the man-nature dialectic in terms of a man-woman relationship, since woman is always conceptualized (under conditions of oppression) as less "human," more "natural" than man. What Marx appears to envision when the man-woman relation is most fully human, is a state wherein nature, without hostility, is perceived to be a part of ourselves, and ourselves to be a part of nature. Nature, including that which is most "natural" in us (our sexuality), becomes humanized, and conversely our humanity becomes naturalized. A Marxist can thus argue that the source of the impulse to dominate and manipulate nature, to regard it as mere utility, lies in our conception of nature as radically different from and opposed to humanity. To the extent to which we come to see nature in ourselves and ourselves in nature (a coming to pass which requires concrete political praxis), the drive to exploit nature will recede. The antagonistic relationship will be replaced by a genuinely human, genuinely natural one:

> Private property has made us so stupid and one-sided that an object is *ours* if we have it . . . . Hence *all* the physical and spiritual senses have been replaced by the simple alienation of them *all*, the sense of *having* . . . . The overcoming of private property means therefore the complete *emancipation* of all human senses and aptitudes . . . . [The senses and aptitudes] try to relate themselves to their *subject matter* for its own sake . . . . Need and satisfaction have thus lost their *egoistic* nature, and nature has lost its mere *utility* by use becoming human use.[43]

This account of the possible resolution of the man-nature confrontation differs radically from Heidegger's. Whereas Marx stresses the *naturalness* of man, Heidegger emphasizes precisely the disparity between man and nature. When we define man as a "rational animal," he writes, we "abandon man to the essential realm of *animalitas* even if we do not equate him with beasts but attribute specific difference to him."[44] What we must do, he urges, is stress the radical *difference* between man and nature, to think man, not on the basis of *animalitas* but in the direction of his *humanitas*.[45] Then man would comprehend himself not as a lord of beings, chief being in a realm of beings, but as that absolutely unique being which can serve as "the shepherd of Being."

Thus we have reached the point of *fundamental* disagreement. In considering Heidegger's critique of Marxism, I have elaborated his argument so as to appeal to *liberatory praxis*. I have presented him as claiming that Marx's humanism is rooted in a technological attitude that leads to a "logic of domination" which blocks off a crucial dimension of reality. I have conceded to Heidegger that Marxism *is* a humanism, but I have also tried to reconstruct a Marxian account of the logic of domination which would imply that a change in this logic comes with the advent of genuine communism. But is this Marxian account more adequate that Heidegger's? Is it better to stress man's uniqueness as the "place" wherein beings are revealed, or to regard man as a natural being capable of humanizing himself and the rest of nature, but prevented from doing so by class-ridden structures of oppression? When appeals to *liberatory praxis* are in conflict, who decides?

For a Marxist such issues cannot be settled abstractly. The debate will continue if people choose sides, talk to one another, and work out the additional implications of the opposing views; but a resolution of the conflict is not finally a purely intellectual matter. I have laid out what I take to be a useful framework for pursuing the Heidegger-Marx intellectual conflicts in a serious way, but I agree with Marx that in the final analysis non-theoretical considerations will determine the issue. "The question whether human thinking can reach objective truth is not a question of theory but a *practical* question. In practice man must prove the truth, that is, the actuality and power, the thissideness of his thinking."[46]

If Marxism remains a living philosophy true to its historical aspirations, it will incorporate the conceptions which best articulate, in a universal manner, the needs and hopes of an oppressed but rising class. As Sartre remarks: "There is no need to readapt a living philosophy to the course of the world; it adapts itself by means of thousands of new efforts, thousands of particular pursuits, for the philosophy is one with the movement of society." If Marxism dies and is not succeeded by a living philosophy of *liberatory praxis,* then one who was a Marxist would probably embrace Heidegger's own assessment of the world: "Only a god can save us now. We can only through thinking and writing prepare for the manifestation of God, or for the absence of God as things go downhill all the way."[47]

Notes

David Schwieckart is an Assistant Professor of Philosophy at Loyola University of Chicago. He holds a Ph. D. in mathematics from the University of Virginia (1969) and a Ph. D. in philosophy from Ohio State University (1977). Among his publications is "Capitalism, Contribution and Sacrifice," *The Philosophical Forum*, VII, Nos. 3-4, pp. 260–276. His forthcoming book is entitled *Capitalism: A Utilitarian Analysis.*

1. "Heidegger's Politics: An Interview with Herbert Marcuse by Frederick Olafson," *Graduate Faculty Philosophy Journal* (Winter, 1977), 29.
2. Ibid., p. 33.
3. Georg Lukács, "Existentialism," in Georg Lukács, *Marxism and Human Liberation* (New York, 1973), 256.
4. Jean-Paul Sartre, *Search for a Method,* trans. Hazel Barnes (New York, 1963), 38.
5. Ibid.
6. Cf. *Search for a Method,* Chapter III, "The Progressive-Regressive Method," pp. 85–166.
7. *Writings of the Young Marx on Philosophy, Politics and Society,* ed. Loyd Easton and Kurt Guddat (Garden City, 1967), 402.
8. Georg Lukács, *History and Class Consciousness* (London, 1971), 203.
9. Ibid., p. 1.
10. Martin Heidegger, *An Introduction to Metaphysics,* trans. Ralph Manheim (New Haven, 1959), 10.
11. Ibid., p. 11.
12. Ibid.
13. Martin Heidegger, "Letter on Humanism," *Basic Writings,* ed. David Farrell Krell (New York, 1977), 202.
14. Ibid.
15. Karl Marx and Friedrich Engels, *The German Ideology: Part One,* ed. C. J. Arthur (New York, 1970), 42.
16. Heidegger, "Letter," p. 210.
17. Ibid., pp. 210, 205.
18. Cf. Thomas Sheehan, "Getting to the Topic: The New Edition of *Wegmarken,*" *Radical Phenomenology: Essays in Honor of Martin Heidegger,* ed., John Sallis (New York, 1978), chap. 18, for more on this interpretation.
19. "Letter on Humanism," p. 210.
20. Ibid., p. 217
21. Ibid.
22. Ibid., p. 228
23. Jean-Paul Sartre, "Existentialism is a Humanism," *Existentialism from Dostoevsky to Sartre,* ed. Walter Kaufmann (New York, 1956), 309.
24. Sartre, *Search,* p. 161
25. Lukács, *History,* p. 148 ff.
26. Ibid., p. xxiii (1967 Preface to the New Edition).
27. Sartre, *Search,* pp. 178–9.
28. Ibid., p. 30.
29. Heidegger, "Letter," p. 220.
30. Ibid.

31. Martin Heidegger, "The Question Concerning Technology," *Basic Writings*, p. 315.
32. Ibid., p. 308.
33. Marx and Engels, p. 86.
34. Cf. Karl Marx, *Capital* (New York, 1967), I, 71ff.
35. Kostas Axelos, in his *Alienation, Praxis and Techne in the Thought of Karl Marx* (Austin, 1976), offers a Heideggerian critique of Marx similar in parts to what follows.
36. Heidegger, "Question," p. 315.
37. The "logic of domination" is a topic to which Horkheimer, Adorno, Marcuse and others of the "Frankfurt School" have devoted much attention. Their various treatments and the relation these bear to Heidegger and Marx are too complex to enter into here, and my treatment does not follow theirs.
38. Martin Heidegger, "The Age of the World Picture," *The Question Concerning Technology and Other Essays,* trans. William Lovitt (New York, 1977), 148.
39. Marx and Engels, p. 52.
40. Marx, *Capital,* I, 390 n.
41. *Writings of the Young Marx,* p. 304.
42. Ibid., p. 303.
43. Ibid., p. 308.
44. Heidegger, "Letter," p. 204.
45. Ibid., p. 205.
46. *Writings of the Young Marx,* p. 401.
47. "Only a God Can Save Us," trans. David Schendler, *Graduate Faculty Philosophy Journal* (Winter, 1977), 18.

Principles Precarious:
On the Origin of the Political
in Heidegger

Reiner Schürmann

The *principia* are such as stands in the first place, in the most advanced rank. The *principia* refer to rank and order.... We follow them without meditation.[1]

Heidegger's writings on the phenomenological Destruction of the history of ontology have been said to be harmful for public life since they deprive political action of its ground.[2] The reasons can be stated briefly. Political action no less than any other experience that we live has its site, its locus, and the very program of situating or localizing fields, the very program of phenomenological topology, excludes reference to any ultimate standard for judgment and legitimation. Indeed, the fields of truth have in common only its hiding-revealing character. Hence political action cannot rely on any extrinsic, foundational, unquestionable ground from which to borrow its credentials. Stated otherwise, the origin of the political does not lie outside the political, and political action is left without recourse for justification. The purpose of this essay is to contribute to the elucidation of the notion of origin as it affects practice in general and political action in particular. The phenomenon of *oriri*, coming to presence, is indeed much more complex than the simple opposition between topology and metaphysical ontology may suggest it is.

Arché, Principium, Ursprung

The content of the "phenomenological destruction of the history of ontology," first announced in *Being and Time*,[3] centers upon the notion of *epoché*. As is well known, Heidegger borrows this term not from Husserl, but from the Stoics.[4]

This word thus does not mean objectification, or the methodic exclusion by a thetical act of consciousness, but a "stop," an interruption, an act of halting. The history of ontologies appears to Heidegger as a multitude of ways in which things render themselves present, in which presence lets them be. It is a history of truth as *aletheia*: a multitude of constellations of unconcealedness and concealment. To speak of "epochs" of presence implies in this line of thinking two things: presence as such reserves itself in what is present; and presence marks "stoppages" that are the thresholds between the fields of intelligibility and of possible life that make up our concrete history.[5] Such halting points in the difference between presence and what is present belong to presence itself, not to man. In this sense, Heidegger's notion of *epoché* is antihumanistic.[6] But this notion also yields an imperative for thinking: the Destruction frees presence so as to restore it to thought which, in turn, "restrains *(an sich halten)* all usual doing and prizing, knowing and looking."[7]

Heidegger's notion of *epoché* thus temporalizes the difference between what is present *(das Anwesende)* and presence (*Anwesen* understood as a verb). The way things are present varies from epoch to epoch, and once a reversal *(Wendung)* has inaugurated a new mode of presence the previous modes are irretrievably lost. We can trace the rise, the sway and the decline of such a mode of presence; that is, we can trace its origin in the sense of *arché*. We can also unearth the theoretical and practical foundations on which a past epoch rested; that is, we can trace its origin in the sense of *principium*. This word designates indeed both the theoretical "principles" of a time and its practical *princeps* ("prince" or authority). But what we shall never be able to trace is the origin as *Ursprung*: the mode in which, at a given age in history, things emerge into presence, linger, have us dream, suffer, pray, make war, trade, etc.,[8] and then, a few decades later, lose that way of being with us. The realm of the political is only the most revelatory of the *pollachos legetai* (the multiple ways something is spoken of) that belongs to the origin: the *arché* of a commonwealth appears as the founding deed that begins and then dominates a polity.[9] The *principium* appears both as propositions held to be self-evident (for example, "the principle of equal rights and self-determination of peoples," Charter of the United Nations), and as the institution retaining ultimate power. The *Ursprung*, finally, appears as the mode in which law, property, but also imponderables such as rhetoric, enter the public realm or "come to presence." The threefold sense of the origin—begin and dominate; rule by first propositions and by a top institution; and come to presence—allows us to take a step further in the direction of the *epoché* as "the thing itself" in the phenomenological Destruction.

OF EPOCHS AND THEIR PRINCIPLES

In the order of authority as in the order of intelligibility, the principles hold the first rank in the field open to an epoch. These principles lay out the paths that the course of exploitations and the discourse of explications will follow. They are observed without question in a given epoch. When questions are raised in their regard, the network of exchange which they have opened becomes confused, and the order that they have founded declines. A principle has its uprise, its period of reign and its ruin. In contrast, the rise or coming-forth of presence requires another type of thought than that which traces the reversals of historical principles. We observe principles unwittingly. The surging forth of presence, the origin as *Ursprung*, demands an inversion of thought. It is this inversion that may appear harmful: with Heidegger's "turn" in thinking, *archai* and *principles* come to be confined to fields in which they obtain. Their site of competence is an epoch opened by ever new constellations of presence. Hence the moorage they provide for theoretical legitimation of action becomes precarious.

If the *epoché* is thus not the method but the matter of the phenomenological Destruction, principles appear in quite a new light. Is not a principle something that inspires reverential fear,[10] that is recognized as prevailing against historical contingencies? Is it not "precious," *axios*, an axiom, therefore, because it is untouchable by chance? In Heidegger's Destruction, on the contrary, one has to speak of the establishment of a principle, and that in the double sense of its founding at the beginning of an epoch and during its reign. Put differently, we are to think the *arché*, the beginning and the domination, of a principle. We are to view an epoch as determined by a code that is unique every time — not a convention, but in the sense the French speak of a "code de la route," a law of *regional* application. The accession of a code to the rank of principle establishes a first, a reference, and thus opens a field of intelligibility. This code regulates the "establishment" of a regional or epochal order in the sense of its putting it in place, and it regulates its "establishment" in the sense of an institution of public utility, of a regime. For instance, the little phrase "Nothing is without reason" attains such a rank at the beginning of the modern era following a long period of incubation.[11] This accession and its consecutive reign allow one to understand the *arché* of modernity; they thus allow one to map out its archeology. The modern era is that period where the principle of sufficient reason is reputed to prevail in thought as well as in action: to think is to "render" reason, *rationem reddere*, and to act is to impose rationality *(arraisonner)* upon nature. We are to understand, it seems, an epoch as the field opened by such an accession and estimation of a principle.

An epoch opens in a "crisis," that is, in a separating *(krinein)* of what will be present for a time from what will be absent. The crises in history institute an economy of presence. But such an economy becomes thinkable only when its grip begins to loosen. At the end of an epoch its economic principle expires. "When, in peril, a reversal produces itself, that can only happen immediately."[12] The principle of an era is that which gives it cohesion, a coherence which for a time applies without discussion or question. At the end of an epoch, however, discussing and questioning such coherence becomes possible; in expiring, a principle renders itself speakable. As long as its economy dominates, and as long as its order disposes of the paths that life and thought follow, one will speak differently than when it withers away, giving way to the establishment of a new order. Their rise, reign and peril reveal epochal principles to be essentially precarious. They have their genealogy and necrology. They set themselves up without a guiding plan and fall without warning. When the habitat that has transitorily become ours decays and falls, questions not posed till then, questions previously impossible to pose, surge forth: if such is its end, what may have been its beginning? The establishments bequeathed us permit talk and questioning above all when they fold, with the result that we know epochs by their reversals.[13]

Intermittent Thinking

What is ranked supreme in an epoch—the code that holds together the activities and discourses in which an epoch recognizes itself—comes into sight for its own sake only in the crises in which it is overturned. At those moments it becomes thinkable. Between epochs, the origin as *arché* and as principle can be thought of as *differing* from the origin as presence. The difference between the order of things present and their presence may thus not be thinkable as long as laws and order apply without question under the unsuspected rule of a given aletheiological economy.[14] A reversal, *Kehre*, in the epochal constellations of truth thus seems to be the condition of a *Kehre* in the thinking of truth. If the reversals in history let themselves be best circumscribed by the retreat of an epochal principle (which until then coded the order of things), then in which direction does this retreat point? The establishment in which a collectivity resides for a time has its order, but not so the sequence itself of these establishments.[15] Thus in these transitions the origin towards which the retreat of a principle points allows us to understand something of its own manner of being. The origin as coming to presence would then be thinkable only intermittently—as *phuein*, showing forth, in pre-classical Greece, and as *Sein*, Being, in the post-modern contemporary world. Throughout the history of metaphysics originary thinking may then have been possible particularly at the moments of scission. Knowing and common sense function best when the common world, the order into which we all fit, is intact. But *thinking* may have its condition in the folds between epochal fields.

It may well be that in these decades of ours the principle that has managed a long epoch is reversing; it becomes thinkable because it is less near. In this caesura an absence may be revealing itself that is the proper space of thought. Thinking would then be opposable to knowing as a fold is to a field, or as the abyss *(Abgrund)* opened by a fold to the ground *(Grund)* on which a field rests. Thinking would require that a "preponderant" epochal principle, that is to say, one "weighing more heavily" for a time upon the life and intelligence of people, be alleviated, that it retire. It may be that, at the threshold dividing one era from the next, ontological anarchism appears, the absence of an ultimate reason in the succession of the numerous principles which have run their course. And it may be that in the self-revelation of this absence human action, notably political practice, becomes thinkable in a way that it is not when life and thought obey the order of things established between two reversals.

EPOCHS MADE OF THINGS, ACTION AND SPEECH

How can one describe the economy of "present" and "absent" imposed by the first in the order of intelligibility, the *principium,* which is also the First in the order of authority, the *princeps?* Such an economy exhibits itself in any domain whatsoever: written texts, painted objects, tattoos, diplomatic treaties, table manners, prisons and asylums; and each of these speaks in its own way of the epochal principle that gives coherence to a culture. But not all cultural facts have an equally revelatory value. For Heidegger, the most revealing traces of past historical fields are preserved in philosophical works.[16] This preference is not something that goes without saying. It is even debatable if one understands these fields as constituting an order of things present, a manifest order (the manifest order is not presence understood as an event, but the modality in which the totality of beings present is epochally posited). Perhaps philosophical works are themselves like tattoos: executed in order to embellish, heavy with meaning for the clan members, signifying a truth to which one dedicates oneself, but using decidedly formalized figures, hence mediated by abstractive spirit. Perhaps the order of an epochal field is even less legible in philosophical works that emanate from it than in tattooed faces. In this case, where is such an order to be read most plainly? In a domain where multiple conducts come together; where things, actions and words join to become accessible to all; at the intersection of the paths of thought and practice; where the collectivity is witness to facts and deeds while being at the same time their protagonist; and in what is at the same time both commonplace and noticeable, that is to say, public. The *obverse* of a field where its principle is *obvious* is the political.[17]

That which gives coherence and cohesion to an epoch reveals itself and becomes legible in the political. One speaks of the political "domain": this *dominium* marks the extent to which the epochal principle dominates. Each of "Western man's various fundamental positions within beings"[18] leads to its own particular economy, which first imposes itself upon beings and then disposes of them during the period that is its own. Imposition and disposition articulate the *arché* of those fundamental positions. Put differently, the founding gesture of a city inaugurates the field of possibles on which it will live and commands that field. Insofar as it commands, such a gesture decrees the code that will remain in effect throughout the epoch. It is the visibility of the origin as *arché* and as *principium* in the political domain that is important here. To act in public is to join words and things in action. The originary field of an epoch becomes obvious when in the midst of his fellowmen a man speaks up about a state of affairs.

Speaking up cannot by itself fully reveal the code that rules an epoch. Such a code is tied to power. Speech alone, without reference to a practical state of affairs and without a call to action, constitutes a domain other than the political; taken in isolation, it constitutes the region of the text.[19] Likewise, if action remains deprived of speech and of reference to other actors, a new domain opens itself; not that of action, but activity among utensils. Neither the presence of other actors nor speech are required for the handling of tools. If other actors join in, the activity becomes work, and if speech makes the work public, it becomes political. The exchange among people finally can also occur uncompounded; a true hatred nourishes itself without words and without actions on things. It belongs to yet another domain, that of the modalities of "being-with." But when the interaction of these three regions comes about (and that is doubtlessly the common case), the principle of an epoch renders itself visible. The political is the correlation, in broad daylight, of speech, of acting, and of a practical state of affairs. This correlation produces the order into which the code obeyed by an epoch translates itself concretely.

THE ORIGIN OF THE POLITICAL

From the recognition of the manifold ways in which Western languages speak of the origin,[20] from its *pollachos legetai,* we have gone over to the notion of an epochal principle and the field of its economy opened up for thinking and living. The history that the phenomenological Destruction deconstructs has appeared as one made of reversals or folds that separate such epochal orders. Whereas knowing and common sense showed themselves to function best under the rules that temporarily ground the things present, thinking — the thinking of the difference between presence and what is present — seems to be at home in an abyss. If it is agreed that the origin, as *arché,* begins and commands; that, as *principium,* it imposes first truths and authority; and that, as *Ursprung,* it brings forth to presence — and if it is agreed that at the moments of reversals its functions of *arché* and of *principium* become uncertain — then we may ask if the origin does not show its true face as "anarchic" and "unprincipled" when an epochal economy comes to whither away. Such a topology of *Ursprung* is all the more crucial since the transmutations of what is originary have appeared to be most legible in the political domain, at the intersection of things, action and speech. If in Heidegger's thinking the origin of the political is indeed anarchic and unprincipled, then we may perhaps be compelled to agree with Werner Marx's observation about its harmfulness.

The "thing itself" of the Destruction now seems to be the reversals, crises, the folds between epochs rather than the epochal fields themselves. What makes the status of these reversals paradoxical is that when they arise and are present, they remain hidden; but when acting, things and speech have entered into their new economy, the reversals, though past, show themselves. It is the owl of Minerva that retrieves them, *ex post facto.* If the political is indeed the domain in which the fixed order of an epoch[21] reveals itself, then phenomenology, in what it may have to say about the political, will have to set out by tracing the subterranean displacements of such an order—of such orders, rather, since all will depend on seeing that nothing permits postulating a primordial order preliminary to the successive or contemporaneous economies of unconcealedness and concealment; on seeing, therefore, that in times of transition the evidence of this absence uproots political acting.[22] The *obverse* of an epoch is the disposition of its political reticulum, the same for as long as it lasts. But the *reverse* is a profound, concealed layer analogous to Foucault's *epistémé*: "anterior to words, perceptions and gestures ... less dubious, always more 'true' than the theories";[23] a layer, the uncovering of which demands the reversal of thought by which philosophy wrests the originary from the archaic and the principiant.

At the thresholds between epochs the orders intermingle and become con-fused—in a confusion that is ever so revelatory. In this blurring of fields the origin shows itself otherwise than as *arché* and as *principium*. The decisive turn-ings may at first go unnoticed, quite as, for Heidegger, the decisive thinkers are the least aware of that which is given to them to think. But these turnings oblige the phenomenologist to raise the question of the political in a different manner than did the ancients. The political is the site where things, actions and speech meet. For the ancients, for the tradition arising out of Attic philosophy, reflection on the political led to the endeavor of translating an ahistorical order, knowable in itself, into public organization to which it served as an *a priori* model and as a criterion of *a posteriori* legitimation. The categories for understanding the body politic were derived from the analysis of sensible bodies and were transposed into practical discourse from speculative or "ontological" discourse. Aristotle's *Physics,* the *Grundbuch,* "foundational book"[24] of Western philosophy, provided practical philosophy with the elementary vocabulary, worked out in the context of movement and its causes. Thus speculative philosophy served as patron and pattern (both words deriv-ing from *pater*, father) for practical philosophy.

What did practical philosophy inherit from speculative philosophy as from its father? Precisely the reference to a first. In order to have knowledge of the sensible there must be a first to which the multiple can be referred and thus be made true, be verified. Likewise, in order that there be action and not merely activities there must be a first that provides action with sense and direction. Political philosophies differ by the way in which they articulate this relation to the one, *pros hen,* but without it the commonwealth would cease to be accessible to metaphysics. This first in reference to which the commonwealth becomes conceivable need not be a supreme power: Aristotle compares the constitution of a principle of action to an army in full retreat, chased by fear, but in which first one, then several soldiers stop, look to the rear where the enemy stands, and regain their courage. They obey orders again, and the activities of each become again the action of all.[25] Aristotle views the command, *arché,* imposing itself on the runaways just as he views the substance, as *arché,* imposing its unity upon the accidents. Such is the filiation between ousiology and practical philosophy. Both obervations retain the relation "to the one." From Plato's philosopher-king to Machiavelli's Prince this *pros hen* reference defines the relations of the many subjects to the one leader as it defines the relations of the many accidents to substance, and in general of the secondary analogates to the prime analogates. Is it not instructive in this regard that Aristotle first analyzes the "proportion," the identity of relation between two terms, in the political context,[26] well before the *Metaphysics*? Political philosophy is not the same, to be sure, when the first to which acting is referred is a man, or a collectivity, or the common good, or a duty. But these are all *archai.* In Heidegger, the destruction of ontologies cuts short all such transpositions of the schema of relations to a first.

The Destruction seeks not to ground but to locate the political. To be concrete, the topology of the reversals in history must trace the mutations of the interplay between action, things and speech. From the ontologies of the body politic to the topology of the political fields, the method is the "step back"[27] from *archai* and principles to presencing; from knowing and obeying to thinking and freedom; from metaphysics to ontological anarchy. The site insofar as it is the space where a phenomenon unfolds, where it is present, is neither the grounding ground nor presencing as such,[28] but the zone of belonging where we are implicated — "folded in" — action, things and speech. By this step back towards the site thinking comes into its own. The origin of the political, understood topologically, cannot be objectified: one thinks correctly only that to which one belongs. The "spring" out of representations such as *archai* and principles into the originary is "the unbridged entry into belonging."[29] Such belonging requires a type of existence. Quite as authentic temporality requires authentic existence if it is to be understood at all, and quite as releasement as a title for Being's way to be requires a released existence if it is to be thought of at all, so anarchic presencing, too, requires anarchic existence. Such existence may imply the deliberate negation of *archai* and principles in the public domain. Such seems to be the consequence if one takes the reciprocity between existing and thinking seriously, which is, together with the subversive power that lies in raising simple questions, the genuinely Socratic strain in Heidegger. The French poet René Char seems to have sensed this same expiring of any First, at the end of the epochal economy structured by *pros hen* relations, when he writes: "Amont éclate" (upstream bursts);[30] "poème pulvérisé" (pulverized poem);[31] "Cette part jamais fixée, en nous sommeillante, d'où jaillira DEMAIN LE MULTIPLE" (That part never fixed, asleep in us, from which will surge TOMORROW THE MANIFOLD).[32]

Notes

Reiner Schürmann is Associate Professor of Philosophy and Chairman, The Graduate Faculty, Department of Philosophy, at the New School for Social Research, New York City. His books include *Meister Eckhart, Mystic and Philosopher* (Indiana U. P., 1978; translation of *Maître Eckhart ou la joie errante*, Paris, 1972), *Les Origines* (Paris, 1976), and *The Origin of Politics: Political Thinking in Heidegger* (forthcoming).

1. Martin Heidegger, *Der Satz vom Grund* (Pfullingen, 1957), pp. 40, 42. (Cited hereafter as SvG).

2. Werner Marx, *Heidegger and the Tradition* (Evanston, 1971), p. 251, speaks of "the extremely perilous character of Heidegger's concept of truth." Karsten Harries claims that "the connections which link the *Rektoratsrede* to *Being and Time* cannot be overlooked." ("Heidegger as a Political Thinker," *Review of Metaphysics*, XXIX, 1976, p. 643.) But the problem consists in localizing that peril, and it is far from established that Heidegger's concept of truth frees the way for totalitarianism. On this point see my "Political Thinking in Heidegger," *Social Research* 45/1 (Spring 1978) pp. 191–221.

3. *Sein und Zeit* (Halle/Saale, 5, 1941), p. 39; *Being and Time* (New York, 1962), p. 63. (These two works are cited hereafter as SZ and BT.)

4. *Holzwege* (Frankfurt, 1950), p. 311; *Early Greek Thinking* (New York, 1975), p. 26f. (These two works are cited hereafter as Hw and EGT.) *Epechein* means to abstain, to cease seeking: the Stoic sage is resigned to not possessing wisdom in the midst of the great number of doctrines concerning truth and that is how he obtains wisdom, i.e., *ataraxia* or tranquility of the soul. See on this matter the excellent article by P. Couissin, "L'origine et l'évolution de l'*epoché*," *Revue des Etudes Grecques*, 42 (1929), pp. 373–397.

5. "The *epoché* of Being belongs to Being itself," Hw 311/EGT 27. "In a steep event, out of its own essence of concealment, Being appropriates its epoch," *Die Technik und die Kehre* (Pfullingen, 1962), p. 43. Neither of the two senses designates "a span of time in occurence, but rather the fundamental characteristic of sending," *Zur Sache des Denkens* (Tübingen, 1969), p. 9; *On Time and Being* (New York, 1972), p. 9. (These two works are cited hereafter as SD and OTB.) Heidegger speaks of a "sequence of epochs in the destiny of Being," SD 9/OTB 9, to dismiss at the same time theories of chance and theories of determinism in history. Several texts spell out the "epochal marks" of Being, or of presence, e.g.: "physis, logos, hen, idea, energeia, Substantiality, Objectivity, Subjectivity, the Will, the Will to Power, the Will to Will," *Iden-*

tität und Differenz (Pfullingen, 1957), p. 64; *Identity and Difference* (New York, 1969), p. 66. (These two works are cited hereafter as IDz and IDce.) Such an epochal deconstruction of Western metaphysics already appears in Heidegger's habilitation thesis of 1916, in which he speaks of the "epochs of the history of the mind," *Frühe Schriften* (Frankfurt, 1972), p. 350.

6. The effort "to think against humanism," in the "Letter in Humanism," is explicitly tied to the phenomenological Destruction: *Platons Lehre von der Wahrheit* (Bern, 1947), pp. 95–97; *Basic Writings* (New York, 1977), pp. 225–227.

7. Hw 54/*Poetry, Language, Thought* (New York, 1971, hereafter cited as PLT), p. 66. This text recalls directly Cicero's advice to "restrain one's assent" *Academica* II, 59, and that formulated by Sextus Empiricus: *epechein peri panton*, "to reserve oneself with regard to all things," *Hypotyposes* I, 232f.

8. In a very Heideggerian fashion, Michel Foucault has complemented the Destruction by an Archeology, first of madness, then of speaking, classifying and exchanging, and lately of the penitentiary systems and of sexuality. Heidegger himself remains largely content with tracing the epochs of presence through philosophical texts.

9. "On the one hand, *arché* means that from which something takes its origin and beginning; on the other it signifies what, *as* this origin and beginning, likewise keeps rein *over*, i.e., preserves and therefore dominates, the other thing that emerges from it. *Arché* means at one and the same time beginning and domination." *Wegmarken* (Frankfurt, 1967, hereafter cited as Wm), p. 317; "On the Being and Conception of *Physis*," *Man and World*, IX (1976), p. 227f. It is this *archein* that Heidegger elsewhere calls "setting into work," Hw 50/PLT 61f. A. Schwan, *Politische Philosophie im Denken Heideggers* (Köln, 1965), develops elements for a political philosophy exclusively from this notion of setting into work. About this enterprise see Jean Michel Palmier, *Les écrits politiques de Heidegger* (Paris, 1968), p. 152.

10. Not an ontic principle, but presence itself is what inspires *Scheu*, the feeling of awe. Cf. Heidegger's interpretation of the first chorus from the *Antigone* of Sophocles, *Einführung in die Metaphysik* (Tübingen, 1953), p. 115; *An Introduction to Metaphysics* (New Haven, 1959), p. 149, and the remarks by Reinhart Maurer, *Revolution und "Kehre"* (Frankfurt, 1975), pp. 41, 48, 212.

11. "In the history of Western thought, which began in the sixth century B.C., it took two thousand three hundred years until that familiar representation 'Nothing is without reason' would be properly thought as a principle and known as a law . . . . Up until the present day we have hardly meditated this state of affairs that this little phrase required such an extraordinarily long period of incubation." SvG, 192.

12. *Die Technik und die Kehre*, op. cit. p. 42.

13. "The reversal *(Wandel)* in Being," understood as "reversal of its destiny," ibid., p. 38.

14. I borrow the term "aletheiological" from Friedrich-Wilhelm von Herrmann, *Die Selbstinterpretation Martin Heideggers* (Meisenheim am Glan, 1964), p. 45.

15. For Heidegger, the reversals between historical epochs are not joints where a reason articulates itself which would be more reasonable yet than the one imposed

by a principle and read phenomenologically in the finite clearing of a given culture. See on this point the remarks by Werner Marx on the "Structure of the History of Being," *Heidegger and the Tradition* (Evanston, 1971), pp. 163–171.

16. Herbert Marcuse speaks of a "fake concreteness" in Heidegger. "Soon I realized," he says, "that Heidegger's concreteness was a phony." "Heidegger's Politics: An Interview with Herbert Marcuse by Frederick Olafson," in *Graduate Faculty Philosophy Journal* VI (1977), pp. 31 and 29. Marcuse's verdict that Heidegger's philosophy was "avoiding reality" is confirmed perhaps by the two instances when Heidegger left the philosophical tradition: the poetry of Hölderlin and modern technology. It is confirmed there since Heidegger understands the one and the other in relation to his unique philosophical problematic, the question of Being.

17. To say that the political is the domain where the principle of an epoch shows itself most visibly signifies neither that all the other phenomena can only be explained politically, nor that phenomenology, when it becomes the destruction of metaphysics, ceases to be regional. The political is only that region *(Gegend)* of phenomena whose essential trait is to join publicly the theoretical and the practical.

18. *Nietzsche* (Pfullingen, 1961), vol. II, p. 421; *The End of Philosophy* (New York, 1973), p. 19.

19. For Heidegger, the problem of the text is reduced most often to that of the poetic text. As he wrote to the literary historian, Emil Staiger, all speech is "that unconcealment that reveals something present," but the poem, in this instance a poem of Mörike, "brings to language that very mode of essentializing" which belongs to language in general. Emil Staiger, *Die Kunst der Interpretation* (Munich, 1971), pp. 35, 40. On the expression "bringing to language," see Beda Allemann, *Hölderlin und Heidegger* (Freiburg, 1954), p. 108.

20. "What is required is a new heedfulness about language and not, as I once thought, the invention of new terms, but rather a return to the originary content of our own language which is always in a process of dying away." Richard Wisser, ed., *Martin Heidegger im Gespräch* (Freiburg, 1970), p. 77.

21. Thus the "theater" is the fixed order of the beginning of the modern era: Hw 84/ "The Age of the World View," *Boundary 2*, IV, 2 (1976), p. 351f; and technology as *"Gestell,"* frame, that of the contemporary age: *Vorträge und Aufsätze* (Pfullingen, 1954), p. 27f.; *Basic Writings*, p. 301f.

22. Here is without doubt the most radical difference which separates Heidegger from the Frankfurt School. One of the preoccupations which makes a "school" of this latter group is its quest for foundations of ultimate legitimation; e.g., Jürgen Haberman, *Legitimation Crisis* (Boston, 1975), p. xxv.

23. Michel Foucault, *The Order of Things* (New York, 1970), p. xxi.

24. Wm 312/ "On the Being and Conception . . .," *Man and World*, p. 224, and SvG 111.

25. Aristotle, *Posterior Analytics*, II, 19; 100 a 11 with the commentary of Hans-Georg Gadamer, *Truth and Method* (New York, 1975), p. 314, and, more specifically, *Kleine Schriften*, vol. I, (Tübingen, 1967), p. 110.

26. *Nicomachean Ethics*, V, 6; 1134 a 26 ff.

27. IDz 47/IDce 51.

28. Presencing differs from what is present as the "locality," *Ortschaft*, differs from the locus, *Ort;* cf. *Vorträge und Aufsätze* (Pfullingen, 1954), p. 255/EGT 99f.

29. IDz 24/IDce 33.

30. *Le nu perdu* (Paris, 1971), p. 48.
31. *La Parole en archipel* (Paris, 1962), p. 73.
32. *Commune présence* (Paris, 1964), p. 255.

Heidegger's Philosophy of Art

Sandra Lee Bartky

Throughout his career Heidegger has shown a persistent interest in topics which belong to the domain of aesthetics: he has discussed the nature of poetic language, compared the functions of poet and philosopher and pondered in depth the ontological significance of poetry.[1] However, not until the appearance of *Holzwege* (1950) with its long leading essay (almost a monograph in itself) entitled "The Origin of the Work of Art" did he produce anything which in breadth, scope and generality might be called a philosophy of art.[2] It is this essay which I shall examine, not primarily for the light it sheds upon Heidegger's later ontology, but in its own right as an independent contribution to our understanding of the nature of art. Since Heidegger's philosophy is notoriously obscure, anyone who wishes to comment on it must first undertake considerable exposition and exegesis. Therefore, in the first four sections I set forth what I take Heidegger to be saying, largely though not entirely without comment, while in the two final sections I examine some of the more striking strengths and weaknesses of the theory.

I. MERE THINGS AND THE "EARTH"

Like so many aestheticians before him, what Heidegger seeks to uncover is the essence of art. Instead of comparing works of art in order to find common characteristics, or trying to derive essential definitions from principles or higher concepts, he proposes that we examine artworks themselves in so far as they are things. For there is some sense in which works of art are things: pictures hang on the wall like hats and are shipped from one place to another like freight; "Beethoven's quartets lie in the storerooms of the publishing house like potatoes in a cellar" (19). Works of art, of course, are not *just* things; clearly they are more. But in order to discover in what sense they are more than merely things, let us try to find out first what "mere" things are.

"Lifeless beings of nature," i.e., stones, clods of earth, pieces of wood, but not flowers or animals, or useful objects such as tools, are what we ordinarily call "things." When we speak of "mere" things, "mere" is understood in a pejorative sense, i.e., a "mere" thing is something which is simply a thing and nothing more. Thus, while we call useful objects things, they are not mere things, nor do any things but mere things count as things "in the strict sense" (22).

But what is a mere thing and in what does the "thingly" character of the mere thing consist? The Western philosophical tradition, Heidegger claims, has produced three fundamental interpretations of the nature of the thing: the thing as substance, as bearer of characteristics; the thing as a "manifold of the given in sensation," i.e., as a collection of sense-data; and the thing as formed matter. The substance theory of the thing derives some of its power from the fact that the schema of substance and accidents which it employs parallels the subject-predicate structure of a simple propositional statement. This fact may vitiate this interpretation of the thing or it may not; but even if it does not, it is clear that the substance-accidents schema can be referred to any entity whatsoever and that therefore it is powerless to distinguish mere things from other things. Furthermore, "attentive dwelling within the sphere of things already tells us that this thing-concept does not hit upon the thingly element of the thing, its independent and self-contained character" (24f.).[3]

Heidegger's objection to the conception of the thing as a collection of sense-data will be familiar to students of analytic philosophy, although it has its origin not in an analysis of language but in a phenomenological examination of perception. Ordinarily we are not presented with a "throng of sensations"; in the appearance of things we never really first perceive tones and noises. We hear the dog barking outside and the airplane overhead, not "acoustical sensations" or bare sounds. "Much closer to us than all sensations are the things themselves . . . . In order to hear a bare sound we have to listen away from things, divert our ear from them, i.e., listen abstractly" (26).

The third conception of the thing — as formed matter — seems closer than the other two to the point of view of common sense because it seems to reflect better than the others the actual visual appearance of things. But does it allow us to grasp the unique character of mere things? The block of granite, admits Heidegger, is something material in a definite form, where by "form" is meant the "distribution and arrangement of the material parts in spatial locations" (28). But objects for use, what Heidegger calls "tools" or "equipment," are also formed matter. Their form is not the accidental result of a prior distribution of matter during some geological process, but it is first determined by the purpose which they are to serve. Furthermore, not only the arrangement of their parts but also the sort of stuff of which they are made depend upon their intended functions. Therefore the notions of matter and form have their proper place in an explication of the nature of things which are produced for use, and they are derived from the experience of making such things. In no case are they "original determinations of the thingness of a mere thing" (28). The matter-form schema seems to apply to mere things; indeed, it seems to apply to any entity whatsoever; but this is so only because we tend to conceive the coming-to-be of things, including mere things, on the analogy of human creation for use. Aristotle's doctrine of final causes in nature would be a case in point; the Christian interpretation of beings as *ens creatum* would be another.

Here Heidegger's case against the matter-form interpretation of the thing is identical with his case against the substance-accidents schema. Both have arisen out of experiences other than the direct confrontation with mere things; neither has grasped the distinctive "thingness" of the thing. The failure of the tradition to grasp the nature of the thing, then, has been a fruitful failure, for it has revealed something important about the mere thing. "The unpretentious thing evades thought most stubbornly" (31). Mere things refuse to reveal themselves; they are "strange and uncommunicative"; they have a "self-contained independence" which is not due to our ignorance but is somehow intrinsic to them (31). This theme, which is repeated with some insistence throughout all of Heidegger's later philosophy, returns later in the essay:

> A stone presses downward and manifests its heaviness. But...this heaviness...denies to us any penetration into it. If we attempt such a penetration by breaking open the rock, it still does not display in its fragments anything inward that has been disclosed. The stone has instantly withdrawn again into the same dull pressure and bulk of its fragments. If we try to lay hold of the stone's heaviness in another way by placing the stone on a balance, we merely bring the heaviness into the form of a calculated weight. This perhaps very precise determination...remains a number, but the weight's burden has escaped us. Color shines and wants only to shine. When we analyze it...by measuring its wavelengths, it is gone. It shows itself only when it remains undisclosed and unexplained. Earth thus shatters every attempt to penetrate into it (46f.).

In this perplexing passage it would seem that Heidegger is attempting to convey the force of a primary encounter with nature—where by "primary encounter" I mean an experience of nature which is pre-analytic and pre-scientific—and the inadequacy of all theoretical constructs to do justice to such an encounter. Mere things such as stones and rocks, things of the earth as we encounter them pre-analytically, either "disintegrate" when they are "explained" by philosophical or scientific theories or else they are returned to us in an unrecognizable form. It is difficult to determine whether these and similar passages are inspired by a view of scientific explanation which I take to be mistaken, i.e., the assumption that scientific explanations of physical phenomena are in competition with descriptions of primary encounters and are meant to replace them. What is not in doubt, however, is that on Heidegger's view the disparity between theoretical accounts of nature and "brute" or "immediate" experience is due to and in fact announces what he calls the "self-refusal of the mere thing" (31).

Although the search for an interpretation of the mere thing has failed, something about the nature of the artwork has, by indirection, been revealed: the artwork, to the extent that it partakes of the "thingly" character of the thing, must share in the impenetrability and mystery of the thing. The self-withholding quality of the things of nature, in turn, is an aspect of a larger phenomenon called the "earth," by which Heidegger understands neither "a mass of matter deposited somewhere" nor "the merely astronomical idea of a planet" (42). The "earth" is a pervasive feature of all being; it is the hidden and essentially self-closing ground of all that appears (48). But we shall return to this theme later.

II. THE WORLD

Since tools or objects, made to be useful — what Heidegger calls "equipment" — occupy an intermediate position between mere things and works of art, perhaps a grasp of their nature will smooth the way for an approach to the essence of the artwork. A familiar piece of equipment, a pair of peasant shoes; is chosen for analysis. We do not need to exhibit an actual pair of shoes; in order to describe them, a pictorial representation will do. Heidegger chooses a painting of a pair of peasant shoes by Van Gogh.[4] It is possible to see in the picture a pair of empty peasant shoes and nothing more. Or it is possible to see much more:

> From the dark opening of the worn insides of the shoes the toilsome tread of the worker stares forth. In the stiffly rugged heaviness of the shoes there is the accumulated tenacity of her slow trudge through the far-spreading and ever-uniform furrows of the field swept by a raw wind. On the leather lie the dampness and richness of the soil. Under the soles slides the loneliness of the field-path as evening falls. In the shoes vibrates the silent call of the earth, its quiet gift of the ripening grain and its unexplained self-refusal in the fallow desolation of the wintry field. This equipment is pervaded by uncomplaining anxiety as to the certainty of bread, the wordless joy of having once more withstood want, the trembling before the impending childbed and shivering at the surrounding menace of death (33f.).

In these shoes, and in the rumination on their character as "footwear," the essence of all equipment—"reliability" or "dependability" *(Verlässlichkeit)*—is revealed. "Dependability" is that by virtue of which the users of equipment are admitted into the sphere of their concerns. To grasp the nature of the peasant shoes as equipment is to be reminded of the life of their wearer; it is to see them within the total domain where they belong. What is essential to the utensil is the capacity it grants to its user to maintain some certain hold on the world, and it is because of this capacity that it can reveal a distinct range of human possibilities.

But not only the peasant shoes have been revealed for what they are. Something crucial to an understanding of the nature of the artwork has also emerged: "This painting spoke. In the vicinity of the work we were suddenly somewhere else than we usually tend to be" (35). This "somewhere else" is the sphere within which the peasant woman lives, works and dies; in showing us the role which peasant shoes play in the life of the peasant, the painting has shown us the world of the peasant. "Towering up within itself, the work opens up a *world* and keeps it abidingly in force" (44).

By "world" Heidegger means neither the physical cosmos nor some particular department of interests; part of the meaning of the term "world" in the essay parallels closely what Husserl and some of his successors have called the *Lebenswelt* or "life-world." For Husserl, the life-world is the comprehensive frame of reference of the living subject, the encompassing horizon within which human experience takes place. The dictionary definition of "world" suggests that the use of the term "life-world" in this tradition is by no means remote from ordinary usage:

> World...the earth and its inhabitants with their concerns; the sum of human affairs and interests..., a state of existence; a sphere or scene of life and action...; individual experience of, or concern with, life on earth; course of life; career; the sum of the affairs which affect the individual....[5]

Heidegger's use of the term "world" carries with it the sense not only of "life-world" but of "historical epoch" as well, with the suggestion that the life-world is an historical structure:

> World is the ever-nonobjective to which we are subject as long as the paths of birth and death, blessing and curse keep us transported into Being. Wherever those decisions of our history that relate to our very being are made, are taken up and abandoned by us, go unrecognized and are rediscovered by new inquiry, there the world worlds (44f.).

To say that a life-world is historical is to say that it occurs or happens (it "worlds"), that it comes and goes.[6] A world makes itself manifest in its philosophy, its science, its political institutions and its art, and a new world occurs when radical changes in these and in other domains are coordinated in a way Heidegger never makes clear. Once revealed, a world continues to "happen" in that the encompassing horizon referred to earlier persists, is taken up, altered, modified. Efforts may even be made by human beings to fix it forever. To be human is to be perpetually at work on the world, even while the world determines the kind and quality of our experience. Perhaps this can be made clearer if we imagine the historical life-world to be a metaphysical, moral, psychological, sociological and political environment which can be modified, even though it represents the framework within which we function.

Part of the essence of an artwork, then, is to disclose the "highest realities," to be a vehicle wherein a world occurs. "The artwork opens up in its own way the Being of beings" (39). Thus, the occurrence of a world, the disclosure of the Being of what-is, cannot be conceived as taking place prior to its manifestations in the forms already mentioned, among which are works of art. The building of the cathedral of Chartres, for example, was no mere consequence of the piety of the age, for it was in and through this act that the religious enthusiasm of the people came to be precisely the sort of enthusiasm it was. Their piety, one might say, consisted not merely in their feelings of devotion, but in their willingness to undertake deeds such as this as well. A people, as well as a person, *is* what it *does*. As a person's acts reveal the truth about that person, so does the artistic expression of a people reveal what is true of its world. Further, since the character of the life-world is neither accidental nor determined by impersonal historical forces, to be a human being and to live in a human community is to be at work on the conservation of certain aspects of the world and on the transformation of others. In the artwork, then, certain fundamental choices are made which determine, in part, the character of the world. "In the tragedy nothing is staged or displayed theatrically, but the battle of the new gods against the old is being fought" (43). The artist does not create the consciousness of an age *ex nihilo,* but neither did the builders of Chartres create the religious fervor which led to its construction.

Since in Heidegger's view the revelations or disclosures which occur in works of art have to do with the highest realities, it is worth noting that in this theory works of art are conceived somewhat on the analogy of religious revelations. But unlike the revealed truths of religion, which are said to be true irrespective of the period in which they are uttered, works of art as Heidegger conceives them are tied to their period in a very fundamental way. If part of the essence of the work of art is to reveal an historical life-world, when the world changes profoundly or — as Heidegger puts it — when a new world comes into being, it must follow that artworks too change radically. When we consider such works as the temple at Paestum or the Bamberg cathedral, we see that they are not the works they *were.* However excellent their state of preservation, their worlds have either withdrawn or perished. We encounter them as belonging to tradition, as works to be conserved. "Henceforth they remain merely such objects" (41).

Two features which belong to the essence of the artwork have now been uncovered: its participation in the self-concealment of the "mere thing," an aspect of the "earth," and its character as discloser of a "world." The precise relationship between "world" and "earth" in the work of art has now to be shown.

III. THE STRIFE OF "WORLD" AND "EARTH"

That manifestation of a world which occurs in the work always occurs in a medium. A work is produced out of some "work-material" such as stone, wood, color, tone, language, etc. Now the matter of a useful object is always determined by its use. Its matter, so to speak, is used up; it "disappears into usefulness" (46). As long as the tool functions, the matter of which it is made does not claim our attention as matter. But just the opposite is true of the work of art. The fundamental character of matter comes forward in the world disclosed by the work and claims our attention. When matter is revealed, it is revealed as it is in itself, i.e., undisclosed and unexplained, in its essential self-concealment. We are shown "the massiveness and heaviness of stone...the firmness and pliancy of wood...the hardness and luster of metal...the lighting and darkening of color...the clang of tone...and the naming power of the word" (46).

Of the two elements in the artwork, then, one — the "world" — is self-revealing and the other — the "earth" — self-concealing. Heidegger characterizes the relationship between the two as a permanent "strife," a "struggle," the "fighting of a battle," and it is this struggle which first makes possible the realization by each element of its own peculiar nature (49 *et passim*). The following considerations may make this clearer.

No artistic conception can be realized except in a medium. In the course of the creative process, artists use the medium in order to realize their artistic conceptions. The sculptor, for example, uses marble to portray folds of cloth. But the medium, in its stubborn self-refusal, will not be subservient to the openness revealed in the work, i.e., it refuses to "disappear into usefulness," and it is because of this very refusal that its own ineradicable character ("the massiveness and heaviness of stone") can first be disclosed at all. Thus, in the "Winged Victory" the attempt to portray folds of cloth has succeeded in making visible not the nature of cloth but the special properties and intrinsic perceptual qualities of marble.

Artistic form *(Gestalt)* is the establishment, the fixing in a medium, of the basic strife between the self-closing medium and the disclosure which the medium bears and supports. All works of art may partake of a single essence for Heidegger, but what distinguishes one work from another is the particular framing or ordering of its material, i.e., its form. The earth, though self-concealing, is not monotonous, for its concealment is neither unvaried nor inflexible. It can take an "inexhaustible variety of simple modes and shapes" and it is part of the function of the artist to exploit these possibilities (47). Artistic excellence, then, will depend not only on the truthfulness, the penetration, the sublimity or profoundity of the artistic disclosure but on the extent to which the materials in the work are liberated so that they can be themselves *for the first time* and not used up or misused (64).

If a critic were to describe the material and the expressive aspects of an artwork as "locked in combat" or engaged in "struggle," we would ordinarily take this to mean that its elements were incompletely or unsuccessfully integrated, that it had failed to achieve unity. But for Heidegger "the unity of the work comes about in the fighting of the battle"; the unity of the work of art is precisely the intimacy of strife (49f.). Clearly, the metaphor of struggle is not meant to suggest disorder or lack of harmony. But just what does it mean? What happens in this struggle is that "the opponents raise each other into the self-assertion of their natures" (49), i.e., neither world nor earth can "assert its nature," which is to say *be* what it is, without the other. "In the struggle, each opponent carries the other beyond itself. Thus the strife becomes ever more intense as strife, and more authentically what it is" (49).

The relationship between world and earth is not dialectical, it should be noted, because neither element arises out of the other nor are the two drawn into some higher synthesis. Each element can be seen for what it is precisely in its commerce with the other. In its attempt to assert itself each element must use the other as instrument; in order to be at all, each element is intimately set against another which embodies a principle to which it is diametically opposed. This is the meaning of "struggle." Thus the world, the principle of disclosure, can only *be* in so far as it is borne by the medium, the self-concealing earth; but the whole notion of a self-concealing element, in turn, would make no sense were there no world, no disclosure, within which a concealment might take place and be recognized as such. Despite the obscurity and apparent difficulty of these passages, it is difficult to avoid the suspicion that Heidegger is saying no more than that for anything to be a work of art its expressive aspect must be embedded in a material medium and—recent experiments notwithstanding—its materials must serve some artistic conception. Here that pervasive obscurity which is so prominent a feature of Heidegger's style ("the opponents raise each other into the self-assertion of their natures") tends to disguise the vacuousness of what is expressed. Moreover, it seems to me that the metaphor of struggle is wholly dispensable and that metaphors of cooperation and accommodation would have served as well. Here again Heidegger's rhetoric is hiding something, this time the absence in the essay of any but the most sketchy account of the relationship between materials and expression.[7]

IV. ART AND TRUTH

These criticisms, however, are somewhat premature, for Heidegger's conception of the artwork has not yet fully emerged. It should be clear from the preceding discussion that Heidegger is a cognitivist of a very emphatic variety. For him an artwork is in essence a disclosure of truth concerning the Being of what-is, a revelation of "world" and "earth," those highest realities, in their interplay. What is peculiar to art and what constitutes it as art is the precise manner in which it discloses the "truth of Being" in contrast to other ways in which an ultimate disclosure may occur. But before pursuing this point further, it will be helpful to consider briefly what Heidegger has to say about the "happening" of truth in general.

The fundamental meaning of truth, or what Heidegger calls "the essence of truth," has been obscured, we are told, but we can best begin to recover it by recalling the Greek term for truth—*aletheia*—which means, literally, "unveiledness" or disclosure, i.e., the unconcealment of that-which-is. When an unconcealment of that-which-is happens, a "world" or disclosure of Being can be said to have occurred. This conception of the nature of truth is not in competition with other theories of truth, although Heidegger often writes as if it were. What Heidegger is after is what makes any conception of truth, indeed any conception at all, first possible, i.e., the widest and most comprehensive framework which is presupposed by philosophical questioning. The conception of truth as, for example, *adaequatio intellectus ad rem* is insufficiently fundamental, not mistaken; it is only possible for intellect to direct itself correctly towards things if that towards which it orders itself is *already* somehow unconcealed, if a whole domain of entities of different types, values, modes of existence and relations has already been disclosed.

> With all our correct representations we would get nowhere, we could not even presuppose that there already is manifest something to which we can conform ourselves, unless the unconcealedness of beings had already exposed us to, placed us in that lighted realm in which every being stands for us and from which it withdraws (52).

Aletheia is the unveiling of that "lighted realm" and it is because of this primordial disclosure that we are first granted access to entities other than ourselves as well as to the entity we ourselves are.

But within the realm of the unconcealed, concealment also prevails. Error and dissimulation are given along with the primordial disclosure so that the occurrence of truth is at the same time an occurrence of untruth: "The nature of truth, that is, of unconcealedness, is dominated throughout by a denial" (54). Concealment is twofold: it occurs as a "refusal" and as a "dissembling." A dissembling occurs when that which is presents itself as other than it is, when one entity counterfeits another, hides or obscures another. Entities are not disclosed first in order to dissemble or be dissembled later: often they are first disclosed as hidden or hiding, as other than they later turn out to be. Appearance and reality, so to speak, are given together: the ambiguous, dissembling character of the disclosure of Being is the condition of human error and illusion.

Of the obscure notion of concealment as "refusal" we are told only this:

> Beings refuse themselves to us down to that one and seemingly least feature which we touch upon most readily when we can say no more of beings than that they are. Concealment as refusal is not simply and only the limit of knowledge in any given circumstance, but the beginning of the clearing of what is lighted (53f.).

Since it is impossible to make sense of the notion of "refusal" on the basis of this passage alone and since the idea of concealing denial, of which "refusal" is an important aspect, is crucial to his philosophy of art, one wonders why Heidegger has failed to develop this theme in the essay and why we are forced to look elsewhere for a clue to its meaning. In another essay from the same collection *(Holzwege)* there is a sentence which Heidegger makes very important by repeating it three times like a *leitmotif:* "Being withdraws as it reveals itself in what-is."[8] This may shed some light on the reason why, in the passage cited above, concealment as refusal is called the "beginning" of the lighting of what is illuminated. The condition of any lighting, so it seems, is the concealing refusal, the withdrawal of Being. To say that Being withdraws in disclosing a world is to deny that Being can be exhausted in its epochs, in what it sends. But this is not to say that Being, the world-ground, is unknowable, a *noumenon,* whose relation to what-there-is would be forever unintelligible. To say that Being "withdraws," that it is not exhausted in its epochs, is, I think, another way of saying that each world-disclosure is *finite,* that *something* remains after the shining forth of a "lighted realm," even though this "something" is nothing other than the possibility that a disclosure other than the disclosure which occurred might have occurred or might yet occur. Since world-disclosures depend upon the choices of an "historical people" and upon those Promethean figures (like artists) who confront the people with its destiny-laden options, to say that the condition of any world-unveiling is that it be finite (that concealing refusal is the beginning of any lighting) is simply to say that whatever is chosen in any act of choosing involves an *exclusion,* a cancelling out of what was not chosen. We can best understand what is meant by the finitude of a world-disclosure when we regard past epochs from the perspective of what succeeded them and when we contemplate how the exercise of certain options in the domain of metaphysics, morals, the arts, politics, etc., determined not only the character of these domains but the range of what could be conceived as alternatives to them as well.

We have now won the vantage-point from which Heidegger's conception of the artwork can be surveyed in its entirety. Truth, as a disclosure of Being, can occur in a number of ways: in the deed that grounds a state; in the fundamental questioning of the thinker; in the ways in which holiness manifests itself; in what Heidegger calls, without explanation, "essential sacrifice" (62); and, as we have seen, in the work of art. The struggle of world and earth, of expression and materials, in the artwork is one way in which the revealing but simultaneously concealing world-event may occur. "World" is the revealing "moment" in the work, while "earth" corresponds to whatever, in the disclosure of world, remains concealed, i.e., the self-closing, twofold-concealing condition of disclosure itself. "Earth juts through the world and world grounds itself on the earth only so far as truth happens as the primal conflict between clearing and concealing" (55). The world disclosed in the work is one way in which there occurs a "clearing of the paths of the essential guiding directions with which all decision complies" (55). World must fight a battle with earth in the work in order to secure the "lighted realm" which it reveals, just as "every decision ... bases itself on something not mastered, something concealed, confusing ..." (55). As the essay progresses the terms "world" and "earth" are expanded so that they no longer refer to aspects of the artwork alone, but to the revealing and concealing moments of any world-disclosure at all.

V. Critical Perspectives: The "Earth"

Heidegger's philosophy of art is cast in a traditional mold. On two counts at least it is strongly reminiscent of the philosophies of art of the great systematic thinkers of the nineteenth century and of the first quarter of this century: first, it is animated by the search for the "essence" of art, a search which is now regarded by many aestheticians as quixotic;[9] second, it springs from and is an extension of a very ambitious ontology. While it is impossible to examine this ontology here, enough of it has been revealed in the foregoing discussion, it is hoped, to sustain the charge that Heidegger's conception of the artwork is not consistent with his larger ontological views.[10]

There is, specifically, an evident lack of symmetry between the notion of the earth as the unpurposed bearer and self-closer, i.e., the thingly aspect of the work, and the twofold concealment (refusal and dissembling) which is part of any disclosure of Being. The struggle of world and earth in the artwork is one way in which the revealing-concealing occurrence of Being takes place. However, if the concealing moment in any disclosure of Being is the finitude of such a disclosure, a finitude which according to *Being and Time* is rooted in the finite character of *Dasein*, the human existent through whom and to whom a disclosure is made, then clearly the finitude of any disclosure is an *historical* aspect of that disclosure. By "historical" is meant this: even though *something* may be "refused" or "dissembled" in every disclosure, the undisclosed possibilities in one era may become part of the content of what is disclosed in the next. Indeed, Heidegger's whole reading of the history of Western metaphysics is a working out of this notion.

But is the "earth," the unpurposed bearer and self-closer which "shatters every attempt to penetrate into it," an *historically* held-back aspect of world-disclosure? Everything we are told early in the essay about the nature of the things of the earth indicates that it is not. There, what Heidegger says not only about mere things but about our "primary encounters" in general suggests that the self-concealing character of what we confront in a primary encounter is permanent and absolute. The earth ("the massiveness and heaviness of stone . . . , the firmness and pliancy of wood . . . , the hardness and luster of metal") is shown in the first part of the essay to be a stubborn and *ineradicable* element in all experience. But by the end of the essay the notion of "earth" has been transformed into an equally ineradicable but entirely *historical* structure.

Is the "thingliness of the thing," which we apprehend in the material medium of the artwork and which Heidegger identifies initially as an aspect of the "earth," meant, perhaps, merely to symbolize what is "earth" in the proper sense, namely the twofold concealment in the disclosure of Being? Indeed once, near the very beginning of the essay, Heidegger refers to the artwork as a symbol, although in the elaborate and lengthy development which follows he makes no mention of this again. The entire passage is worth quoting:

> . . .the artwork is something else over and above the thingly element. This something else in the work constitutes its artistic nature. The artwork is, to be sure, a thing that is made, but it says something other than the mere thing itself is, *allo agoreuei*. The work makes public something other than itself; it manifests something other; it is an allegory. In the work of art something other is bought together with the thing that is made. To bring together is, in Greek, *sumballein*. The work is a symbol (19f.).

Just prior to this passage Heidegger has referred to the fact that "there is something stony in a work of architecture" and "wooden in carving," i.e. that artworks partake of the thingly character of the sorts of manufactured items which in fact they are. But, we are told here, in addition to being examples of handicraft, artworks have an "artistic nature" whereby something is made public other than the fact that there exists here and now this certain manufactured item. What is made public in the work, we learn later, is the world which it discloses. Thus the work is a "symbol" in that it brings together *(sumballein)* the thingly character of handicraft with the revelatory character which is peculiar to art. Except in this limited etymological sense I can find no indication in the essay that Heidegger holds what might be called a "symbolic" theory of art. If the material medium were meant merely to symbolize "earth," and since "world" and "earth" can be distinguished for purposes of analysis only but do not exist as independent elements in the work, then it would follow that the struggle of "world" and "earth" would have to be symbolic too. But what could such a strife symbolize? A disclosure of Being, perhaps, conceived to occur elsewhere, i.e. somewhere apart from the work? Here Heidegger's meaning is unmistakable. The work does not symbolize some aspect of a world which is already fixed and finished. To create a work of art is to be at work on the world; creating works — and "preserving" them, which is a function of the audience — is one important way in which a world "occurs." In this sense the artwork does not disclose Being mediately and indirectly, by virtue of its correspondence to another disclosure, but immediately and directly. This is its *essence*. Indeed towards the end of the essay Heidegger suggests that since poets are instrumental in forging the very language of an "historical people," that comprehension of Being articulated in poetry first makes possible other sorts of disclosures (72).

Heidegger has fitted his account of the nature of the art object to his notion of the revealing-concealing Being-event as Procrustes fitted luckless travellers to his bed. It is not difficult to see how this came about. Since the "twofold concealment" makes possible any disclosure of truth, it too must have a concealing element, which will make its disclosure first possible by setting its limits. The "thingly" aspect, the material medium of the artwork, seems to perform this function. Not only is there no work without a medium, but the character of the medium determines and sets limits to the kind of content or expression which is possible in a work. Further, the relationship between materials and content in an artwork can be described as a kind of tension or "struggle" (although as I pointed out earlier, it need not be so described) just as truth for Heidegger, in his larger account of the Being-event, is conceived to be a combat between disclosure and concealment.

The necessity for finding an absolute congruence between artistic disclosure and the "happening of truth" has two unhappy results. Not only does it lead to inconsistency in the development of the theme of the "earth" but it also encourages Heidegger to make quasi-mystical and misleading statements about the nature of the medium in art. The medium, we recall, partakes of the "self-refusal of the mere thing," i.e., it has the character of something self-closing or self-concealing. But what can this mean when applied to clay, to language or to tone? In what way does the discovery of its "self-refusal" enlarge our understanding of the nature or the role of the medium in the total work?

Earlier I tried to make the notion of a self-concealing medium somewhat less opaque by associating it with the disparity between certain sorts of scientific accounts of things and things as they ordinarily appear, a disparity which philosophers have tried to account for in a number of ways. But whether there is or is not such a disparity is not relevant here, and it is difficult to see how our comprehension of art or the medium of art hangs on its solution. Heidegger has transformed this disparity, the fact — if it is a fact — that things "withhold themselves," into a mysterious property of things. What lies behind this transformation is the demand implicit in Heidegger's "architectonic" that the "twofold concealment" be exemplified in the artwork itself. We are hard put to discover what *more* "self-concealment" might be than just the fullness and richness of the appearance of things in our ordinary commerce with them, a fullness, to be sure, which is retained, explored and made vivid in the artwork and "lost" in physical explanation. Thus while Heidegger seems to have much insight into the ontological character of the medium, in fact he says nothing about it which is not commonplace.

VI. Critical Perspectives: The "World"

It should be clear from the preceding discussion that Heidegger's treatment of the theme of the "earth" is unsatisfactory. But the notion of the artwork as a disclosure of the "world" is far more fruitful and it is here that we encounter what is most valuable and illuminating in the essay.

Although they reveal the world, works of art for Heidegger neither express propositions about it nor, by possessing some feature which resembles a similar feature in experience, do they set up a correspondence to it.[11] In spite of this there is a sense in which the artist holds the mirror up to nature, to human nature and to human experience: "Genuinely poetic projection is the opening up or disclosure of that into which human being as historical is already cast" (75). The act of artistic disclosure, whereby the artist chooses a new perspective or creates a unique vantage-point from which the nature of our situation can be grasped is one way of finding out the truth about "that into which human being . . .is already cast." There is, in effect, no situation, no world as the *human* world at all, unless it is grasped *as* the world, and this is possible only from some perspective from which the whole has significance. The introduction of novel elements, i.e. the creative activity of artists themselves, determines (together with other factors) the truth about the situation which they disclose, and it is precisely *in* this creative activity that the artist is "at work" on the world. It is in this way that art can be at once genuine innovation and faithful record. To do what the artist does, to take up a position in regard to what-there-is, is just to disclose the character of the world into which human existence is thrown: the artist's discovery of meaning is at the same time a founding of meaning.

In some artworks, "the battle of the new gods against the old is being fought" (43). In the Greek theater, for example, there is no mere repetition of metaphysical, moral and theological truths arrived at elsewhere. What happens instead is that these truths are reaffirmed by the audience in a complex of acts and experiences. In apprehending the central truths of the drama the audience is also overwhelmed by their force, and it chooses to consecrate itself again to that manner of existence which a recognition of these truths implies. Without this reaffirmation these truths would not continue to be the truths they are, for they are part of the total framework—the life-world—within which Greek experience as such is possible. Thus the drama both reveals the world of the Greeks and is itself a significant factor in the genesis and perpetuation of that world.

Heidegger's "model" for truth in art is not scientific truth but what might be called "existential truth," the truth about one's own existence as it emerges in the attempt to grasp the significance of that existence. This "move" allows Heidegger to bypass some of the traditional problems which beset cognitive theories of art and to clear the way for a more refined and subtle comprehension of the way in which art discloses the truth about life. "Existential" knowledge of the self is not fragmentary; it involves more than the recovery of facts about one's past or the determination of the real nature of one's motives in some specific situation. To grasp the significance of my existence as a whole, and the meaning of the experiences I have had, I must discover who I am and what I truly value. But in order to uncover the truth about myself in this sense I must choose a perspective from which to regard myself; I must *take a stand* in regard to who I am and what I want, and what I take to be true about my history and situation will depend in large measure upon the nature of this stand. The stand I take in regard to my identity and my values which makes it possible for me to regard myself in a new light is analogous to artistic creation which discloses Being. Here, in the case of existential knowledge as in the case of art, the disclosure of the meaning of a situation and the bestowal of significance upon it are seen to be aspects of the same act.

Heidegger's account of the nature of truth in art makes less mysterious that sense of awe which often overtakes us in the presence of truly great art. The phenomenon of awe, often slighted or even ignored in traditional accounts of the nature of the aesthetic response, is not ordinarily called forth by expressions of emotion, by pleasing forms or by occasions which afford us satisfaction in the exercise of our own faculties. Indeed, most traditional accounts of the artwork fail to explain why art evokes in us a sense of awe at all. But awe is an emotion appropriate to the unveiling of mysteries, to the revelation of the "highest realities," and if a frequent ingredient in our response to art is in fact an awed recognition that truths of a very high order have been disclosed, then certain aspects of our conduct in regard to art, which were hitherto regarded as merely fortuitous, are now seen to bear an intimate relation to the works themselves. Two such types of conduct are the ritual and ceremonial behavior which often surrounds the display or performance of artworks and the elevation of artists to the status of heroes or demigods. The lives of artists are the stuff of legends and their persons, real or symbolic, often the object of cults: one has only to think of the cult of Byron in the last century and the cults of

Lawrence and Hemingway in our own. This exaltation of the artist is not confined to the Romantic period, although in modern times it is most closely associated with the Romantic Movement. In ancient times Homer was revered as a seer, and the idea that the artist is in touch with divine powers which allow him to apprehend the highest realities is found in the *Ion* and the *Phaedrus*. If the artwork does indeed disclose the nature of Being, then the impulse to revere the artist, which springs from a sense of awe before the profundity of his disclosures, is a wholly natural and appropriate response even though it may take forms which are vulgar or grotesque. Heidegger has, in effect, provided us with an account of the artwork which grants legitimacy to the conception of the artist as seer or prophet.

While artworks may make the sorts of disclosures Heidegger claims they make and provoke in us types of responses appropriate to such disclosures, does it follow that this capacity to disclose the "highest realities" is *essential* to art, that it defines it *as* art? In order to answer this question let us return briefly to that passage in the essay in which the concept of art as disclosure of Being first emerges. Heidegger discovers that art reveals the world by discovering first the nature of peasant shoes and then the nature of the world of the peasant in Van Gogh's painting. The scrutiny of the painting is guided by an end, the desire to discover what is revealed about the inner nature of the subject. That this painting or any painting can disclose the "real" nature of any object is assumed beforehand, not demonstrated or found out by examination. Nevertheless Heidegger pretends that he has discovered the essence of Van Gogh's painting (and thereby of all paintings) by an application of the phenomenological method: he looks closely at the painting and describes what he sees; he tries to "let the painting speak." The sustained attack in the essay on inappropriate conceptual schemes which distort our vision of things as they are, combined with this attentive turning to the painting itself, gives the impression that the essence of the artwork can just be "seen" by the receptive viewer. But this is a false impression. The purely formal aspects of the work, its arrangement of spaces or pattern of lines, can be "seen" in it too, and there is no reason to regard these aspects of the work as less essential to it than others. Whether I see the work as "significant form" or as the disclosure of the peasant's world depends in part on decisions arrived at prior to looking about what paintings are. What I take the painting to be, in turn, depends on the character of my world and how I am situated within it. While it may be true that artworks disclose the nature of the world, it is also true that the nature of our world determines not only our response to specific works of art but our larger conception of the nature of art as well.[12]

But is it true that every art, including music and non-objective painting, has a world-revealing function? It is not clear how music might reveal a world—not, at least, without the introduction of *ad hoc* hypotheses in the style of Spengler about the relationship between the forms of musical expression and general modes of cultural expression. Certainly the music of an age reveals something about the age, but how central to the work itself is this revelation? How constitutive of its essence? There is a trivial sense in which every product of human art or craft reveals something about its maker or about the age in which it is made. Bad popular art is often said to reveal more about its age than great art. What sorts of disclosures are integral to the work itself and what sorts are not? *Hamlet* makes profound revelations about human character and human destiny, but it also reveals a great deal about the conventions of the Elizabethan theater and current concepts of revenge. And what of a religious believer who is seized and made witness to what for him is the highest reality — the passion of Christ — by a very bad painting of the Crucifixion? What of another believer with better taste who is brought face to face with the constitutive realities of his world by Grünewald's Isenheimer Altar? Is he better situated than the atheist art critic to apprehend the purely aesthetic values of the painting? These are some of the difficulties to which Heidegger's philosophy of art gives rise. Questions such as these reveal more than that Heidegger has failed to uncover the essence of art; what they indicate, I think, is that however illuminating and fruitful Heidegger's analysis of the world-revealing function of art may be, his aesthetic theory as a whole is very much in need of further elaboration.

Notes

Sandra Lee Bartky is Associate Professor of Philosophy at the University of Illinois at Chicago Circle. Her studies of Heidegger's later philosophy have appeared in *Inquiry* and *Philosophy and Phenomenological Research*. She is currently working in the areas of phenomenological Marxism and philosophy of feminism. An earlier version of this paper appeared in *The British Journal of Aesthetics*.

1. See Martin Heidegger, *Erläuterungen zu Hölderlins Dichtung*, 2nd ed. (Frankfurt/M. 1951). English translations of two essays from this collection, *"Heimkunft/An die Verwandten,"* and *"Hölderlin und das Wesen der Dichtung"* appear in the volume *Existence and Being*, with an introduction by Werner Brock (Chicago, 1949). *"Wozu Dichter?"* from *Holzwege* (Frankfurt/M. 1950) and *". . .dichterisch wohnet der Mensch"* from *Vorträge und Aufsätze* appear in translation in Heidegger, *Poetry, Language, Thought*, translations and introduction by Albert Hofstadter (New York, 1971). *"Die Sprache im Gedicht"* from *Unterwegs zur Sprache* (Pfullingen, 1959) appears in English in Heidegger, *On the Way to Language*, trans. by Peter Hertz (New York, 1971). See also *Hebel der Hausfreund* (Pfullingen, 1957) and *"Hölderlins Erde und Himmel"* in *Hölderlin-Jahrbuch*, II (1958-60).
2. In *Poetry, Language, Thought*. Hereafter, all page references to the essay in this volume will be included in the body of the paper.
3. Heidegger's first objection to this interpretation is clearly premature: the thing, one might reply, bears special characteristics which distinguish it from other entities or else it is a special kind of substance.

4. The painting is Van Gogh's "Les Souliers," Stedelijk Museum, Amsterdam.

5. *Webster's New International Dictionary* (Springfield, 1930), p. 2350.

6. There are precedents for this too in ordinary discourse, e.g., "the world of the middle ages vanished overnight."

7. For a fine account of the integration of four elements in the artwork—materials, form, expression and function—and a description of the way in which each in its interaction with the others makes possible what Heidegger would call the "self-assertion of the natures" of all, see D. W. Gotshalk, *Art and the Social Order* (Chicago, 1947), Chaps. IV–VII.

8. *Holzwege*, p. 310. The sentence is from the essay *"Der Spruch des Anaximander."* An English translation of this essay appears in Heidegger, *Early Greek Thinking*, trans. David Farrell Krell and Frank Capuzzi (New York, 1975).

9. See in particular William E. Kennick, "Does Traditional Aesthetics Rest on a Mistake?" in *Contemporary Studies in Aesthetics*, ed. Francis J. Coleman (New York, 1968); see also, in the same volume, Paul Ziff, "The Task of Defining a Work of Art."

10. For a critical examination of some dominant themes in Heidegger's later philosophy, see my articles *"Seinsverlassenheit* in the Later Philosophy of Heidegger," *Inquiry*, X (1967); "Originative Thinking in the Later Philosophy of Heidegger," *Philosophy and Phenomenological Research*, Vol. XXX, no. 3, March, 1970; and "Heidegger and the Modes of World Disclosure," in *Philosophy and Phenomenological Research*, Vol. XL, no. 2, Dec., 1979.

11. This version of cognitivism is developed by John Hospers, in *Meaning and Truth in the Arts* (University of North Carolina Press, 1946).

12. It might be objected that this view is entirely in line with Heidegger's notion of the "circle of understanding" as it is developed in the analysis of *Dasein*. However, in "The Origin of the Work of Art" Heidegger avoids discussion of the way in which an artist's world influences his conception of art because he wishes to show how the Being-event occurs through the medium of art. A world must "happen" somehow and the elaboration of the various modes of its happening is a central theme in Heidegger's later philosophy. But the "circularity" in the circle poses questions which are not answered in the essay. What, for example, is the status of Heidegger's own conception of art? And how, if artistic disclosure depends upon the world and the world on artistic disclosure, can anything genuinely new break the circle? See *Sein und Zeit*, 7th ed. (Tübingen, 1953), sections 2, 31 and 32. English translation, *Being and Time*, trans. Macquarrie and Robinson (New York, 1962).

VI. BIBLIOGRAPHIES

Heidegger: Translations in English, 1949-1977

H. Miles Groth

Represented in the following bibilography are substantial texts by Heidegger which have been translated into English. The entries are arranged alphabetically by German title. Following the entry title the most recent source of the item in a German publication is given. On the second line of each entry the most recent (or preferred) translation in English is given, followed by its current and most accessible source citation. Occasionally a double reference is given. In all cases, immediately following the entry title the date of the first translation is given in parentheses, though it may not be the date of the translation and its source as represented in the entry. Following the first translation date, the translator's name appears. English titles preceded by an asterisk are bilingual editions.

Omitted from this bibliography are some brief excerpts of communications from Heidegger, letters, conversations, interviews and other fragments of Heidegger's recorded utterances, and a protocol prepared by students of Heidegger in a seminar in which Heidegger participated.

The criteria for selection have been (1) that the published words constitute a substantial text and are not so fragmentary that they are of only incidental or anecdotal interest to the Heidegger scholar, and (2) that the text appeared in a German publication under Heidegger's authorship. The single exception to the latter is the newspaper article "Schöpferische Landschaft: Warum bleiben wir in der Provinz?" which appears in Guido Schneeberger's *Nachlese zu Heidegger* (1962). For a full account of the publication history of Heidegger's works which have been translated into English, along with some materials about the composition and occasion of the texts' preparation, see this bibliographer's *Study and Research Bibliography of Heidegger Translations in English* (unpublished). In that bibliography, arranged by English translation title, both the substantial texts and the fragments are accounted for, amounting to 86 entries for the years 1949–1977.

For the sake of completeness, ten additional translations of brief or "third person" accounts or occasional pieces drawn from letters and conversations with Heidegger, and the protocol mentioned above, are presented directly below. Many of the fragments are highly interesting and add to our understanding of the published translations.

1. Written replies (1970) to questions posed by J. Glenn Gray and Joan Stambaugh, in the latter's "Introduction" to *The End of Philosophy* (1973) (Tr. Joan Stambaugh) New York: Harper and Row, xi-xiv.

2. Zygmunt Adamczewski's "On the Way to Being. Reflecting on Conversations (1968) with Martin Heidegger" (Tr. Zygmunt Adamczewski), in *Heidegger and the Path of Thinking* (1970) (Sallis, J., ed.) Pittsburgh: Duquesne University Press, 12–36.

3. Excerpt of a letter to Manfred S. Frings of 6 August 1964, in the editor's note to Max Scheler's "Reality and Resistance: on *Being and Time,* Section 43" (Tr. Thomas Sheehan), in *Listening* 12 (3), 1977, 61, and here, above.

4. Excerpts from letters (1921–29) to Karl Löwith in the latter's "The Nature of Man and the World of Nature. For Heidegger's 80th Birthday" (Tr. R. Philip O'Hara), in *Martin Heidegger: In Europe and America* (1973) (Ballard, E. G. *et al.,* eds.) The Hague: Martinus Nijhoff, 37–46. The article appeared first in 1970 in *The Southern Journal of Philosophy* 8 (4).

5. Excerpt of a letter to J. Glenn Gray of 10 October 1972, in William Lovitt's "Introduction" to *The Question Concerning Technology and Other Essays* (1977) New York: Harper and Row, xxxv, n. 2, the excerpt translated by Lovitt.

6. Hermann Noack's record of "Conversation (1953) with Martin Heidegger," in *The Piety of Thinking* (1976) (Tr. James Hart and John Maraldo) Bloomington: Indiana University Press, 59–76.

7. Fragments from *Heraklit* (1970), in a review article by David Farrell Krell, "The Heraclitus Seminar (1966–67)," in *Research in Phenomenology* 1, 1971, 137–146.

8. Richard Wisser's "Martin Heidegger: An Interview (1969)" (Tr. Vincent Guardliano and Robert Pambrun), in *Listening* 6, 1971, 34–40.

9. Excerpts from speeches and newspaper articles (1933–34), in *German Existentialism* (1965) (Tr. and ed. Dagobert Runes) New York: Wisdom Library.

10. Otto F. Bollnow and J. Ritter's account of "A Discussion (1929) Between Ernst Cassirer and Martin Heidegger" (Tr. Francis Slade), in *The Existentialist Tradition: Selected Writings* (Languilli, D., ed. (1971) Garden City: Doubleday, 192–203. An earlier translation of the protocol appeared in *Philosophy and Phenomenological Research* 25, 1964–65, 208–222, translated by Carl Hamburg.

Note

Professor H. Miles Groth teaches at St. Vincent College, Latrobe, Pennsylvania. His article, "Messkirch: Martin Heidegger: June, 1976" appeared in *Philosophy Today,* 20 (1976), 259ff. and was reprinted in *Anglican Theological Review,* 59 (1977), 43 ff. More recent articles are his "On the Fundamental Experience of Voice in Language," *Philosophy Today* (1980), and "The Riddle of the Laughing Shepherd: On Nietzsche's *Zarathustra* III," *American Imago* (1980).

Bibliography:
Heidegger Translations in English

"Abendgang auf der Reichenau" (1917) *Das Bodenseebuch* (Konstanz) 4, 1917, 152.

*"Eventide on Reichenau" (1963) (Tr. William J. Richardson). In William J. Richardson, *Heidegger: Through Phenomenology to Thought* (1963, 2nd edition, 1967, The Hague: Martinus Nihoff), 1.

"Alētheia (Heraklit, Fragment B 16)" (1954). In *Vorträge und Aufsätze* III (3. Aufl., 1967, Pfullingen: Neske), 53–78.

"Alētheia (Heraclitus, Fragment B 16)" (1975) (Tr. Frank Capuzzi). In *Early Greek Thinking* (1975, New York: Harper and Row), 102–123.

"Anmerkungen über die Metaphysik" (1954). In *Vorträge und Aufsätze* I ("Überwindung der Metaphysik," I–XXV, XXVII–XXVIII) (3. Aufl., 1967, Pfullingen: Neske), 63–83, 89–91.

"Overcoming Metaphysics" (1973) (Tr. Joan Stambaugh). In *The End of Philosophy* (1973, New York: Harper and Row), 84–103, 109–110.

"Ansprache zum Heimatabend" (1962). In *700 Jahre Stadt Messkirch* (1962, Freiburg: K. Aker), 7–16.

*"Messkirch's Seventh Centennial" (1971) (Rev. tr. Thomas Sheehan) *Listening* 8, 1973, 40–54.

"Antrittsrede" (1959) *Jahresheft der Heidelberger Akademie der Wissenschaften* (Heidelberg) 48, 1959, 20–21.

"Martin Heidegger: A Recollection" (1970) (Tr. Hans Seigfried). *Man and World* 3, 1970, 3–4, and in this volume, above.

Aus der Erfahrung des Denkens (1954, Pfullingen: Neske), (2. Aufl., 1965).

"The Thinker as Poet" (1971) (Tr. Albert Hofstadter). In *Poetry, Language, Thought* (1971, New York: Harper and Row), 3–14.

"Aus der letzten Marburger Vorlesung" (1964). In *Wegmarken* (*Gesamtausgabe* 9, 1976, Frankfurt: Klostermann), 79–101.
"From the Last Marburg Lecture Course" (1971) (Tr. John Macquarrie). In *The Future of Our Religious Past: Essays in Honor of Rudolf Bultmann* (Robinson, E., ed.) (1971, New York: Harper and Row), 317–332.

"Aus einem Gespräch von der Sprache. Zwischen einem Japanen und einem Fragenden" (1959). In *Unterwegs zur Sprache* (4. Aufl., 1971, Pfullingen: Neske), 83–155.
"A Dialogue on Language" (1971) (Tr. Peter D. Hertz). In *On the Way to Language* (1971, New York: Harper and Row), 1–54.

"Bauen Wohnen Denken" (1954). In *Vorträge und Aufsätze* II (3. Aufl., 1967, Pfullingen: Neske), 19–36.
"Building Dwelling Thinking" (1971) (Tr. Albert Hofstadter). In *Basic Writings* (1977, New York: Harper and Row), 323–339.

"Brief an Edmund Husserl vom 22 Oktober 1927" (1962). In Edmund Husserl, *Phänomenologische Psychologie* (*Husserliana* 9) (1962, Den Haag: Martinus Nijhoff), 600–601.
"The Idea of Phenomenology, With a Letter to Edmund Husserl" (1977) (Tr. Thomas Sheehan). *Listening* 12 (3), 1977, 118–119.

"Brief an Arthur Schrynemakers. Freiburg im Breisgau den 20 September 1966" (1970). In *Heidegger and the Path of Thinking* (Sallis, J., ed.) (1970, Pittsburgh: Duquesne University Press), 9–10.
*"A Letter from Martin Heidegger" (1970) (Tr. Arthur H. Schrynemakers). *Ibid.*, 10–11.

"Brief an Albert Borgmann (1969, Freiburg)" (unpublished in German).
"Letter from Martin Heidegger" (1970) (Tr. Albert Borgmann). *Philosophy East and West* 20, 1970, 221.

"Brief vom 20 October 1966 an Manfred S. Frings" (1968). In *Heidegger and the Quest for the Truth* (Frings, M. S., ed.) (1968, Chicago: Quadrangle), 19–21.
*"A Letter from Heidegger" (1968) (Tr. William J. Richardson). *Ibid.*, 17–19.

"Brief über den Humanismus" (1947). In *Wegmarken* (*Gesamtausgabe* 9, 1976, Frankfurt: Klostermann), 313–364.
"Letter on Humanism" (1962). In *Basic Writings* (1977) (Tr. Frank A. Capuzzi and J. Glenn Gray) (New York: Harper and Row), 193–242.

"Curriculum Vitae" (1914). In *Die Lehre vom Urtreil im Psychologismus* (1914, Leipzig: Barth), 111.
"Curriculum Vitae" (1965) (Tr. Therese Schrynemakers). *Listening* 12 (3), 1977, 110.

"...dichterisch wohnt der Mensch..." (1954). In *Vorträge und Aufsätze* II (3. Aufl., 1967, Pfullingen: Neske), 61–78.
"...Poetically Man Dwells..." (1971) (Tr. Albert Hofstadter). In *Poetry, Language, Thought* (1971, New York: Harper and Row), 213–229.

"Das Ding" (1951). In *Vorträge und Aufsätze* II (3. Aufl., 1967, Frankfurt: Klostermann), 37–59.
"The Thing" (1971) (Tr. Albert Hofstadter). In *Poetry, Language, Thought* (1971, New York: Harper and Row), 165–186.

Einführung in die Metaphysik (1953). (Tübingen: Nicmeyer, 3. Aufl., 1966).
An Introduction to Metaphysics (1959) (Tr. Ralph Manheim). (1961, Garden City: Doubleday).

"Einige Hinweise auf Hauptgeschichtspunkte für das theologische Gespräch über 'Das Problem eines nichtobjektivierenden Denkens und Sprechens in der heutigen Theologie'" (1969). In *Phänomenologie und Theologie* (1970, Frankfurt: Klostermann), 37–46.
"The Problem of a Non-objectifying Thinking and Speaking in Contemporary Theology" (1968). In *The Piety of Thinking* (Tr. James Hart and John Maraldo). (1976, Bloomington: Indiana University Press), 22–31.

"Einleitung zu 'Was ist Metaphysik?'" ("Der Rückgang in der Grund der Metaphysik") (1949). In *Wegmarken* (*Gesamtausgabe* 9, 1976, Frankfurt: Klostermann), 365–383.
"The Way Back into the Ground of Metaphysics" (1957) (Tr. Walter Kaufmann). In *Existentialism from Dostoevsky to Sartre* (Kaufmann, W., ed.) (2nd ed., 1975, New York: New American Library), 265–279.

"Das Ende der Philosophie und die Aufgabe des Denkens" (1966). In *Zur Sache des Denkens* (1969, Tübingen: Niemeyer), 61–80.
"The End of Philosophy and the Task of Thinking (1972) (Tr. Joan Stambaugh). In *Basic Writings* (1977, New York: Harper and Row), 373–392.

"Entwurfe zur Geschichte des Seins als Metaphysik" (1961). In *Nietzsche* II (1961, Pfullingen: Neske), 458–480.
"Sketches for a History of Being as Metaphysics" (1973) (Tr. Joan Stambaugh). In *The End of Philosophy* (1973, New York: Harper and Row), 55–74.

"Die Erinnerung in die Metaphysik" (1961). In *Nietzsche* II (1961, Pfullingen: Neske), 481–490.
"Recollection in Metaphysics" (1973) (Tr. Joan Stambaugh). In *The End of Philosophy* (1973, New York: Harper and Row), 75–83.

Der Feldweg (1950). (Frankfurt: Klostermann, 4. Aufl., 1969.)
*"The Pathway" (1967). (Rev. tr. Thomas Sheehan) *Listening* 8, 1973, 32–39, and in this volume, above.

Die Frage nach dem Ding. Zu Kants Lehre von den transzendentalen Grundsätzen (1962, Tübingen: Niemeyer).
What is a Thing? (1967) (tr. W. B. Barton and Vera Deutsch). (1969, Chicago: Regnery, 1969.) [Section B 5 (a-f 3), pp. 66–108, reprinted in *Basic Writings* (1977, New York: Harper and Row), 247–282, as "Modern Science, Metaphysics and Mathematics."]

"Die Frage nach der Technik" (1954). In *Die Technik und die Kehre* (Opuscula aus Wissenschaft und Dichtung I) (3. Aufl., 1976, Pfullingen: Neske), 5–36.
"The Question Concerning Technology" (1977) (Tr. William Lovitt). In *The Question Concerning Technology and Other Essays* (1977, New York: Harper and Row), 3–35. [Also in *Basic Writings* (1977) New York: Harper and Row, 284–317.]

"Gedachtes. Für René Char in freundschaftlichem Gedanken" (1972). In *Homage à René Char* (Fourcade, E., ed.) (1972, Paris: L'Herne), 170–187. ("Zeit, " "Wege," "Winke," "Cézanne," "Vorspiel," "Dank.")
*"Thoughts" (1976) (Tr. Keith Hoeller). *Philosophy Today* 20 (4), 1976, 286–290.

"Gelassenheit" (1959). In *Gelassenheit* (2. Aufl., 1960, Pfullingen: Neske), 11–28.
"Memorial Address" (1966) (Tr. John M. Anderson and E. Hans Freund). In *Discourse on Thinking* (1966, New York: Harper and Row), 43–57.

"Grundsätze des Denkens" (1958) *Jahrbuch für Psychologie und Psychotherapie* (Munich) 6, 1958, 33–41.
"Principles of Thinking" (1976) (Tr. James Hart and John Maraldo). In *The Piety of Thinking* (1976, Bloomington: Indiana University Press), 46–58.

"Heimkunft! An die Verwandten" (1944). *Erläuterungen zu Hölderlins Dichtung* 4. Aufl., 1971, Frankfurt: Klostermann), 9–30.
"Remembrace of the Poet" (1949) (Tr. Douglas Scott). In *Existence and Being* (Brock, W., ed.) (1968, Chicago: Regnery), 232–269.

"Hegels Begriff der Erfahrung" (1950). In *Holzwege* (*Gesamtausgabe* 5, 1977), 115–208.
Hegel's Concept of Experience (1970) (Tr. J. Glenn Gray). (1970, New York: Harper and Row.)

"Hölderlin und das Wesen der Dichtung" (1936). In *Erläuterungen zu Hölderlins Dichtung*. (4. Aufl., 1971,Frankfurt: Klostermann), 33–48.
"Hölderlin and the Essence of Poetry" (1949) (Tr. Douglas Scott). In *Existence and Being* (Brock, W., ed.) (1968, Chicago: Regnery), 270–291.

"In memoriam Max Scheler" (1975) In *Max Scheler im Gegenwartsgeschehen der Philosophie* (Good, P., Hrsq.) (1975, Munich: Francke), 9–10.
"In Memory of Max Scheler" (1978) (Tr. Thomas Sheehan), in this volume, above.

Kant und das Problem der Metaphysik (1929). (Frankfurt: Klostermann, 4. Aufl., 1973).
Kant and the Problem of Metaphysics (1962) (Tr. James S. Churchill). (1962, Bloomington: Indiana University Press.)

"Kants These über das Sein" (1962). In *Wegmarken* (*Gesamtausgabe* 9, 1976, Frankfurt: Klostermann), 445–480.
"Kant's Thesis About Being" (1973) (Tr. Ted E. Klein and William E. Pohl). *The Southwestern Journal of Philosophy*, 4, 1973, 7–33.

"Die Kehre" (1962). In *Die Technik und die Kehre* (Opuscula aus Wissenschaft und Dichtung I) (3. Aufl., 1976, Pfullingen: Neske), 37–47.
"The Turning" (1971) (Tr. William Lovitt). In *The Question Concerning Technology and Other Essays* (1977, New York: Harper and Row), 36–49.

Die Kunst und der Raum (1969, St. Gallen: Erker).
"Art and Space" (1973) (Trans. Charles Seibert). *Man and World* 6, 1973, 3–8.

"Logos (Heraclitus, Fragment B 50)" (1951). In *Vorträge und Aufsätze* III (3. Aufl., 1967, Pfullingen: Neske), 3–25.
"Logos (Heraclitus, Fragment B 50)" (1975) (Tr. David Farrell Krell). In *Early Greek Thinking* (1975, New York: Harper and Row), 59–78.

"Mein Weg in die Phänomenologie" (1969). In *Zur Sache des Denkens* (1969, Tübingen: Niemeyer), 81–90.
"My Way to Phenomenology" (1972) (Tr. Joan Stambaugh). In *Existentialism from Dostoevsky to Sartre* (Kaufmann, W., ed.) (2nd ed. 1975, New York: New American Library), 234–241.

"Die Metaphysik als Geschichte des Seins" (1961). In *Nietzsche* II (1961, Pfullingen: Neske), 399–457.
"Metaphysics as History of Being" (1973) (Tr. Joan Stambaugh). In *The End of Philosophy* (1973, New York: Harper and Row), 1–54.

"Moira (Parmenides, Fragment VIII, 34–41)" (1954). In *Vorträge und Aufsätze* III (3. Aufl., 1967, Pfullingen: Neske), 27–52.
"Moira (Parmenides VIII, 34–41)" (1975) (Tr. Frank Capuzzi). In *Early Greek Thinking* (1975, New York: Harper and Row), 79–101.

"Nachwort zu 'Was ist Metaphysik?'" (1943). In *Wegmarken* (*Gesamtausgabe* 9, 1976, Frankfurt: Klostermann), 303–312.
"Postscript" to "What is Metaphysics?" (1949) (Tr. R. F. C. Hull and Alan Crick). In *Existentialism from Dostoevsky to Sartre* (Kaufmann, W., ed.) (2nd ed., 1975, New York: New American Library), 257–264.

"Nietzsches Wort 'Gott ist tot'" (1950). In *Holzwege* (*Gesamtausgabe* 5, 1977, Frankfurt: Klostermann), 209–267.
"The Word of Nietzsche: 'God Is Dead'" (1977) (Tr. William Lovitt). In *The Question Concerning Technology and Other Essays* (1977, New York: Harper and Row), 53–112.

"Nur noch ein Gott kann uns retten" (1976). *Der Spiegel* (Hamburg) 23, 31 May 1976, 193–219.
"Only a God Can Save Us" (1976) (Tr. Maria P. Alter and John D. Caputo). *Philosophy Today* 20 (4), 1976, 267–284. "Only a God Can Save Us" (1978) (Tr. William J. Richardson) in this volume, above.

"Die onto-theo-logische Verfassung der Metaphysik" (1957). In *Identität und Differenz* (2. Aufl., 1957, Pfullingen: Neske), 35–73.
*"The Onto-theo-logical Nature of Metaphysics" (1960). In *Identity and Difference* (Tr. Joan Stambaugh). (1969, New York: Harper and Row), 42–74.

"Phänomenologie und Theologie" (1969). In *Wegmarken* (*Gesamtausgabe* 9, 1976, Frankfurt: Klostermann), 45–77.
"Phenomenology and Theology" (1976) (Tr. James Hart and John Maraldo). In *The Piety of Thinking* (1976, Bloomington: Indiana University Press), 5–21. (Includes a translation of the "Vorwort" to the German edition on pp. 3–4.)

"Platons Lehre von der Wahrheit" (1942). In *Wegmarken* (*Gesamtausgabe* 9, 1976, Frankfurt: Klostermann), 203–238.
"Plato's Doctrine of Truth" (1962) (Tr. John Barlow). In *Philosophy in the Twentieth Century* II (Barrett, W. *et. al.*, eds.) (1962, New York: Random House), 251–270.

"Protokoll zu einem Seminar über den Vortrag 'Zeit und Sein'" (1969). In *Zur Sache des Denkens* (1969, Tübingen: Niemeyer), 27–60.
"Summary of a Seminar on the Lecture 'Time and Being'" (1972) (Tr. Joan Stambaugh). In *On Time and Being* (1972, New York: Harper and Row), 25–54.

"Das Realitätsproblem in der modernen Philosophie" (1912). *Philosophisches Jahrbuch* (Fulda) 25, 1912, 353–363.
"The Problem of Reality in Modern Philosophy" (1973) (Tr. Phillip J. Bossert). *Journal of the British Society for Phenomenology* (Manchester) 4, 1973, 64–71.

"Rezension: E. Cassierer, *Philosophie der symbolischen Formen* (2. Teil: *Das mythische Denken*)" (1928). *Deutsche Literaturzeitung* (Berlin) 5, 1928, 1000–1012.
"Review of Ernst Cassirer's *Mythical Thought* (1925)" (1976) (Tr. James Hart and John Maraldo). In *The Piety of Thinking* (1976, Bloomington: Indiana University Press), 32–45.

"Des Satz der Identität" (1957). In *Identität und Differenz* (2. Aufl., 1957, Pfullingen: Neske), 11–34.
*"The Principle of Identity" (1960). In *Identity and Difference* (Tr. Joan Stambaugh.) (1969, New York: Harper and Row), 21–41.

"Der Satz vom Grund" (1956). In *Der Satz vom Grund* (4. Aufl., 1971, Pfullingen: Neske), 189-211.
"The Principle of Ground" (1974) (Tr. Keith Hoeller). *Man and World* 7, 1974,
207-222.

"Schöfperische Landschaft: Warum bleiben wir in der Provinz?" (1934). In
Nachlese zu Heidegger (Schneeberger, G., Hrsg.) (Bern: Francke),
216-218.
"Why Do I Stay in the Provinces?" (1977) (Tr. Thomas Sheehan). *Listening*
12 (3), 1977, 122-124, and in this volume, above.

Sein und Zeit (1927). In *Gesamtausgabe* 2 (1977, Frankfurt: Klostermann).
Being and Time (1962) (Tr. John Macquarrie and Edward Robinson) Oxford:
Blackwell, 1967. ["Introduction" only, SZ, pp. 3-53, newly translated by
Joan Stambaugh, J. Glenn Gray and David Farrell Krell, in *Basic Writings*
(1977, New York: Harper and Row), 41-89.]

"Seinsverlassenheit und Irrnis" (1951). In *Vorträge und Aufsätze* I ("Überwin-
dung der Metaphysik," XXVI) (3. Aufl., 1967, Pfullingen: Neske), 83-89.
"Overcoming Metaphysics" (1973) (Tr. Joan Stambaugh). In *The End of
Philosophy* (1973, New York: Harper and Row), 103-109.

"Die Sprache" (1959). In *Unterwegs zur Sprache* (4. Aufl., 1971, Pfullingen:
Neske), 9-33.
"Language" (1971) (Tr. Albert Hofstadter). In *Poetry, Language, Thought* (1971,
New York: Harper and Row), 189-210.

"Sprache" (1976). In *Philosophy Today* 20 (4), 1976, 291. (A reproduction of
Heidegger's manuscript of the poem appears in *Erinnerung an Martin
Heidegger* (Neske, G., Hrsg.) (1977, Pfullingen: Neske), 177.
"Language" (1976) (Tr. Thomas Sheehan), *Ibid.*

"Die Sprache im Gedicht. Eine Erörterung von Georg Trakls Gedicht" (1953).
In *Unterwegs zur Sprache* (4. Aufl., 1971 Pfullingen: Neske), 35-82.
"Language in the Poem" (1971) (Tr. Peter D. Hertz). In *On the Way to Language*
(1971, New York: Harper and Row), 159-198.

"Der Spruch des Anaximander" (1950). In *Holzwege* (*Gesamtausgabe* 5, 1977,
Frankfurt: Klostermann), 321-373.
"The Anaximander Fragment" (1975) (Tr. David Farrell Krell). In *Early Greek
Thinking* (1975, New York: Harper and Row), 13-58.

"Der Ursprung des Kunstwerkes" (1950). In *Holzwege* (*Gesamtausgabe* 5, 1977, Frankfurt: Klostermann), 1–74.
"The Origin of the Work of Art" (1965) (Tr. Albert Hofstadter). In *Basic Writings* (1977, New York: Harper and Row), 149–187.

"Versuch einer zweiten Bearbeitung. Einleitung. Die Idee der Phänomenologie und der Rückgang auf das Bewusstsein" (1962). In Edmund Husserl, *Phänomenologische Psychologie* (*Husserliana* 9, 1962, Den Haag: Martinus Nijhoff), 256–262.
"The Idea of Phenomenology, With a Letter to Edmund Husserl" (1970) (Tr. Thomas Sheehan). *Listening* 12 (3), 1977, 111–117.

"Vom Wesen der Wahrheit" (1943). In *Wegmarken* (*Gesamtausgabe* 9, 1976, Frankfurt: Klostermann), 177–202.
"On the Essence of Truth" (1949). In *Basic Writings* (Tr. John Sallis). (1977, New York: Harper and Row), 117–141.

"Vom Wesen des Grundes" (1929). In *Wegmarken* (*Gesamtausgabe* 9, 1976, Frankfurt: Klostermann), 123–175.
The Essence of Reasons (1969) (Tr. Terrence Malick). (1969, Evanston: Northwestern University Press.)

"Vom Wesen und Begriff der *Physis*. Aristoteles, Physik B, 1" (1958). In *Wegmarken* (*Gesamtausgabe* 9, 1976, Frankfurt: Klostermann), 239–301.
"On the Being and Conception of *Physis* in Aristotle's *Physics* B, 1" (1976) (Tr. Thomas Sheehan). *Man and World* 9, 1976, 219–270.

"Vorbemerkungen des Herausgebers" zu: Edmund Husserls *Vorlesungen zur Phänomenologie des inneren Zeitbewusstseins* (1928). In Edmund Husserl, *Zür Phänomenologie des inneren Zeitbewusstseins* (*Husserliana* 10, 1966) (Boehm, R., Hrsg.) (Den Haag: Martinus Nijhoff), XXIV–XXV.
"Editor's Foreword" to Edmund Husserl, *The Phenomenology of Internal Time-Consciousness* (1928). In Edmund Husserl, *The Phenomenology of Internal Time-Consciousness* (1964) (Tr. James S. Churchill). (1964, Bloomington: Indiana University Press), 15–16.

"Ein Vorwort. Brief an P. William J. Richardson" (1963). In William J. Richardson, *Heidegger: Through Phenomenology to Thought* (2nd ed., 1967, The Hague: Martinus Nijhoff), IX–XXIII.
*"Preface" (1963) (Tr. William J. Richardson). *Ibid.*, XVIII–XXII.

Was heisst Denken? (1954). (Tübingen: Niemeyer, 3. Aufl., 1971).
What is Called Thinking? (1968) (Tr. Fred D. Wieck and J. Glenn Gray). (New York: Harper and Row, 1972, Torchbook Edition). (Part I, Lecture I, and Part II, Lecture II [excluding, from the latter, the "Summary and Transition"] pp. 3-18 and 113, reprinted in *Basic Writings* (1977, New York: Harper and Row), 345-367, as "What Calls for Thinking?").

Was ist das—die Philosophie? (1956) (Pfullingen: Neske, 3. Aufl., 1963).
* What Is Philosophy? (1958) (Tr. William Kluback and Jean T. Wilde). (1968, London: Vision Press).

"Was ist Metaphysik?" (1929). In *Wegmarken* (*Gesamtausgabe* 9, 1976, Frankfurt: Klostermann), 103-122.
"What Is Metaphysics?" (1949). In *Basic Writings* (1977) (Tr. David Farrell Krell). (1977, New York: Harper and Row), 95-112. (This address, in the translation by R. F. C. Hull and Alan Crick, appears with its "Postscript" (1943) and the 1949 "Einleitung"—"The Way Back into the Ground of Metaphysics," translated by Walter Kaufmann—in the second edition of *Existentialism from Dostoevsky to Sartre* (Kaufmann, W., ed.) (1975, New York: New American Library), 242-279.

"Der Weg zur Sprache" (1959). In *Unterwegs zur Sprache* (4. Aufl., 1971, Pfullingen: Neske), 239-268.
"The Way to Language" (1971) (Tr. Peter D. Hertz). In *On the Way to Language* (1971, New York: Harper and Row), 111-136.

"Wer ist Nietzsches Zarathustra?" (1954). In *Vorträge und Aufsätze* I (3. Aufl., 1967, Pfullingen: Neske), 93-118.
"Who is Nietzsche's Zarathustra?" (1967) (Tr. Bernd Magnus). *Review of Metaphysics* 20, 1967, 411-431.

"Das Wesen der Sprache" (1959). In *Unterwegs zur Sprache* (4. Aufl., 1971, Pfullingen: Neske), 157-216.
"The Nature of Language" (1971) (Tr. Peter D. Hertz). In *On the Way to Language* (1971, New York: Harper and Row), 57-108.

"Der Wille zur Macht als Erkenntnis" (1961). In *Nietzsche* I (1961, Pfullingen: Neske), 473-658 (excerpt translated: pp. 473-481).
"Nietzsche as Metaphysician" (1973) (Tr. Joan Stambaugh). In *Nietzsche: A Collection of Critical Essays* (Solomon, R.C., ed.) (1973, Garden City: Doubleday Anchor), 108-113. (Translated with an excerpt from "Der Wille zur Macht als Kunst.")

"Der Wille zur Macht als Kunst" (1961). In *Nietzsche* I (1961, Pfullingen: Neske), 11–254 (excerpt translated: pp. 11–14).

"Nietzsche as Metaphysician" (1973) (Tr. Joan Stambaugh). In *Nietzsche: A Collection of Critical Essays* (Solomon, R. C., ed.) (1973, Garden City: Doubleday Anchor), 105–108. (Translated with an excerpt from "Der Wille zur Macht als Erkenntnis.") (Complete trans., 1979, D. F. Krell.)

"Wissenschaft und Besinnung" (1954). In *Vorträge und Aufsäzte* I (3. Aufl., 1967, Pfullingen: Neske), 45–70.

"Science and Reflection" (1977) (Tr. William Lovitt). In *The Question Concerning Technology and Other Essays* (1977, New York: Harper and Row), 155–182.

"Das Wort" (1958). In *Unterwegs zur Sprache* (4. Aufl., 1971, Pfullingen: Neske), 217–238.

"Words" (1971) (Tr. Peter D. Hertz). In *On the Way to Language* (1971, New York: Harper and Row), 139–156.

"Wozu Dichter?" (1950). In *Holzwege* (*Gesamtausgabe* 5, 1977 Frankfurt: Klostermann), 269–320.

"What Are Poets For?" (1971) (Tr. Albert Hofstadter). In *Poetry, Language, Thought* (1971, New York: Harper and Row), 91–142.

"Die Zeit des Weltbildes" (1950). In *Holzwege* (*Gesamtausgabe* 5, 1977, Frankfurt: Klostermann), 75–113.

"The Age of the World Picture" (1951) (Tr. William Lovitt). In *The Question Concerning Technology and Other Essays* (1977, New York: Harper and Row), 115–154. (The 1951 translation by Marjorie Grene, under the title "The Age of the World View," is reprinted in *Boundary 2*, IV (2), 1976, 341–355.)

"Zeit und Sein" (1968). In *Zur Sache des Denkens* (1969, Tübingen: Niemeyer, 1–25.

"Time and Being" (1972) (Tr. Joan Stambaugh). In *On Time and Being* (1972, New York: Harper and Row), 1–24.

"Zur Erörterung der Gelassenheit. Aus einem Feldweggespräch über das Denken" (1959). In *Gelassenheit* (2. Aufl., 1960, Pfullingen: Neske), 27–71.

"Conversation on a Country Path About Thinking" (1966) (Tr. John Macquarrie and Edward Robinson). In *Discourse on Thinking* (1969, New York: Harper and Row), 58–90.

"Zur Seinsfrage" (1955). In *Wegmarken* (*Gesamtausgabe* 9, 1976, Frankfurt: Klostermann), 385–426.

The Question of Being (1958) (Tr. William Kluback and Jean T. Wilde). (1959, London: Vision Press.)

Heidegger:
Secondary Literature in English, 1929-1977

H. Miles Groth

Contents

A. Periodical Literature on Heidegger

B. Collections of Essays on Heidegger

C. Articles in Heidegger Collections

D. Essays and Articles in Non-Heidegger Collections

E. Book-length Studies of Heidegger

F. Comparative and Selected Related Studies:
   Heidegger, Phenomenology, Existentialism

A. Periodical Literature on Heidegger

Abbagnano, N. "Outline of a Philosophy of Existence." *Philosophy and Phenomenological Research,* 9, 1948, 200-211.

Adamczewski, Zygmunt. "Martin Heidegger and Man's Way to Be." *Man and World,* 1, 1968, 363-379.

Adamczewski, Zygmunt. "Commentary on Calvin O. Schrag's 'Heidegger on Repetition and Historical Understanding.'" *Philosophy East and West,* 20, 1970, 297-301.

Adkins, Arthur W. "Heidegger and Language." *Philosophy,* 37, 1962, 229-237.

Ahlers, R. "Is Technology Inherently Repressive?" *Continuum,* 8, 1970, 111-122.

Alderman, Harold G. "Heidegger's Critique of Science." *Journal of Aesthetic Education,* 2, 1968, 101-107.

Alderman, Harold G. "Heidegger: Necessity and Structure of the Question of Being." *Philosophy Today,* 14, 1970, 141-147.

Alderman, Harold G. "Heidegger on Being Human." *Philosophy Today,* 15, 1971, 16-29.

Alderman, Harold G. "Heidegger: Technology as Phenomenon." *Personalist,* 51, 1971, 535-545.

Alderman, Harold G. "Heidegger on the Nature of Metaphysics." *Journal of the British Society for Phenomenology,* 2, 1971, 12-22.

Allers, Rudolf. "Heidegger on the Principle of Sufficient Reason." *Philosophy and Phenomenological Research,* 20, 1959-60, 365-373.

Allers, Rudolf. "The Meaning of Heidegger." *New Scholasticism,* 36, 1962, 445-474.

Anderson, James F. "Bergson, Aquinas and Heidegger on the Nothing of Nothingness." *Proceedings of the American Catholic Philosophical Association,* 41, 1967, 143-148.

Anderson, John M. "On Heidegger's *Gelassenheit*: A Study of the Nature of Thought." *Journal of Existentialism,* 5, 1964–65, 339–351.

Anderson, T. "The Rationalism of Absurdity: Sartre and Heidegger." *Philosophy Today,* 21, 1977, 263–272.

Arendt, Hannah. "Martin Heidegger at Eighty." *New York Review of Books,* 17, 21 October 1971, 50–54.

Aronson, Ronald. "Interpreting Husserl and Heidegger: The Root of Sartre's Thought." *Telos,* 5, 1972, 47–67.

Awerkamp, Dion. "Heidegger and the Problem of God." *Annual Report of the Duns Scotus Philosophical Association,* 29, 1965, 75–97.

Baerwald, F. "Sociological View of Depersonalization." *Thought,* 31, 1956, 55–78.

Ballard, Edward G. "A Brief Introduction to the Philosophy of Martin Heidegger." *Tulane Studies in Philosophy* 12, 1963, 106–151.

Ballard, Edward G. "On the Pattern of Phenomenological Method." *Southern Journal of Philosophy,* 8, 1970, 421–431.

Barrett, William. "Homelessness in the World." *Commentary* 61, 1976, 34–43.

Bartky, Sandra L. " Heidegger's Philosophy of Art." *British Journal of Aesthetics,* 9, 1969, 353–371, and in this volume, above.

Bartky, Sandra L. "Originative Thinking in the Later Philosophy of Heidegger." *Philosophy and Phenomenological Research,* 30, 1970, 368–381.

Bartlett, Steven. "Phenomenology of the Implicit." *Dialectica,* 29, 1975, 173–188.

Barton, W. B., Jr. "An Introduction to Heidegger's *What is a Thing?*" *Southern Journal of Philosophy,* 11, 1973, 15–25.

Baumgardt, D. "Rationalism and the Philosophy of Despair: Pre-Nazi German Ethics, 1913–1933." *Swanee Review,* 55, 147, 223–237.

Beaufret, Jean. "Heidegger Seen from France." *Southern Journal of Philosophy*, 8, 1970, 433–438.

Behl, L. "Wittgenstein and Heidegger." *Annual Report of the Duns Scotus Philosophical Association*, 27, 1963, 70–115.

Benkston, Benkt Erik. "Martin Heidegger in Memoriam." *Svenska Teologisk Kvartalskrift* (Lund), 1, 1977, 47–48.

Berg, Richard. "Heidegger on Language and Poetry." *Kinesis*, 7, 1977, 75–89.

Bertman, Martin A. "Truth as Mystic *Coulisse* in Nietzsche." *Philosophy Today*, 18, 1974, 41–46.

Biemel, Walter. "Heidegger and Metaphysics." *Listening*, 12 (3), 1977, 50–60, and in this volume, above.

Bixler, J.S. "The Failure of Martin Heidegger." *Harvard Theological Review*, 56, 1963, 121–143.

Blaisdell, Chuck. "Heidegger's Structure of Time and Temporality—A New Repudiation of the Classical Conception." *Dialogue* (Montreal), 18, 1976, 44–53.

Boelen, Bernard J. "Martin Heidegger's Approach to Will, Decision, and Responsibility." *Review of Existential Psychology and Psychiatry*, 1, 1961, 197–204.

Boliek, Lynn. "The Integrity of Faith." *Philosophia Reformata* (Kampen), 39, 1974, 41–68.

Bollnow, Otto F. "The Objectivity of the Humanities and the Essence of Truth." *Philosophy Today*, 18, 1974, 3–18.

Booth, Stella. "The Temporal Dimension of Existence." *Journal of Philosophy*, 7, 1970, 48–62.

Borgmann, Albert. "The Transformation of Heidegger's Philosophy." *Journal of Existentialism*, 1966–67, 161–180.

Borgmann, Albert. "Philosophy and the Concern for Man." *Philosophy Today*, 1966, 236–246.

Borgmann, Albert. "Language in Heidegger's Philosophy." *Journal of Existentialism*, 1966-67, 161-180.

Bossart, William H. "Heidegger's Theory of Art." *Journal of Aesthetics and Art Criticism*, 27, 1968, 57-66.

Bossert, Phillip J. "A Note on Heidegger's 'Opus One.'" *Journal of the British Society for Phenomenology*, 4, 1973, 61-63.

Boukaert, Luk. "Ontology and Ethics: Reflections on Levinas' Critique of Heidegger." *International Philosophical Quarterly*, 10, 1970, 402-419.

Breton, S. "From Phenomenology to Ontology." *Philosophy Today*, 4, 1960, 227-237.

Breton, S. "Ontology and Ontologies: The Contemporary Situation." *International Philosophical Quarterly*, 3, 1963, 339-369.

Brown, R. H. "Existentialism, a Bibliography." *Modern Schoolman*, 31, 1953, 19-33.

Bruzina, Ronald. "Heidegger on the Metaphor and Philosophy." *Cultural Hermeneutics*, 1, 1973, 305-322.

Buchanan, James. "Heidegger and the Problem of Ground." *Philosophy Today*, 17, 1973, 232-245.

Buckley, Frank M. "The Everyday Struggle for the Leisurely Attitude." *Humanitas*, 8, 1972, 307-321.

Bungay, Stephen. "On Reading Heidegger." *Mind*, 86, 1977, 423-426.

Burch, Robert W. "Heidegger and the Bounds of Sense." *Southwestern Journal of Philosophy*, 6, 1975, 27-30.

Byrum, Charles Steven. "Philosophy as Play." *Man and World*, 8, 1975, 315-326.

Camele, Anthony. "Martin Heidegger and Meaning for Man." *Listening*, 1, 1966, 140-149.

Camele, Anthony. "Time in Whitehead and Heidegger: Some Comparisons." *Process Studies,* 5, 1975, 83–105.

Camele, Anthony. "Time in Merleau-Ponty and Heidegger." *Philosophy Today,* 19, 1975, 256–268.

Camele, Anthony. "Heideggerian Ethics." *Philosophy Today,* 21, 1977, 284–293.

Caputo, John D. "Being, Ground and Play in Heidegger." *Man and World,* 3, 1970, 26–48.

Caputo, John D. "The Rose is Without Why: The Later Heidegger." *Philosophy Today,* 15, 1971, 3–15.

Caputo, John D. "Heidegger's Original Ethics." *New Scholasticism,* 45, 1971, 127–138.

Caputo, John D. "Time and Being in Heidegger." *Modern Schoolman,* 50, 1973, 325–349.

Caputo, John D. "Phenomenology, Mysticism and the *Grammatica Speculativa:* A Study in Heidegger's *Habilitationsschrift.*" *Journal of the British Society for Phenomenology,* 5, 1974, 101–117.

Caputo, John D. "Meister Eckhart and the Later Heidegger: The Mystical Element in Heidegger's Thought." *Journal of the History of Philosophy,* Part I, 12, 1974, 479–494; Part II, 13, 1975, 61–80.

Caputo, John D. "The Principle of Sufficient Reason: A Study of Heideggerian Self-Criticism." *Southern Journal of Philosophy,* 13, 1975, 419–426.

Caputo, John D. "The Problem of Being in Heidegger and the Scholastics." *Thomist,* 41, 1977, 62–91.

Caputo, John D. "The Poverty of Thought: A Reflection on Heidegger and Eckhart." *Listening,* 12 (3), 1977, 84–91, and in this volume, above.

Cerf, W.H. "An Approach to Heidegger's Ontology." *Philosophy and Phenomenological Research,* 1, 1940, 177–190.

Child, Arthur. "Hiddenness: Simple Concealment and Disguise." *Metaphilosophy*, 1, 1970, 223–257.

Chung-Yuan Chang. "Commentary on J. Glenn Gray's 'Splendor of the Simple.'" *Philosophy East and West*, 20, 1970, 241–246.

Chung-Yuan Chang. "Pre-rational Harmony in Heidegger's Essential Thinking and Ch'an Thought." *The Eastern Buddhist* (Kyoto), 5 (2), 1972, 153–170.

Chung-Yuan Chang. "'The Essential Source of Identity' in Wang Lung-Chi'i's Philosophy." *Philosophy East and West*, 23, 1973, 31–47.

Chung-Yuan Chang. "Tao: A New Way of Thinking." *Journal of Chinese Philosophy*, 1, 1974, 127–152.

Chung-Yuan Chang. "Taoist Philosophy and Heidegger's Poetic Thinking." *Indian Philosophical Quarterly* (Poona), 4, 1977, 305–311.

Clark, Orville. "Pain and Being: An Essay on Heideggerian Ontology." *Southwestern Journal of Philosophy*, 4, 1973, 179–190.

Cleveland, Harlan. "Welcome (to Conference on 'Heidegger and Eastern Thought')." *Philosophy East and West*, 20, 1970, 223–225.

Cohen, E. "The Ontological Position of God in Existentialist Philosophy." *Iyyum* (Jerusalem), 16, 1965, 3–38.

Cohn, P. N. "Are Philosophers Difficult? Apropos of Heidegger's Theory of Truth." *Texas Quarterly*, 17, 1974, 73–95.

Collins, James. "German Neoscholastic Approach to Heidegger." *Modern Schoolman*, 21, 1944, 143–152.

Corcoran, P. "The Influence of Existentialism on Contemporary Theology, III: Waiting for the Later Heidegger." *Irish Ecclesiastical Record* (Dublin), 108, 1967, 1–18, 105–113.

Coreth, E. "From Hermeneutics to Metaphysics." *International Philosophical Quarterly*, 11, 1971, 249–259.

Corngold, Stanley. *"Sein und Zeit:* Implications for Poetics." *Boundary 2,* IV (2), 1976, 439–454.

Cowan, Joseph L. "Cans and Can'ts." *Philosophy Research Archives,* 3, 1977, 1171.

Cress, Donald W. "Heidegger's Critique of 'Entitative Metaphysics' in his Later Works." *International Philosophical Quarterly,* 12, 1972, 69–86.

Cumming, J. "Martin Heidegger." *Tablet,* 230, 5 June 1976, 551.

Curtin, John. "Waiting and Truth." *New Scholasticism,* 47, 1973, 469–477.

Curtin, John. "Death and Presence: Martin Heidegger." *Philosophy Today,* 20, 1976, 262–266.

Dauenhauer, Bernard P. "An Approach to Heidegger's Way of Philosophizing." *Southern Journal of Philosophy,* 9, 1971, 265–275.

Dauenhauer, Bernard P. "On Death and Birth." *Personalist,* 57, 1976, 162–170.

Dauenhauer, Bernard P. "Heidegger, the Spokesman for the Dweller." *Southern Journal of Philosophy,* 15, 1977, 189–199.

Dean, T. "Heidegger, Marx and Secular Theology." *Union Seminary Quarterly Review,* 22, 1967, 191–204.

Deely, John N. "The Situation of Heidegger in the Tradition of Christian Philosophy." *Thomist,* 31, 1967, 159–244.

DeGennaro, Angelo A. "Heidegger's Vision of the Human." *Christian Century,* 93, 7 July 1976, 620.

Delp, A. "Modern German Existential Philosophy." *Modern Schoolman,* 21, 1944, 143–152.

Demske, J. M. "Heidegger's Quadrate and the Revelation of Being." *Philosophy Today,* 7, 1963, 245–257.

Demske, J. M. "Martin Heidegger at 86." *America,* 134, 13 March 1976, 206–207.

Deutsch, Eliot. "Commentary on J. L. Mehta's 'Heidegger and the Comparison of Indian and Western Philosophy.'" *Philosophy East and West,* 20, 1970, 319–321.

Derrida, Jacques. "The Ends of Man." *Philosophy and Phenomenological Research,* 30, 1957, 31–57.

DeWalhens, Alphonse. "Reflections on Heidegger's Development: A Review of *Heidegger: Through Phenomenology to Thought* by William J. Richardson." *International Philosophical Quarterly,* 5, 1965, 475–502.

Discussion (of John Wild's "An English Version of Martin Heidegger's *Being and Time*"). *Review of Metaphysics,* 16, 1963, 780–785; 17, 1963, 296–300; 17, 1964, 610–161.

Douglas, George H. "Heidegger's Notion of Poetic Truth." *Personalist,* 47, 1966, 500–508.

Douglas, George H. "Heidegger on the Education of Poets and Philosophers." *Educational Theory,* 22, 1972, 443–449.

Doyle, John P. "Heidegger and Scholastic Metaphysics." *Modern Schoolman,* 49, 1972, 201–220.

Dreyfus, H.L. "The Priority of *the* World to *my* World: Heidegger's Answer to Husserl (and Sartre)." *Man and World,* 9, 1975, 121–130.

Driscoll, Giles. "Heidegger: A Response to Nihilism." *Philosophy Today,* 2, 1967, 17–37.

Driscoll, Giles. "Heidegger's Ethical Monism." *New Scholasticism,* 42, 1968, 497–510.

Earle, William. "Wahl on Heidegger and Being." *Philosophical Review,* 67, 1958, 85–90.

Edwards, Paul. "Heidegger and Death as 'Possibility.'" *Mind,* 84, 1975, 548–566.

Edwards, Paul. "Heidegger and Death: A Deflationary Critique." *Monist,* 59, 1976, 161–186.

Ehman, Robert R., "Temporal Self-Identity." *Southern Journal of Philosophy,* 12, 333–341.

Elliston, F. "Phenomenology Reinterpreted: From Husserl to Heidegger." *Philosophy Today,* 21, 1977, 273–283.

Emad, Parvis. "Heidegger on Schelling's Concept of Freedom." *Man and World,* 8, 1975, 157–174.

Erickson, Steven A. "Martin Heidegger." *Review of Metaphysics,* 19, 1966, 462–492.

Erickson, Steven A. "Meaning and Language." *Man and World,* 1, 1968, 563–586.

Erickson, Steven A. "Worlds and World Views." *Man and World,* 2, 1969, 228–247.

Fabro, C. "The Problem of Being and the Destiny of Man: Heidegger and Hegel." *International Philosophical Quarterly,* 1, 1961, 407–436.

Faber, Marvin. "Heidegger on the Essence of Truth." *Philosophy and Phenomenological Research,* 18, 1957–58, 523–532.

Farber, Marvin. "The Phenomenological Tendency." *Journal of Philosophy,* 59, 1962, 429–439.

Farrelly, John. "Religious Reflection and Man's Transcendence." *Thomist,* 37, 1963, 1–68.

Fay, Thomas A. "Heidegger: Thinking as *Noein.*" *Modern Schoolman,* 51, 1973, 17–18.

Fay, Thomas A. "Early Heidegger and Wittgenstein on World." *Philosophical Studies* (Maynooth), 21, 1973, 161–171.

Fay, Thomas A. "Heidegger on Logic: A Genetic Study of his Thought on Logic." *Journal of the History of Philosophy,* 12, 1974, 77–94.

Fell, Joseph P. "Heidegger's Notion of Two Beginnings." *Review of Metaphysics,* 25, 1971, 213–237.

Ferguson, Frances C. "Reading Heidegger: Jacques Derrida and Paul de Man." *Boundary 2*, IV (2), 1976, 593-610.

Fletcher, J. "The Being Question." *Month*, 9, 1976 (August), 279-281.

Fox, D. A. "Being and Particularity." *Religion in Life*, 35, 1966, 587-602.

Franks, Dean. "An Interpretation of Technology through the Assertorial-Problematic Distinction." *Kinesis*, 4, 1971, 22-29.

Franquiz, J. A. "An Appaisal of Heidegger's Epistemology as a Foundation for a Metaphysics of Religion." *Wesleyan Studies in Religion*, 57, 1965, 23-29.

Franz, H. "Heidegger's Relevance for Theology: A Protestant View." *Theological Digest*, 10, 1962, 87-93.

Freund, E. H. "Man's Fall in Martin Heidegger's Philosophy." *Journal of Religion*, 24, 1944, 180-187.

Friedman, M. "Phenomenology and Existential Analysis. Existential Phenomenology: Temporality, Distancing and Immediacy." *Review of Existential Psychology and Psychiatry*, 9, 1968, 151-168.

Frings, Manfred S. "Heidegger and Scheler." *Philosophy Today*, 12, 1968, 21-30.

Frings, Manfred S. "Insight — Logos — Love (Longeran — Heidegger — Scheler)." *Philosophy Today*, 14, 1970, 106-115.

Frings, Manfred S. "Protagoras Re-discovered: Heidegger's Explication of Protagoras' Fragment." *Journal of Value Inquiry*, 8, 1974, 112-123.

Fu, Charles Wei-Hsun. "Creative Hermeneutics: Taoist Metaphysics and Heidegger." *Journal of Chinese Philosophy*, 3, 1976, 114-143.

Fulton, James S. "The Event of Being." *Southwestern Journal of Philosophy*, 6, 1975, 7-13.

Futrell, J. C. "Myth and Message: A Study of the Biblical Theology of Rudolf Bultmann." *Catholic Biblical Quarterly*, 21, 1959, 283-315.

Gadamer, Hans-Georg. "Concerning Empty and Ful-filled Time." *Southern Journal of Philosophy*, 8, 1970, 341–353.

Gadamer, Hans-Georg. "The Problem of Historical Consciousness." *Graduate Faculty Philosophy Journal*, 5, 1975, 8–52.

Gans, Steven. "Ethics or Ontology: Levinas and Heidegger." *Philosophy Today*, 16, 1972, 117–121.

Gaidenko, P. P. "The Problem of Time in Martin Heidegger's Ontology." (Summary in English.) *Voprosy Filosofi* (Moscow), 12, 1965, 109–120.

Gaidenko, P. P. "The 'Fundamental Ontology' of Heidegger as a Basis of Philosophical Irrationalism." *Soviet Studies in Philosophy* (New York), 4 (3), 1965–66, 44–45.

Gelley, A. de. "Staiger, Heidegger and the Task of Criticism." *Modern Language Quarterly*, 23, 1962, 195–216.

Gelven, Michael. "Guilt and Human Meaning." *Humanitas*, 9, 1972, 69–81.

Gelven, Michael. "Eros and Projection." *Southwestern Journal of Philosophy*, 4, 1973, 125–136.

Gelven, Michael. "Heidegger and Tragedy." *Boundary 2*, IV (2), 1976, 555–568.

George, R. T. de. "Heidegger and the Marxists." *Studies in Soviet Thought* (Dordrecht), 5, 1965, 289–298.

Gerber, Rudolf J. "Heidegger: Thinking and Thanking Being." *Modern Schoolman*, 44, 1967, 205–222.

Gerber, Rudolf J. "Focal Points in Recent Heidegger Scholarship." *New Scholasticism*, 42, 1968, 561–577.

Gerhard, William A. and Gupta, Brijen. "Literature: The Phenomenological Art." *Man and World*, 3, 1970, 102–115.

Gibson, W. R. Boyce. "Excerpts from a 1929 Freiburg Diary." *Journal of the British Society for Phenomenology*, 2, 1971, 63–76.

Gleason, Robert. "Toward a Theology of Death." *Thought*, 32, 1957, 39–68.

Glicksman, M. "A Note on the Philosophy of Heidegger." *Journal of Philosophy*, 35, 1938, 93–104.

Goff, Robert Allen. "Wittgenstein's Tools and Heidegger's Implements." *Man and World*, 1, 1968, 447–462.

Goff, Robert Allen. "Saying and Being with Heidegger and Parmenides." *Man and World*, 5, 1972, 62–78.

Graff, Willem L. "Rilke in the Light of Heidegger." *Laval Théologique et Philosophique* (Quebec), 17, 1961, 165–172.

Gray, J. Glenn. "The Idea of Death in Existentialism." *Journal of Philosophy*, 48, 1951, 113–127.

Gray, J. Glenn. "Heidegger's 'Being.'" *Journal of Philosophy*, 49, 1952, 415–422.

Gray, J. Glenn. "Heidegger 'Evaluates' Nietzsche." *Journal of the History of Ideas*, 14, 1953, 304–309.

Gray, J. Glenn. "Heidegger's Course: From Human Existence to Nature." *Journal of Philosophy*, 54, 1957, 197–207.

Gray, J. Glenn. "Martin Heidegger: On Anticipating my Own Death." *Personalist*, 46, 1965, 439–458.

Gray, J. Glenn. "Homelessness and Anxiety: Sources of the Modern Mode of Being." *Virginia Quarterly Review*, 48, 1972, 24–39.

Gray, J. Glenn. "Splendor of the Simple." *Philosophy East and West*, 20, 1970, 227–240.

Greef, D. de. "Philosophy and its 'Other.'" *International Philosophical Quarterly*, 10, 1970, 252–275.

Greif, J. C. G. "Some Aspects of Hermeneutics: A Brief Survey." *Religion*, 1, 1971, 131–151.

Grene, Marjorie. "Heidegger: Philosopher and Prophet." *Twentieth Century*, 164, 1958, 545–555.

Groth, H. Miles. "Messkirch: Martin Heidegger: June 1976." *Philosophy Today*, 20, 1976, 259-261. [*Anglican Theological Review*, 59, 1977, 43-46 (reprint).]

Gründer, K. "Heidegger's Critique of Science in its Historical Background." *Philosophy Today*, 7, 1963, 15-32.

Guerrière, Daniel. "Ontology as the Symbolism of the Future." *Philosophy Today*, 17, 1973, 213-219.

Gupta, Kumar, R. "What is Heidegger's Notion of Time?" *Revue Internationale de Philosophie* (Bruxelles), 14, 1960, 163-193.

Hall, R. L. "Heidegger and the Space of Art." *Journal of Existentialism*, 8, 1967, 91-108.

Hammet, Jenny Y. "Thinker and Poet: Heidegger, Rilke, and Death." *Soundings*, 60, 1977, 166-178.

Hamrick, William S. "Heidegger and the Objectivity of Aesthetic Truth." *Journal of Value Inquiry*, 5, 1970, 120-130.

Hamrick, William S. "Fascination, Fear, and Pornography." *Man and World*, 7, 1974, 52-66.

Harries, Karsten. "Heidegger and Hölderlin: The Limits of Language." *Personalist*, 44, 1963, 5-23.

Harries, Karsten. "A Note on John Wild's Review of *Being and Time*." *Review of Metaphysics*, 17, 1964, 296-300.

Harries, Karsten. "Heidegger's Conception of the Holy." *Personalist*, 47, 1966, 169-184.

Harries, Karsten. "Wittgenstein and Heidegger: The Relationship of the Philosopher to Language." *Journal of Value Inquiry*, 2, 1968, 281-291.

Harries, Karsten. "Heidegger as a Political Thinker." *Review of Metaphysics*, 29, 1975-76, 642-669.

Harries, Karsten. "Language and Silence: Heidegger's Dialogue with Georg Trakl." *Boundary 2*, IV (2), 1976, 495-511.

Hart, R. L. "Heidegger's Being and Time in Phenomenology." *Encounter*, 26, 1965, 281–291.

Hartmann, Klaus. "The German Philosophical Scene." *Journal of the British Society for Phenomenology*, 3, 1972,. 11–14.

Hartmann, Klaus. "The Logic of Deficient and Eminent Modes in Heidegger." *Journal of the British Society for Phenomenology*, 5, 1974, 118–134.

Hassett, Joseph D. "Heidegger, Being and World in Turmoil." *Thought*, 36, 1961, 537–554.

Hayes, D. G. "Nietzsche's Eternal Recurrence: A Prelude to Heidegger." *Journal of Existentialism*, 6, 1965–66, 189–196.

Heaton, J.M. "Saying and Showing in Heidegger and Wittgenstein." *Journal of the British Society for Phenomenology*, 3, 1972, 42–45.

Hedwig, Klaus, "German Idealism in the Context of Light Metaphysics." *Idealistic Studies*, 2, 1972, 16–38.

Heinemann, F. H. "What is Alive and What is Dead in Existentialism?" *Revue Internationale de Philosophie* (Bruxelles), 3, 1949, 306–319.

Hellerich, Gert. "What is Often Overlooked in Existentialist Situation Ethics." *Journal of Thought*, 5, 1970, 46–54.

Hermann, R. D. "Heidegger and Logic." *Sophia* (Padova), 29, 1961, 353–357.

Hinners, R. C. "The Freedom and Finiteness of Existence in Heidegger." *New Scholasticism*, 33, 1959, 32–48.

Hinners, R.C. "Being and God in Heidegger's Philosophy." *Proceedings of the American Catholic Philosophical Association*, 31, 1957, 157–162.

Hirsch, Elisabeth Feist. "Martin Heidegger and the East." *Philosophy East and West*, 20, 1970, 247–263.

Hodgson, P. C. "Heidegger, Revelation, and the Word of God." *Journal of Religion*, 49, 1969, 228–252.

Hoeller, Keith. "Phenomenological Foundations for the Study of Suicide." *Omega*, 4 (3), 1973, 195–208.

Hoeller, Keith. "Heidegger Bibliography of English Translations." *Journal of the British Society for Phenomenology*, 6, 1975, 206–208.

Hofstadter, Albert. "Truth and Being." *Journal of Philosophy*, 62, 1965, 167–183.

Hofstadter, Albert. "Enownment."*Boundary 2*, IV (2), 1976, 357–377.

Hood, Webster F. "The Latent Dimension of Experience." *Main Currents*, 27, 1971, 84–88.

Hopkins, Jasper. "Are Moods Cognitive? A Critique of Schmitt on Heidegger." *Journal of Value Inquiry*, 6, 1972, 64–71.

Horgby, I. "The Double Awareness in Heidegger and Wittgenstein." *Inquiry*, 2, 1952, 235–264.

Hornedo, Florentino H. "Truth, Man, and Martin Heidegger." *St. Louis University Research Journal* (Baguio City), 2, 1971, 1–18.

Hoy, David Couzens. "The Owl and the Poet: Heidegger's Critique of Hegel." *Boundary 2*, IV (2), 1976, 393–410.

Hyland, Andrew A. "Art and the Happening of Truth: Reflections on the End of Philosophy." *Journal of Aesthtics and Art Criticism*, 30, 1971, 177–187.

Ihde, Don. "Language and the Two Phenomenologies." *Southern Journal of Philosophy*, 8, 1970, 399–408.

Ihde, Don and Slaughter, T.F. "Studies in the Phenomenology of Sound: Listening, on Perceiving Persons, God and Sound." *International Philosophical Quarterly*, 10, 1970, 232–251.

Ihde, Don. "Phenomenology and the Later Heidegger." *Philosophy Today*, 18, 1974, 19–31.

Jacques, J. H. "Heidegger and the Greeks." *Listener* (London), 76, 1966, 773–774.

Jacques, J. H. "The Phenomenology of Temporal Awareness." *Journal of the British Society for Phenomenology*, 1, 1970, 38–45.

Jaeger, Hans. "Heidegger's Existential Phenomenology and Modern German Literature." *Publications of the Modern Language Association,* 67, 1952, 655–683.

Jaeger, Hans. "Heidegger and the Work of Art." *Journal of Aesthetics and Art Criticism,* 17, 1958–59, 58–71.

Janicaud, Dominique. "Heidegger and Method." *Man and World,* 9, 1976, 140–152.

Johnson, R. F. "More on Heidegger and Bultmann." *Encounter,* 18, 1967, 209–211.

Jonas, Hans. "Gnosticism and Modern Nihilism." *Social Research,* 19, 1952, 430–452.

Jung, H. Y. "Confucianism and Existentialism: Intersubjectivity as the Way of Man." *Philosophy and Phenomenological Research,* 30, 1969, 186–202.

Jung, H. Y. and Jung, P. "To Save the Earth." *Philosophy Today,* 19, 1975, 108–117.

Kaelin, E. F. "Merleau-Ponty, Fundamental Ontologist." *Man and World,* 3, 1970, 102–115.

Kates, Carol A. "Heidegger and the Myth of the Cave." *Personalist,* 50, 1969, 532–548.

Kaufman, F. W. "The Value of Heidegger's Analysis of Existence for Literary Criticism." *Modern Language Notes,* 48, 1933, 487–491.

Kaufmann, Walter. "German Thought Today." *Kenyon Review,* 19, 1957, 15–30.

Kelley, Derek A. "The Earth as Home." *Religious Humanism,* 6, 1972, 178–179.

Kerr, Fergus. "Heidegger Among the Theologians." *New Blackfriars,* 40, 1965, 396–403.

Kerr, Fergus. "Liberation and Contemplativity." *New Blackfriars,* 50, 1969, 356–366.

Kerr, Fergus. "Metaphysics After Heidegger: For his Eighty-Fifth Birthday." *New Blackfriars*, 55, 1974, 344–357.

Kersten, Fred. "Heidegger and Transcendental Phenomenology." *Southern Journal of Philosophy*, 11, 1973, 202–215.

Kestenbaum, Victor. "Phenomenology and Dewey's Empiricism: A Response to Leroy Troutner." *Educational Theory*, 22, 1972, 99–108.

Keyes, C. D. "An Evaluation of Levinas' Critique of Heidegger." *Research in Phenomenology*, 2, 1972, 63–93.

Jhan, Mohammed Ahman. "*Daseinsanalyse* and Existential Analysis." *Pakistan Philosophical Journal* (Lahore), 12, 1973, 60–68.

Khoobyar, Helen. "The Educational Import of Heidegger's Notion of Truth as Letting-be." *Proceedings: Philosophy of Education*, 30, 1974, 47–58.

King, Magda. "Heidegger Reinterpreted." (Review of L. Versenyi's *Heidegger, Being and Truth*) *International Philosophical Quarterly*, 6, 1966, 483–491.

King, Magda. "Truth and Technology." *Human Context*, 5, 1973, 1–34.

Kirkland, Frank M. "Gadamer and Ricoeur: The Paradigm of the Text." *Graduate Faculty Philosophy Journal*, 6, 1977, 131–144.

Kisiel, Theodore. "The Happening of Tradition: The Hermeneutics of Gadamer and Heidegger." *Man and World*, 2, 1969, 358–385.

Kisiel, Theodore. "On the Dimensions of a Phenomenology of Science in Husserl and the Young Doctor Heidegger." *Journal of the British Society for Phenomenology*, 4, 1973, 217–234.

Kisiel, Theodore. "Towards the Topology of Dasein." *Listening*, 12 (3), 1977, 38–49, and in this volume, above.

Klein, Ted. "Being as an Ontological Predicate: Heidegger's Interpretation of Kant's Thesis about Being.'" *Southwestern Journal of Philosophy*, 4, 1973, 35–51.

Klein, Ted. "A Shared Paradox." *Southwestern Journal of Philosophy*, 6, 1975, 21–25.

Kockelmans, Joseph J. "Heidegger on Time and Being." *Southwestern Journal of Philosophy*, 8, 1970, 319–340.

Kockelmans, Joseph J. "Heidegger on Theology." *Southwestern Journal of Philosophy*, 4, 1973, 85–108.

Kockelmans, Joseph J. "Toward an Interpretative or Hermeneutic Social Science." *Graduate Faculty Philosophy Journal*, 5, 1975, 73–96.

Kohak, Erazim V. "I, Thou and It. A Contribution to the Phenomenology of Being-in-the-World." *Philosophy Forum* (Dekalb), 1, 1968, 36–72.

Kraft, J. "Philosophy of Existence, Its Structure and Significance." *Philosophy and Phenomenological Research*, 1, 1941, 339–358.

Kraft, J. "In Reply to Kaufmann's Critical Remarks about my Paper, 'Philosophy of Existence.'" *Philosophy and Phenomenological Research*, 1, 1941, 364–365.

Kreeft, Peter. "Zen in Heidegger's *Gelassenheit*." *International Philosophical Quarterly*, 11, 1971, 521–545.

Krell, David Farrell. "Toward an Ontology of Play." *Research in Phenomenology*, 2, 1972, 63–93.

Krell, David Farrell. "Heidegger and Zarathustra." *Philosophy Today*, 18, 1974, 306–311.

Krell, David Farrell. "Nietzsche in Heidegger's *Kehre*." *Southern Journal of Philosophy*, 13, 1975, 197–204.

Krell, David Farrell. "On the Manifold Meaning of *a-lētheia*: Brentano, Aristotle, Heidegger." *Research in Phenomenology*, 5, 1975, 77–94.

Krell, David Farrell. "Toward *Sein und Zeit*: Heidegger's Early Review (1919–21) of Jaspers' *Psychologie der Weltanschauungen*." *Journal of the British Society for Phenomenology*, 6, 1975, 147–156.

Krell, David Farrell. "Heidegger, Nietzsche, Hegel. An Essay in Descensional Reflection." *Nietzsche-Studien* (Berlin), 5, 1976, 255–262.

Krell, David Farrell. "Art and Truth in Raging Discord: Heidegger and Nietzsche on the Will to Power." *Boundary 2*, IV (2), 1976, 379–392.

Kroner, R. J. "Existentialism and Christianity." *Encounter*, 17, 1956, 219-244.

Kroner, R. J. "Heidegger's Private Religion." *Union Seminary Quarterly*, 11, 1956, 23-37.

Ladrière, J. "History and Destiny." *Philosophy Today*, 9, 1965, 3-25.

Lampert, Lawrence. "On Heidegger and Historicism." *Philosophy and Phenomenological Research*, 34, 1974, 586-590.

Lambert, Lawrence. "Heidegger's Nietzsche Interpretation." *Man and World*, 7, 1974, 353-378.

Lang, Zane A. "Preontological Mistakes." *Kinesis*, 5, 1973, 79-86.

Langan, Thomas. "Heidegger in France." *Modern Schoolman*, 33, 1955-56, 114-118.

Langan, Thomas. "Transcendence in the Philosophy of Heidegger." *New Scholasticism*, 32, 1958, 45-60.

Langan, Thomas. "A Note in Response to Rukavina's Comment ('Being and Things in Heidegger')." *New Scholasticism*, 33, 1959, 358-369.

Langan, Thomas. "Heidegger Beyond Hegel: A Reflexion on the 'Onto-theo-logical Constitution of Metaphysics.'" *Filosofia* (Torino), 19, 1968, 735-746.

Langan, Thomas. "Heidegger and the Possibility of Authentic Christianity." *Proceedings of the American Catholic Philosophical Association*, 46, 1972, 101-112.

Lauer, Quentin. "Heidegger and Being." *Proceedings of the American Catholic Philosophical Association*, 31, 1957, 163-165.

Lauer, Quentin. "Four Phenomenologists. Scheler, Heidegger, Sartre, Merleau-Ponty." *Thought*, 33, 1958, 183-204.

Lawler, James. "Heidegger's Theory of Metaphysics and Dialectics." *Philosophy and Phenomenological Research*, 35, 1975, 363-375.

Lechner, Robert. "Martin Heidegger." *Philosophy Today*, 19, 1975, 78.

Leonard, Linda. "Toward an Ontological Analysis of Detachment." *Philosophy Today*, 16, 1972, 268–280.

Leonard, Linda. "The Belonging-together of Poetry and Death." *Philosphy Today*, 19, 1975, 137–145.

Levine, Steven K. "On Origins." *Abraxas*, 1, 1970, 25–29.

Lewis, Donald F. "Aristotle's Theory of Time: Destructive Ontology from Heideggerian Principles." *Kinesis*, 2, 1970, 81–92.

Lichtheim, George. "On the Rim of the Volcano: Heidegger, Bloch, Adorno." *Encounter*, 22, 1964, 98–105.

Lichtigfeld, Adolph. "Imagination in Kant and Heidegger: A Survey." *Filosofia* (Torino), 18, 1967, 807–836.

Lingis, Alphonso. "Truth and Art." *Philosophy Today*, 16, 1972, 112–134.

Long, W. "Existentialism, Christianity and Logos." *Personalist*, 47, 1966, 149–168.

Long, E. T. "Being and Thinking." *Southern Journal of Philosophy*, 8, 1971, 131–140.

Long, E. T. "Jaspers' Philosophy of Existence as a Model for Theological Reflection." *International Journal for Philosophy of Religion*, 1, 1972, 35–43.

Loscerbo, J. "Martin Heidegger. Remarks Concerning Some Earlier Texts on Modern Theology." *Tijdschrift voor Filosophie* (Leuven), 39, 1977, 104–129.

Lovitt, William. "A *Gespräch* with Heidegger on Technology." *Man and World*, 6, 1973, 44–59.

Löwith, Karl. "Heidegger and F. Rosenzweig on Temporality and Eternity." *Philosophy and Phenomenological Research*, 3, 1942, 53–77.

Löwith, Karl. "Heidegger: The Problem and Background of Existentialism." *Social Research*, 15, 1948, 345–369.

Löwith, Karl. "The Nature of Man and the World of Nature. For Heidegger's 80th Birthday." *Southern Journal of Philosophy*, 8, 1970, 309–318.

Lowry, Atherton C. "Merleau-Ponty and Fundamental Ontology." *International Philosophical Quarterly*, 15, 1975, 397–409.

Luipjen, W. "Heidegger and the Affirmation of God." *Doctor Communis* (Rome), 18, 1965, 303–310.

Macquarrie, John. "Bultmann's Existential Approach to Theology." *Union Seminary Quarterly Review*, 12, 1960, 17–27.

Macquarrie, John. "Heidegger's Earlier and Later Work Compared." *Anglican Theological Review*, 49, 1967, 3–16.

Macquarrie, John. "The Idea of a Theology of Nature." *Union Seminary Quarterly Review*, 30, 1975, 69–75.

Magerauer, Robert. "Toward Reading Heidegger's *Discourse on Thinking*." *Southwestern Journal of Philosophy*, 8, 1977, 143–156.

Magnus, Bernd. "Heidegger and the Truth of Being." *International Philosophical Quarterly*, 4, 1964, 245–264.

Magnus, Bernd. "Nihilism, Reason, and the 'Good.'" *Review of Metaphysics*, 25, 1971, 292–310.

Malik, Charles H. "A Christian Reflection on Heidegger." *Thomist*, 41, 1977, 1–61.

Maly, Kenneth. " Toward *Ereignis*. An Initiatory Thinking Through of the Granting in Heidegger's Essay 'Zeit und Sein.'" *Research in Phenomenology*, 3, 1973, 63–93.

Maly, Kenneth. " Subject, Dasein, and Disclosure." *Research in Phenomenology*, 5, 1975, 183–193.

Manchester, Peter B. " Time in Whitehead and Heidegger: A Reply (to Mason, David R. 'Time in Whitehead and Heidegger: Some Comparisons')." *Process Studies*, 1975, 106–113.

Marshall, Donald G. "The Ontology of the Literary Sign: Notes Toward a Heideggerian Revision of Semiology." *Boundary 2*, IV (2), 1976, 611–634.

Martin, F. David. "Heidegger's Being of Things and Aesthetic Education." *Journal of Aesthetic Education*, 8, 1974, 87–105.

Marcuse, Herbert and Olafson, Frederick. "Heidegger's Politics: An Interview." *Graduate Faculty Philosophy Journal*, 6, 1977, 28–40.

Marx, Werner. "Heidegger's New Conception of Philosophy. The Second Phase of 'Existentialism.'" *Social Research*, 22, 1955, 450–474.

Mason, David R. "Time in Whitehead and Heidegger: Some Comparisons." *Process Studies*, 5, 1975, 83–105.

Masson, Robert. "Rahner and Heidegger: Being, Hearing, and God." *Thomist*, 37, 1973, 455–488.

Maurer, Reinhart. "From Heidegger to Practical Philosophy." *Idealistic Studies*, 3, 1973, 133–162.

McCool, Gerald A. "The Christian Hegelianism of George Morel." *Modern Schoolman*, 47, 1970, 279–304.

McCormick, Peter. "Heidegger's Meditation on the Word." *Philosophical Studies* (Maynooth), 18, 1969, 79–99.

McCormick, Peter. "Interpretation in the Later Heidegger." *Philosophical Studies* (Maynooth), 19, 1970, 83–101.

McCormick, Peter. "Saying and Showing in Heidegger and Wittgenstein." *Journal of the British Society for Phenomenology*, 3, 1972, 27–35.

McCormick, Peter. "Heidegger on Hölderlin." *Philosophical Studies* (Maynooth), 22, 1973, 7–16.

McCormick, Peter. "A Note on 'Time and Being.'" *Philosophy Today*, 19, 1975, 95–99.

McEvilly, W. "Kant, Heidegger and the *Upanishads*." *Philosophy East and West*, 12, 1969, 311–317.

McGaughey, D. "Husserl and Heidegger on Plato's Cave Allegory: A Study of Philosophical Influence." *International Philosophical Quarterly*, 16, 1976, 331–348.

McGinley, John. "The Essential Thrust of Heidegger's Thought." *Philosophy Today*, 15, 1971, 242–249.

McGinley, John. "Heidegger's Concern for the Lived-World in his Dasein-analysis." *Philosophy Today,* 16, 1972, 92–115.

Mehta, J. L. "Heidegger and the Concept of Indian and Western Philosophy." *Philosophy East and West,* 20, 1970, 303–317.

Meier, P.J. "Fundamental Ontology and Positive Theology. Heidegger's Way of Thinking." *Journal of Religious Thought,* 17, 1960, 101–115.

Meissner, W. W. "The Temporal Dimension in the Understanding of Human Experience." *Journal of Existentialism,* 7, 1966–67, 129–160.

Merlan, P. "Time-Consciousness in Husserl and Heidegger." *Philosophy and Phenomenological Research,* 8, 1947, 23–54.

Mermall, Thomas. "Spain's Philosoper of Hope." *Thought,* 45, 1970, 103–120.

Metzger, Arnold. "Freedom and Death." *Human Context,* 4, 1975, 215–243.

Micelli, V. "Heidegger and Bultmann: Keepers of the Cosmic Age." *L'Osservatore Romano* (Rome), 25 (221), 22 June 1972.

Millikan, James. "Wild's Review of *Being and Time.*" *Review of Metaphysics,* 16, 1962–63, 780–785.

Mitchell, Donald W. "Commentary on Elisabeth Feist Hirsch's 'Martin Heidegger and the East.'" *Philosophy East and West,* 20, 1970, 265–269.

Moehling, Karl A. "Heidegger and the Nazis." *Listening,* 12 (3), 1977, 92–105, and in this volume, above.

Moeller, J. "'Nietzsche and Metaphysics': Heidegger's Interpretation of Nietzsche." *Philosophy Today,* 8, 1964, 118–132.

Molnar, Thomas. "Heidegger and Humanism." *Commentary,* 68, 1958, 343–345.

Mood, J. J. "Poetic Language and Primal Thinking: A Study of Barfield." *Encounter,* 26, 1965, 417–433.

Mood, J. J. "Leadbelly on *Angst:* Heidegger on the Blues." *Philosophy Today,* 14, 1970, 161–167.

Moore, A. "Existential Phenomenology." *Philosophy and Phenomenological Research,* 27, 1967, 408–414.

Morrison, James C. "Heidegger's Critique of Wittgenstein's Conception of Truth." *Man and World,* 2, 1969, 551–573.

Morriston, Wesley. "Heidegger on the World." *Man and World,* 5, 1972, 452–466.

Moser, Simon. "Toward a Metaphysics of Technology." *Philosophy Today,* 15, 1971, 129–156.

Munson, Thomas N. "Heidegger's Recent Thought on Language." *Philosophy and Phenomenological Research,* 21, 1960–61, 361–372.

Murray, Michael. "Heidegger and Ryle: Two Versions of Phenomenology." *Review of Metaphysics,* 27, 1973, 88–111.

Murray, Michael. "A Note on Wittgenstein and Heidegger." *Philosophical Review,* 83, 1974, 501–503.

Muto, K. "New Possibilities for a Philosophy of Religion." *Northeast Asia Journal of Theology* (Tokyo), 5/6, 1970–71, 57–70.

Nagley, W. E. "Introduction to the Symposium and Reading of a Letter from Martin Heidegger." *Philosophy East and West,* 20, 1970, 221.

Nakagawa, N. "On 'Analogical Characteristics' in Heidegger's Philosophy." *Journal of Religious Studies* (Tokyo), 33 (162), 1960, 55-56.

Nanajivako, Bhikku. "Karma — The Ripening Fruit." *Main Currents,* 29, 1972, 28–36.

Natanson, Maurice. "The Problem of Anonymity in Gurwitsch and Schutz." *Research in Phenomenology,* 5, 1975, 51–56.

Nicholson, Graeme. "The Commune of *Being and Time.*" *Dialogue,* 10, 1971, 708–726.

Nicholson, Graeme. "Camus and Heidegger: Anarchists." *University of Toronto Quarterly.* 41 (1), 1971, 14–23.

Nicholson, Graeme. "Disclosure in Heidegger." *Studi Internazionali di Filosofia* (Torino), 4, 1972, 139–154.

Nicholson, Graeme. "Heidegger on Thinking." *Journal of the History of Philosophy*, 13, 1973, 491–503.

Nielsen, Niels C. "Demythologizing and the *philosophia perennis:* Bultmann, Jaspers and Heidegger." *Rice University Studies*, 50, 1964, 55–67.

Nishitani, Keiji. "Preliminary Remarks (to Heidegger's *Zwei Ansprachen in Messkirch*')." *The Eastern Buddhist* (Kyoto), 1 (2), 1966, 48–59.

Nokes, D. "Pope and Heidegger: A Forgotten Fragment." *Review of English Studies*, 23, 1972, 308–313.

Nwodo, Christopher S. "The Work of Art in Heidegger: A World Disclosure." *Cultural Hermeneutics*, 4, 1976–77, 61–73.

Nwodo, Christopher S. "The Role of Art in Heidegger." *Philosophy Today*, 21, 1977, 294–304.

Olafson, Frederick A. "Interpretation and Personal Structure of Language." *Journal of Philosophy*, 69, 1972, 718–734.

Olafson, Frederick A. "Consciousness and Intentionality in Heidegger's Thought." *American Philosophical Quarterly*, 12, 1975, 91–103.

O'Mahoney, B. E. "Martin Heidegger's Existential of Death." *Philosophical Studies* (Maynooth), 18, 1969, 58–75.

O'Meara, Thomas F. "Tillich and Heidegger: A Structural Relationship." *Harvard Theological Review*, 61, 1968, 249–261.

O'Meara, Thomas F. "Heidegger on God." *Continuum*, 5, 1968, 686–698.

Orr, J. "German Social Theory and the Hidden Face of Technology." *European Journal of Sociology* (Paris), 2, 1974, 312–336.

Oshima, S. "Barth's *analogia relationis* and Heidegger's Ontological Difference." *Journal of Religion*, 53, 1973, 176–194.

Oshima, S. "The Ontological Stuructures of Human Existence in Barth and Heidegger. Toward a Theology of Fellowship." *Rice University Studies,* 60 (1), 1974, 103–129.

Ott, Heinrich. "Language and Understanding." *Union Seminary Quarterly Review,* 21, 1966, 275–293.

Palmer, Richard E. "The Postmodernity of Heidegger." *Boundary 2,* IV (2), 1976, 411–432.

Paluch, S. J. "Heidegger's *What is Metaphysics?*" *Philosophy and Phenomenological Research,* 30, 1970, 603–609.

Paluch, S. J. "Heidegger and the 'Scandal of Philosophy.'" *Journal of the British Society for Phenomenology,* 6, 1975, 168–172.

Paskow, Alan. "The Meaning of My Own Death." *International Philosophical Quarterly,* 14, 1974, 51–69.

Paskow, Alan. "What do I Fear Facing My Own Death?" *Man and World,* 8, 1975, 146–156.

Patricca, Nicholas A. "Martin Heidegger's Understanding of Theology." *Listening,* 10, 1975, 59–72.

Philippoussis, J. "Heidegger and Plato's Notion of Truth." *Dialogue,* 15, 1976, 502–504.

Piorkowski, Henry. "The Path of Phenomenology: Husserl, Heidegger, Sartre, Mcrleau-Ponty." *Annual Report of the Duns Scotus Philosophical Association,* 30, 1966, 177–221.

Pöggeler, Otto. "Heidegger Today." *Southern Journal of Philosophy,* 8, 1970, 273–308.

Pöggeler, Otto. " 'Historicity' in Heidegger's Later Work." *Southwestern Journal of Philosophy,* 4, 1973, 53–73.

Pöggeler, Otto. "Being as Appropriation." *Philosophy Today,* 19, 1975, 152–178.

Pöggeler, Otto. "Metaphysics and Topology of Being in Heidegger." *Man and World,* 8, 1975, 3–27, and in this volume, above.

Powell, R. "Has Heidegger Destroyed Metaphysics?" *Listening*, 2, 1967, 52–59.

Rahner, Karl. "The Concept of Existential Philosophy in Heidegger." *Philosophy Today*, 13, 1969, 126–137.

Rather, L. J. "Existential Experience in Whitehead and Heidegger." *Review of Existential Psychology and Psychiatry*, 1, 1961, 113–119.

Reiser, William E. "An Essay on the Development of Dogma in a Heideg-gerian Context: A Non-theological Explanation of Theological Heresy." *Thomist*, 39, 1975, 471–495.

Rice, Ervin K. "Pedagogic Theory and the Search for Being: Denton's Direction in the Epistemology of Education." *Educational Theory*, 25, 1975, 389–396.

Richardson, William J. "Heidegger and the Problem of Thought." *Revue Philosophique de Louvain*, 60, 1962, 58–78.

Richardson, William J. "Heidegger and the Origin of Language." *International Philosophical Quarterly*, 2, 1962, 404–416.

Richardson, William J. "Heidegger and God—and Professor Jonas." *Thought*, 40, 1965, 13–40.

Richardson, William J. "Heidegger and Theology." *Theological Studies*, 26, 1965, 86–100.

Richardson, William J. "The Place of the Unconscious in Heidegger." *Review of Existential Psychology and Psychiatry*, 5, 1965, 265–290.

Richardson, William J. "Heidegger and the Quest for Freedom." *Theological Studies*, 28, 1967, 286–307.

Richardson, William J. "Heidegger's Critique of Science." *New Scholasticism*, 42, 1968, 511–536.

Richardson, William J. "Heidegger and Plato." *Heythrop Journal*, 4, 1963, 273–279.

Richardson, William J. "Heidegger and Aristotle." *Heythrop Journal*, 5, 1964, 58–64.

Richardson, William J. "Martin Heidegger: In Memoriam." *Commonweal,* 104, 7 January 1977, 16-18.

Richardson, William J. "Heidegger's Way Through Phenomenology to the Thinking of Being." *Listening,* 12 (3), 1977, 21-37, and in this volume, above.

Richey, C. W. "On the Intentional Ambiguity of Heidegger's Metaphysics." *Journal of Philosophy,* 55, 1958, 1144-1148.

Ricoeur, Paul. "The Task of Hermeneutics." *Philosophy Today,* 17, 1973, 112-128.

Riddel, Joseph N. "From Heidegger to Derrida: Doubling and (Poetic) Language." *Boundary 2,* IV (2), 1976, 571-592.

Rintelen, F. J. von. "The Existentialism of Martin Heidegger." *Personalist,* 38, 1957, 238-247; 376-382.

Rohatyn, D.A. "A Note on Heidegger and Wittgenstein." *Philosophy Today,* 15, 1971, 69-71.

Rohatyn, D.A. "An Introduction to Heidegger: Truth and Being." *Sapienza* (Rome), 28, 1975, 211-218.

Rollin, Bernard E. "Heidegger's Philosophy of History of *Being and Time.*" *Modern Schoolman,* 49, 1972, 97-112.

Rombach, H. "Reflections on Heidegger's Lecture 'Time and Being.'" *Philosophy Today,* 10, 1960, 19-29.

Rorty, Richard. "Overcoming the Tradition: Heidegger and Dewey." *Review of Metaphysics,* 30, 1976-77, 280-305.

Rosen, S. H. "Curiosity, Anxiety, Wonder." *Giornale di Metafisica* (Torino), 14, 1959, 465-474.

Rosen, S. H. "Heidegger's Interpretation of Plato." *Journal of Existentialism,* 7, 1967, 477-504.

Rosen, S. H. "Philosophy and Ideology: Reflections on Heidegger." *Social Research,* 35, 1968, 260-285.

Rosenfeld, Alvin H. " 'The Being of Language and the Language of Being': Heidegger and Modern Poetics." *Boundary 2,* IV (2), 1976, 535-553.

Rosenstein, Leon. "The Ontological Integrity of the Art Object from the Ludic Point of View." *Journal of Aesthetics and Art Criticism,* 34, 1976, 323–336.

Rotenstreich, Nathan. "The Ontological Status of History." *American Philosophical Quarterly,* 9, 1972, 49–58.

Rotenstreich, Nathan. "Schematics and Freedom." *Revue Internationale de Philosophie* (Bruxelles), 28, 1974, 464–474.

Rukavina, Thomas F. "Being and Things in Heidegger's Philosophy: A Rejoinder." *New Scholasticism,* 33, 1959, 184–201.

Rukavina, Thomas F. "Heidegger's Theory of Being." *New Scholasticism,* 40, 1966, 423–446.

Ryle, Gilbert. "Review of *Sein und Zeit.*" *Mind,* 38, 1929, 355–370.

Ryle, Gilbert. "Martin Heidegger: *Sein und Zeit.*" *Journal of the British Society for Phenomenology,* 1, 1970, 3–13.

Sabatino, Charles J. "Heidegger Commentary: Faith and Human Meaning." *Listening,* 10, 1975, 51–58.

Sallis, John C. "World, Finitude, Temporality in the Philosophy of Martin Heidegger." *Philosophy Today,* 9, 1965, 40–51.

Sallis, John C. "Art within the Limits of Finitude." *International Philosophical Quarterly,* 7, 1967, 285–297.

Sallis, John C. "Language and Reversal." *Southern Journal of Philosophy,* 8, 1970, 381–397.

Sallis, John C. "Towards the Showing of Language." *Southwestern Journal of Philosophy,* 4, 1973, 75–83.

Scanlon, John D. "The *epochē* and Phenomenological Anthropology." *Research in Phenomenology,* 2, 1972, 95–109.

Schacht, Richard L. "Husserlian and Heideggerian Phenomenology." *Philosophical Studies* (Dordrecht), 23, 1972, 293–314.

Schaper, Eva. "Saying and Showing in Heidegger and Wittgenstein." *Journal of the British Society for Phenomenology*, 3, 1972, 36–41.

Scharff, Robert C. "'On 'Existentialist' Readings of Heidegger." *Southwestern Journal of Philosophy*, 2, 1971, 7–20.

Scheler, Max. "Reality and Resistance: On *Being and Time*, Section 43 (1927)." *Listening*, 12 (3), 1977, 61–73, and in this volume, above.

Scheltens, D. "Reflections on Natural Theology." *International Philosophical Quarterly*, 11, 1971, 75–86.

Schimanski, Stefan. "On Meeting a Philosopher." *Partisan Review*, 15, 1948, 506–509.

Schmitt, Richard. "Phenomenology and Metaphysics." *Journal of Philosophy*, 59, 1962, 421–428.

Schmitt, Richard. "Heidegger's Analysis of 'Tool.'" *Monist*, 49, 1965, 70–86.

Schmitt, Richard. "Can Heidegger be Understood?" *Inquiry*, 10, 1967, 53–73.

Schmitz, Kenneth. "Father Richardson, S.J., on Heidegger." *Modern Schoolman*, 44, 1967, 247–259.

Schneider, Herbert W. "Hegel, Heidegger, and 'Experience': A Study in Translation." *Journal of the History of Philosophy*, 10, 1972, 347–350.

Schoenborn, Alexander von. "Heideggerian Everydayness." *Southwestern Journal of Philosophy*, 3, 1972, 103–110.

Schrader, G. A. "Heidegger's Ontology of Human Existence." *Review of Metaphysics*, 10, 1956, 35–36.

Schrader, G.A. "Conditions of Alienation." *Philosophy Forum* (DeKalb), 11, 1972, 341–363.

Schrag, Calvin O. "Phenomenology, Ontology, and History in the Philosophy of Heidegger." *Revue Internationale de Philosophie* (Bruxelles), 12, 1958, 119–132.

Schrag, Calvin O. "Whitehead and Heidegger: Process Philosophy and Existential Philosophy." *Philosophy Today*, 4, 1960, 26–35.

Schrag, Calvin O. "Heidegger and Cassirer on Kant." *Kant-Studien* (Bonn), 58, 1967, 87–100.

Schrag, Calvin O. "Heidegger on Repetition and Historical Understanding." *Philosophy East and West,* 20, 1970, 287–295.

Schrag, Calvin O. "Time and Being in Heidegger." *Modern Schoolman*, 50, 1973, 325–249.

Schrag, Calvin O. "The Transvaluation of Aesthetics and the Work of Art." *Southwestern Journal of Philosophy,* 4, 1973, 109–124.

Schulz, Walter. "God of the Philosophers in Modern Metaphysics." *Man and World,* 6, 1973, 353–371.

Schürmann, Reiner. "Heidegger and Meister Eckhart on Releasement." *Research in Phenomenology,* 3, 1973, 95–119.

Schürmann, Reiner. "Situating René Char: Hölderlin, Heidegger, Char and the 'There Is.'" *Boundary 2,* IV (2), 1976, 513–534.

Schwerer, Armand. "Three Poems: 'The Point,' 'Blood,' 'A Setting Up in the Unconcealed.'" *Boundary 2,* IV (2), 1976, 489–493.

Scott, Charles E. "Heidegger Reconsidered: A Response to Professor Jonas." *Harvard Theological Review,* 59, 1966, 175–185.

Scott, Charles E. "Heidegger, the Absence of God, and Faith." *Journal of Religion,* 46, 1966, 365–373.

Scott, Charles E. "Heidegger's Attempt to Communicate a Mystery." *Philosophy Today,* 10, 1966, 132–141.

Scott, Charles E. "Heidegger and Consciousness." *Southern Journal of Philosophy,* 8, 1970, 355–372.

Scott, Charles E. "Truth Without Dialectic." *Journal of the American Academy of Religion,* 38, 1970, 304–309.

Scott, Charles E. "Heidegger, Madness, and Well-Being." *Southwestern Journal of Philosophy,* 4 (3), 1973, 157–177.

Scott, N.A. "Eliot and the Orphic Way." *Journal of the American Academy of Religion,* 42, 1974, 203–231.

Seeburger, Francis F. "Heidegger and the Phenomenological Reduction." *Philosophy and Phenomenological Research,* 36, 1975, 212–221.

Sefler, George F. "Heidegger's Philosophy of Space." *Philosophy Today,* 17, 1973, 246–254.

Seidel, George J. "Heidegger: Philosopher for Ecologists?" *Man and World,* 4, 1971, 93–99.

Seidel, George J. "Heidegger on Schelling." *Studi Internazionale di Filosofi* (Torino), 6, 1974, 170–174.

Seigfried, Hans. "Descriptive Phenomenology and Constructivism." *Philosophy and Phenomenological Research,* 37, 1976–77, 248–261.

Sendaydiego, Henry B. "Heideggerian Metaphysics, Logic and Emotion-ism." *Journal of the West Virginia Philosophical Society,* V, 1973, 14–17.

Sendaydiego, Henry B. "Applying Heidegger's '*Entschlossenheit*' to a Political Matrix." *Journal of the West Virginia Philosophical Society,* VI, 1974, 15–17.

Sendaydiego, Henry B. "Heidegger's Thoughts on the Aesthetic." *Journal of the West Virginia Philosophical Society,* X, 1976, 14–16.

Sendaydiego, Henry B. "Heidegger on the Teaching-Learning Process." *Journal of the West Virginia Philosophical Society,* XI, 1976, 23–26.

Seyppel, J. H. "The Comparative Study of Truth in Existentialism and Pragmatism." *Journal of Philosophy,* 50, 1953, 229–241.

Seyppel, J. H. "A Criticism of Heidegger's Time Concept with Reference to Bergson's *durée.*" *Revue Internationale de Philosophie* (Bruxelles), 10, 1956, 503–508.

Shearson, William A. "The Common Assumptions of Existential Philosophy." *International Philosophical Quarterly,* 15, 1975, 131–147.

Sheehan, Thomas. "Heidegger: From Beingness to the Time-Being." *Listening,* 8, 1973, 17–31.

Sheehan, Thomas. "Notes on a lovers' quarrel: Heidegger and Aquinas." *Listening,* 9, 1974, 137–143.

Sheehan, Thomas. "Heidegger, Aristotle, and Phenomenology." *Philosophy Today,* 19, 1975, 87–94.

Sheehan, Thomas. "Heidegger's Early Years: Fragments for a Philosophical Biography." *Listening,* 12 (3), 1977, 3–20, and in this volume.

Sheehan, Thomas. "Getting to the Topic: The New Edition of *Wegmarken.*" *Research in Phenomenology,* 7, 1977, 299–316.

Shepard, L. A. "Verbal Victory and Existential Anguish." *Philosophical Journal,* 6, 1969, 95–111.

Sherover, Charles M. "Heidegger's Ontology and the Copernican Revolution." *Monist,* 51, 1967, 559–573.

Sherover, Charles M. "Kant's Transcendental Object and Heidegger's *Nichts.*" *Journal of the History of Philosophy,* 7, 1969, 413–422.

Shouery, Imad. "Phenomenological Analysis of Waiting." *Modern Schoolman,* 50, 1973, 159–182.

Shmueli, Efraim. "Contemporary Philosophical Theories and Their Relation to Science and Technology." *Philosophy in Context,* 4, 1975, 37–60.

Sikora, J. J. "Articulation in Being and Consciousness." *Science et Esprit* (Montreal), 21, 1969, 231–251.

Silverman, Hugh J. "Man and Self as Identity of Difference." *Philosophy Today,* 19, 1975, 131–136.

Slote, Michael A. "Existentialism and the Fear of Dying." *American Philosophical Quarterly.* 12, 1975, 17–28.

Smith, F. Joseph. "The Meaning of the 'Way' in Heidegger." *American Church Quarterly,* 3, 1962, 89–102.

Smith, F. Joseph. "Insights Leading to a Phenomenology of Sound." *Southern Journal of Philosophy,* 5, 1967, 187–199.

Smith, F. Joseph. "Heidegger's Kant Interpretation." *Philosophy Today,* 11, 1967, 257–264.

Smith, F, Joseph. "Further Insights Leading to a Phenomenology of Sound." *Journal of Value Inquiry,* 3, 1969, 136–146.

Smith, F. Joseph. "Two Heideggerian Analyses." *Southern Journal of Philosophy,* 8, 1970, 409–421.

Smith, F. Joseph. "A Critique of Martin Heidegger." *Southwestern Journal of Philosophy,* 4, 1973, 137–156.

Smith, James L. "Nihilism and the Arts." *Journal of Aesthetics and Art Criticism,* 33, 1975, 329–338.

Smith, Joseph H. "The Heideggerian and Psychoanalytic Concepts of Mood." *Human Inquiries,* 10, 1970, 101–111.

Smith, Christopher P. "Heidegger, Hegel, and the Problem of *das Nichts.*" *International Philosophical Quarterly,* 8, 1968, 379–405.

Smith, Christopher P. "Heidegger's Critique of Absolute Knowledge." *New Scholasticism,* 45, 1971, 56–86.

Smith, Christopher P. "Heidegger's Break with Nietzsche and the Principle of Subjectivity." *Modern Schoolman,* 52, 1975, 227–248.

Smith, Christopher P. "A Poem of Rilke: Evidence for the Later Heidegger." *Philosophy Today,* 21, 1977, 250–262.

Smith, V.E. "Existentialism and Existence." *Thomist,* 11, 1948, 160–171.

Smolko, John F. "Philosophy and Theology." *Proceedings of the American Catholic Philosophical Association,* 44, 1970, 31–45.

Sontag, F. "Heidegger and the Problem of Metaphysics." *Philosophy and Phenomenological Research,* 24, 1964, 410–416.

Sontag, F. "Heidegger, Time and God." *Journal of Religion,* 47, 1967, 279–294.

Spanos, William V. "Heidegger, Kierkegaard, and the Hermeneutic Circle: Towards a Postmodern Theory of Interpretation and Dis-closure." *Boundary 2,* IV (2), 1976, 455–488.

Spanos, William V. "Martin Heidegger and Literature: A Preface." *Boundary 2,* IV, (2), 1976, 337–339.

Spiegelberg, Herbert. "From Husserl to Heidegger." *Journal of the British Society for Phenomenology,* 1, 1973, 58–62; 77–83.

Stack, George J. "Concern in Heidegger and Kierkegaard." *Philosophy Today,* 13, 1969, 26–35.

Stack, George J. "The Being of the Work of Art in Heidegger." *Philosophy Today,* 13, 1969, 159–173.

Stack, George J. "Human Possibility." *Idealistic Studies,* 2, 1972, 1–15.

Stack, George J. "Existence and Possibility." *Laval Théologique et Philosophique* (Quebec), 28, 1972, 149–170.

Stack, George J. "The Language of Possibility and Existential Possibility." *Modern Schoolman,* 50, 1973, 159–182.

Stack, George J. "Heidegger's Concept of Meaning." *Philosophy Today,* 17, 1973, 255–266.

Stahl, Gerry. "Attuned to Being: Heideggerian Music in Technological Society." *Boundary 2,* IV (2), 1976, 637–664.

Stambaugh, Joan. "Commentary on Takeski Umehara's 'Heidegger and Buddhism.'" *Philosophy East and West,* 20, 1970, 283–286.

Stambaugh, Joan. "Time and Dialectic in Hegel and Heidegger." *Research in Phenomenology,* 4, 1974, 87–97.

Stambaugh, Joan. "A Heidegger Primer." *Philosophy Today,* 19, 1975, 79–86.

Steffney, J. "Heidegger and Buber: Ontology and Philosophical Anthropology." *Religion in Life,* 43, 1974, 33–41.

Steffney, J. "Transmetaphysical Thinking in Heidegger and Zen Buddhism." *Philosophy East and West,* 27, 1977, 323–335.

Stern, G. "On the Pseudo-Concreteness of Heidegger's Philosophy." *Philosophy and Phenomenological Research,* 9, 1948, 200–211.

Stewart, David. "Heidegger and the Greening of Philosophy." *Southwestern Journal of Philosophy,* 6, 1975, 15–19.

Strasser, Steven. "The Concept of Dread in the Philosophy of Heidegger." *Modern Schoolman,* 35, 1957, 1–20.

Stratton, Jon D. "Identity and Difference as *Austrag:* Hegel and Heidegger." *Kinesis,* 3, 1971, 81–92.

Strauss, Leo. "Philosophy as Rigorous Science and Political Philosophy." *Interpretation,* 2, 1971, 1–9.

Stulberg, Robert J. "Heidegger and the Origin of the Work of Art." *Journal of Aesthetics and Art Criticism,* 32, 1973, 257–265.

Sturm, F. G. "Authenticity and Other Persons." *Christian Century,* 80, 1963, 340–342.

Symposium: Martin Heidegger. (American Philosophical Association, Eastern Division). *Journal of Philosophy,* 60, 1963, 651–684.

Taubes, Susan A. "The Gnostic Foundations of Heidegger's Nihilism." *Journal of Religion,* 34, 1954, 155–172.

Thomas, J. H. "Immortality and Humanism (Existentialism)." *Modern Churchman,* 3, 1959, 33–40.

Thulstrup, N. K. E. "Logstrup's Comparison Between Kierkegaard and Heidegger." *Theology Today,* 12, 1955, 303–305.

Tiebout, Harry M. "Subjectivity in Whitehead: A Comment on Whitehead and Heidegger." *Dialectica,* 13, 1959, 350–353.

Til, C. van. "The Later Heidegger and Theology." *Westminster Theological Review,* 26, 1964, 121–161.

Tillich, Paul. "Existential Philosophy." *Journal of the History of Ideas,* 5, 1944, 44–70.

Times Literary Supplement. "Philosopher of Frustration." *London Times Literary Supplement,* 21 December 1962, 13.

Tint, H. "Heidegger and the 'Irrational.'" *Proceedings of the Aristotelian Society,* 57, 1956–57, 235–268.

Tollenaere, M. de. "Immortality: A Reflective Exploration." *International Philosophical Quarterly,* 10, 1970, 556–569.

Tracy, David. "A Response and Commentary (to Patricca and Sabatino)." *Listening,* 10, 1975, 73–77.

Tranoy, K. "Contemporary Philosophy: Analytic and Continental." *Philosophy Today,* 8, 1964, 155–168.

Trivers, H. "Heidegger's Misinterpretation of Hegel's Views on Spirit and Time." *Philosophy and Phenomenological Research,* 3, 1942, 162–168.

Troutner, Leroy F. "The Confrontation Between Experimentalism and Existentialism, from Dewey to Heidegger and Beyond." *Proceedings: Philosophy of Education,* 24, 1968, 186–194.

Troutner, Leroy F. "The Dewey-Heidegger Comparison Re-Visited: A Reply and Comparison." *Proceedings: Philosophy of Education,* 27, 1971, 213–224.

Troutner, Leroy F. "The Dewey-Heidegger Comparison Re-Visited: A Perspectival Partnership for Education." *Proceedings: Philosophy of Education,* 28, 1972, 28–44.

Troutner, Leroy F. "Toward a Phenomenology of Education: An Exercise in the Foundations." *Proceedings: Philosophy of Education,* 30, 1974, 148–164.

Turnbull, R. G. "Heidegger on the Nature of Truth." *Journal of Philosophy,* 54, 1957, 559–565.

Umehara, Takeshi, "Heidegger and Buddhism." *Philosophy East and West,* 20, 1970, 515–520.

Vail, Loy M. "Heidegger's Conception of Philosophy." *New Scholasticism,* 42, 1968, 470–496.

Vandenberg, Donald. "Who is 'Pseudo?' " *Educational Theory,* 24, 1974, 183–193.

Vandenberg, Donald. "Reply to Wingertner's 'Reply to Vandenberg's "Not Who but What is 'Pseudo'?' " *Educational Theory,* 25, 1975, 202.

Van de Pitte, F. P. "The Role of Hölderlin in the Philosophy of Heidegger." *Personalist,* 43, 1962, 168–179.

Van Kaam, Adrian. "Clinical Implications of Heidegger's Concept of Will, Decision and Responsibility." *Review of Existential Psychology and Psychiatry,* 1, 1961, 205–216.

Vater, Michael G. "Heidegger and Schelling: The Finitude of Being." *Idealistic Studies*, 5, 1975, 20–58.

Versényi, Laszlo. "The Quarrel Between Philosophy and Poetry." *The Philosophical Forum* (Boston), 2, 1970–71, 200–212.

Vick, George R. "Heidegger's Linguistic Rehabilitation of Parmenides' Being." *American Philosophical Quarterly*, 8, 1970, 139–150.

Vick, George R. "The New 'Copernican Revolution.'" *Personalist*, 52, 1971, 630–642.

Vietta, Egon. "Being, World, and Understanding. A Comment on Heidegger." *Review of Metaphysics*, 5, 1951–52, 157–172.

Walsh, J. H. "Heidegger's Understanding of No-thingness." *Cross Currents*, 13, 1963, 305–323.

Warnock, Mary. "Packaged Inauthenticity." *New Society*, 22 July 1971, 159.

Water, Lambert van de. "The Work of Art, Man and Being: A Heideggerian Theme." *International Philosophical Quarterly*, 9, 1969, 214–235.

Water, Lambert van de. "Being and Being Human: An Impasse in Heidegger's Thought?" *International Philosophical Quarterly*, 13, 1973, 391–402.

Watson, James R. "Heidegger's Hermeneutic Phenomenology." *Philosophy Today*, 15, 1971, 30–43.

Watson, James R. "Being . . . There: The Neighborhood of Being." *Philosophy Today*, 19, 1975, 118–130.

Weber, Renée. "A Critique of Heidegger's Concept of Solicitude." *New Scholasticism*, 42, 1968, 537–560.

Weiler, Gershon. "On Heidegger's Notion of Philosophy." *Hermathena* (Dublin), 93, 1959, 16–25.

Weiss, H. "The Greek Conception of Time and Being in the Light of Heidegger's Philosophy." *Philosophy and Phenomenological Research*, 2, 1941, 173–187.

Welch, Cyril. "Commentary on '*Ontologie du Signifier*' (Rioux)." *Man and World*, 4, 1971, 258–261.

Weldhen, Margaret. "The Existentialists and Problems of Moral and Religious Education." *Journal of Moral Education,* 1, 1971, 19–26.

Welte, Bernhard. "Seeking and Finding: The Speech at Heidegger's Burial." *Listening,* 12 (3), 1977, 106–109, and in this volume, above.

Werkmeister, W. H. "An Introduction to Heidegger's 'Existential Philosophy.'" *Philosophy and Phenomenological Research,* 2, 1941, 79–87.

Werkmeister, W.H. "Heidegger and the Poets." *Personalist,* 52, 1971, 5–22.

White, David A. "World and Earth in Heidegger's Aesthetics." *Philosophy Today,* 12, 1968, 282–286.

White, David A. "Revealment: A Meeting of Extremes in Aesthetics." *Journal of Aesthetics and Art Criticism.*" 28, 1970, 515–520.

White, David A. "Truth and Being: A Critique of Heidegger on Plato." *Man and World,* 7, 1974, 118–134.

White, David A. "A Refutation of Heidegger as Nihilist." *Personalist,* 56, 1975, 278–288.

Wienpahl, P. D. "Philosophy and Nothing." *Chicago Review,* 13, 1959, 59–74.

Wild, John. "The New Empiricism and Human Time." *Review of Metaphysics,* 7, 1953–54, 537–557.

Wild, John. "An English Version of Martin Heidegger's *Being and Time.*" *Review of Metaphysics,* 16, 1962–63, 296–315.

Wild, John. "The Philosophy of Martin Heidegger." *Journal of Philosophy,* 60, 1963, 664–677.

Wild, John. "Being and Time: A Reply." *Review of Metaphysics,* 17, 1964, 610–616.

Wild, John. "'Being,' Meaning and the World." *Review of Metaphysics,* 18, 1965, 411–429.

Will, Frederic. "William James and Existential Authenticity (James — Heidegger)." *Personalist,* 43, 1962, 157–167.

Williams, John R. "Heidegger and the Theologians." *Heythrop Journal,* 12, 1971, 258-280.

Williams, John R. "Heidegger, Death, and God." *Studies in Religion (Sciences Religieuses)* (Toronto), 1, 1970, 298-320.

Wingerter, J. Richard. "Pseudo-Existential Writings on Education." *Educational Theory,* 24, 1974, 291-296.

Winter, Gibson. "Human Science and Ethics in a Creative Society." *Cultural Hermeneutics,* 2, 1973, 145-174.

Wolz, Henry G. "The Paradox of Piety in Plato's *Euthyphro* in the Light of Heidegger's Conception of Authenticity." *Southern Journal of Philosophy,* 12, 1974, 493-511.

Wren, Thomas E. "Heidegger's Philosophy of History." *Journal of the British Society for Phenomenology,* 3, 1972, 111-125.

Wurzer, William Stefan. "Nietzsche's Dialectic of Intellectual Integrity: A Propaedeutic." *Southern Journal of Philosophy,* 13, 1975, 235-245.

Wyschogrod, Michael. "Heidegger's Ontology and Human Existence." *Diseases of the Nervous System,* 22 (4), 1961, 50-56.

Zimmerman, Michael E. "Heidegger, Ethics and National Socialism." *Southwestern Journal of Philosophy,* 5, 1974, 97-105.

Zimmerman, Michael E. "The Foundering of *Being and Time.*" *Philosophy Today,* 19, 1975, 100-107.

Zimmerman, Michael E. "Heidegger on Nihilism and Technique." *Man and World,* 8, 1975, 394-414.

Zimmerman, Michael E. "On Discriminating Everydayness, Unownedness, and Falling in *Being and Time.*" *Research in Phenomenology,* 5, 1975, 109-127.

Zimmerman, Michael E. "The Unity and Sameness of the Self as Depicted in *Being and Time.*" *Journal of the British Society for Phenomenology,* 6, 1975, 157-167.

Zimmerman, Michael E. "A Comparison of Nietzsche's Overman and Heidegger's Authentic Self." *Southern Journal of Philosophy,* 14, 1976, 213-231.

Zimmerman, Michael E. "Heidegger's New Conception of Authentic Selfhood." *Personalist,* 57, 1976, 198–212.

Zimmerman, Michael E. "Beyond 'Humanism': Heidegger's Understanding of Technology." *Listening,* 12 (3), 1977, 74–83, and in this volume.

Zuidma, S. U. "The Idea of Revelation with Karl Barth and with Martin Heidegger. The Comparability of Their Patterns of Thought." *Free University Quarterly,* 4, 1955, 71–84.

B. Collections of Essays on Heidegger.
Abbreviations in parentheses following the titles in this section are keyed to some articles in Section C, below.

Ballard, Edward G. and Scott, Charles E. (eds.) *Martin Heidegger: In Europe and America* (HEA). The Hague: Martinus Nijhoff, 1973.

Frings, Manfred S. (ed.) *Heidegger and the Quest for Truth* (HQT). Chicago, Quadrangle Books, 1968.

Kockelmans, Joseph J. (ed.) *On Heidegger and Language* (HL). Evanston: Northwestern University Press, 1972.

Robinson, J. M. and Cobb, B. J. (eds.) *The Later Heidegger and Theology* (LHT). New York: Harper and Row, 1962.

Sallis, John C. (ed.) *Heidegger and the Path of Thinking* (HPT). Pittsburgh: Duquesne University Press, 1970.

C. Articles in Heidegger Collections [B].

Adamczewski, Zygmunt. "On the Way to Being." In *HPT,* 1970, 12–36.

Alderman, Harold. "The Work of Art and Other Things." In *HEA,* 1973, 157–170.

Aler, J. "Heidegger's Conception of Language in *Being and Time.*" In *HL,* 1972, 33–62.

Anderson, J. M. "Truth, Process, and Creature in Heidegger's Thought." In *HQT,* 1968, 28–61.

Ballard, Edward G. "Heidegger's View and Evaluation of Nature and Natural Science." In *HPT,* 1970, 37–64.

Biemel, Walter. "Poetry and Language in Heidegger." In *HL,* 1972, 147–168.

Boelen, Bernard J. "The Question of Ethics in the Thought of Martin Heidegger." In *HQT,* 1968, 76–105.

Borgmann, Albert. "Heidegger and Symbolic Logic." In *HQT,* 1968, 139–162.

Brock, Werner. "Introduction: A Brief Outline of the Career of Martin Heidegger. Account of *Being and Time.* Account of the four essays ("On the Essence of Truth," "Hölderlin and the Essence of Poetry," "Remembrance of the Poet," "What is Metaphysics?"). In Martin Heidegger. *Existence and Being,* Chicago: Regnery, 1949, 13–248.

Cobb, John B. "Is the Later Heidegger Relevant for Theology?" In *LHT,* 1962, 177–197.

Gray, J. Glenn. "Introduction." In Martin Heidegger's *What is Called Thinking?,* New York: Harper and Row, 1968, xii–xxvii.

Keyes, C. D. "Truth as Art. An Interpretation of Heidegger's *Sein und Zeit* (Section 44) and *'Der Ursprung des Kunstwerkes.'*" In *HPT,* 1970, 65–84.

Kisiel, Theodore. "The Language of the Event: The Event of Language." In *HPT,* 1970, 85–104.

Kisiel, Theodore. "The Mathematical and the Hermeneutical: On Heidegger's Notion of the *a priori.*" In *HEA,* 1973, 109–120.

Kockelmans, Joseph J. "Ontological Difference, Hermeneutics, and Language." In *HL,* 1972, 195–234.

Krell, David Farrell. "The Question of Being (General Introduction)." In Martin Heidegger. *Basic Writings,* New York: Harper and Row, 1977, 3–35.

Langan, Thomas. "The Problem of the Thing." In *HPT,* 1970, 105–115.

Lingis, Alphonso. "On the Essence of Technique." In *HQT,* 1968, 126–138.

Lohman, J. "Martin Heidegger's 'Ontological Difference' and Language." In *HL*, 1972, 303–363.

Lovitt, William. "Introduction." In Martin Heidegger. *The Question Concerning Technology and Other Essays*, New York: Harper and Row, 1977, xiii–xxxix.

Marx, Werner. "The World in Another Beginning: Poetic Dwelling and the Role of the Poet." In *HL*, 1972, 235–259.

Ott, Heinrich. "Hermeneutic and Personal Structure of Language." In *HL*, 1972, 169–193.

Pöggeler, Otto. "Heidegger's Topology of Being." In *HL*, 1972, 107–146.

Powell, R. "The Later Heidegger's Omission of the Ontic-Ontological Structure of Dasein." In *HPT*, 1970, 116–137.

Ricoeur, Paul. "The Critique of Subjectivity and the *cogito* in the Philosophy of Heidegger." In *HQT*, 1968, 511–536.

Robinson, James M. "The German Discussion of the Later Heidegger." In *LHT*, 1962, 3–76.

Sallis, John C. "Toward the Movement of Reversal: Science, Technology, and the Language of Homecoming." In *HPT*, 1970, 138–168.

Schöfer, E. "Heidegger's Language: Metalogical Forms of Thought and Grammatical Specialties." In *HL*, 1972, 281–301.

Schoenborn. Alexander von. "Heidegger's Question: An Exposition." In *HEA*, 1973, 47–54.

Schrag, Calvin O. "Introduction." In Edmund Husserl, *Phenomenology of Internal Time-Consciousness*, Bloomington: Indiana University Press, 1964, 9–13.

Schrag, Calvin O. "Rethinking Metaphysics." In *HQT*, 1968, 106–125.

Schuwer, André. "Prolegomena to 'Time and Being': Truth and Time." In *HPT*, 1970, 169–190.

Smith, F. Joseph. "In-the-World and On-the-Earth: A Heideggerian Interpretation." In *HQT*, 1968, 184–203.

Tymieniecka, A.-T. "Cosmos, Nature and Man, and the Foundations of Psychiatry." In *HPT,* 1970, 191–220.

Volkmann-Schluck, K.-H. "The Problem of Language." In *HEA,* 1973, 121–128.

Wild, John. "Heidegger and the Existential *a priori.*" In *HPT,* 1970, 221–234.

D. Essays and Articles in Non-Heidegger Collections.

Barrett, William. "Dialogue on Anxiety." In *The New Partisan Reader 1945–1953.* (Phillips, W. *et. al.,* eds.) New York: Harcourt, Brace, 1953, 221–229.

Barrett, William. Introduction, Part Four, "Phenomenology and Existentialism." In *Philosophy in the Twentieth Century* II (W. Barrett and H. Aiken, eds.), New York: Random House, 1962, 125–169.

Barrett, William. "The Flow of Time." In *The Philosophy of Time. A Collection of Critical Essays* (Gale, R. M., ed.), Garden City, N.Y.: Doubleday/Anchor Books, 1967, 354–376.

Binswanger, Ludwig. "Heidegger's Analytic of Existence and its Meaning for Psychiatry." In Ludwig Binswanger. *Being-in-the-World,* New York: Harper and Row, 1968, 206–221.

Boelen, Bernard J. "Heidegger as a Phenomenologist." In *Phenomenological Perspectives* (Bossert, P. J., ed.), The Hague: Martinus Nijhoff, 1975, 93–114.

Blackham, H. J. "Martin Heidegger." In H. J. Blackham. *Six Existentialist Thinkers,* London: Routledge, Kegan Paul, 1952, 86–109.

Brock, Werner. "Present Day Philosophy." In Werner Brock. *Introduction to Contemporary Philosophy,* New York: Cambridge University Press, 1935, 87–118.

Bruns, G. L. "Poetry as Reality: The Orpheus Myth and its Modern Counterparts." In G. L. Bruns. *Modern Poetry and the Idea of Language,* New Haven: Yale University Press, 1974, 206–231.

Calas, N. "Truth and Albert Hofstadter." In N. Calas. *Art in the Age of Risk, and Other Essays,* New York: E. P. Dutton, 1968, 121–125.

Derrida, Jacques. "*Ousia* and *grammē:* A Note to a Footnotes in *Being and Time.*" In *Phenomenology in Perspective* (Smith, F., ed.) The Hague: Martinus Nijhoff, 1970, 54–93.

Dreyfus, H. L. and Todes, S. "The Existential Critique of Objectivity: Kierkegaard, Nietzsche, and Heidegger." In *Patterns of the Life-World* (Edie, J., ed.) Evanston: Northwestern University Press, 1971, 346–381.

Edwards, Paul. "Existentialism and Death: A Survey of Some Confusions and Absurdities." In *Philosophy, Science and Method* (Morgenbesser, S. *et al.*, eds.), New York: St. Martins Press, 1969, 473–507.

Frings, Manfred S. "Max Scheler: Focusing on Rarely Seen Complexities of Phenomenology." In *Phenomenology in Perspective* (Smith, F., ed.), The Hague: Martinus Nijhoff, 1970, 54–93.

Gray, J. Glenn. "The New Image of Man in Martin Heidegger's Philosophy." In *European Philosophy Today* (Kline, T., ed.), New York: Quadrangle, 1965, 31–60.

Gray, J. Glenn. "Poets and Thinkers: Their Kindred Roles in the Philosophy of Martin Heidegger." In *Phenomenology and Existentialism* (Lee, E. N. *et al.*, eds.), Baltimore: Johns Hopkins Press, 1967, 93–111.

Grene, Marjorie G. "Sartre and Heidegger: The Free Resolve." In Marjorie G. Grene, *Dreadful Freedom* (1959: *Introduction to Existentialism*), Chicago: University of Chicago Press, 1948, 41–66.

Grene, Marjorie G. "Heidegger's Return to Being." In *Ibid.,* 1948, 67–94.

Grene, Marjorie G. "A Note on the Philosophy of Heidegger: Confessions of a Young Positivist." In Marjorie G. Grene, *Philosophy In and Out of Europe*, Berkeley: University of California Press, 1976, 38–49.

Grene, Marjorie G. "The German Existentialists." In *Ibid.,* 1976.

Hartshorne, Charles. "Croce, Heidegger, and Hartmann." (1937) In Charles Hartshorne, *Beyond Humanism,* Lincoln: University of Nebraska Press, 1968, 298–311.

Henry, J. "The Term 'Primitive' in Kierkegaard and Heidegger." In *The Concept of the Primitive* (Montagu, A., ed.), New York: Free Press, 1968, 212–228.

Jaeger, Hans. "Heidegger's Existential Philosophy and Modern German Literature." In Hans Jaeger, *Essays on German Literature 1935-1962,* Bloomington: Indiana University Press, 1968, 103–136.

Jaeger, Hans. "Heidegger and the Work of Art." In *Ibid.,* 1968, 137–158.

Johnstone, H. W. "Rhetoric and Communication in Philosophy." In *Contemporary Philosophic Thought* III (Kiefer, H. E. *et al.,* eds.), Albany: State University of New York Press, 1970, 351–364.

Kaelin, E. F. "Notes Toward an Understanding of Heidegger's Aesthetics." In *Phenomenology and Existentialism* (Lee, E. N. *et al.,* eds.), Baltimore: Johns Hopkins Press, 1967, 59–92.

Kaufmann, Walter. "Heidegger's Castle." In Walter Kaufmann, *From Shakespeare to Existentialism: Studies in Poetry, Religion, and Philosophy,* Boston: Beacon Press, 1959, 302–330.

Kersten, Fred. "Heidegger and the History of 'Platonism.'" In *Der Idealismus und Seine Gegenwart* (Guzzoni, A. *et al.,* eds.), Hamburg: F. Meiner, 1976, 272–296.

Kisiel, Theodore. "Phenomenology as the Science of Sciences." In *Phenomenology and the Natural Sciences* (Kockelmans, J. and Kisiel, T., eds), Evanston: Northwestern University Press, 1970, 5–44.

Kisiel, Theodore. "Science, Phenomenology and the Thinking of Being." In *Ibid.,* 1970, 167–183.

Kockelmans, Joseph J. "Heidegger on the Essential Difference and Necessary Relation Between Philosophy and Science." In *Ibid.,* 1970, 147–166.

Kockelmans, Joseph J. "Language, Meaning and Ek-sistence." In *Phenomenology in Perspective* (Smith, F., ed.), The Hague: Martinus Nijhoff, 1970, 94–121.

Langan, Thomas. "Two German Existentialists." In *Recent Philosophy, Hegel to the Present* (Gilson, E. H., ed.), New York: Random House, 1966, 145–168.

Langan, Thomas. "The Future of Phenomenology." In *Phenomenology in Perspective* (Smith, F., ed.), The Hague: Martinus Nijhoff, 1970, 1–15.

Lynch, Lawrence. "Martin Heidegger: Language and Being." In *An Étienne Gilson Tribute* (O'Neill), Milwaukee: Marquette University Press, 1959, 135–147.

Moenkenmeyer, H. "Martin Heidegger." In *Existential Thinkers and Thought* (Patka, F. E., ed.), New York: Philosophical Library, 1962, 93–110.

Needleman, Jacob. "A Critical Introduction to Ludwig Binswanger's Existential Psychoanalysis (1963)." In Ludwig Binswanger, *Being-in-the-World,* New York: Harper and Row, 1968, viii–xx; 1–145.

Nielsen, Niels. "Zen Buddhism and the Philosophy of Martin Heidegger (1958)." In *Filosophie Orientale e Pensiero Occidentale* [X], Florence: Sansoni, 1960, 131–137.

Passmore, J. A. "Existentialism and Phenomenology." In J. A. Passmore. *A Hundred Years of Philosophy* (2nd ed.), New York: Basic Books, 1966, 476–516.

Prufer, T. "Martin Heidegger: Dasein and the Ontological Status of the Speaker of Philosophical Discourse." In *Twentieth Century Thinkers* (Ryan, J. K., ed.), Staten Island: Alba House, 1965, 159–173.

Richardson, William J. "Kant and the Late Heidegger." In *Phenomenology in America* (Edie, J., ed.), Chicago: Quadrangle, 1967, 125–147.

Richardson, William J. "Being for Longeran: A Heideggerian View." In *Language, Truth, and Meaning* (McShane, P., ed.), Notre Dame: University of Notre Dame Press, 1970, 272–283.

Roberts, D. E. "Heidegger." In D. E. Roberts. *Existentialism and Religious Belief,* New York: Oxford University Press, 1959 (1957), 145–191.

Shapiro, Meyer. "The Still Life and Personal Object—A Note on Heidegger and Van Gogh." In Marianne L. Simmel, *The Reach of Mind: Essays in Memory of Kurt Goldstein,* New York: Springer, 1969, 203–209.

Sherover, Charles. "Heidegger and the Reconstruction of the Kantian Ethic (summary)." In *Akten des XIV. Internationales für Philosophie* (1968), Vienna: Herder, 1970, 527–534.

Smith, V. E. "Heidegger's Return to Being." In V. E. Smith, *Idea-Men of Today,* Milwaukee: Bruce Publishing Company, 1950, 265–287.

Smith, F. Joseph. "Being and Subjectivity: Heidegger and Husserl." In *Phenomenology in Perspective* (Smith, F., ed.), The Hague: Martinus Nijhoff, 1970, 122–156.

Spiegelberg, Herbert. "Martin Heidegger." In Herbert Spiegelberg, *The Phenomenological Movement* I (2nd ed.) (*Phaenomenologica*, 6), The Hague: Martinus Nijhoff, 1960, 271–357.

Spiegelberg, Herbert. "On Some Human Uses of Phenomenology." In *Phenomenology in Perspective* (Smith, F., ed.), The Hague: Martinus Nijhoff, 1970, 16–31.

Troutner, Leroy F. "John Dewey and the Existential Phenomenologist." In *Existentialism and Phenomenology in Education: Collected Essays* (Denton, E., ed.), New York: Teachers College Press, 1974, 9–50.

Troutner, Leroy F. "Time and Education." In *Ibid.*, 1974, 159–181.

Warnock, Mary. "Existentialist Ethics." In *New Studies in Ethics* II (Hudson, ed.), New York: St. Martins Press, 1974, 397–464.

Werkmeister, W. H. "Hegel and Heidegger." In *New Studies in Hegel's Philosophy* (Steinkraus, ed.), New York: Holt, Rinehart and Winston, 1971, 142–155.

Will, F. "Heidegger and the Gods of Poetry." In F. Will, *Literature Inside Out,* Cleveland: Western Reserve University Press, 1966, 25–35.

E. Book Length Studies of Heidegger.

Biemel, Walter. *Martin Heidegger: An Illustrated Study.* New York: Harcourt, Brace, Jovanovich, 1976 (1973).

Cousineau, Robert Henri. *Humanism and Ethics: An Introduction to Heidegger's "Letter on Humanism," with a Critical Bibilography.* Paris: Béatrice-Nauwelaerts, 1972.

Deely, John N. *The Tradition Via Heidegger: An Essay on the Meaning of Being in the Philosophy of Martin Heidegger.* New York: Humanities Press, 1972.

Demske, J. M. *Being, Man and Death: A Key to Heidegger.* Lexington: University Press of Kentucky, 1970 (1963).

Gelven, Michael. *A Commentary on Heidegger's "Being and Time": A Section-by-Section Interpretation.* New York: Harper and Row, 1970.

Grene, Marjorie. *Martin Heidegger.* New York: Hillary House, 1957.

King, Magda. *Heidegger's Philosophy: A Guide to His Basic Thought.* New York: Dell, 1964.

Kockelmans, Joseph J. *Martin Heidegger: A First Introduction to His Philosophy.* Pittsburgh: Duquesne University Press, 1965.

Langan, Thomas. *The Meaning of Heidegger: A Critical Study of an Existentialist Phenomenology.* New York: Columbia University Press, 1959.

Macomber, W. B. *The Anatomy of Disillusion: Martin Heidegger's Notion of Truth.* Evanston: Northwestern University Press, 1967.

Macquarrie, John. *Martin Heidegger.* Richmond: John Knox Press, 1968.

Magnus, Berd. *Heidegger's Metahistory of Philosophy:* Amor Fati, *Being and Truth.* Atlantic Highlands: Humanities Press, 1970.

Marx, Werner. *Heidegger and the Tradition.* Evanston: Northwestern University Press, 1971 (1961).

McCormick, Peter J. *Heidegger and the Language of the World: An Argumentative Reading of the Late Heidegger's Meditations on Language.* Ottowa: University of Ottowa Press, 1976.

Mehta, J. L. *The Philosophy of Martin Heidegger.* New York: Harper and Row, 1971 (1967).

Perotti, James L. *Heidegger and the Divine: The Thinker, the Poet, and God.* Athens (Ohio): Ohio University Press, 1974.

Powell, R. A. *Heidegger's Retreat from the Transcultural Structure of Dasein.* Chicago: St. Xavier College Press, 1966.

Richardson, William J. *Heidegger: Through Phenomenology to Thought (Phaenomenologica, 13).* The Hague: Martinus Nijoff, 1967 (1963).

Schmitt, Richard. *Martin Heidegger on Being Human: An Introduction to "Sein und Zeit."* New York: Random House, 1969.

Seidel, George J. *Heidegger and the Pre-Socratics.* Lincoln: University of Nebraska Press, 1964.

Skirbekk, Gunnar. *Truth and Preconditions Approached Via an Analysis of Heidegger.* Bergen: Verlag Universitat i Bergen, 1972.

Vakakethala, Francis J. *Discovery of Being*. Bangalore: Dharmaran College Press, 1970.

Vail, L. M. *Heidegger and the Ontological Difference*. University Park: Pennsylvania State University Press, 1972.

Versenyi, Laszlo. *Heidegger, Being and Truth*. New Haven: Yale University Press, 1965.

Vycinas, Vincent. *Earth and Gods: An Introduction to the Philosophy of Martin Heidegger*. The Hague: Martinus Nijhoff, 1961.

F. Comparative and Related Studies: Heidegger, Phenomenology, Existentialism.

Abbagnano, N. *Critical Existentialism*. Garden City: Doubleday/Anchor Books, 1969.

Anderson, James F. *The Bond of Being*. New York: Greenwood Press, 1969.

Barrett, William. *What is Existentialism?* New York: Grove Press, 1964 (1947).

Barrett, William. *Irrational Man: A Study in Existential Philosophy*. Garden City: Doubleday Anchor, 1958.

Barnes, W. *Philosophy and Literature of Existentialism*. Woodbury: Barron's Educational Service, 1968.

Blackham, H. J. *Six Existentialist Thinkers*. New York: Macmillian: 1952.

Binswanger, Ludwig. *Being-in-the-World*. New York: Harper and Row, 1968 (1963).

Boelen, Bernard J. *Existential Thinking: A Philosophical Orientation*. Pittsburgh: Duquesne University Press, 1968.

Borzaga, R. *Contemporary Philosophy. Phenomenology and Existentialism*. Milwaukee: Bruce Publishing Company, 1966.

Boss, Medard. *Psychoanalysis and Daseinsanalysis*. New York: Basic Books, 1963 (1957).

Brock, Werner. *An Introduction to Contemporary German Philosophy*. Cambridge: University Press, 1947.

Brown, James. *Kierkegaard, Heidegger, Buber and Barth: Subject and Object in Modern Theology*. New York: Collier Books, 1962 (1953).

Cochrane, Arthur C. *The Existentialists and God*. Philadelphia: Westminster Press, 1956.

Collins, James. *The Existentialists: A Critical Study*. Chicago: Regnery, 1952.

Erickson, Steven A. *Language and Being: An Analytical Phenomenology*. New Haven: Yale University Press, 1970.

Farber, Marvin. *Phenomenology and Existence: Toward A Philosophy Within Nature*. New York: Harper and Row, 1967.

Gilson, Étienne. *Being and Some Philosophers*. Toronto: Pontifical Institute of Medieval Studies, 1952 (1949).

Grene, Marjorie. *Dreadful Freedom* (1948). Reissued as *Introduction to Existentialism*. Chicago: Regnery, 1959.

Grimsley, Ronald. *Existentialist Thought*. Cardiff: University of Wales Press, 1955.

Harper, Ralph. *Existentialism: A Theory of Man*. Cambridge: Harvard University Press, 1948.

Heinemann, F. H. *Existentialism and the Modern Predicament*. New York: Harper and Row, 1953.

Hines, Thomas J. *The Later Poetry of Wallace Stevens: Phenomenological Parallels with Husserl and Heidegger*. Lewisburg: Bucknell University Press, 1976.

Horosz, W. *The Promise and Peril of Human Purpose*. St. Louis: W. H. Green, 1970.

Horvath, Nicholas. *Essentials of Philosophy: Hellenes to Heidegger*. Woodbury: Barron's Educational Service, 1974.

Howey, R. L. *Heidegger and Jaspers on Nietzsche*. The Hague: Martinus Nijhoff, 1973.

Hunnex, M. D. *Existentialists and Christian Belief.* Chicago: Moody Press, 1969.

Hunsinger, George. *Kierkegaard, Heidegger, and the Concept of Death.* Stanford: University Press, 1968.

Ihde, Don. *Hermeneutic Phenomenology.* Evanston: Northwestern University Press, 1971.

Kaelin, E. F. *Art and Existence: A Phenomenological Aesthetics.* Lewisburg: Bucknell University Press, 1969.

Kuhn, H. *Encounter with Nothingness: An Essay on Existentialism.* Chicago: Regnery, 1949.

Landgrebe, Ludwig. *Major Problems in Contemporary European Philosophy.* New York: Ungar Publishing Company, 1966.

Langan, Thomas. *Heidegger Beyond Hegel.* Torino: Editioni di Filosofia, 1970.

LeCoco, R. P. *The Radical Thinkers: Heidegger and Sri Aurobindo.* Pondicherry: Sri Aurobindo Society, 1972.

Löwith, Karl. *Nature, History, and Existentialism.* Evanston: Northwestern University Press, 1966.

Luipjen, W. A. *Phenomenology and Humanism: A Primer in Existential Phenomenology.* Pittsburgh: Duquesne University Press, 1966.

Macquarrie, John. *An Existentialist Theology: A Comparison of Heidegger and Bultmann.* New York: Harper and Row, 1965.

Marray, M. *Modern Philosophy of History, Its Origin and Destination.* The Hague: Martinus Nijhoff, 1970.

Mascall, E. L. *Existence and Analogy.* Hamden: Archon Books, 1967.

May, Rollo (ed.) *Existence.* New York: Basic Books, 1958.

Molina, F. R. (ed.) *The Sources of Existentialism as Philosophy.* Englewood Cliffs: Prentice-Hall, 1969.

Naess, Arne. *Four Modern Philosophers: Carnap, Wittgenstein, Heidegger, and Sartre.* Chicago: University of Chicago Press, 1968.

Nauman, S. E. *The New Directions of Existentialism.* New York: Philosophical Library, 1971.

Olafson, F. A. *Principles and Persons: An Ethical Interpretation of Existentialism.* Baltimore: Johns Hopkins Press, 1967.

Palmer, Richard E. *Hermeneutics: Interpretation Theory in Schleiermacher, Dilthey, Heidegger, and Gadamer.* Evanston: Northwestern University Press, 1969.

Patka, F. E. *Existentialist Thinkers and Thought.* New York: Citadel Press, 1962.

Reinhardt, K. F. *The Existentialist Revolt: The Main Themes and Phases of Existentialism. Kierkegaard, Nietzsche, Heidegger, Jaspers, Sartre, Marcel.* Milwaukee: Bruce Publishing Company, 1952.

Ricoeur, Paul. *The Conflict of Interpretations.* Evanston: Northwestern University Press, 1974 (1969).

Ricoeur, Paul. *Freud and Philosophy.* New Haven: Yale University Press, 1970 (1965).

Rintelen, F. J. *Contemporary German Philosophy and Its Background.* Bonn: Bouvier, 1970.

Rosen, Stanley. *Nihilism: A Philosophical Essay.* New Haven: Yale University Press, 1969.

Ruggiero, Guido de. *Existentialism.* London: Seeker and Warurg, 1946.

Sanborn, P. *Existentialism.* New York: Pegasus Books, 1968.

Sartre, Jean-Paul. *Being and Nothingness.* New York: Philosophical Library, 1956 (1943).

Sefler, George. *Language and World: A Methodological-Structural Synthesis Within the Writings of Martin Heidegger and Ludwig Wittgenstein.* Atlantic Highlands: Humanities Press, 1974.

Sherover, Charles. *Heidegger, Kant and Time.* Bloomington: Indiana University Press, 1971.

Sinari, R. *Reason in Existentialism*. New York: Humanities Press, 1968 (1967).

Sonnemann, Ulrich. *Existence and Therapy*. New York: Humanities Press, 1968 (1954).

Sontag, F. *The Existentialist Prolegomena to a Future Metaphysics*. Chicago: University of Chicago Press, 1969.

Spiegelberg, Herbert. *Phenomenology in Psychology and Psychiatry*. Evanston: Northwestern University Press, 1972.

Starr, David E. *Entity and Existence: An Ontological Investigation of Aristotle and Heidegger*. New York: Franklin, 1975.

Ussher, Arland. *Journey Through Dread: A Study of Kierkegaard, Heidegger and Sartre*. New York: Biblo and Tannen, 1968.

Wahl, Jean André. *Philosophies of Existence. An Introduction to the Basic Thought of Kierkegaard, Heidegger, Jaspers, Marcel, Sartre*. New York: Schocken Books, 1969.

Warnock, Mary. *Existentialist Ethics*. New York: St. Martins Press, 1967.

Warnock, Mary. *Existentialism: Kierkegaard, Nietzsche, Heidegger, Sartre, Marcel, Merleau-Ponty*. New York: Oxford University Press, 1970.

Wyschogrod, Micahel. *Kierkegaard and Heidegger. The Ontology of Existence*. New York: Humanities Press, 1969.

Zaner, Richard and Ihde, Don (eds.). *Phenomenology and Existentialism*. New York: G. P. Putman, 1973.